Victory Over the Kingdom of Darkness

> From ghoulies and ghosties
> And long-leggedy beasties
> And things that go bump in the night,
> Good Lord, deliver us!
> ~ Traditional Scottish Prayer

Rev. Gordon Williams

Edited by
Diane Roblin-Lee & Rev. Dennis Baker

VICTORY OVER THE KINGDOM OF DARKNESS
© 2015 Rev. Gordon Williams

Library and Archives Canada Cataloguing in Publication

Williams, Gordon, 1937-, author
Victory over the kingdom of darkness / Rev. Gordon Williams;
with Diane Roblin-Lee.

From ghoulies and ghosties, and long-leggedy beasties, and things that go bump in the night, Good Lord, deliver us!
--traditional Scottish prayer.
Includes bibliographical references.
Issued in print and electronic formats.
ISBN 978-1-896213-76-7 (pbk.).-- ISBN 978-1-896213-83-5 (epub)

1. Demonology. 2. Demoniac possession.

BT975.W54 2015   235'.4   C2015-900628-7
                                        C2015-900629-5

PUBLISHED IN CANADA
byDesign Media
www.bydesignmedia.ca

COVER & INTERIOR DESIGN – Diane Roblin-Lee
LOGO DESIGN – Rick and Sharon Janzen
EDITORS – Rev. Dennis Baker and Diane Roblin-Lee

ISBN 978-1-896213-76-7 – Paperback
ISBN 978-1-896213-83-5 - EPUB

Revised Standard Version of the Bible (RSV), copyright © 1946, 1952, and 1971 the Division of Christian Education of the National Council of the Churches of Christ in the United States of America. Used by permission. All rights reserved. Unless otherwise noted, all references are from the RSV.

The New Jerusalem Bible (NJB) Published in 1985 by Darton, Longman & Todd and Les Editions du Cerf, and edited by the Reverend Henry Wansbrough

Greek definitions from *A Greek-English Lexicon of the New Testament and other Early Christian Literature* Second, Third and Fourth Editions. Revised and edited by Fredrick William Danker, based on Walter Bauer's previous English Editions by W.F. Arndt, F.W. Gingrich, and F. W. Danker. The University of Chicago Press/ Chicago and London. Published 2000.

Disclaimer: The opinions expressed in this book are those of the author and do not constitute part of the curriculum of any program. The development, preparation and publication of this work has been undertaken with great care. However, the author, publisher, editor and agents of the G.W.E.A. are not responsible for any errors contained herein or for consequences that may ensue from use of materials or information contained in this work. The information contained herein is intended to assist individuals in establishing and maintaining positive Christian lives and is distributed with the understanding that it does not constitute legal or medical advice. References to quoted sources are only as current as the date of the publications and do not reflect subsequent changes in law.

All rights reserved. No part of this publication may be reproduced, stored in a retrieval system, or transmitted in any form or by any means without prior permission of the copyright owner.

Dedication

This book is dedicated to the Person who visited me the night of April 17, 1957, to call me into ministry – my Savior and Lord, Jesus Christ. He said, "Gordon I want you to come and work for Me. I want you to be a fisher of men. If you will come and work for Me, I will supply all of your needs according to My riches in Glory."

It is dedicated to my Heavenly Counselor, the Holy Spirit, who opened up the Scriptures to reveal things that many people have never seen – and to my Heavenly Father, whose plans for my life have been beyond anything I could have hoped or imagined:

"For consider your call, brethren; not many of you were wise according to worldly standards, not many were powerful, not many were of noble birth; but God chose what is foolish in the world to shame the wise, God chose what is weak in the world to shame the strong, God chose what is low and despised in the world, even things that are not, to bring to nothing things that are, so that no human being might boast in the presence of God. He is the source of your life in Christ Jesus, whom God made our wisdom, our righteousness and sanctification and redemption; therefore, as it is written, 'Let him who boasts, boast of the Lord.'" (1 Corinthians 1:26–31)

This book is also dedicated to those who have encouraged me over the years in my ministry: to my wife Ruth Williams and our children – Geoffrey and his wife Margaret, our daughter Margaret, Douglas and his wife Gylian and our son Karl; to Miss Hazel Grimmon, Dr. Ed Mol and my good friend and classmate, Rev. Dennis Baker; to my Board of Directors, all men of great faith: Wayne Sproule, Arthur Kelly, Bryan DeMarchi and Donald Railton; and to all who faithfully pray and support our ministry.

Table of Contents

Foreword 7

Introduction 9

Chapter One 11
Foundational Issues for Exploring the Subject of Demons
God, Satan and Demons

Chapter Two 43
Drawing the Lines
The Old Testament Spiritual Structure

Chapter Three 91
A Fight to the Finish
God's Plan, Purpose and Provision for our Victory

Chapter Four 105
Defeating the Kingdom of Darkness
The Flawed Plans of Satan

Chapter Five 145
Victory Day
Resurrection and the Coming of the Holy Spirit

Chapter Six 165
Today's Warfare
Living on Daily Alert

Chapter Seven 221
Tactics of Demons
Tactics, Characteristics, Weapons and Agendas of Demons

Chapter Eight 291
Hand to Hand Combat With the Enemy Forces
Tactical Operations

Chapter Nine *311*
Skilled Warfare
Sending Demons to the Abyss

Chapter Ten *345*
The War Comes Home
The Battles Within

Appendix *383*
The Origin of Demons

Bibliography *411*

Foreword

I first met Gordon Williams when I was Directing the Teen Challenge ministry in Toronto, Ontario, back in the seventies. Gordon was a regular host on the *100 Huntley Street* telecast.

I was deeply touched by his sincerity and dynamic faith in the living Christ. Gordon's emphasis on the power of the Holy Spirit in his preaching and sharing, was exactly what we needed to emphasize to the addicts and abuse victims in our in our Teen Challenge ministry.

Over the last few years, I have had more opportunities to spend time with Gordon. He is such an encouragement to me personally. It has been so exciting to see how God has continued to bless and empower him with the Holy Spirit. We have lunch as often as we can. He is full of joy and great humor and it is always a refreshing break for me. I leave our luncheons, each time, inspired and determined to pour myself into our Breakthrough ministry, having received a fresh touch from God as I have spent time with a real man of God, Gordon Williams!

I am presently reading one of his devotional books entitled *Spirit-led Days*. This book has inspired me greatly to draw closer, daily, through prayer and worship, to our Heavenly Father and our Lord Jesus Christ, through the indwelling Holy Spirit. God is using Gordon Williams to awaken the church to recognize all that the Lord has provided for us and to spur us on to press into His marvelous provision through our total surrender to the Holy Spirit's leadership in our daily living.

I thank God for allowing me to have Gordon Williams as a friend and as a great inspiration in my life. Read his books and hear him preach at every opportunity you can; God will meet you there!

Rev. Maury Blair
Executive Director of Breakthrough Ministries Canada

Introduction

One of the most troubling issues of the Bible, is the problem of demon possession. For the most part, people today have dismissed it as the product of over-worked imaginations attempting to put a label on a psychological or physical problem that cannot be otherwise identified.

Demon possession is regarded by many as being symptomatic of a primitive civilization, poor theology and an antiquated belief system. Unfortunately, our sophisticated society has starved people spiritually, telling them that such things are not real, leaving them without the necessary knowledge and tools to deal with their issues. Because of this, people who have been possessed or harassed by demons, have learned not to discuss their core issues with doctors, psychiatrists, counselors or clergy, for fear of being wrongly judged or treated inappropriately. When pressed by those in whom they do confide, however, many describe experiences in which evil spirits have actually entered their bodies. They may tell of a demon, or demons, talking to them and persuading them to do things that are dangerous – either for themselves or for other people.

When demons enter a person, they will often manifest as emotional, physical or psychological disorders. People who seek professional help, risk being placed in psychiatric hospitals where they are given drugs that cloud their minds and leave them in stupors. Others live in poverty and disgrace, because most doctors – and even most religious counselors – do not recognize the existence of such beings. Victims who avoid this fate, generally live tormented lives. They often have little, or no, control over their physical bodies.

Our society, unlike so-called "primitive" countries that recognize the reality of demons, has left many of its people trapped in a damned condition, dominated by the kingdom of darkness. In sharp contrast, it is not unusual for many citizens of primitive societies to actually worship demons and spend their lives trying to placate them, because the unbelievers there, as here, have no authority for dealing with such things.

During my studies in university and seminary, I received no teaching about demonology; but I noticed that the subject came up often, on the pages of the Bible. Through years of study and ministry experience, I learned that demons, evil spirits and unclean spirits are very real and are simply different names for the same beings. They are creatures which affect people's lives badly, whether the people affected believe in their existence or not. Sometimes, they make themselves visible; but often, they remain invisible. They are spiritual beings who can move things, damage property and go inside people's bodies; often controlling them like a hand inside a glove, forcing them to do and say outrageous things. Some people become preoccupied with demons and see them as the excuse for every problem in the world – but most do not believe in their existence and so are easily victimized. The main problem is that too many Christians do not understand the authority they have in Jesus Christ, and so are incapable of dealing effectively with them.

The purpose of this book is to expose demons for what they are and to bring balance, awareness and clarity to the issue. Further, it is an up-to-date manual for dealing with them in the 21st Century.

By the time you finish reading this book, you will be able to see through the façade that has been raised by our enemy to mislead, deceive and defeat you. As you, as a Spirit-filled Christian, learn how to deal with the members of the kingdom of darkness, you will discover Jesus is not only your Savior, LORD, Healer and Deliverer, but also your Commander who, through the Holy Spirit (your Counselor), can direct your warfare.

> *I have yet many things to say to you, but you cannot bear them now.*
> *When the Spirit of Truth comes, He will guide you into all the truth;*
> *for He will not speak on His own authority, but whatever He hears*
> *He will speak, and He will declare to you the things that are to come.*
> *He will glorify Me, for He will take what is Mine and declare it to*
> *you. All that the Father has is Mine; therefore I said that He will take*
> *what is Mine and declare it to you.* (John 16:12-15)

Foundational Issues for Exploring the Subject of Demons

God, Satan & Demons

We have an enemy. We are in a battle for our souls. Looking around at the beautiful trees, skies and blessings of our lives, it's sometimes difficult to believe that we are the focus of two opposing kingdoms, contending for our eternal souls. While the kingdom of God defeated the kingdom of Satan at the moment of Resurrection, our defeated foe will continue to tempt and test us until the end of time.

In my service to Jesus Christ, I am constantly confronted by the needs of people who have come under attack by Satan or his demons. Sadly, most have had no teaching on how to deal with the kingdom of darkness and live in a perpetual state of vulnerability to his evil purposes.

Boot Camp

In the early days of my ministry, like many ministers today, I had little understanding of the realities of spiritual warfare. While studying for the ministry at Princeton Theological Seminary in New Jersey, USA and at Waterloo Lutheran University in Waterloo, Ontario, Canada, I had good teaching in Christian counseling. I studied psychology and learned how to apply the Scriptures so that I could, with the guidance of the Holy Spirit, find healing for those whom I counseled. I also discovered the importance of creating a network of professional counselors, doctors, psychiatrists, pastors, and psychologists who could help my people find health and healing. Part of my study involved learning how to diagnose patients at the Pennsylvania State Hospital in Philadelphia. Consequently, when I graduated and was ordained, I was well prepared to deal with sin and sickness according to the Scriptures.

However, the one area for which I had absolutely no preparation, was in the area of what has come to be known as deliverance ministry, or the casting out of evil spirits. It was while I was pastoring the First Presbyterian Church of Englishtown, New Jersey, U.S.A., that I was introduced to the critical need for this kind of ministry. Fortunately, I had received no teaching against it. The instruction that I had received was, "Do what the Bible says. Follow Jesus' example."

When I arrived in Englishtown, I began to receive telephone calls from an elderly woman. She was not involved in our congregation and was a total stranger to me. She begged me to go to her house and help her. I went to visit and she proceeded to tell me a weird story about a spirit that was supposedly in her house. She claimed that it cursed and swore at her and kept her awake at night – taunting her, pushing her out of bed and off of chairs.

I thought this all had to be her imagination working overtime. Consequently, I tried to talk to her about Jesus Christ and her need for salvation. In great agitation, she cursed and swore at me and demanded that I leave her house.

So I left and went home. Before I arrived, she was calling again, asking me to go back. She called continuously.

The next morning I went to see her again. This time, I suggested she should read the Bible. Again she went into a rage, screaming at me to leave.

Again I went home. Again she started calling before I got there, begging me to go back and help her. She called over and over again that day.

The next morning, I went to see her again. This time, I tried to be more careful and suggested that she read a Christian book which I thought would help her. Again she raged, cursing and swearing, demanding that I leave her house.

Of course I left. However, before I got home, she was telephoning again, begging me to go and help her. I was definitely puzzled about what was wrong with this woman.

In my efforts to get a handle on what was happening, I called a fellow classmate from seminary, Rev. Dennis Baker, and asked his opinion. He asked me to describe the woman's symptoms, which I did.

"Oh, it's just a simple case of demon possession," he said.

I replied, "Come on, Dennis, you know I don't believe in such a thing."

"Well," he said, "if you want to help the woman, you had better treat it as if you do."

Disappointed with his diagnosis, I called one of the pastoral counselling professors at my seminary, the Rev. Earl Jabay, to ask for his advice. Earl had written several books on counselling and had a tremendous ministry at the New Jersey Neuro-Psychiatric Institute, just outside of Princeton, New Jersey. He had always been a very congenial, helpful professor. I explained my problem to him. After listening carefully, he said, "Well, Gordon, it sounds like a simple case of demon possession."

"Do you mean to tell me there is really such a thing as demon possession?" I asked.

"Yes, there definitely is, and many people are trapped and hopeless, because too many Christians do not want to accept the Bible's teaching about them." Earl recommended some books, which contained accurate teaching about possession and harassment by evil spirits.

After I read the books and gained understanding of the warfare that needed to be fought, I went back to the house of the woman who had called me, looking for her. Her neighbors said that an ambulance had come and taken her away to a psychiatric hospital. Unfortunately, despite all my searching, I was unable to find her again.

However, I was now prepared to help anyone else who was being victimized by demons. I had learned to tell the difference between real evil spirits and imagined evil spirits; between possession and oppression (or harassment) and between the work of the Holy Spirit and evil spirits.

As it turned out, I was not going to have to wait very long to put my new understanding of demon possession to work.

A young family, who had just moved to Englishtown, rented a two-story house with a walk-in attic. The couple had three little girls ages eight, five, and three. They were excited, as the movers unpacked their furniture and placed each piece in its assigned room. Because they had been late unpacking, the parents put the three girls into one of the four bedrooms for their first night in the house. About three o'clock in the morning, the parents heard the three girls screaming as they ran into their parents' room, terrified. All three were pointing behind them, to the room from which they had just escaped, talking and crying all at once. They were jabbering about something that had come out of the closet. Both parents went to check out the room, but could see nothing. The girls unanimously refused to go back into that room. That was how it all began.

The problem didn't go away. In the coming days, the mother began to hear music coming from different rooms at different times. Occasionally, she could hear voices in different parts of the house. Trying to maintain her equilibrium, she wrote the music and voices off as freak occurrences, caused by stray radio signals. A few days later, as she was moving boxes to store in the attic, she began to hear voices up there. She went to talk with her pastor about what was going on, but he passed it off as the fruit of an over-active imagination. Nevertheless, she continued to hear the voices, as did her husband and children. The woman and her husband looked all through the attic, but could find nothing amiss. Despite the evidence to the contrary, there was no one there.

On another occasion, while carrying a box of clothing up into the attic, she heard a voice ask, "Would you like to see Jesus?"

"Of course, I would!" she responded.

"Then jump out the window and you will see Jesus," the voice said. The woman was half-way out of the attic window before she realized what she was doing. Climbing back in, she was so terrified that she refused to go into the attic again.

I have learned, through years of experiences like this, that evil spirits invade houses to possess, terrorize and harass people to the point of committing suicide.

The family members were afraid, but did not know where to turn for help. Their pastor had never encountered this kind of problem. It seemed all they could do was pray – and pray they did.

During a joint worship service, where several of the churches in town had joined together, the woman happened to be sitting next to my wife, Ruth. While they were waiting for the service to begin, she told Ruth what she and her family had been experiencing. Ruth said, "You had better speak with my husband about this. He will be able to help you." That was my introduction to the situation.

The woman came to see me a few days later and told me what had been happening since they'd moved into their newly rented house. After listening to her, I explained that they had unknowingly moved into a house that was occupied by evil spirits. I offered to go through it and get rid of the evil spirits, if they wished me to do so.

I explained that some people called this exorcism, but that I liked to call it "blessing out the house." Further, I explained that, in order to be protected from the evil spirits, she and her husband and children would need to receive Jesus Christ as their Savior and Lord and pray that He would baptize them in the Holy Spirit. The woman talked it over with her husband and they invited me over to their house. When I arrived, I asked them to step outside, so that if the demons reacted, they would avoid being frightened or hurt. I went through every room in the house and commanded every unclean spirit to leave and to go to the abyss in the Name of Jesus Christ. Then, I invited the Holy Spirit to fill every room with His presence.

There was peace in the house from that day on. Both husband and wife received salvation and the baptism of the Holy Spirit, with the signs following (see Mark 16:17-18).

The family became part of our church. The first time the woman attended our Wednesday evening Bible study, she was welcomed warmly. However, one long-time resident of Englishtown, asked her, "Where do you live?"

Unhesitatingly, the woman told her.

The woman who had posed the question became very serious, "Oh! You live in *that house?!*" That ended their conversation.

The next morning, I asked my secretary, Ethel Vass, who had been born and raised in the town, if she knew anything about "that house."

"Yes," she said, "I know quite a bit about it. My parents lived there. My mother tried to murder my father in that house. She shot him with a gun. The family who lived there most recently, had four children whom they forced to live in the attic, where they beat them and fed them dog food. The Children's Aid Society took the children away and the parents were arrested and are in jail. The man who lived there, before my parents, hanged himself in the attic. That house has a long, bad history. Why are you asking about it?"

I explained that the young family who was living in that house were having some troubles, but that I had been able to get rid of the source of the problems. It was now a good house.

The family never had any more problems as long as they lived there, nor did anyone who followed them.

The previous inhabitants of the house had been victimized by evil spirits. Apparently, no one was ever taken seriously when they sought help from pastors, other Christians and a variety of counselors.

Demons are a reality which must be dealt with today, as they were in Bible times and in all the intervening years of history. I shall be forever grateful to Jesus Christ for the sensitive way He taught and led me, regarding the problem of demonic involvement in people's lives.

Taking the offensive, in the kingdom of God, requires us to introduce people to Jesus Christ – give them an opportunity to receive Him and accept Him as the sacrifice for their sins – and give Him the opportunity to forgive their sins and make them into new people. Unfortunately, many of us, who have been raised in and around churches, never had anyone tell us we could have a personal relationship with Jesus Christ. Sadly, it could have been because many of the people in those churches didn't know that they, themselves, could have one. Without knowing Him themselves, it would have been impossible for them to introduce us to Him. While I was growing up, I had a long list of Christian Sunday School teachers and youth leaders. Unfortunately, if they knew Jesus personally, they didn't know how to introduce others to Him, because I didn't get the message.

A friend who had met Christ through Billy Graham, told me about his experience. At the time, I didn't know that anybody could have a personal relationship with God, where they could actually have a conversation. Certainly, I had heard the Bible stories where God spoke to specially chosen people, but I never considered the possibility that I could, or would, be one of those. I did not know that God talked to anybody today. Consequently, it was somewhat of a shock when I skeptically followed my friend Bob Webb's instructions about how to get to know Jesus. I really didn't expect anything to happen.

Bob said, "All you have to do is call on the Name of Jesus and, even though you cannot see Him, He is here. Then, ask Him to forgive you for any sin or wrong you have done and invite him to come into your heart and your life."

I asked him how I was supposed to do this: sitting, standing or kneeling.

He said I could do it any way I liked and then he asked, "Can I pray with you?"

I had noticed that he had that strange look in his eyes that Christians get when they think they've got a live one; so I said, "No! If this works, it will work if I'm alone."

Bob agreed, left the church and went home. Bob's instructions didn't make sense to me, but I followed them. I sat down on a chair and prayed as he had instructed me. I was going to give it only this one chance. After saying the prayer, I sat and waited for about a half hour, expecting nothing to happen – but, suddenly, it happened! I discovered Jesus Christ is real and can talk to us personally. I experienced what He talked about in John 3:3,5,7.

> *Jesus answered him, "Truly, truly, I say to you, unless one is born anew, he cannot see the kingdom of God.... Truly, truly, I say to you, unless one is born of water and the Spirit, he cannot enter the kingdom of God.... Do not marvel that I said to you, 'You must be born anew.'"* (John 3:3,5,7)

Jesus forgave me for all my sin and filled me with the Holy Spirit.

> *And they were all filled with the Holy Spirit and began to speak in other tongues, as the Spirit gave them utterance.* (Acts 2:4)

Then I went home.

The next morning, I woke up and saw a *new me* reflected in the mirror. Later that day, I met a friend on the main street of Kirkland Lake and invited him for coffee in a nearby restaurant. As we talked, he asked, "Gordon, what has happened to you?"

I asked what he meant.

"First of all, you offered to buy the coffee! Secondly, you've stopped your swearing."

I had had a problem with my mouth and, despite having tried to stop cursing and swearing, I'd been unsuccessful. Besides forgiving me and giving me a new life, Jesus had given me a spiritual mouthwash that has lasted throughout my life.

Whenever we introduce someone to Jesus Christ, and they ask Him to be their Savior and Lord, we're taking the offensive in victorious spiritual warfare. It's another defeat for the devil and his kingdom of darkness.

In order to demonstrate what Christians can do to overcome the enemy, I will share more stories in later chapters.

But first, it's necessary to expose and reveal the roots of the conflict in which we will be embroiled until the end of time. In order not to fall prey to the plans of the enemy and to live victoriously, we need to have a solid understanding of who God is and be able to recognize our adversary, the devil.

Roots of Conflict

After God finished creating the world and all that surrounded it, Adam and Eve blissfully enjoyed the blessings of Eden. While God had given them instructions for maintaining the bliss, the rules didn't sound too complicated. Really, there was only one: they were not to eat the fruit of the tree of the knowledge of good and evil. With all the fruit on all the other trees available to them, one would think it shouldn't have been too hard to stay away from one tree.

But a third character appeared in the garden – a serpent. He engaged Eve in pleasant conversation.

"Did God say, 'You shall not eat of any tree of the garden?'"

And the woman said to the serpent, "We may eat of the fruit of the trees of the garden; but God said, 'You shall not eat of the fruit of the tree which is in the midst of the garden, neither shall you touch it, lest you die.'"

But the serpent said to the woman, "You shall not die. For God knows that when you eat of it your eyes will be opened, and you will be like God, knowing good and evil." (Genesis 3:3–5)

Not only did the serpent question God's Word, but he lied. Eve did what many people continue to do today; she accepted the serpent's word over God's Word. Of course the serpent was Satan (the devil) in disguise and the result was that he was cursed by God.

> *The Lord God said to the serpent, "Because you have done this, cursed are you above all cattle, and above all wild animals; upon your belly you shall go, and dust you shall eat all the days of your life. I will put enmity between you and the woman, and between your seed and her seed; He shall bruise your head, and you shall bruise his heel.* (Genesis 3:14,15)

He was doing what he was created to do. He was tempting Eve, and eventually Adam, to test their faithfulness to God. Testing faithfulness is his job. After he proved Adam and Eve to be unfaithful, the devil laid charges against them to God for breaking the law. The root of the title "devil," references the prosecuting attorney for the state in the Greek judicial system.

Although it has been Satan's responsibility to catch law-breakers and sinners, he was never given any legal authority to sin himself. Nevertheless, even though he was an angel (albeit a rebellious one), he sinned on his very first assignment; he lied to Eve. To this day, he still seems to get the best mileage out of lies.

While Satan deceived Eve, her fault lay in believing Satan instead of believing God. She was tempted and sinned. Adam followed suit.

> *He who commits sin is of the devil; for the devil has sinned from the beginning.* (1 John 3:8)

It is clear that, in the beginning, the devil had access to God's throne around the clock, so he was able to report to God about those who failed when he tempted them every day.

> *And I heard a loud voice in heaven, saying, "Now the salvation and the power and the kingdom of our God and the authority of His Christ have come, for the accuser of our brethren has been thrown*

down, who accuses them day and night before our God."
(Revelation 12:10)

Many years after his world-changing encounter with Adam and Eve, we find the enemy of man stirring up more trouble – this time, with God's servant, Job. The Book of Job reveals Satan talking with God. Apparently, like the other angels, he was reporting in on his work.

Now there was a day when the sons of God came to present themselves before the LORD, and Satan also came among them. The LORD said to Satan, "Whence have you come?"
Satan answered the LORD, "From going to and fro on the earth, and from walking up and down on it."
And the LORD said to Satan, "Have you considered my servant Job, that there is none like him on the earth, a blameless and upright man, who fears God and turns away from evil?"
Then Satan answered the LORD, "Does Job fear God for nought? Hast Thou not put a hedge about him and his house and all that he has, on every side? Thou hast blessed the work of his hands, and his possessions have increased in the land. But put forth Thy hand now, and touch all that he has, and he will curse Thee to Thy face."
And the LORD said to Satan, "Behold, all that he has is in your power; only upon himself do not put forth your hand."
So Satan went forth from the presence of the LORD. (Job 1:6-12, KJV)

When God asked him about His faithful servant Job, Satan asked for and was given permission to test him. His contention was that the only reason Job was faithful, was because God had blessed him. He wanted to prove that if Job were not blessed, he would reject God. While God allowed the testing, there was a condition to the permission. God told Satan that, while he could put Job's faithfulness to the test, he could not kill him.

Satan was certain he could hurt Job so badly that he would curse God. In one day, Satan killed Job's ten children and totally bankrupted him. Job lost everything.

In all this Job did not sin or charge God with wrong. (Job 1:22)

Temptation is crafted to entice a person to sin and turn away from God. Amazingly, Job did not do this – not even after his friends tried to tell him how he sinned (in their opinions). Not only did Job not fall away, but he remained steadfast in his faith.

Behold, He will slay me; I have no hope; yet I will defend my ways to His face. This will be my salvation, that a godless man shall not come before Him. (Job 13:15,16)

Unlike Job, when Satan attacks and tempts us, it is common for us to either sin or blame God for what was actually the work of Satan. Sin breaks our relationship with God. Because Job did not sin, his relationship with God remained intact – even after Satan had taken his best shot.

God reprimanded Job's three friends for cooperating (even though they did not realize it) with Satan.

And the Lord *restored the fortunes of Job, when he had prayed for his friends; and the* Lord *gave Job twice as much as he had before.* (Job 42:10)

From the earliest days, the battle raged between our Creator and the enemy of our souls, Satan.

Foundational Issues for Gaining Knowledge About Our Enemy

Recognizing our enemy, whose most successful strategy involves getting people to believe he doesn't exist, is critical to living the victorious, abundant life Jesus came to give us.

Unmasking and exposing Satan and his demons can render him powerless, as we become skillful in using the weapons God has given us.

In order to properly explore this issue, we have to understand three foundational issues:

1. Who the one true God is
2. Who Satan is
3. The origin and nature of demons

Recognition of the One True God

There is only one God who created the world we live in, and who directs the course of people's lives – with or without their cooperation. His Name, which He first gave to the Jews, is "Yahweh." Speaking to Moses, He said:

> *"I am the* LORD *(Hebrew – 'Yahweh'). And I appeared to Abraham, to Isaac and to Jacob as God Almighty (Hebrew – 'El Shaddai') and by My Name 'The* LORD*' (Yahweh) I never made Myself known to them."* (Exodus 6:2-3)

The history of Yahweh's involvement with the created world is described in the Old Testament portion of the Bible, which contains the old covenant – the agreement Yahweh made with the Jews. (He established the new covenant when He entered history in the physical body of Jesus Christ and became Emmanuel (which means, "God with us").

Because of a misinterpretation of one verse of Scripture, the Jews stopped speaking God's Name, "Yahweh."

> *He who blasphemes the Name of the* LORD *(Yahweh) shall be put to death; all the congregation shall stone him; the sojourner as well as the native, when he blasphemes the Name, shall be put to death.* (Leviticus 24:16)

The Jews were afraid that speaking God's Name would bring a curse – and possibly even death – to them. They dealt with the situation by speaking the Hebrew word for LORD, "Adonai," whenever they saw His written Name, "Yahweh."

When the Old Testament was translated into Greek a few centuries before Christ, it was called the Septuagint. "Yahweh" was completely removed from the translations 6,823 times and replaced with "Adonai." The result was that God's Name was never used and was lost to general use and knowledge. In 1611, the translators of the King James Version wanted to use God's Name in some way. Their idea of compromise was a composite of the consonant letters of Yahweh and the vowel letters of

Adonai, which resulted in the non-name, "Jehovah," that appears about seven times in the King James Version. The only English versions that restored God's real Name back into the Old Testament are the Jerusalem Bible and its updated version, the New Jerusalem Bible. Most English Bibles signal the presence of the Name "Yahweh" in the text by printing the word "Lord" instead of "Lord." This change in typography involves small capital letters after the initial capital "L."

Today, many people have begun to call God "Yeshua / Yeshuah" which actually means "Joshua." "Joshua" means "Yahweh's grace," which is just one attribute of God and does not address the full person of who God is. Joshua cannot answer prayer. Such prayer goes unheard.

Yahweh, the only God, had to reintroduce His Name to Israel and the rest of the world when He came to earth as Jesus.

... became flesh and dwelt amongst us. (John 1:14)

He reintroduced it as "Jesus," which means, "Yahweh is salvation."

On the Day of Pentecost, after God had sent the Holy Spirit into believers' lives, Peter said:

"And it shall be that whoever calls on the Name of the Lord shall be saved." (Acts 2:21)

He was referring to Jesus Christ in quoting from the Old Testament.

Then everyone who calls on the Name of the Lord (Yahweh) shall be saved ... (Joel 2:32)

Jesus is Yahweh in the flesh. Consequently, the only Name through which we can be saved is that of Jesus Christ.

There is salvation in no one else, for there is no other Name under Heaven given among men by which we must be saved. (Acts 4:12)

God does not change His Name as He moves from country to country or from time to time. His Hebrew Name, Yahweh, and His Greek Name, Jesus, are so irritating to unbelievers that they react strongly against it. No other name, of any other so-called god, is an alternative to the Name of Jesus. Jesus said:

> *"I am the way, and the truth, and the life: no one comes to the Father but by Me."* (John 14:6)

It is untrue that other religions are simply different roads headed in the same direction. Any other spirit that sets itself up as a god, according to the Bible, is an evil spirit.

> *Do not be mismated with unbelievers. For what partnership have righteousness and iniquity? Or what fellowship has light with darkness? Or what accord has Christ with Belial? Or what has a believer in common with an unbeliever? What agreement has the Temple of God with idols? For we are the Temple of the living God; as God said, "I will live among them, and move among them, and I will be their God, and they shall be My people. Therefore come out from them, and be separate from them," says the* L<small>ORD</small>, *"and touch nothing unclean; then I will welcome you, and I will be a father to you, and you shall be My sons and daughters," says the* L<small>ORD</small> *Almighty. Since we have these promises, beloved, let us cleanse ourselves from every defilement of body and spirit, and make holiness perfect in the fear of God.* (2 Corinthians 6:14-7:1)

John warns us to keep ourselves from idols,[1] which means to stay away from all things which are supposedly images of other gods, but are in fact, evil spirits. When people worship other gods, they break God's first commandment, which has never been amended or compromised:

> *I am Yahweh your God, who brought you out of Egypt, out of the house of bondage. You shall have no other gods before Me. You shall not make for yourself a graven image of anything that is in Heaven above, or that is in the earth beneath, or that is in the water under the earth; you shall not bow down to them; for I Yahweh your God am a jealous God.* (Exodus 20:1-5)

---

[1] 1 John 5:21

This warning was repeated.

For you shall not bow down to another god, for Yahweh's Name is "Jealous," He is a jealous God. (Exodus 34:14)

God does not tolerate rivalry between Himself and other so-called gods. He is the only God who has authority over everything and everyone. The Mosaic law forbids any material representations of God.

In Revelation, the final book of the Bible, we read that after the seven trumpets have been blown and judgment has come to the earth, there will still be those who refuse to repent of worshipping the idols they serve. They will perish in their rebellion.

The rest of mankind, who were not killed by these plagues, did not repent of the work of their hands or give up worshipping demons and idols of gold and silver and bronze and stone and wood, which cannot either see or hear or walk; nor did they repent of their murders; of their sorceries, or their immorality or their thefts. (Revelation 9:20-21)

There is only one road, one God, and one Name leading to Heaven. That Name is Jesus Christ. His instructions for how to get to Him, are so pivotal – so critical – that they bear repeating.

I am the way (hodos[2])*, and the truth* (aletheia)*, and the life* (zoe)*; no one* (oudes: not one) *comes to the Father but by Me.* (John 14:6)

Jesus Christ alone is the judge and has the authority to determine who can have eternal life in Heaven. No demons who misrepresent themselves as gods, regardless of their names, have any authority to offer anybody a place in Heaven.

Only Jesus Christ gives us authority to deal with demons. He gives this authority to Christian believers when they are baptized with the Holy Spirit with the proof of the signs following:

And these signs will accompany those who believe: in My Name they will cast out demons; they will speak in new tongues ... (Mark 16:17)

---

[2] Meaning "road."

Sadly, today, as in ancient Israel, there are people who think that they can worship and serve the God of the Bible – and worship and serve other gods at the same time; but Yahweh tolerates no rivals, nor does Jesus.

Thomas answered Him, "My Lord and my God!" (John 20:28)

And God spoke all these words, saying, "I am the Lord (Yahweh) your God, who brought you out of the land of Egypt, out of the house of bondage. You shall have no other gods before Me. You shall not make for yourself a graven image, or any likeness of anything that is in Heaven above, or that is in the earth beneath, or that is in the water under the earth; you shall not bow down to them or serve them; for I the Lord (Yahweh) your God am a jealous God, visiting the iniquity of the fathers upon the children to the third and the fourth generation of those who hate Me, but showing steadfast love to thousands of those who love Me and keep My commandments ... Take heed to all that I have said to you; and make no mention of the names of other gods, nor let such be heard out of your mouth." (Exodus 20: 1-6; 23:13)

The Pharisees mistakenly accused Jesus of receiving authority from Beelzebub,[3] the devil.[4] They made this mistake because they did not recognize who Jesus really was, in spite of His ministry and the signs He performed. In their spiritual blindness, they saw simply an ordinary carpenter from Nazareth, who had no recognized spiritual authority.

Without recognizing the God of Abraham, Isaac and Jacob as the one true God, it is impossible to explore the subject of demons with any validity, as His Scriptures are the source of our knowledge of the evil kingdom.

Recognition of Who Satan Really Is

Belial, the name commonly used as a synonym for Satan, is the personification of evil. Paul contrasted Belial, the prince of darkness, with Christ, the Light of the World.

---

[3] The devil likes to be called "Beelzebul" which means "Lord of the land" or "Lord who should be honored," but the Jews called him "Beelzebub" which means "Lord of the flies" or "manure pile."
[4] Matthew 12:24; Mark 3:22; Luke 11:15

What agreement does Christ have with Belial? Or what does a believer share with an unbeliever? (2 Corinthians 6:15)

The Bible depicts Belial as a powerful demon who seduces people into any type of sin. His name means "wicked and worthless." It has also been translated as "lord of arrogance" or "lord of pride" (Baalial) and "the angel of lawlessness."[5]

Belial attracted people to worship him as a god. His followers were called "sons of Belial." Yahweh, our God, warned that the followers of Belial could be identified if they encouraged Israel to serve other gods.

... that scoundrels from among you have gone out and led the inhabitants of the town astray, saying, "Let us go and worship other gods," whom you have not known, then you shall inquire and make a thorough investigation. If the charge is established that such an abhorrent thing has been done among you, you shall put the inhabitants of that town to the sword, utterly destroying it and everything in it – even putting its livestock to the sword. (Deuteronomy 13:13-15)

Before we delve into the mystery of demons, it is important to understand that "the devil" or "Satan" is not an evil spirit; God created him as an angel – but he sinned and fell, becoming the god of the kingdom of darkness.

When Satan attempted a rebellion in Heaven against God, he allowed his arrogance and pride to catapult him into such wicked delusions of grandeur that he actually thought he could successfully take God's position, and was cast out of Heaven.

And I heard a loud voice in Heaven, saying, "Now the salvation and the power and the kingdom of our God and the authority of His Christ have come, for the accuser of our brethren has been thrown down, who accuses them day and night before our God." (Revelation 12:10)

Since then, Satan has been known as the accuser and deceiver of God's people. The title or name "Satan" actually means, "the accuser or

---
[5] Catholic Encyclopedia and Wikipedia.com

the adversary." Even in his disobedience, he must complete the work assigned to him in the beginning – until his sentence is carried out. Then, the humiliated devil, the false prophet, the unrepentant sinners and fallen angels will be cast into the Lake of Fire. The devil's judgment is written in the Bible for all to see.

> *... and the devil who had deceived them was thrown into the Lake of Fire and sulphur where the beast and the false prophet were, and they will be tormented day and night for ever and ever.*
> (Revelation 20:10)

The devil is no longer free to travel to Heaven. He who once had daily access to God's throne, can no longer go there. The once mighty tempter is confined to the earth, without his former angelic followers. Here he prowls around, tempting people, to see whom he can destroy. At the present time, he is the only fallen angel who is allowed to move around; but he is on a short leash. Peter describes him as a roaring lion.

> *Be sober, be watchful. Your adversary the* devil *prowls around like a roaring lion, seeking someone to devour.* (1 Peter 5:8)

In no place in the Bible, are we told the devil was an archangel, as many have claimed. I suspect he passed that story around himself, in an attempt to make himself appear more important than he is. Nor did he hold any other position (such as the leader or director of the angelic, heavenly music) other than the one which is clearly described in the Bible as "tempter."

Paul describes him as:

> *... the ruler of the power of the air, the spirit that is now at work among those who are disobedient.* (Ephesians 2:2)

This sounds like an impressive title, but it is not. It speaks of his alienation from Heaven by God and defines the limits of his movements.

There are two Greek words translated as "air." The first one, the one used to define Satan's territory, is "aer." "Aer" describes the space from the earth's surface to the highest mountaintop. The second Greek word translated as "air," is "aither," which describes the space from the mountaintops to as far out in space as it is possible to travel. The use of "aer" in this passage, means that the devil cannot travel higher than Mount Everest.

He is neither omnipresent, nor all-powerful; these are attributes of only Yahweh. The devil can be in just one place at a time, tempting or tricking one person at a time. He may be fast, but he is not fast enough to be in all the places he is attributed to be.

Capitalizing on the fallen nature of man, Satan leaves a lot of (if not most) so-called temptations to our own imaginations. He knows that our own guilt from our unfaithfulness to God will keep most of us immobilized and in rebellion against God. Consequently, he gets the credit for tempting us, when in actual fact, he wasn't within miles of us.

James writes that most temptation comes from within ourselves.

... but each person is tempted when he is lured and enticed by his own desire. Then desire when it has conceived gives birth to sin; and sin when it is full-grown brings forth death. Do not be deceived, my beloved brethren. (James 1:14-16)

Nevertheless, some temptation does comes from the devil and demons. The kingdom of darkness is highly competitive. Both the devil and demons love to be worshipped.

... and he said to Him, "All these I will give You, if You will fall down and worship me." (Matthew 4:9)

If You, then, will worship me, it shall all be Yours. (Luke 4:7)

They sacrificed to demons which were no gods, to gods they had never known, to new gods that had come in of late, whom your fathers had never dreaded. (Deuteronomy 32:17)

... the sacrifices of pagans are offered to demons, not to God, and I do not want you to be participants with demons. You cannot drink the cup of the Lord *and the cup of demons too; you cannot have a part in both the* Lord*'s table and the table of demons.*
(1 Corinthians 10:20-21 NIV)

The devil liked to be called "Beelzebul" which means "lord of the land" or "lord who should be honored," but the Jews preferred to call him "Beelzebub" which means "lord of the flies" or "manure pile." They knew Yahweh was the only true God and they would worship only Him.[6] Interestingly, the translators of the King James Version of the Bible always used "Beelzebub" in their translation, when the Greek text used "Beelzebul."[7] They evidently thought it was important to maintain the tradition of belittling the devil.

The Jews also referred to the devil as Belial, meaning "worthlessness," because to follow him was a worthless endeavor which led people to Hell. Paul asked:

"What accord has Christ with Belial?" (2 Corinthians 6:15)

In other words, what agreement or involvement has Christ with the devil? The answer, of course, is none; and, just as Jesus has nothing to do with the devil, neither should we, particularly by participating in any form of religious worship or service that is offered to the devil.

The devil serves one other important purpose: it is his responsibility to test and tempt everyone whom Jesus has called to do ministry, to prove whether or not they're going to be faithful to God. The Greek word for devil (diabolos) is actually a legal title that comes to us from the Greek courts. It means the prosecuting attorney. Satan, himself, sinned the first time he was sent on assignment.[8]

The Greek word for temptation (peirazo) means, "to entice a man to do wrong, to seduce him to sin, to persuade him to take the wrong way," but it also means "to test a person in order to see if he or she can succeed in what he or she has been equipped to do."

He who commits sin is of the devil; *for the* devil *has sinned from the beginning. The reason the Son of God appeared was to destroy the works of the* devil. (1 John 3:8)

---

[6] Exodus 20:1-5
[7] Matthew 10:25; 12:27; Mark 3:22; Luke 11:15,18,19
[8] Genesis 3:1-8

In the Old Testament, we see Satan as the lying tempter. In the course of trying to tempt those people whom God wishes to use, Satan causes sickness, natural disasters and sometimes even death. He challenges God's people and encourages them to be disobedient to God's commands. He resists God's judgments to His face and is repeatedly rebuked by God and the archangel Michael.

Jesus, like all of us, had to be tempted by the devil in order to prove that He could complete His ministry. He passed the test and there, in the wilderness, He defeated the devil.

> *The Spirit immediately drove Him out into the wilderness. And He was in the wilderness forty days, tempted by Satan; and He was with the wild beasts; and the angels ministered to Him.* (Mark 1:12-13)
> (see also Matthew 4:1-11)

In the same manner we, who are called to be the children of God, must be tempted and tested by the devil. We can be assured of passing the test only after we have been baptized with both water and the Holy Spirit.

When the devil comes to test us, we must remember that, although he is a fallen angel, he is nevertheless still an angel, one of the "glorious ones," who carries out his work of testing us under the authority of our God. This means we must show him the respect and courtesy with which all people and angels are to be treated. To curse and deride him and make negative remarks about him is to fail his testing of us. That is why Jude reminds us about the archangel Michael's modeling of the protocols of dealing with Satan.

> *But when the archangel Michael, contending with the devil, disputed about the body of Moses, he did not presume to pronounce a reviling judgment upon him, but said, "The Lord rebuke you."* (Jude 8-9)

The principle of respecting Satan's right to his God-given position is a principal of spiritual warfare that has been carried over from the Old Testament into the New Testament. We need to recognize the legal position of the tempter (and any other spiritual dignities) and deal with him authoritatively, without pride.

And the angels that did not keep their own position but left their proper dwelling have been kept by Him in eternal chains in the nether gloom until the judgment of the great day; just as Sodom and Gomorrah and the surrounding cities, which likewise acted immorally and indulged in unnatural lust, serve as an example by undergoing a punishment of eternal fire. Yet in like manner these men in their dreamings defile the flesh, reject authority, and revile the glorious ones. But when the archangel Michael, contending with the devil, disputed about the body of Moses, he did not presume to pronounce a reviling judgment upon him, but said, "The LORD rebuke you." But these men revile whatever they do not understand, and by those things that they know by instinct as irrational animals do, they are destroyed. (Jude 1:6-10)

So, we have a choice when the devil comes to tempt and test us. We can go through all of the questioning Jesus went through – or we can simply say, *"The LORD rebuke you."* Either way, we pass the test. This is what "the Angel of the LORD" (Yahweh) said to Satan when he tried to tempt Joshua, the high priest:

The LORD (Yahweh) rebuke you, O Satan. (Zechariah 3:2)

The devil is under the authority of any born-again believer who is baptized with the Holy Spirit.

And Jesus came and said to them, "All authority in Heaven and on earth has been given to Me." (Matthew 28:18)

And these signs will accompany those who believe: in My Name they will cast out demons; they will speak in new tongues; they will pick up serpents, and if they drink any deadly thing, it will not hurt them; they will lay their hands on the sick, and they will recover. So then the LORD Jesus, after He had spoken to them, was taken up into Heaven, and sat down at the right hand of God. And they went forth and preached everywhere, while the LORD worked with them and confirmed the message by the signs that attended it. (Mark 16:17-20)

Resist the devil and he will flee from you. (James 4:7)

By the authority of God's Scriptures, if we resist Satan and cast out demons, they have to leave us alone.

The devil's ground forces are evil spirits or demons, two names for the same things. The King James Version translates them as "devils," not to be confused with the devil or Satan, two titles for the same person. Satan is the name of the devil. "Devil" is the description of his activity.

In order to deal effectively with demons, it is important not to mistake the work of the devil for the work of demons. Many misinformed Christians attempt to cast out the devil when he is not the entity at work. It is not his job to possess people – it is to tempt and test people in order to see if they are going to be faithful to God through Jesus Christ. Evil spirits (demons) come to possess people or to haunt houses so they can torment the occupants.

The Origin and Nature of Demons[9]

Demons are not creatures from outer space; nor are they the spirits or ghosts of people who have died. While most people have overlooked what the Bible says about their origin, there's no question that it acknowledges their existence and that they are beings with whom people must deal.

The Scriptures do tell us that they are under the ultimate authority of God and know, without any question, who Jesus Christ is and that He has authority over them.

Jesus then asked him, "What is your name?"
And he said, "Legion;" for many demons had entered him.
(Luke 8:30)

Demons are the servants of the devil, the god of the kingdom of darkness. We need to be thankful that they are not fallen angels. We have a major problem dealing with one fallen angel – imagine if we had to deal with *all* of the fallen angels who were cast out of Heaven!

---

[9] For further information, see the Appendix

Now war arose in Heaven, Michael and his angels fighting against the dragon; and the dragon and his angels fought, but they were defeated and there was no longer any place for them in Heaven. And the great dragon was thrown down, that ancient serpent, who is called the devil and Satan, the deceiver of the whole world – he was thrown down to the earth, and his angels were thrown down with him. And I heard a loud voice in Heaven, saying, "Now the salvation and the power and the kingdom of our God and the authority of His Christ have come, for the accuser of our brethren has been thrown down, who accuses them day and night before our God. And they have conquered him by the blood of the Lamb and by the word of their testimony, for they loved not their lives even unto death. Rejoice then, O Heaven and you that dwell therein! But woe to you, O earth and sea, for the devil has come down to you in great wrath, because he knows that his time is short!" (Revelation 12:7-12)

Evil spirits, like all beings, are always subject to God's authority. This was evident when Jesus dealt with the demon-possessed man named "Legion." That name meant that the man had about 6,000 demons living inside him, which is why he had such superhuman strength. He shouted to Jesus,

What have You to do with me, Jesus, Son of the Most High God? I beseech You, do not torment me. (Luke 8:28)

They knew exactly what Jesus had to do with them. He had come to send them to the place of judgment and punishment. In another incident, when Jesus dealt with two demoniacs, as in Luke 8:28, they said to Jesus,

"What have you to do with us, O Son of God? Have you come here to torment us before the time?"
Now a herd of many swine was feeding at some distance from them. And the demons begged him, "If You cast us out, send us away into the herd of swine."
And He said to them, "Go."
So they came out and went into the swine; and behold, the whole

> herd rushed down the steep bank into the sea, and perished in the waters. The herdsmen fled, and going into the city they told everything, and what had happened to the demoniacs. (Matthew 8:29-33)

Whenever Jesus, or a Christian with His authority, comes to deal with any evil spirit, it is their time.

We know also, that demons can differentiate between those of us who operate with the power and authority of Jesus Christ – and those who don't.

> And these signs will accompany those who believe: in My Name they will cast out demons; they will speak in new tongues ... (Mark 16:17)

> But the evil spirit answered them, "Jesus I know, and Paul I know; but who are you?" (Acts 19:15)

Just as the Scriptures do not tell us the number of fallen angels who were cast out of Heaven, we are not told how many demons exist. We are told that demons harass and possess people and occupy houses and buildings.

> When the unclean spirit has gone out of a man, he passes through waterless places seeking rest; and finding none he says, "I will return to my house from which I came." And when he comes he finds it swept and put in order. Then he goes and brings seven other spirits more evil than himself, and they enter and dwell there; and the last state of that man becomes worse than the first. (Luke 11:24-26)

The good news is that we Christians who are baptized with the Holy Spirit do have authority to cast them out and send them to the abyss. Jesus sent the seventy disciples to do ministry, and when they returned they reported,

> "Lord, even the demons are subject to us in Your Name!" And He said to them, "I saw Satan fall like lightning from Heaven. Behold, I have given you authority to tread upon serpents and scorpions, and over all the power of the enemy; and nothing shall hurt you. Nevertheless do not rejoice in this, that the spirits are

subject to you; but rejoice that your names are written in Heaven." (Luke 10:17-20)

Demons are often wrongly assumed by people to be God's unfaithful "fallen angels" who, in their rebellion against God, were defeated by Michael and God's "faithful angels." Evil spirits are not the heavenly angels who rebelled against God. This misunderstanding has led people to believe that the rebellious angels, who supported the devil's rebellion, were cast down to earth with him, where they became demons. In actual fact, when the rebellious heavenly angels were thrown down, they were not free to move around and harm people.

Those rebellious angels have been chained up in a temporary Hell (Tartarus) until they are cast in the Lake of Fire with the devil. Peter tells us specifically where they were sent.

For if God did not spare the angels when they sinned, but cast them into Hell and committed them to pits of nether gloom to be kept until the judgment ... then the LORD knows how to rescue the godly from trial, and to keep the unrighteous under punishment until the day of judgment, and especially those who indulge in the lust of defiling passion and despise authority. (2 Peter 2:4,9-10)

Jude agreed with Peter when he wrote,

And the angels that did not keep their own position but left their proper dwelling have been kept by Him in eternal chains in the nether gloom until the judgment of the great day; just as Sodom and Gomorrah and the surrounding cities, which likewise acted immorally and indulged in unnatural lust, serve as an example by undergoing a punishment of eternal fire. (Jude 6-7)

Paul recognizes that:

... even Satan disguises himself as an angel of light. So it is not strange if his servants disguise themselves as servants of righteousness. Their end will correspond to their deeds.
(2 Corinthians 11:14-15)

Some of Satan's servants are human beings and others are demons. These demons often pretend to be angels who have been sent by Jesus. God's authentic angels come to assist us in our ministries of helping people to know Jesus Christ as their Savior, LORD, Healer and Deliverer,

Are they not all ministering spirits sent forth to serve, for the sake of those who are to obtain salvation. (Hebrews 1:14)

The thief comes only to steal and kill and destroy; I (Jesus) *came that they may have life, and have it abundantly.* (John 10:10)

As we have the same purpose as our Leader, Jesus Christ, so also, demons have the same purpose as their leader.

We could not possibly deal with any angels in our own strength, whether faithful or fallen, because they are too powerful. The only fallen heavenly angel we have to deal with is the devil, and we cannot deal with him without the help of our appointed Counselor, the Holy Spirit. Only when we, as Christians, have been baptized with the Holy Spirit, can we do spiritual warfare with confidence.

But when the Counselor comes, whom I shall send to you from the Father, even the Spirit of Truth, who proceeds from the Father, He will bear witness to Me; and you also are witnesses, because you have been with Me from the beginning ... Nevertheless I tell you the truth: it is to your advantage that I go away, for if I do not go away, the Counselor will not come to you; but if I go, I will send Him to you." (John 15:26-27; 16:7)

In both Hebrew and Greek, the word for "angel" also means "messenger." It can mean "a human messenger serving as an envoy; an envoy; one who is sent" by humans or by God. While angels can be messengers of God, evil spirits are messengers of Satan. Although demons do not have the power of the heavenly angels, they do have some power to harass, inflict torment, cause sickness, and even kill people.

Evil spirits are *spirits*, but that does not mean they cannot move furniture or push people or throw articles around or go inside people's bodies, as we will see in a later chapter.

So – where do demons or evil spirits come from? The Bible answers that question. It tells us they are the inventions of a "base mind." This will be explained more fully later in the book.

And since they did not see fit to acknowledge God, God gave them up to a base mind and to improper conduct. They were filled with all manner of wickedness, evil, covetousness, malice. Full of envy, murder, strife, deceit, malignity, they are gossips, slanderers, haters of God, insolent, haughty, boastful, inventors of evil,[10] disobedient to parents, foolish, faithless, heartless, ruthless. Though they know God's decree that those who do such things deserve to die, they not only do them but approve those who practice them. (Romans 1:28-32)

A "base mind" in Greek (adokimon, os) describes a person who has not passed the test and so is unqualified, worthless or base: in short, a person who is unfit for any good deed.

They profess to know God, but they deny him by their deeds; they are detestable, disobedient, unfit for any good deed. (Titus 1:16)

While some may question the idea of demons being the "invention" of base minds, suggesting that places them in the realm of simple imagination, the word "invention" or "inventions" (epheuretes) are the proper translations both in Greek and Hebrew. While thoughts and ideas may be simple inhabitants of the mind (all in one's head), when they develop into inventions, they have substance apart from the mind that brought them into existence.

"Epheuretes" are not simply the ordinary works of a base mind which results in sinful behaviour. The English translation is "to think up, devise or fabricate in the mind; try to invent an alibi; to think out or produce (a new device, process, etc.); originate, as by experiment; devise for the first time, as Edison invented the phonograph." The word "invention" is defined as "something invented; specifically: a) something thought up or mentally fabricated; falsehood. b) something originated by experiment, etc; a new device or contrivance."

---
[10] Greek: Inventors of evil things

Demons are not easily invented. They are not the ordinary manifestations of the base mind or the simple works of the flesh, but the product of creating an evil being called a "tulpa" or "tulpas." They have a life of their own apart from the mind that conceived them. These are called "mind creatures" (demons) that are invented and let loose in the world and have an existence of their own apart from their inventors. If they were simply manifestations of the fruit of a base mind, a different Greek word (phaino) would have been used. This is the only place in the New Testament where the Greek word "epheuretes," meaning "invention," is used.

The evil spirits invented by people with base minds can be dangerous if not handled correctly by Christians who have been baptized with the Holy Spirit and who are knowledgeable about their spiritual authority over evil.

The bottom line is this: all messengers of Satan – whether they be the rebellious heavenly angels chained up until the final judgement or demons whom we, with the authority given to us by Jesus, could send into the abyss – will, in the end, be cast into the Lake of Fire with the devil. There, too, will go everyone who does not receive Jesus Christ as Savior and LORD and whose name is not written in, or has been removed from, the Book of Life.

> *And they begged him not to command them to depart into the abyss.* (Luke 8:31)

> *... and the* devil *who had deceived them was thrown into the Lake of Fire and sulphur where the beast and the false prophet were, and they will be tormented day and night for ever and ever.* (Revelation 20:10)

> *He who conquers shall be clad thus in white garments, and I will not blot his name out of the Book of Life; I will confess his name before my Father and before His angels.* (Revelation 3:5)

> *... and all who dwell on earth will worship it, every one whose name has not been written before the foundation of the world in the Book of Life of the Lamb that was slain.* (Revelation 13:8)

... and the dwellers on earth whose names have not been written in the Book of Life from the foundation of the world, will marvel to behold the beast, because it was and is not and is to come. (Revelation 17:8)

And I saw the dead, great and small, standing before the throne, and books were opened. Also another book was opened, which is the Book of Life. And the dead were judged by what was written in the books, by what they had done ... and if any one's name was not found written in the Book of Life, he was thrown into the Lake of Fire. (Revelation 20:12,15)

*... and if any one takes away from the words of the book of this prophecy, God will take away his share in the tree of life and in the holy city, which are described in this book. (*Revelation 22:19)

And so will be the end of the devil, his demons and everybody who does not receive Jesus Christ as Savior and Lord – not a fate to risk!

Drawing the Lines ...

The Old Testament Spiritual Structure

In order to get a clear picture of the kingdom of God and the kingdom of the devil, it's important to understand the structure of each.

God's Network

In the Old Testament, "Yahweh" is the Name by which God revealed Himself. Under the old covenant, God ruled His people directly, as their King. He liked to visit His people Himself. When He met with people in the Old Testament, He most often revealed Himself in the form of "the Angel of the Lord." It was as Though He would not send His angels to do anything which He Himself wouldn't do, so He would take on the appearance of an angelic being.

God's visits were too numerous in the Old Testament to mention them all; however, He spoke to Hagar (see Genesis 16), Moses (see Exodus 3:2), Balaam (see Numbers 22:22, 35), Samson's mother (see Judges 13:3) and Elijah (see 1 Kings 19:7), to name a few.

In the form of the Angel of the Lord, God often destroyed Israel's enemies – such as the Assyrians when they surrounded Jerusalem. He visited their camp at night and killed 185,000 of them – evidently the entire army.[11] Perhaps the reason for Satan's mistake in thinking he could defeat God, was that God looked like an ordinary angel when He visited His people. It would be easy to mistake Him for someone weak and insignificant who could easily be defeated when He came to earth in the humble form of Jesus Christ.

> *... He had no form or comeliness that we should look at Him, and no beauty that we should desire Him.* (Isaiah 53:2)

God set up an order in the spiritual realm that resembled a military organization. His angels are His army. (The word "hosts" in many English versions means "army.") He established a chain of command, with Himself as the Commander-in-Chief. An archangel, Michael,[12] is next in command as His field-marshal. Michael is the only archangel mentioned by name in the Bible and may be the one who will shout when the LORD descends.

> *For the LORD Himself will descend from Heaven with a cry of command, with the archangel's call, and with the sound of the trumpet of God.* (1 Thessalonians 4:16)

In this simple military structure, it would appear that God set up a network of angels to cover the whole earth, and probably the whole of creation. They have territorial assignments that include both cities and countries and are assigned to both individuals and to national ethnic groups, like the Jews. While not normally visible to people, they can be seen when they, or God, determine it to be necessary.

Three Kinds of Angels in the Kingdom of God

All angels are under God's command. It is their responsibility to help, serve and give direction from God to those who are heirs of salvation.

> *Are they not all ministering spirits sent forth to serve, for the sake of those who are to obtain salvation?* (Hebrews 1:14)

The Bible does not tell us how many angels there are. It indicates only that there are a lot of them; for instance, we are told that a million of

---

[11] See 2 Kings 19:35
[12] See Jude 1:9

them ministered to God while a billion stood before His throne. There are more angels than we can count: thousands upon thousands.

> *... a thousand thousands served Him, and ten thousand times ten thousand stood before Him; the court sat in judgment, and the books were opened.* (Daniel 7:10)

In order to understand how God uses His angels, it is necessary to examine their assignments as described in the Old Testament. There are three kinds of angels in the kingdom of God:

- Seraphim
- Cherubim
- Regular angels

The Seraphim and the Cherubim both have wings, while the regular angels do not.

The Seraphim

Isaiah reported seeing the seraphim angels surrounding God's throne. Some people think they were guarding God's throne, but I cannot believe God needs any kind of protection. According to Isaiah, these angels led in worship around God's throne by crying,

> *Holy, holy, holy, is the LORD of hosts: the whole earth is full of His glory.* (Isaiah 6:2)

When Isaiah confessed his sin, it was one of the seraphim who took a coal from the altar with tongs. With it, he touched Isaiah's lips to purge his sin. He had to be cleansed if he were to be used by God as a prophet.

The seraphim are the worship leaders or high priests of God's heavenly Temple which, of course, is His throne. They are the same four beasts of Revelation 4:8.

> *... who are full of eyes all round and within, and day and night they never cease to sing, "Holy, holy, holy, is the LORD God Almighty, who was and is and is to come!"* (Revelation 4:8)

Above Him stood the seraphim; each had six wings: with two He covered His face, and with two He covered his feet, and with two He flew." (Isaiah 6:2)

O LORD of hosts, God of Israel, who art enthroned above the cherubim, Thou art the God, Thou alone, of all the kingdoms of the earth; Thou hast made Heaven and earth. (Isaiah 37:16)

The Cherubim

The cherubim are involved in carrying out other assignments as God determines. They carry God's glory with them to prepare a place for Him to meet with His people or to do anything which requires the glory of God to be there.

Then the cherubim lifted up their wings, with the wheels beside them; and the glory of the God of Israel was over them.
(Ezekiel 11:22; see also Ezekiel 10:1-22)

God placed the cherubim at the east of the garden of Eden, one of whom had a flaming sword to guard the way to the tree of life.

He drove out the man; and at the east of the garden of Eden He placed the cherubim, and a flaming sword which turned every way, to guard the way to the tree of life. (Genesis 3:24)

Two golden figures of cherubim were made to form a part of the mercy seat and placed on the Ark of the Covenant where God promised to meet with Israel.

And you shall make two cherubim of gold; of hammered work shall you make them, on the two ends of the mercy seat. Make one cherub on the one end, and one cherub on the other end; of one piece with the mercy seat shall you make the cherubim on its two ends. The cherubim shall spread out their wings above, overshadowing the mercy seat with their wings, their faces one to another; toward the mercy seat shall the faces of the cherubim be. And you shall put the mercy seat on the top of the ark; and in the ark you shall put the testimony that I shall give you. There I will meet with you, and from above the mercy seat, from between the two cherubim that are upon the ark of the testimony, I will speak with you of all that I will give you in commandment for the people of Israel. (Exodus 25:18-22)

When Solomon built the Temple, he had cherubim carved out of olive wood (see 1 Kings 6:23-35) and overlaid with gold. They remind God's people that God dwelt between the cherubim.

Give ear, O Shepherd of Israel, Thou who leadest Joseph like a flock! Thou who art enthroned upon the cherubim, shine forth.
(Psalm 80:1)

God gave Ezekiel a vision of cherubim and wheels flying and with them came the glory of the LORD (see Ezekiel 10).

Regular Angels

The third class of angels look like regular people. They do not have wings. They are God's messengers, They carry out His instructions and guide His people so they can know His will. They often confirm what God has already told someone. They look like people, but with a difference; there's a glow about them which comes from spending time with God. After being with God, Moses' face shone from the fellowship. Like him, these angels usually appear to shine a little brighter or be a little different from ordinary people.

Perhaps the best-known angel, is Gabriel. He was sent to Daniel to interpret a vision and give him skill in understanding the prophecy concerning the Messiah.

And I heard a man's voice between the banks of the U'lai, and it called, "Gabriel, make this man understand the vision." (Daniel 8:16)

... while I was speaking in prayer, the man Gabriel, whom I had seen in the vision at the first, came to me in swift flight at the time of the evening sacrifice." (Daniel 9:21)

Later on, he would announce to Elizabeth the birth of her son, John the Baptist; and to Mary the birth of her son, Jesus, who would fulfill the prophecy Gabriel explained to Daniel. Gabriel is never called an archangel in the Bible.

It was the regular type of angels who visited Sodom and urged Lot to leave the city when God was about to destroy it because of the wickedness of the people.

> *The two angels came to Sodom in the evening; and Lot was sitting in the gate of Sodom. When Lot saw them, he rose to meet them, and bowed himself with his face to the earth ... When morning dawned, the angels urged Lot, saying, "Arise, take your wife and your two daughters who are here, lest you be consumed in the punishment of the city."* (Genesis 19:1,15)

These are the kind of angels Jacob saw in his dream, ascending and descending the ladder which reached from Heaven to earth.[13] Those angels, I am convinced, were going from Heaven down to their assignments and returning after completing them. It was two such angels who visited Lot in Sodom, to warn him about the forthcoming destruction of the city[14] so that he and his family could escape. It was these angels who talked with Mary Magdalene and other women in Jesus' empty tomb.

> *But Mary stood weeping outside the tomb, and as she wept she stooped to look into the tomb; and she saw two angels in white, sitting where the body of Jesus had lain, one at the head and one at the feet. They said to her, "Woman, why are you weeping?" She said to them, "Because they have taken away my* LORD, *and I do not know where they have laid Him."*
> (John 20:11-13; see also Luke 24:23)

The archangel Michael is in charge of the regular angels. He, himself, is one. They are just a little higher than men in God's chain of command.[15]

God places them in charge of us in order to guard us wherever we go.

> *For He will give His angels charge of you to guard you in all your ways. On their hands they will bear you up, lest you dash your foot against a stone.* (Psalm 91:11-12)

---
[13] See Genesis 28:12
[14] See Genesis 19:13
[15] See Psalm 8:5

Regular angels are encouraged to bless Yahweh, for they are the mighty ones who carry out His commandments and who listen to the voice of His Word.

Bless the LORD (Yahweh), O you His angels, you mighty ones who do His Word, hearkening to the voice of His Word! (Psalm 103:20)

They are spirits, but they are also physical beings who carry out God's directions. They are encouraged to join with all of creation to praise Him.

Praise Him, all His angels, praise Him, all His host! (Psalm 148:2)

Angels are God's unseen army. They are always on duty looking after His interests. They defend His people, whether the people have the eyes to see them or not. When the Syrian army surrounded the city of Dothan in an attempt to capture Elisha, Elisha had the spiritual eyes to see the angelic army, but his servant was afraid and blind to it until God opened his eyes.

He said, "Fear not, for those who are with us are more than those who are with them." Then Elisha prayed, and said, "O LORD (Yahweh), I pray Thee, open his eyes that he may see." So the LORD opened the eyes of the young man, and he saw; and behold, the mountain was full of horses and chariots of fire round about Elisha. And when the Syrians came down against him, Elisha prayed to the LORD, and said, "Strike this people, I pray Thee, with blindness." So He struck them with blindness in accordance with the prayer of Elisha. (2 Kings 6:16-18)

The Syrians, of course, were all blinded to this. In spiritual warfare, we must learn the all-important lesson, that those who are on our side are always greater in number than those who are on the enemy's side. The only way we can be defeated is to believe the deceptions of the enemy.

There is no record in the Old Testament of any angel of God ever being defeated by the kingdom of darkness. There is no record of God's faithful angels ever failing to carry out His commands. The only so-called failure is that of the *unfaithful* angels who sinned. They, and Satan, are the only subjects of any record of angelic failure.

Satan's Network

Just as God's spiritual network gives structure to the kingdom of God, the devil's network comprises the kingdom of darkness. It appears that it has a parallel structure to that of the kingdom of God, another evidence of Satan's counterfeiting schemes. However, it was dealt a severe deathblow by Emmanuel, Jesus Christ, when Satan was foolish enough to confront God in outright rebellion. Let us take a closer look at his allies.

Evil Angels

It appears that a number of angels sinned and became evil angels. Through their pride, Satan wove them together into the kingdom of darkness and formed his network.

He let loose on them his fierce anger, wrath, indignation, and distress, a company of destroying angels. (Psalm 78:49)

The kingdom of darkness is comprised of these evil beings. We do not know all the circumstances or nature of their sinning; however, we do know some of them came to earth, took wives and had children (nephilim) against God's will.

When men began to multiply on the face of the ground, and daughters were born to them, the sons of God saw that the daughters of men were fair; and they took to wife such of them as they chose. Then the LORD *(Yahweh) said, "My spirit shall not abide in man for ever, for he is flesh, but his days shall be a hundred and twenty years." The Nephilim were on the earth in those days, and also afterward, when the sons of God came in to the daughters of men, and they bore children to them. These were the mighty men that were of old, the men of renown.* (Genesis 6:1-4)

When the Scripture speaks of the devil and his messengers, it refers to two types of evil angels:

1. Rebellious heavenly angels that were cast out of Heaven down to Tartarus where they remain chained.[16]

---
[16] 2 Peter 2:4,9; Jude 6; Luke 10:18

2. Demons or evil spirits. These are mistakenly called Satan's angels, but are not real angels, but are the inventions of evil minds.[17]

It can be confusing, because when Paul wrote to the Church at Corinth about his struggles, the Greek word translated "messenger" is (aggelos), otherwise translated as "angel." Nevertheless, evil spirits are not angels.

And to keep me from being too elated by the abundance of revelations, a thorn was given to me in the flesh, a messenger of Satan, to harass me, to keep me from being too elated. (2 Corinthians 12:7)

Unclean and Familiar Spirits (Demons or Evil Spirits)

These evil, unclean and "familiar"[18] spirits or demons are not fallen angels. The Bible gives details of their origin. They are a unique class, created by evil (base) minds, which Satan uses in his fight against the Kingdom of God.

Evil, unclean, and familiar spirits (demons) like to possess or take up residence in individuals, houses or buildings, where they can control, intimidate, harass, and kill people. These seem to be the most uncontrollable and unpredictable group in the kingdom of darkness.

Some demons are called "shadow people," because they appear in the form of shadowy figures. Some people have assumed them to be from another planet.

A familiar spirit (so called because they appear to be familiar) pretends to be the ghost of someone known – like a family member, a friend, an acquaintance or a famous person. The Bible makes it clear that people who die cannot return to earth because they go either to Paradise (a temporary Heaven) or to Tartaros (a temporary Hell) until Jesus returns. Death is a one way experience.[19]

---

[17] See Appendix
[18] Leviticus 19:31; 20:6,27; Deuteronomy 18:11; 1 Samuel 28; 2 Kings 21:6; 1 Chronicles 10:13; Isaiah 19:3, 29:4 (KJV)
[19] See Luke 16:26

These familiar spirits deceive people through impersonation. They can make a man talk with a woman's voice or a woman talk with a man's voice. Since many demons have lived for many centuries, they can be familiar with a whole host of people known to a victim through history and they have no trouble speaking different languages.

I have seen demons in human form that looked like people; even one in a black form that gave the appearance of being a monk. Sometimes they look like shapes covered with bed sheets of varying colors. For the most part, they are ugly and unattractive, although there are those that are very attractive. Some are funny looking. Some appear very small about the size of a rat. Others take on animal or bird shapes. Some appear like various shaped or colored clouds. Some resemble Halloween masks and costumes. They may appear in varying shapes and sizes to either frighten the people they want to control – or to disarm them by not frightening them, so they can possess or harass them after it's too late to escape.

Regardless of what they may look like, or whether they can be seen at all by the human eye, their purpose is to harass, possess, manipulate, frighten, hurt, and destroy people.

For the most part, evil spirits, which can manifest in varying shapes and sizes, seem to prefer to remain invisible to the human eye. At times, they will materialize to frighten people; usually bothering children first, making themselves visible and terrorizing them. But there is no rule of thumb. They will attack people of all ages.

When they become visible, they will often assume the outward appearance of some deceased person known to the intended victim in the past, such as a family member or friend. It's not unusual for them to take on the appearance of someone who may once have lived in a particular house and be assumed to be "phantoms" or "ghosts" of the former occupants. The purpose of these evil spirits is not only to harass and control people, but "to steal, kill and destroy."

The thief comes only to steal and kill and destroy. I (Jesus) came that they may have life, and have it abundantly. (John 10:10)

To believers who know the authority we have in Jesus Christ, these are all vain attempts to defeat the kingdom of God. Nevertheless, the wiles of the enemy must be taken seriously because they can be dangerous. Not only are souls at stake; physical lives can also be in danger.

Familiar spirits like to visit and harass people when they are grieving the death of a loved one, pretending to be the spirit of the deceased person. Often working through mediums who supposedly can make contact with the dead, they give people messages from, or about, dead people. They may visit grieving people with advice that will cause them to make bad decisions regarding their daily living, making their victims appear to be unstable. God has warned us not to seek advice from mediums because they will defile anybody who goes to them.[20]

And when they say to you, "Consult the mediums and the wizards who chirp and mutter," should not a people consult their God? Should they consult the dead on behalf of the living? (Isaiah 8:19)

By gaining their victim's confidence, familiar spirits give advice that may at first seem helpful; but because their hidden purpose is to torment the victims, the advice eventually proves to be destructive. They usually have many followers who are misled and who, unless they repent, like the familiar spirits, will not go to Heaven.

Familiar spirits can take on the appearance of people who have died and imitate children, adults, strange looking people, animals, rats, bats, birds and other creatures. When they possess people, they can cause them to be dehumanized and degrade them so that they will imitate animals' movements and make animal-like noises.

I was once at a Full Gospel Business Men's Fellowship meeting in a motel in Fredericton, New Brunswick. I was praying with some people, when I saw over-sized rats running under some tables and through a wall. At first I thought I was imagining this, but when it happened several times, I discovered there was a bar on the other side of the wall where the demons had gone to seek out new victims.

---

[20] (See Leviticus 19:31; 20:6; Deuteronomy 18:11; 1 Samuel 28:3,7-9; 2 Kings 21:6; 23:24; Isaiah 8:19; 19:3)

Sometimes, familiar spirits imitate the symptoms of physical and psychological disorders. Frequently, they cause a possessed person to have epileptic-like seizures, often causing him or her to have pain and live in a tortured state. When given medical tests, nothing abnormal is discovered in such people. However, if the demons are not cast out, the victims will suffer the consequences of the imitated disorder which usually eventuates in death.

The first time I was a guest on the Richard Syrette Show, a call-in radio talk show on station CFRB in Toronto, Canada, I mentioned that in my experience, the most frequently imitated psychological disorder is schizophrenia.

A listener called in and said, "If what you have described is true, it sounds to me as though my sister has been misdiagnosed for over twenty years. She has often tried to tell us about a spirit that went into her. No one believes her, because no one thinks such a thing could be possible. Now she doesn't talk about it, for fear she'll end up back in the hospital with heavier medication. Can you help her?"

While it's true that there is a legitimate disorder called schizophrenia, some so-called schizophrenia is actually a spiritual disorder. True schizophrenia can be caused by a variety of things, such as a chemical disorder or prolonged abuse. Visual and audio hallucinations are often involved. When the source is an evil spirit, the possessed person can generally identify a time or incident when the spirit entered his or her body and began to cause problems, often forcing the person to do things out of his or her control. Whenever such a person tries to tell doctors, psychologists, psychiatrists, pastors or counselors about the situation, he or she is often categorized as having an emotional or psychological disorder. Many are subjected to drug therapy and confined to a hospital for treatment. Because of this, a possessed person will learn very quickly not to mention the spirits and settle into a very lonely and tormented life. Because of the bizarre behavior caused by the evil spirits, he or she usually becomes socially isolated, not unlike the man in the Gadarenes.

In this case, I told the man that if his sister would like to see me, she would have to call me, because I do not solicit ministry.

The sister called, and I made an appointment to visit her in the west end of Toronto. When I arrived at her apartment, her two brothers were with her. She looked like a worn-out woman in her sixties. I asked her to tell me what had happened. She explained that, about twenty years prior to this, she had accompanied a friend to a meeting in a church where there was a special speaker. She had gone there to broaden her spiritual horizons. She continued, "The speaker was a Buddhist monk. He walked over to me and placed his hand on my head and a spirit came into me. It took control over my body movements. I tried to contact the monk for help, but he wouldn't call me back. I sought help from a minister and then went to see my doctor. He sent me to a psychiatrist, who hospitalized me. I can't get anyone to listen and understand."

I asked, "In what ways has this affected your daily living?"

She explained that this spirit would make her scream and fall down in public. It had gotten so bad that she had had to stop doing her grocery shopping during the day and now she did it at night instead, when there were very few people around. Most of her time was spent locked up in her apartment. The only people she ever saw were her family. She looked at me and asked, "Can you help me?"

I explained that Jesus Christ could help her. I told her she had been possessed by an evil spirit. For her safety, before I could deal with this evil spirit, it was going to be necessary for her to invite Jesus Christ to be her Savior and receive what is called the baptism of the Holy Spirit, so that God's Holy Spirit would come into her heart and protect her from evil possession. I explained that in every person there is a place for the Holy Spirit, but that if we do not have the Holy Spirit living in us, we will have an empty space that makes us feel as though "something is missing." Without the protection and infilling of the Holy Spirit, this empty space can be filled with an evil spirit, just as happened to her.

I told her that she could replace the evil spirit with the Holy Spirit, if she so desired. She thought for a few moments and then said, "I have been living with a bad spirit for twenty years and the Holy Spirit is a good spirit, isn't He?"

I said, "Yes."

She replied, "That would be a welcome change; so, my answer is yes."

I then took authority over the spirit and, in the Name of Jesus Christ, I commanded the evil spirit to leave her body and to go to the abyss. When it left, I laid hands on her and she prayed along with me to ask Jesus to forgive her sin and be her Savior and Lord. Next, we prayed and asked Jesus to baptize her with the Holy Spirit. She received Him and began to speak in tongues, continuing for several minutes. It was after praying with her, that I realized her whole appearance had changed. She no longer looked old and worn out. I could see that she was just in her mid-forties. The evil spirit left her forever. Later, she called me to say, "Thanks to Jesus, I have found myself again."

Another woman called about her sister, who was acting strangely and not making any sense when she talked. I suggested the woman should ask her sister if what she was going through, might have anything to do with a spirit. So, she did and her sister replied, "Yes," and went on to say, "At first there was only one, but since then, many more have come. I'm at the place where I can hardly control my body and what I say. Nobody will listen to me. Nobody will take me seriously. My psychiatrist thinks I'm schizophrenic. I feel like I'm going out of my mind."

I met with the sister and, with her permission, I commanded the demons in her to leave her body and go to the abyss and stay there. They left and we prayed, asking Jesus to become her Savior and to baptize her with the Holy Spirit so she could be protected and know His plan for her life. As we prayed, the Holy Spirit took the place of the demons. She was immediately in her right mind and speaking in a new language.[21]

Her sister asked, "Can I receive the Holy Spirit too?"

"Of course!" I replied. We prayed and she, too, received salvation and the baptism in the Holy Spirit. She, too, began to speak in the new language which the Holy Spirit gave her.

The woman then remarked, "Now we are both in our right minds!"

---

[21] See Mark 16:17

The Old Testament law required that a person with a familiar spirit had to be stoned to death.

A man or a woman who is a medium or a wizard shall be put to death; they shall be stoned with stones, their blood shall be upon them. (Leviticus 20:27)

Today, however, because of Jesus, we can expel the demons and set people free. Although we have the authority to expel them, we have to stay on the lookout for their efforts to wreak havoc in our lives. That is why Peter warns:

Discipline yourselves, keep alert. Like a roaring lion, your adversary the devil *prowls around, looking for someone to devour.*
(1 Peter 5:8)

Bolder evil spirits are called "poltergeists." While they may occasionally seem like playful ghosts, they can be very destructive and irritating; turning on or off lights, radios and television sets, moving furniture, causing people to be sick, throwing articles across a room and breaking objects. Sometimes, they hide clothes and other things, causing confusion and bringing terrible fear to the people who live in the affected house. They can whisper gossip into people's ears and cause dissension. Their presence can contaminate a building by causing terrible smells, the source of which cannot be detected. They will often enter a house or building with the people whom they are afflicting. Their goal is to intimidate, control and kill the inhabitants.

The thief comes only to steal and kill and destroy ... (John 10:10)

Three Kinds of Demons (Evil Spirits)

Satan's mighty angels are chained up in their prison, so all he has left to do his bidding are his evil and unclean spirits. While the kingdom of darkness is only a shadow of its former Old Testament power, that is no reason to think it is any less dangerous. We must know who our enemies are. We need to recognize the devil's allies in the war in which we are engaged.

There are three different kinds of demons, identified by Paul in Ephesians 6:12. They are demons of:
1. Principalities
2. Powers
3. World rulers (elemental spirits of the universe)

> *For we are not contending* (Greek "pale": engaged in a challenging contest, wrestling, fighting) *against flesh and blood, but against principalities, against powers, against world rulers of this present darkness, against the spiritual hosts in heavenly places.* (Ephesians 6:12)

This is the army of wickedness which used to be in heavenly places, but which now has hellish plans for our lives.

These three kinds of evil spirits – principalities, powers, and world rulers – are the so-called *"hosts of wickedness in heavenly places."* The heavenly places are the hearts and minds of people for which Jesus died and rose again. He wants them to be part of His Temple, His Body, and His Church.

Yes, the devil has power. And, yes, the evil spirits have power. And, yes, they are dangerous. However, Christians have more power. Christians are more dangerous to the enemy than the enemy is to us. But, we have to be clear that we are engaged in spiritual warfare. We must learn to recognize the enemy and how to put on the whole armor of God so that we can *"stand against the wiles of the devil"* (see Ephesians 6:11).

Let's look at these different kinds of evil spirits and the realms in which they operate and attack people.

1. Principalities

First of all, "principalities" are a class of evil spirits which operates in the occult world, through practices which are defined by God as "abhorrent," and which attempt to lead people into the kingdom of darkness.

> *... you shall not learn to follow the abominable practices of those nations. There shall not be found among you any one who burns his son or his daughter as an offering, anyone who practices divination,*

a soothsayer, or an augur, or a sorcerer, or a charmer, or a medium, or a wizard, or a necromancer. For whoever does these things is an abomination to the LORD; and because of these abominable practices the LORD your God is driving them out before you.
(Deuteronomy 18:9-12)

What God is warning us about here, in modern terms, is any involvement in Satanism, fortune telling, foretelling the future, forecasting the future using omens, white witchcraft, communicating with the spirit world, black witchcraft and claiming to communicate with the dead. All of these occult practices are directed and controlled by evil spirits called principalities. Through people who are involved in these occult practices, millions of people are led away from God and given a false hope. Many of them become possessed.

In 1974, a young woman, who was involved in witchcraft, came to see me one evening in my church office in Brampton, Ontario. She told me she was involved in a coven and that she was supposed to take over the leadership of it. However, she had become more and more frightened as she learned about and experienced the power of the evil spirit that guided her and gave her power. What had started out to be exciting and fun, had suddenly turned on her and she felt the spirit, that was directing her, threatened her life. She had been talking with a young Christian woman from our church, who had told her that Jesus Christ could set her free from the spirit that was dominating her life. As I talked with her, using the Name of Jesus in our conversation, the demon that controlled her began to react.

Suddenly, she jumped up screaming and ran out of my office. I followed her. She was bouncing from wall to wall, turning and twisting down the hallway toward the side entrance of the church. The principality spirit was trying to escape. She was thrown against the side doors and fell to the floor writhing and screaming. When I caught up to her I commanded the evil spirit to leave her. It left immediately. I then prayed with her to invite Jesus to be her Savior and LORD and to be baptized in the Holy Spirit. She was set free. However, the next morning, when she woke up, she discovered her arm had been broken from being thrown against the church doors.

Knowing the power of the spirit that had possessed her through witchcraft, she was fearful of what the coven of witches might try to do to her and to me. I assured her that they had absolutely no power to hurt either of us. Jesus Christ had given us power over them. They might try to shoot some of their fiery darts at us, but they could do us no harm. Sure enough, the head of the coven, whom she was supposed to replace, contacted her and threatened to curse both of us if she did not return to witchcraft. Almost immediately, I received written curses stuck to my car and the door of my home. I was told later that the witches began to curse us in their coven meetings.

Now, any witch, or anybody involved in any kind of occult practices, who has not learned about the danger involved in trying to curse a Holy Spirit-baptized Christian with the "signs following[22]," has not learned his or her craft very well. Any witch or warlock, who knows his or her business, knows they must never try to curse a born-again, Spirit-filled Christian, because curses cannot affect a Christian. Not only that, but a curse will bounce off a Christian and boomerang back on the sender.

Like a sparrow in its flitting, like a swallow in its flying, an undeserved curse goes nowhere. (Proverbs 26:2)

As Balaam discovered when he tried to curse Israel, unless God gives permission to curse His people, they cannot be cursed.[23]

The witch broke this cardinal rule. She tried to curse Christians – her former coven-member and me. The result was that she died. She was killed by her own curse as it rebounded back against her. Like Lot's wife, she could not believe that the God of Israel could do such a mighty thing. God is our defense. We have the shield of faith with which we can extinguish curses.

... take the shield of faith, with which you will be able to quench all the flaming arrows of the evil one. (Ephesians 6:16)

---

[22] Mark 16:17,18
[23] See Numbers 23: 17-24

We have the authority to set people free from principality demons.

Christians have nothing to fear when we hear about people in the occult putting curses against individual Christians and churches. I have to laugh when I hear Christians getting upset when they hear such things. The enemy knows they cannot risk a frontal attack against our churches and ministries or else they will be destroyed. Consequently, their most predictable tactic is to start a rumor designed to short-circuit an effective ministry and cause Christians live in fear of them. Principality demons have suffered enough defeats that they are constantly trying to warn their cohorts not to attack Christians, but like all self-willed and rebellious people they do not take direction very well – even from other demons.

2. Powers

The second type or class of evil spirits is called powers. These demons attempt to possess people and control them physically. They do so by going inside a person's body and overriding his or her control by taking control of their body movements – like a hand-puppeteer.

Most often, these demons will imitate psychological disorders in the people who they possess. They will frequently imitate schizophrenia. When a person is possessed by such a demon, they will demonstrate all the normal symptoms of whatever disorder is being copied. Unfortunately, a doctor will usually prescribe heavy medication that allows the evil spirit to have even greater control over the will of the possessed person. If such a person who is possessed goes into a church building or attempts to participate in a Christian worship service, it's not uncommon for them to have a violent uncontrollable reaction or breakdown that will require hospitalization. If they try to explain to a doctor what is going on with them, they will often be heavily medicated, and possibly placed in a psychiatric ward until they calm down. Possessed people learn very quickly to be careful about to whom they talk regarding their condition. Most people will think they are crazy. Evil spirits, of the "powers" variety, will victimize whomever they possess and will often drive the possessed person to injure, hurt, or even murder other people; whether family members, friends, or strangers.

The Gadarene man, whom Jesus met, had demons that were called "powers" evil spirits.[24] He had supernatural strength, which allowed him to break chains. When Jesus asked the man what his name was, he replied, "'Legion,' because he had many demons.[25] A Roman legion consisted of up to 6,000 soldiers, so that was a lot of demons. Jesus cast them out and set the man free, restoring him to his right mind.

Although a born-again, Spirit-filled Christian cannot be internally possessed by any kind of demon, he or she can be harassed from outside. Sometimes evil spirits "ride" like monkeys on people they are harassing, causing pain or lack of control over some part of their bodies. Jesus has given Christians authority over powers so that we can cast them out and set people free to know Jesus Christ as their Savior and Lord.

Shortly after our arrival in Brampton, Ontario, Canada, where I became the Senior Pastor of St. Paul's United Church, I went to the local hospital, Peel Memorial, to visit some patients affiliated with our congregation. On my list, were a young man and a young woman in their twenties, who were patients in the psychiatric ward. They were neither related nor acquainted with each other.

First, I found the young man and asked a nurse for a room where I could talk and pray with him. She graciously accommodated me. While talking with the young man, I realized he did not have a psychiatric problem. He was possessed with an evil spirit. With his permission, I cast the demon out of him and prayed with him to receive Jesus Christ as his Savior and Lord. He was baptized with the Holy Spirit and began to speak in tongues, which indicated that he was set free.

After leaving the young man, I located the young woman and took her into the same room, in which I had just prayed. Much to my surprise, after talking with her about her problem, I discovered that she, too, was possessed by an evil spirit. With her permission, I cast out the evil spirit and prayed with her to receive Jesus Christ as her Savior and Lord. She, too, began to speak in a different language. I was surprised to encounter

---

[24] Ephesians 6:12
[25] See Luke 8:26-39

two people who had been possessed by demons during my first hospital visit in my new church, but I thanked Jesus that they had been set free.

I then went on to visit several other people in the hospital and prayed with them for healing of their sicknesses and, when appropriate, for the success of surgery.

The next day, I received a telephone call from the head nurse in the psychiatric ward. She said, "The psychiatrists would like to have a meeting with you to discuss this new therapeutic technique you have."

I told her I would go up and discuss it with her first. She agreed. However, as soon as I mentioned evil spirits and demons, her facial expression made it clear that she didn't want to hear anything about my – ahem – "new therapeutic technique."

She said, "We'll call you if we think we need your help."

I knew I would never receive a call from the psychiatrists, because most medical practitioners see no value in spiritual approaches. They believe that the idea of demon possession is an emotionally rooted, psychological or physical issue. That opinion has placed demon-possessed people in a position where they are subjected to the direction of the kingdom of darkness, with no place to escape. They are drugged and left to vegetate in the haze of a prescription-defined world.

That same year, I was asked by the morning news television program, *Canada A.M.* on the C.T.V. Network, to preview the new movie, *The Exorcist*. It was being released at the University Theatre in Toronto.

I was amazed at the story. It demonstrated one of the common ways (playing with a ouija board) by which people can be possessed, and showed the effects of the demon upon the little girl. Of course Hollywood added their sizzle, with the girl's head twirling around. But for me, the most twisted aspect of the movie was the lie with which it ended – that Christians cannot effectively cast out demons.

I had observed most of the things demonstrated in the movie through the course of my ministry, and so was invited several times to discuss the movie and the consequences of getting involved in occult practices, on *Canada A.M.* and many other television and radio talk shows. Usually invited along with me, were occult practitioners (satanists, witches and warlocks, mediums and others too numerous to mention) to discuss the movie and the topic of possession. When I stop to think about it, I am often amazed that Jesus would make my introduction to national television in Canada, through reviewing and discussing a movie about exorcism.

The *Toronto Star* newspaper printed my review. Fortunately, someone gave it to a young mother who was concerned for her three-year-old daughter, after having seen the movie. What the young mom had seen on the screen, was exactly what had been happening to her daughter for six months. She had run out of the theatre, frightened for the life of her daughter. She lost weight and was on the verge of a nervous breakdown by the time she read my review. After reading it, she realized there was hope for her daughter.

The mother brought her little girl to my church office on a Sunday afternoon. The child was uncontrollable. She cursed and swore at me with a vocabulary worse than any of the miners I had worked with prior to going into the ministry. She was obviously possessed.

I asked the mother where this had all started. She told me it had begun in their apartment when, on a hot afternoon, an unusual cold wind came in through the open patio door. It was then that her daughter began to act weirdly and became uncontrollable.

I decided that the best place to deal with the little girl, was in their apartment where it had all begun. I told the mother to go to their apartment and I would follow them there.

It was a rather hot day and the apartment had no air conditioning. When I entered the girl's bedroom, she was sitting in her crib, bouncing up and down like a basketball – without moving a muscle. She was cursing and swearing and the bedroom was so cold that I could see my breath. Such phenomena are common when demons possess a person.

I took authority over the evil spirit and, in the Name of Jesus Christ, commanded the demon to leave her. It immediately left and she suddenly reverted back to being a normal three-year-old girl. I then prayed with her and her mother to receive Jesus as their Savior and Lord and to receive the Holy Spirit. They were set free.

That little girl has grown up serving Jesus Christ and I had the privilege of officiating at her wedding to a Christian man. She has a beautiful music ministry. Today, she is the mother of two children and she and her husband are serving Jesus Christ.

It is of the utmost importance that if we cast evil spirits out of a person, we understand that person has an empty place that needs to be replaced by the Holy Spirit, or else the evil spirit, after wandering around trying to find a new residence, will come back. Jesus warned about this when He said,

> *When the unclean spirit has gone out of a person, it wanders through waterless regions looking for a resting place, but not finding any, it says, "I will return to my house from which I came." When it comes, it finds it swept and put in order. Then it goes and brings seven other spirits more evil than itself, and they enter and live there; and the last state of that person is worse than the first.* (Luke 11:24-26)

A Spirit-filled Christian can easily drive out the powers type of evil spirits from a person who wants to be set free. When we cast out evil spirits, unclean spirits or demons (all are different words describing the same beings), the person needs to have the demon replaced by the Holy Spirit. This does not normally occur automatically. As I described earlier, for many people, the experience of salvation is often a separate experience from that of the baptism of the Holy Spirit. If the person does not receive the baptism of the Holy Spirit, they are in jeopardy of having the unclean spirit come back, along with seven other evil spirits, and his or her life will be eight times worse than before.

To put it another way: after the evil spirit leaves a person and he or she experiences salvation, he or she becomes a new wineskin,[26] prepared

---
[26] See Luke 5:37-39

and waiting for the new wine of the Holy Spirit to fill him or her. When a person receives forgiveness for sins, he or she is cleaned, swept and put in order – with no occupant – but prepared for the occupancy of the Holy Spirit. The new wineskin requires the new wine that only He can bring.

> *Neither is new wine put into old wineskins; if it is, the skins burst, and the wine is spilled, and the skins are destroyed; but new wine is put into fresh wineskins, and so both are preserved.* (Matthew 9:17; see also Mark 2:22; Luke 5:37-38)

After receiving the baptism of the Holy Spirit with the "signs following,"[27] we are no longer possessable by any evil spirit. Although they can harass us or invade (haunt) our homes, buildings or cars – trying to intimidate and influence those who live and work in those places – the Spirit-baptized person has the authority to send them to the abyss. If the person is not baptized in the Holy Spirit, he or she is in jeopardy of re-infestation.

Although Spirit-filled Christians cannot be possessed, powers can harass and attack them, and, if they are not careful, these spirits can physically hurt them. Christians are a threat to the kingdom of darkness. Some people are even killed. Powers will sometimes get violent when they are commanded to leave a person or building; but, no matter how they react, when commanded to do so, they have to leave in the Name of Jesus Christ.

One misunderstanding many people have, concerning power type evil spirits, is that they are non-sexual – neither male nor female. While it seems most evil spirits are not, with some this is not the case. There are some that attack people sexually. A demon that attacks women is called an "incubus," while a demon that attacks men is called a "succubus." Usually, they will attempt to seduce their victims when they are asleep; when their victims wake up, they are held down and, unless the victim calls on the Name of Jesus, rendered incapable of warding off their attackers.

It's not uncommon for either men or women to be sexually molested, or even raped, by demons. An incubus is generally thought to be male,

---

[27] See Mark 16:17-20

because it usually lies with a woman (who is either awake or sleeping) with whom it seeks sexual intercourse. A succubus is generally considered to be a female demon which usually seeks to have sexual relations with a man (who is either awake or sleeping). They seem to have heterosexual tendencies.

But there are also demons with a bi-sexual tendency. Demons will try to force themselves upon people of all ages, from children to adults. They are usually very brutal. I have dealt with a number of women who have been raped, over and over again, and who, when they tried to find a counselor or pastor who could help them, were not taken seriously. Most often, they were accused of making up a story, suffering from an overworked imagination or having a psychological disorder.

The first time I had a woman come to me seeking help in this regard, she explained, through her terror, that since moving into a new home with her family, she was being raped repeatedly at almost any time of the day or night. She was surprised that I took her seriously. I told her that I could get rid of the evil spirit who was attacking her, but I could not do so unless she was willing to ask Jesus Christ to be her Savior and Lord and receive the baptism of the Holy Spirit, with the evidence of speaking in tongues. Only then would she have authority over any demon who attempted to abuse her or invade her house again. If she were not willing to do those two things, then I would not be willing to get rid of the evil spirit, because Jesus tells us that it will gather together seven more spirits and come back, making her life even worse.

She said desperately, "I want Jesus to be my Savior and Lord. We prayed and she received salvation and the baptism of the Holy Spirit, with the evidence of speaking in tongues. I then went through her house and cast out the incubus demon and sent it to the abyss.

Men are completely devastated when they are attacked, overpowered and sodomized (male rape) by an unseen physical being. A man came to see me and described how he was wakened in the middle of the night by some being that held him paralyzed, while it carried out different sexual deviations upon his body. He was completely defeated, demoralized and dehumanized. When the succubus spirit left him, he ran to his bathroom and vomited and cried for hours. I explained what had occurred and that it could be stopped. I assured him that Jesus Christ was the only Person who could protect him against more attacks. I told him he needed to repent for his own sins, ask Jesus to be his Savior and LORD and receive the baptism of the Holy Spirit. Then, he would have authority to cast out any demon or evil spirit that tried to attack or harm him again.

He agreed. We prayed and he received the baptism of the Holy Spirit and began to speak in tongues – the proof that he had the authority to deal with evil spirits.

Although they normally do not make themselves visible to their victims, demons are physical beings. They are like the "invisible man" or "invisible woman." They can be belligerent and attack people, whether they are awake or asleep. Their victims live in terror. It's not unusual for family members or friends to witness victims being attacked but be unable to help or defend them, because the attacker is invisible and may attack them as well – or throw them aside or beat them up. All demons have physical powers, and although they like to remain unseen in most cases, they will appear if they believe it will further their objectives and lead their victims to cooperate with them.

No matter how corrupt, mean or threatening evil spirits are – whether seen or unseen – they are under the authority of any Christian who has received the baptism of the Holy Spirit – with the evidence to prove it.[28] Even if they know they are under the authority of certain Christians, demons will often argue, as they did with Jesus, in an effort not to be sent to the abyss.[29] Sometimes, they will throw things at us, try to push us away, try to trip us so we will fall down stairs, or threaten us – as though they have authority over us.

Nevertheless, when we command demons to leave in the Name of Jesus Christ, they must go and we must insist that they go. And, they will!

---

[28] See Mark 16:17-20
[29] See Mark 5:10–12; Luke 8:31

3. World Rulers

The third type of evil spirits is called "world rulers." These demons develop religions and political parties. They strive to rule countries by causing chaos, revolutions and wars, both civil and international. They pretend they are gods, or goddesses and long to be worshipped and receive prayer.

Again, the devil *took Him to a very high mountain, and showed Him all the kingdoms of the world and the glory of them; and he said to Him, "All these I will give You, if You will fall down and worship me."*
(Matthew 4:8-9; see also Luke 4:7)

Paul used the words "world rulers" to denote demons called "elemental spirits" (stoicheia) in the letter to the Galatians.

So with us; when we were children, we were slaves to the elemental spirits of the universe (Greek: kosmos) ... *So through God you are no longer a slave but a son, and if a son an heir. Formerly, when you did not know God, you were in bondage to beings that by nature are no gods. Now, however, that you have come to know God, or rather, to be known by God, how can you turn back again to the weak and beggarly elemental spirits, whose slaves you want to be once more? You observe days, and months, and seasons, and years!"*
(Galatians 4:3,7-10)

Evil spirits use their powers to try to control world events by means of the four elements of the natural world, which are earth, fire, air, and water.

Failing to recognize the powers, principalities or spirits of world rulers that come against us, makes us vulnerable to becoming victims of their schemes and evil work, but once we have received Jesus Christ as Savior and LORD, and have been baptized with the Holy Spirit, we have authority even over the elemental spirits of the universe. James explained it this way:

The prayer of a righteous man has great power in its effect. Elijah was a man of like nature with ourselves and he prayed fervently that it might not rain, and for three years and six months it did not rain on the earth. Then he prayed again and the Heaven gave rain, and the earth brought forth its fruit. (James 5:16-18)

These elemental spirits are deceitful demons and certainly have some authority to affect the earth, fire, air and water. Paul warned the Colossian Church:

Therefore let no one condemn you in questions of food and drink or with regard to a festival or a new moon or sabbath. These are only a shadow of what is to come; but the substance belongs to Christ. Do not let anyone disqualify you by philosophy and empty deceit, according to human tradition, according to the elemental spirits of the universe, and not according to Christ. (Colossians 2:16-17)

While elemental spirits try to use the weather to control us, we can pray, take authority over them and change the threatening weather patterns.

We have friends who were living in Woodstock, Ontario, when a tornado went through the town and countryside. One of the farmers there, gathered his family to pray and asked Jesus to turn the tornado away from his farm. The tornado came up to his property, followed the property line around the perimeter and continued in a straight line, wreaking havoc on the rest of the countryside.

A couple in our fellowship was living in a house in a rural housing development north of Orangeville, Ontario. When they saw a tornado headed through their subdivision, destroying one house after another and headed straight to their house, they prayed and asked Jesus to turn it away from their house. They videotaped the tornado as it came up to their property line and skirted around their property, destroying the house next to them, as it continued on its path.

Some years ago, when I was a board member of a retreat center, a tornado, traveling from west to east, destroyed a shopping mall and continued east up to the retreat center's property line. Those in the retreat center began to pray and take authority over the tornado, asking Jesus to divert it around the property. Again, it came up to the property line and went south, then east and north and finally continued east on its original course. Not a building or tree of that center was damaged by the tornado!

One time I was conducting a funeral in Brampton, Ontario. After the service, we had to drive to a small country cemetery about twenty miles away. Heavy rain fell all the way there. As we approached the cemetery, one of the funeral directors remarked, "I wish this rain would stop or we are all going to get soaked."

I asked, "Do you want the rain to stop?"

"Well, I guess so!" he remarked with sarcasm.

I said, "Jesus, will You please stop the rain?"

The rain immediately stopped. When we were leaving the cemetery, I said, "Jesus, You can let the rain start again." Immediately, the rain started, as if a water tap had been turned on. Neither of the funeral directors spoke another word as we drove home.

When a Christian, who is baptized with the Holy Spirit (with the evidence of the signs following), gets hold of the knowledge that he or she can take authority over elemental spirits and change weather patterns in order to protect people and do the work of Jesus Christ, it can be life-changing in terms of effectiveness of ministry and the power to change negative circumstances.

Many people have been taught that even born-again, Spirit-filled Christians do not necessarily have authority over every kind of demon or evil spirits. The truth is, that any demon is the same as any other demon, in terms of all being under our authority. When Jesus told His disciples (and us) that they would cast out demons in His Name, He did not say, "There are three different kinds or classes of demons or evil spirits, some of which you do not have authority over." While demons may try to persuade Christians that we have no authority over them, there's no point in listening, because they are all liars. Jesus has given us all authority to do His ministry.

When they saw Him, they worshiped Him; but some doubted. And Jesus came and said to them, "All authority in Heaven and on earth has been given to Me. Go therefore and make disciples of all nations, baptizing them in the Name of the Father and of the Son and of the Holy Spirit, and teaching them to obey everything that I have commanded you. And remember, I am with you always, to the end of the age." (Matthew 28:17-20)

And He said to them, "Go into all the world and proclaim the good news to the whole creation. The one who believes and is baptized will be saved; but the one who does not believe will be condemned. And these signs will accompany those who believe: by using My Name they will cast out demons; they will speak in new tongues; they will pick up snakes in their hands, and if they drink any deadly thing, it will not hurt them; they will lay their hands on the sick, and they will recover." So then the Lord *Jesus, after He had spoken to them, was taken up into Heaven and sat down at the right hand of God. And they went out and proclaimed the good news everywhere, while the* Lord *worked with them and confirmed the message by the signs that accompanied it.* (Mark 16:15-20)

Paul recognized that there is a strong pull to fall back to former religions, whose gods are evil spirits and who make up rules to control and condemn people through guilt.

Let no one disqualify you, insisting on self-abasement and worship of angels, taking his stand on visions, puffed up without reason by his sensuous mind, and not holding fast to the head, from whom the whole body, nourished and knit together through its joints and ligaments, grows with a growth that is from God. If with Christ, you died to the elemental spirits of the universe, why do you live as if you still belonged to the world? Why do you submit to regulations, 'Do not handle, Do not taste, Do not touch.' All these regulations refer to things that perish with use; they are simply human precepts and doctrines. These have indeed an appearance of wisdom in promoting rigor of devotion and self-abasement and severity to the body, but they are of no value in checking self-indulgence. (Colossians 2:18-23)

World ruler demons will do anything to interrupt genuine services of worship to the God of the Bible. It's not unusual for them to use the people whom they have possessed, to accomplish this task.

In 1974, I was the Senior Pastor at St. Paul's Church, Brampton, Ontario. We were delighted when the church sent my wife and me on a holiday to the Bahamas. One tropical Sunday morning, we attended a worship service in one of the local churches. As the service began, we observed that a man who was sitting in one of the pews, second from the front and about fifteen pews ahead of us, seemed to be suffering from epilepsy. His body started to shake and his arms began to move in an uncontrollable manner. His voice was slurred and he started to make some indistinguishable sounds and utterances that caught our attention. It was obvious that most of the people were accustomed to his apparent health problem. However, as the service proceeded, his voice grew from a whisper to louder sounds. When the pastor began to preach, the man's voice began to get louder and he began to distract people from the pastor's message.

I finally realized that the man was demon possessed and nobody, including the pastor, recognized the problem. I turned to my wife and said, "That man has an evil spirit!"

"Are you sure?" she asked.

I replied, "Yes! Watch this."

In a whisper, which could not be heard by anybody sitting around us, I said, "Evil spirit, I command you to stop and leave this church building." Evil spirits, I have discovered, have excellent hearing. Suddenly, the man's jerking movements stopped, as did the vocal noises. The man suddenly appeared to be in control of himself. He stood up, turned around and looked at me. He then made his way quietly out of the row of pews, into the aisle, keeping his eyes firmly fixed on me. He walked up the aisle, past where we were sitting, and exited the church. The pastor completed his message without any further interruption.

The people in that church had been putting up with the interruptions from the demon-possessed man for many years. They had been under the false assumption that he was suffering from epilepsy. An imitation of epilepsy is a very common manifestation of demon possession.

When a demon-possessed person is examined by a doctor, there will be nothing physical to confirm a diagnosis of epilepsy or any other disease. Because doctors are at a loss to explain disorders that have no physical cause, sufferers will often be diagnosed as having psychological problems and will be given drugs or electric shock treatments. Without Christians who operate in churches in the gift of discerning of spirits, the door is open to a myriad of disruptions in worship services and meetings.

To one is given through the Spirit the utterance of wisdom, and to another the utterance of knowledge according to the same Spirit, to another faith by the same Spirit, to another gifts of healing by the one Spirit, to another the working of miracles, to another prophecy, **to another the ability to distinguish between spirits,** *to another various kinds of tongues, to another the interpretation of tongues. All these are inspired by one and the same Spirit, who apportions to each one individually as He wills.* (1 Corinthians 12:8-11)

World ruler demons have no problem giving people religious experiences, in which repentance plays no part. Initially, the experience appears to be good and feels good – but after a while, the demon or demons turn on the person and begin to take control and torment him or her, often driving the person to distraction, depression and even suicide.

Former drug addicts have told me that the first seven or eight times of using illegal drugs seems non-addictive, but then addiction sets in and the person cannot control the drug; the drug controls him or her. This resembles the experience some people have when they become possessed with demons. Evil spirits promise the world; but deliver failure, sin, sickness, death, destruction and, in the end, their followers end up in Hell, rather than in Heaven.

When given the opportunity, demons will possess people whom they put in positions of leadership; such as priests, clergy or anyone in rebellion against God. These people disregard the gospel of Jesus Christ and refuse to recognize Jesus as their Savior, Lord, Healer and Deliverer. Paul referred to the people who worship in such demonic religions when he wrote,

> *Therefore God gave them up in the lusts of their hearts to impurity, to the degrading of their bodies among themselves, because they exchanged the truth about God for a lie and worshiped and served the creature rather than the Creator, who is blessed forever!* (Romans 1:24-25)

> *Therefore, my beloved, shun the worship of idols ... No, I imply that what pagans sacrifice they offer to demons and not to God. I do not want you to be partners with demons. You cannot drink the cup of the Lord and the cup of demons. You cannot partake of the table of the Lord and the table of demons.* (1 Corinthians 10:14, 20–21)

Like the devil and all sinners, world ruler spirits feel the need to be worshipped in one way or another. They get their worship thrills by influencing and controlling not only religious leaders, but also political leaders, whose egos hunger and thirst for power. World ruler spirits are involved in every political system in the world. Their influence and control of political arenas usually go unrecognized, but surface whenever the governments they influence begin to involve themselves in persecuting individual Christians and churches. They influence governments to pass immoral legislation which gives people permission to break God's commandments. Their influence can be seen in legislation that permits people to murder other people through such issues as assisted suicide, abortion and legalized drug usage. Any government that passes unscriptural or anti-Christian laws, shows evidence of the unseen influence of "world rulers" demons.

Their influence becomes clear when one country goes to war with another country to gain control of their material and economic resources. It's obvious when races turn against each other or when world religions (with their so-called god's permission) persecute, control and kill members of religious groups that do not worship their god or gods. The unacknowledged influence of world rulers is evident in every level of government, because they want to be gods, ruling over people. Many politicians consider themselves to be gods who rule people. In their own rebellion, they drive people to participate in their rebellion against Jesus Christ. There are no governments in existence today that operate fully under the Lordship of Jesus Christ and seriously, corporately, consult Him and wait for the guidance of the Holy Spirit before passing legislation. Certainly, there are some who acknowledge His existence in their charters and constitutions. They will tolerate Christians who have been elected to represent their constituencies but, essentially, the influence of Jesus Christ is kept to a minimum or is ignored altogether by the majority. The world of politics is a Godless religion that the world rulers type of demons fight to control. Some of our most recent demonic political systems, such as Communism and Nazism, have been more zealously religious than the Christians they have ruthlessly persecuted.

World ruler demons are in constant war with the God of the Bible, who desires to give guidance to His people according to His plan. Christians in politics and business, who turn to Jesus Christ for guidance, discover that He has a plan to make countries prosper and to bless their citizens. It is evident who is guiding politicians by the kind of decisions and laws they make. Jesus warned,

No one can serve two masters; for either he will hate the one and love the other, or he will be devoted to the one and despise the other. You cannot serve God and mammon. (Matthew 6:24; see also Luke 16:13)

"Mammon" (which signifies wealth) is such a world ruler. The apostle Paul described such "world ruler demons" when he said,

No, I imply that what pagans sacrifice they offer to demons and not to God. I do not want you to be partners with demons.
(1 Corinthians 10:20)

World ruler clichés include, "Christians should not be involved in politics" and "There must be a separation of church and state." The devil loves to be worshipped and had the audacity to try to tempt Jesus to worship him, as do demons. He tried to make a deal with Him. After showing him all the kingdoms of the world, he offered them to Him, if He would just bow down and worship him.

> *Jesus said to him, "Begone, Satan! For it is written, 'You shall worship the L{{ORD}} your God and Him only shall you serve.'"*
> (Matthew 4:10; see also Luke 4:5–8)

Jesus knew who He was and is and will always be: He is the L{{ORD}} our God. Satan and evil spirits are constantly trying to persuade people to worship them. They misrepresent themselves as gods – but they know and recognize Jesus as the Most High God: Yahweh.[30]

One of the ladies involved in the Harriston, Ontario, church, where I was the pastor, came to see me about a friend to whom she had been witnessing about her need to receive the baptism of the Holy Spirit. She had told her friend about how, through speaking and praying in tongues, the Holy Spirit was speaking to her and giving her direction for every day.

The friend said, "Oh, I don't need that. I have it already. I don't *speak* in tongues, but I write messages in tongues. When the spirit comes over me, I get messages from God in writing. They are in a different language, but I get them every day. I can't read them, but I know they are from God. Someday, He will bring somebody to me who can interpret them."

The woman asked me, "Does God do this?"

I replied, "Speaking and praying in tongues, is a verbal gift of the Holy Spirit, through which the Holy Spirit gives us a real language.[31] The only kind of supernatural writing I've heard about, is something called "automatic handwriting," which is found in the occult world. It is a method sometimes used by evil spirits, to communicate through possessed people. Ask your friend if she would let me see these letters she received."

The friend agreed to let me see the letters. The woman brought a file, filled with over fifty hand-written messages. The format looked like

---
[30] See Mark 5:7; Acts:16:17
[31] See Mark 16:17; 1 Corinthians 12:10

a letter; however, it was written in another language, which used our Roman alphabet. I had no idea what they were saying. So, I prayed and asked, "Holy Spirit, is this a real language?"

He said, "Yes, it is."

I then asked, "What language is it?"

"It is a biblical language," came the answer.

"Which biblical language?"

"Hebrew."

I was then able to transliterate the messages. Each letter was signed with a name I did not recognize. I looked it up in my Hebrew lexicon, and found it. It was the name of the god of the Amorites, one of the enemies of Israel. The Amorites worshipped the moon-gods Sin and Amurru.

I called the woman who had brought them and explained, "Your friend is in big trouble. She is being possessed by an ancient demon."

The woman called her friend and, after ministry by which the demon was cast out, she was set free and received Jesus Christ as her Savior and God. The ancient demon was replaced by the Holy Spirit, who gave her the authentic gift of speaking in tongues. She asked me to destroy the original letters. I did; however, I made photocopies of a few of them for my files, for future reference.

The three different kinds of demons (powers, principalities and world rulers) may be the unseen enemy, but they are no match for a believer who has been baptized with the Holy Spirit and is equipped by Jesus with the gifts of the Holy Spirit. The spiritual power gifts Jesus gives, empower us to have authority over every kind of demon spirit. When we receive the evidence that we have been baptized in the Holy Spirit, the gift of speaking tongues, it eliminates any question of whether or not the baptism has been received. Once the evidence is there, the believer has the confidence to go forward, exercising his or her authority, knowing that the full authority of Heaven backs up the words he or she speaks in dealing with spiritual warfare. The ministry package we receive, proves, beyond question, that we are authentic believers.

In My Name they will cast out demons; they will speak in new tongues (languages); *they will pick up serpents, and if they drink any deadly thing, it will not hurt them; they will lay hands on the sick and they will be healed.* (Mark 16:17-18)

It is interesting that the first of the four signs of being authentic believers[32] is, *"In My Name they will cast out demons."* The second sign is, *"they will speak in new tongues* (languages)." The third is, *"they will pick up serpents, and if they drink any deadly thing, it will not hurt them"* (which is a promise of protection). The fourth sign is, *"they will lay their hands on the sick, and they will recover."* One of the most authenticating proofs is found in the fourth chapter of James, where victory over the enemy is assured for a believer.

Submit yourselves therefore to God. Resist the devil *and he will flee from you.* (James 4:7)

While it is crucial to be able to recognize demonic interference in our lives, the good news is that it is not always necessary to identify what kind or type of demons are involved. All classes of demons: principalities, powers and world rulers, are under the authority of Jesus Christ and those Christians to whom He has given the authority – those who have received the baptism of the Holy Spirit and who have the "signs following."[33]

The Imposter Syndrome

The devil and his demons imitate the work of the Holy Spirit by trying to counterfeit[34] His ministering gifts.[35]

Because most pastors and Christians have never seen the authentic gifts of the Holy Spirit being used in ministry, they have an unhealthy fear of *counterfeit* gifts. If these people actually knew the Holy Spirit and the gifts He distributes,[36] they would know that the idea that the devil or

---

[32] *A Greek-English Lexicon of the New Testament and Other Early Christian Literature* by Walter Bauer, edited and revised by Frederick William Danker, pages 920-921
[33] See Mark 16:17-20
[34] See also *The Challenging Counterfeit*, by Raphael Gasson
[35] See Romans 12:6-8; 1 Corinthians 12:8-10
[36] See 1 Corinthians 12:11

evil spirits could counterfeit the gifts of the Holy Spirit *convincingly*, is simply laughable.

The counterfeit gifts all originate from the occult world and do not look or sound anything like the fifteen authentic gifts of the Holy Spirit. Our protection from the so-called counterfeit gifts, is to learn to use the real gifts under the guidance of the Holy Spirit with confidence, so that we can carry out the ministry that God intended.

The counterfeit gifts are very poor imitations of the genuine gifts of the Holy Spirit, as outlined in Romans and 1 Corinthians.

Having gifts that differ according to the grace given to us, let us use them: if prophecy, in proportion to our faith; if service, in our serving; he who teaches, in his teaching; he who exhorts, in his exhortation; he who contributes, in liberality; he who gives aid, with zeal; he who does acts of mercy, with cheerfulness ... To one is given through the Spirit the utterance of wisdom, and to another the utterance of knowledge according to the same Spirit, to another faith by the same Spirit, to another gifts of healing by the one Spirit, to another the working of miracles, to another prophecy, to another the ability to distinguish between spirits, to another various kinds of tongues (languages), *to another the interpretation of tongues* (languages). (Romans 12:6-8; 1 Corinthians 12:8-10)

Besides their miserable efforts to produce counterfeit *gifts* of the Spirit, demons also try to counterfeit the genuine *fruit* of the Spirit.

But the (genuine) *fruit of the Spirit is love, joy, peace, patience, kindness, goodness, faithfulness, gentleness, self-control; against such there is no law.* (Galatians 5:22-23)

The demonic versions of the fruit of the Spirit are called the *"works of the flesh,"* as described in Galatians:

Now the works of the flesh are plain: fornication, impurity, licentiousness, idolatry, sorcery, enmity, strife, jealousy, anger, selfishness, dissension, party spirit, envy, drunkenness, carousing, and the like. I warn you, as I warned you before, that those who do such things shall not inherit the kingdom of God. (Galatians 5:19-21)

The demonic form of religion lacks and denies the power of the one true God.

> *... holding the form of religion but denying the power of it. Avoid such people.* (2 Timothy 3:5)

People who involve themselves in demonic religions are *"holding to the outward form of godliness but denying its power"* (see 2 Timothy 3:5). Every cult and every religion (with the exception of Christianity and, to some extent, Judaism) is led by, and worships, world rulers.

In the beginning, God was positioned as LORD over all. Had His people recognized and worshipped Him as their rightful, authentic King, things would have turned out much differently. However, the leaders of Israel told Samuel to give them a human king to govern them.

> *But the thing displeased Samuel when they said, "Give us a king to govern us."*
> *Samuel prayed to the LORD, and the LORD said to Samuel, "Listen to the voice of the people in all that they say to you; for they have not rejected you, but they have rejected Me from being king over them."* (1 Samuel 8:6-7)

When Samuel told them what the consequences of having an earthly (imposter) king would be, the people refused to listen to him and said,

> *No! But we are determined to have a king over us, so that we also may be like other nations, and that our king may govern us and go out before us and fight our battles.* (1 Samuel 8:19-20)

Consequently, the LORD told Samuel to listen to the people and to give them a king.[37] God chose Saul and thus began the sad story of the kings of Israel.[38]

Under the new covenant, God, through Jesus Christ, re-established Himself as the authentic "King of kings and LORD of lords,"[39] whose kingdom *"is not of this world,"*[40] but is within each of us who believe.[41] We

---

[37] See 1 Samuel 8:22
[38] See 1 Samuel 9:17
[39] See Revelation 17:14; 19:16
[40] See John 18:36
[41] See Luke 17:21

enter His kingdom and take out citizenship[42] when we allow Jesus Christ to be our Savior and LORD and receive the baptism of the Holy Spirit.[43]

Although the devil is called (mistakenly) "the god of this world,"[44] when Paul wrote this passage, he was not referring to the devil as the *true* God of this world.[45-46] The devil is not a god of anything. He is only a fallen angel who must carry on his assigned duty of tempting and testing people to see whether they are being faithful to the only God. He cannot be trusted. His kingdom is in chaos, largely because he lacks the power to be omnipresent (able to be in more than one place at one time).

> *And even if our gospel is veiled, it is veiled only to those who are perishing. In their case the god of this world has blinded the minds of the unbelievers, to keep them from seeing the light of the gospel of the glory of Christ, who is the likeness of God.* (2 Corinthians 4:3-4)

The devil/Satan is nothing but a thief.

> *The thief comes only to steal and kill and destroy; I came that they might have life, and have it abundantly.* (John 10:10)

Our God blinded the eyes of unbelievers. Therefore they could not believe. Jesus quoted Isaiah:

> *In the year that King Uzzi'ah died I saw the Lord sitting upon a throne, high and lifted up; and his train filled the temple ... And he said, "Go, and say to this people: 'Hear and hear, but do not understand; see and see, but do not perceive.' Make the heart of this people fat, and their ears heavy, and shut their eyes; lest they see with their eyes, and hear with their ears, and understand with their hearts, and turn and be healed."* (Isaiah 6:1,9,10)

> *Who has believed what we have heard? And to whom has the arm of the Lord been revealed?* (Isaiah 53:1)

Paul is clear:

---

[42] See Ephesians 2:19
[43] See John 16:7-15, Acts 19:1-7
[44] 2 Corinthians 4:3-4
[45] Greek "age"
[46] ...who is Jesus.

And then the lawless one will be revealed, and the Lord Jesus will slay him with the breath of His mouth and destroy him by His appearing and His coming. The coming of the lawless one by the activity of Satan will be with all power and with pretended signs and wonders, and with all wicked deception for those who are to perish, because they refused to love the truth and so be saved. Therefore God sends upon them a strong delusion, to make them believe what is false, so that all may be condemned who did not believe the truth but had pleasure in unrighteousness. (2 Thessalonians 2:8-12)

World ruler demons pretend to be gods and demand that people worship them. However, there is only **one** God in this world. His Name in the Old Testament is "Yahweh." In the New Testament, it is "Jesus," the only true "God of this world." A god by any other name is just a demon.

And it shall be that whoever calls on the Name of the LORD shall be saved. (Acts 2:21; see also Romans 10:13)

And there is salvation in no one else, for there is no other name under Heaven given among men by which we must be saved. (Acts 4:12)

The Old Testament references which are applied to Jesus refer to Yahweh.

About seven years ago, I met with a man in the former Soviet Republic of the Ukraine. He was the leader of a Christian political party and had spent thirty years in a Communist prison. His only crime had been that he was a Christian. All he would have had to do, in order to be released, was to renounce his faith in Jesus Christ. When I asked him why he didn't do that and then immediately turn back to Jesus after being released, he replied, with tears in his eyes, "How could I have done that to Jesus, after all He has done for me?"

Some years ago, when pastoring in Englishtown, New Jersey, U.S.A., I had the opportunity to examine a witch's handbook. It had a centerfold that extended about six feet out of the book, on which there was a chart of the way the kingdom of darkness was organized. On the chart was every religion, every occult practice, and every non-Christian spiritual practice. It showed everything from simple occult practices, to witchcraft, right through to all of the world religions. It showed where each level fit into the scheme of the devil's network. I found it fascinating. The only two names not listed were Judaism and Christianity. That made perfect sense to me, because it was to Abraham, Isaac and Jacob, that God began to reveal Himself. That revelation found its completion in the New Testament:

> *But as it is, Christ has obtained a ministry which is as much more excellent than the old as the covenant He mediates is better, since it is enacted on better promises. For if that first covenant had been faultless, there would have been no occasion for a second. For He finds fault with them when He says: "The days will come," says the* Lord, *"when I will establish a new covenant with the house of Israel and with the house of Judah; not like the covenant that I made with their fathers on the day when I took them by the hand to lead them out of the land of Egypt; for they did not continue in My covenant, and so I paid no heed to them," says the* Lord. *"This is the covenant that I will make with the house of Israel after those days," says the* Lord: *"I will put My laws into their minds, and write them on their hearts, and I will be their God, and they shall be My people. And they shall not teach every one his fellow or every one his brother, saying, 'Know the* Lord,' *for all shall know Me, from the least of them to the greatest. For I will be merciful toward their iniquities, and I will remember their sins no more." In speaking of a new covenant He treats the first as obsolete. And what is becoming obsolete and growing old is ready to vanish away.* (Hebrews 8:6-13)

The worshippers of Baal, perhaps the most famous demon, (the Nicolaitans, mentioned in Revelation 2:6,15) infiltrated the churches in Ephesus and Pergamos and persist, to this day, in their attempts to get people to worship them. Baal's name comes up over and over again, from the Old Testament book of Numbers, through to the New Testament book of Romans. The Apostle Paul wrote the Galatian church, saying:

> *So with us; when we were children, we were slaves to the elemental spirits of the universe ... Formerly, when you did not know God, you were in bondage to beings that by nature are no gods; but now that you have come to know God, or rather to be known by God, how can you turn back again to the weak and beggarly elemental spirits* (Greek: stoicheia), *whose slaves you want to be once more?* (Galatians 4:3,8,9)

Many people are controlled and possessed by world rulers, but, again, any Spirit-filled Christian can set people free from any world ruler spirit – but only if the person wishes to be set free (see Mark 16:17).

A Healthy, Balanced View of Demons

C. S. Lewis said, "There are two equal and opposite errors into which our race can fall about the devils (demons). One is to disbelieve in their existence. The other is to believe, and to feel an excessive and unhealthy interest in them. They themselves are equally pleased by both errors, and hail a materialist or a magician with the same delight."[47] He was absolutely correct.

It's not unusual to find people who are totally preoccupied with demons. They imagine that almost everything wrong in a person's life, is evidence of the work of an evil spirit. They imagine them to be here, there and everywhere – assuming every sin has its root in demons and every physical, mental, and emotional sickness is the manifestation of an evil spirit. They blame every problem in churches on demonic interference and so busy themselves in casting out evil spirits before starting any meeting. Because they don't understand the pruning and (sometimes difficult) changes the Holy Spirit may be working in Christians' lives, they are unable to differentiate between the work of a demon and the working of the Holy Spirit.

---

[47] Screwtape Letters, Dec., 1946, C. S. Lewis, The Macmillan Company, Foreword, p. 9

We must not get preoccupied with any one part of ministry. To do so would leave people vulnerable and hopeless.

While preoccupation with demons is dangerous and off-balance, we can't ignore the issue. Ignorance, apathy and denial will not dissolve the problems we must face with the kingdom of darkness. If there were no problems in this area, or no need to learn how to deal with the devil, Jesus would have been off-kilter in His teachings. On the contrary, He was anything but wrong in His evaluation of people's spiritual needs and problems. We know He knew the difference between sin and demon involvement, because it was written of Him:

> *... and they brought Him all the sick, those afflicted of various diseases and pains, demoniacs, epileptics and paralytics, and He healed them.* (Matthew 4:24b)

The correct approach is somewhere in the middle, where we believe in the existence of demons but keep them in view only from the corner of our eyes. We pay them only enough attention to cast them out from people's lives and buildings.

Paul warns us not to be unequally yoked.

> *No, I imply that what pagans sacrifice they offer to demons and not to God. I do not want you to partners with demons.*
> (1 Corinthians 10:20)

> *What agreement does Christ have with Belial? Or what does a believer share with an unbeliever? What agreement has the Temple of God with idols? For we are the Temple of the living God.*
> (2 Corinthians 6:15-16)

A preoccupation with demons was blatantly apparent when I participated in one of the Richard Syrette shows. One of the callers said, "I think every member of my family is demon possessed."

I asked the man what had caused him to come to that conclusion. His response was that every time he tried to talk with his family members about inviting Jesus to be their Savior and Lord, they didn't want to hear anything about it.

I said, "I'm sorry to have to tell you this, but your family is suffering from what the Bible describes as, "old-fashioned sin." You will have to continue to be patient and to let your witness show them that Jesus has changed you. When they see what Jesus has done for you, they will want to invite Jesus to be their Savior and Lord, just as He is yours."

He responded, "Oh, I thought it would be easier if they were demon possessed."

There is no quick fix for our convenience.

After another episode of guesting on the Richard Syrette Show, I received a telephone call from a man asking for help. His five-year-old daughter was being hurt by "a mean boy" who had attacked her in her bedroom and their bathroom. She would no longer go into either room without one of her parents. They thought she simply had a vivid imagination – until they came home one afternoon and discovered all of their living and dining room furniture piled up in the center of the room. Not only that, but one of their two small dogs had been put in the closet by the front door. The second dog, still yelping in pain, had been locked in a kitchen cupboard, with its tail sticking out the door.

I agreed to go to the home to deal with the situation. Before I went through their house to get rid of the evil spirit, I explained that, for their protection, it would be necessary for them to receive the baptism of the Holy Spirit. They would need to be able to speak in tongues so the demon could not possess them. After they agreed, I asked them to step outside while I exorcised the apartment. The evil spirit tried to push me out the door, but I commanded it to leave in the Name of Jesus Christ and to go to the abyss and stay there. It left. Then, I asked the Holy Spirit to fill the apartment with His presence. I called the couple to come back in and prayed for them to receive the baptism of the Holy Spirit. They both began to speak in tongues.[48] Now they have peace.

Following another Richard Syrette Show, I received phone calls from both the best friend and a daughter of a ninety-three-year-old woman.

---
[48] See Acts 2:4; 8:17; 19:6

She had told them about the frightening things happening in her apartment every night. Whenever she went to bed, she would hear someone, or something, moving about in her apartment. Whatever it was, threw dishes out of her china cabinet, breaking some. The daughter initially thought her mother was hallucinating, and so took her to see her doctor who explained that, at her age, her various glands stop functioning as they should and were probably causing her to see things that were not there. He prescribed some medication, which she took as directed.

However, the problem continued. Every night, more dishes would come flying out of the china cabinet. Finally, the daughter spent a night with her mother and observed the strange phenomena. The next day, she called the radio show, asking for me.

When I went to the lady's apartment to get rid of the evil spirit, she told me she was a Pentecostal Christian who spoke in tongues. She had spoken to her pastor, but he didn't believe in demons. As far as he was concerned, it was just her imagination. (Sadly, many people continue to be victimized by evil spirits because their clergy do not want to accept the fact that evil spirits are a reality.) Nevertheless, she had had the personal protection of the Holy Spirit.

I went through her apartment and got rid of the evil spirit. She telephoned me a week later to let me know her dishes were no longer flying out of her china cabinet and she was no longer taking the medication. Furthermore, she was having a peaceful sleep each night.

A preoccupation with demons has left many people trapped in their sins and feeling hopeless. They feel powerless to effect change in their lives because they attribute their problems to an outside power that they can't control. They ignore the tools God has given us to deal with the sin in our lives.

Judson Cornwall warns us about getting our attention filled with demons. In his book, *Let Us Praise*[49], he shares about what happened when he became preoccupied with demons. When he was a pastor in

---

[49] *Let Us Praise,* Judson Cornwall, Bridge-Logos Publishers, 2006, ISBN 0882701347, p. 71-73

A Fight to the Finish

God's Plan, Purpose and Provision for our Victory

Recognizing the fact that we have an enemy and are in a battle isn't enough. We have to be able to protect and defend ourselves. Christians are faced with five major obstacles to knowing how to engage the enemy effectively and actually doing it.

1. Ignorance about the kingdom of darkness and its authority

2. Being sure of what God says about the devil, demons and sin, and what authority they actually have

3. Knowing what the Bible really says about what Jesus Christ accomplished on the Cross to bring the new covenant into effect

4. Understanding the place of angels and the church in spiritual warfare under the new covenant

5. Understanding what authority individual believers have and their position in this war.

To solve these problems, we have to recognize the two distinct historical periods of the Bible.

Two Distinct Historical Periods of the Bible

The Old Testament period runs from the creation of the universe up to the ministry of Jesus Christ. The New Testament period covers the time since Jesus Christ was born until He returns.[50]

The Old Testament world, and the spiritual forces of the kingdom of darkness, are much different from the New Testament world that Jesus left behind after His death, Resurrection and Ascension. Without acknowledging the difference, many Christians are fighting a non-war of vain imaginations that are no longer reality.

The Old Testament is a covenant of law God designed to deal with sinful humanity. That covenant has been replaced with a new one. The terms of the old one no longer apply; not because God has changed, but because the situation has changed.

Jesus' ministry separated the old world (B.C., meaning "Before Christ") from the new world (A.D. meaning "Anno Domini" or "Year of Our Lord"), with the Cross of Calvary marking the dividing point. Unfortunately, because the requirements of God regarding the old world are included in the Biblical records (to remind us of our history), many people assume they apply to serving God today. They don't. They have been dismantled. Those requirements were given to the Jews and have no authority today. Their value lies in demonstrating how God dealt with sin, the devil, His chosen people and the kingdom of darkness prior to giving His new covenant. They foreshadowed God's plan for the new covenant.

The Old Testament world is gone; the New Testament world has come! Paul said,

Therefore, if any one is in Christ, he is a new creation; the old has passed away, behold, the new has come. (2 Corinthians 5:17)

The Old Testament prepared the way for the New Testament. While we must know it and study it to understand what Jesus Christ has done for us, only the New Testament has any authority now. This means that,

---

[50] John 5:25-29; 1 Corinthians 15:51-57; 1 Thessalonians 4:13-18; Revelation 20:4-5, 11-15

in terms of the way we practice Christianity today, Christians can set the Old Testament aside. While it is invaluable in understanding the significance of elements of the New Testament, our study of the promises and penalties of the New Testament is where our focus should be. It contains all the necessary direction for salvation and clear instructions for how to maintain a personal relationship with God. This was not available to people under the old covenant.

The kingdom of darkness has been defeated. It has lost its power, its sting and its threat. The devil has been put on a short leash and is under strict supervision. The kingdom of darkness has been shattered. Whenever its defeated forces attack God's overwhelmingly superior forces, they are defeated. Satan has been humiliated and his strong angels have been imprisoned. Nevertheless, no matter how embarrassing the defeats may be, the skirmishes continue today, forcing us to deal with our enemy. The good news is that any Spirit-filled Christian, regardless of age, can thrash demon forces at any engagement.

The Old Testament of law has been replaced with a New Testament covenant of grace.

In Zechariah 11:4-14, God (Yahweh) prophesied the ending or annulling[51] of the Old Testament covenant He had established with His people. At the same time, He annulled the brotherhood between Judah and Israel. With Jesus' death on the Cross of Calvary, He paid off those who did not want Him to be their Shepherd. This was fulfilled when Judas threw the thirty shekels of silver into the Temple's treasury. Jesus explained when He said:

"The law and the prophets were until John; since then the good news of the kingdom of God is preached, and every one enters it violently." (Luke 16:16)

But as it is, Christ has obtained a ministry which is as much more excellent than the old as the covenant He mediates is better, since it is enacted on better promises. For if the first covenant had been faultless, there would have been no occasion for a second. (Hebrews 8:6,7)

---

[51] The word "annul" means to "do away with; make of no effect; make null and void; cancel; abolish."

In speaking of a new covenant He treats the first as obsolete. And what is becoming obsolete and growing old is ready to vanish away. (Hebrews 8:13)

Jesus' death on the Cross of Calvary changed everything. As one professor said, "God strained the Old Testament through the Cross of Calvary and everything that came through, and which is necessary, is in the New Testament."

The replacement of the old, with the new covenant, was necessary if we were to be victorious in spiritual warfare. The central issue of spiritual warfare concerns dealing with sin. It is giving in to sin – the breaking of God's law through rebellion – that gives the devil his authority. It is the sin of mankind that gives him the confidence to challenge God.

Jesus changed the way spiritual warfare must be conducted. His strategy, founded on His sacrifice of blood on the Cross to pay for sin, is always victorious.

Our Sin Debt

Jesus explains the seriousness and hopelessness of our sin debt in the Parable of the Unforgiving Servant.[52] There, He tells about a servant who owed a king 10,000 talents of gold. A talent was a measurement of gold weighing 158 pounds. In Biblical times, there were two types of talents: ordinary business trading talent that weighed 131 pounds and the King's talent that weighed 158 pounds. At today's gold price of $1,276.90 dollars per ounce, that would be an incredible sin debt of $32,380,042,000.00. The king shows him mercy and forgives the whole amount. However, the servant goes out and meets a fellow servant who owes him 100 denarii, the equivalent of about three months' wages, just a pittance compared with what he himself had owed. When the fellow servant protests that he cannot pay it back, the first servant refuses to forgive the debt, despite the astounding mercy that has just been bestowed upon him. The king, upon hearing of this, calls the first servant back and reinstates the 10,000 talent debt. He then turns him over to the tormentors for punishment, until the

---
[52] See Matthew 18:23-35

man can pay back what he owes the king – which would be never. Jesus concludes the parable by saying,

> *So also My Heavenly Father will do to every one of you, if you do not forgive your brother from your heart.* (Matthew 18:35)

Jesus introduced us to a new power to forgive sin when the Pharisees got angry and accused Him of speaking blasphemies for saying, "*Man, your sins are forgiven you,*"[53] to the man he healed:

> *"But that you may know that the Son of Man has authority on earth to forgive sins"* – *He said to the man who was paralyzed* – *"I say to you, rise, take up your bed and go home."* (Luke 5:24)

If Jesus had been any other man, He would have been a sinner with absolutely no authority to forgive anybody's sin. But He was not just any ordinary man. He was Emmanuel – God with us.

> *Behold, a virgin shall conceive and bear a son, and His Name shall be called Emmanuel (which means, God with us).* (Matthew 1:23)

Jesus (Emmanuel) was God in the flesh.

> *And the Word became flesh and dwelt among us, full of grace and truth; we have beheld His glory as of the only Son from the Father.* (John 1:14)

John the Baptist said of Him,

> *Behold, the Lamb of God who takes away the sin of the world!* (John 1:29; see also verse 36)

Peter said,

> *You know that you were ransomed from the futile ways inherited from your fathers, not with perishable things such as silver or gold, but with the precious blood of Christ, like that of a lamb without blemish or spot.* (1 Peter 1:18-19)

Jesus is the sacrificial lamb who alone could pay for the sins of the world: yours and mine.

---
[53] Luke 5:20

... we have not a High Priest who is unable to sympathize with our weaknesses, but One who in every respect has been tempted as we are, yet without sin. (Hebrews 4:15)

Repentance + Blood Sacrifice ... the Key to Forgiveness

Repentance alone is not enough to find forgiveness for our sins. Repentance relies on the offering of a blood sacrifice.

But when Christ had offered for all time a single sacrifice for sins, He sat down at the right hand of God, then to wait until His enemies should be made a stool for His feet. For by a single offering He has perfected for all time those who are sanctified. (Hebrews 10:12-14)

Jesus provided the only blood sacrifice God will accept to grant forgiveness for our sin. He replaced the daily sacrifices with His own death on the Cross of Calvary.

For God so loved the world that He gave His only Son, that whoever believes in Him should not perish but have eternal life. (John 3:16)

Only by the blood of Jesus Christ, can citizens of the dominion of darkness be transferred into the kingdom of God.

He has delivered us from the dominion of darkness and transferred us to the kingdom of His beloved Son, in whom we have redemption, the forgiveness of sins. (Colossians 1:13-14)

Jesus turned the Cross of Calvary into the altar upon which He paid for all the sin of the world. When He shouted, "*It is finished*" (John 19:30), He was actually saying, "It is paid in full." He paid for all the sin of the world with His sinless blood, thereby becoming our perfect sacrifice by which we can, with the godly sorrow that leads to repentance, find daily forgiveness of our sin.

For godly grief produces a repentance that leads to salvation and brings no regret ... (2 Corinthians 7:10)

Further, with the baptism of the Holy Spirit, we can be living witnesses of the goodness and grace of God. That is why Jesus said,

> *The law and the prophets were until John; since then the good news of the kingdom of God is preached, and every one enters it violently.*
> (Luke 16:16)

The Greek word "biázetai," which occurs in Luke 16:16 means to "go after something with enthusiasm, seek fervently, try hard"[54] This is what Jesus meant when He answered the rich man who asked, *"Good teacher, what shall I do to inherit eternal life?"* His answer was,

> *"One thing you still lack. Sell all that you have and distribute to the poor, and you will have treasure in Heaven; and come, follow Me."*
> (Luke 18:22)

A true believer will do whatever it costs to inherit eternal life, no matter how difficult it may seem. This is the point of the parables of the hidden treasure.

> *The kingdom of Heaven is like treasure hidden in a field, which a man found and covered up; then in his joy he goes and sells all that he has and buys that field. Again, the kingdom of Heaven is like a merchant in search of fine pearls, who, on finding one pearl of great value, went and sold all that he had and bought it.*
> (Matthew 13:44-46)

The point is not that anyone can buy his or her way into Heaven, but that he or she will do whatever possible to own the forgiveness, peace and eternal life Jesus offers.

The Scriptures are clear:

> *Indeed, under the law almost everything is purified with blood, and without the shedding of blood there is no forgiveness of sins.*
> (Hebrews 9:22)

Jesus warned,

> *So when you see the desolating sacrilege* (abomination of desolation – KJV) *spoken of by the prophet Daniel, standing in the holy place (let the reader understand), then let those who are in Judea flee to the*

[54.] P. 175, Greek-English Lexicon, Bauer-Danker

mountains; let him who is on the housetop not go down to take what is in his house; and let him who is in the field not turn back to take his mantle. And alas for those who are with child and for those who give suck in those days. Pray that your flight might not be in winter or on the Sabbath. (Matthew 24:15-20; see also Mark 13:14-18)

In this Scripture, Jesus was not talking about some frightening destruction of the world at the end of time. He was quoting a prophecy Daniel had given about a frightening event that would happen which would bring destruction to Jerusalem and the Temple.

According to the prophet Daniel, *"the desolating sacrilege"* (abomination of desolation KJV) would be evident when:

... the people of the prince who is to come shall destroy the city and the sanctuary. Its end shall come with a flood, and to the end there shall be war; desolations are decreed. And he shall make a strong covenant with many for one week; and for half of the week he shall cause sacrifice and offering to cease; and upon the wings of abominations shall come one who makes desolate, until the decreed end is poured out on the desolator. (Daniel 9:26-27)

Daniel restates this in 21:11:

... the time that the continual burnt offering is taken away, and the abomination that makes desolate is set up ...

For the Jews (to whom Daniel was speaking) there could be no greater abomination than taking away the ability to make daily sacrifices to deal with sin. Without being able to offer these sacrifices in the Temple, under the old covenant, they had no hope of receiving forgiveness of sin – and without the forgiveness of sin, they had no hope; there was only the expectation of receiving "the wages of sin" which is "death."

For the wages of sin is death ... (Romans 6:23)

This kind of death had to do with the death that ends up in

... the lake that burns with fire and sulphur, which is the second death. (Revelation 21:8)

The *"abomination of desolation"* in Greek means "the detestable thing causing the desolation or destruction" (Greek verb eremoo; noun: eremosis: devastation, destruction) of the holy place, which included the Temple and the city of Jerusalem. That destruction occurred when the Roman army destroyed Jerusalem in A.D. 70 and ended the sacrifices forever. To Gentiles (non-Jewish people), this might not seem like any big problem. But for those who understood the ramifications of sin, as the Jews did, having no way to deal with it was untenable.

For those who understood they could not be saved by good works or the keeping of laws (even God's laws) without sacrificing innocent blood, there was the knowledge that only Hell could await them at the end of life. For the Jews, having no way to deal with their sin was most frightening.

What About the Rebuilding of the Temple and Resumption of Daily Sacrifices?

This new covenant of grace, whereby sin is forgiven as a result of godly repentance and the appropriation of Jesus' once-for-all-time blood sacrifice, replaces the old covenant, where individual sins required individual sacrifices.

Obviously, those who are preparing to rebuild the Temple in Jerusalem are badly mistaken in the idea that once the Temple is rebuilt, they can resume animal sacrifices to pay for their sin and receive forgiveness. God has moved on from that stage in history and will never again accept the blood of innocent birds and animals.

However, Jesus prophesied that the Temple in Jerusalem was going to be destroyed once and for all time.[55] His sacrifice on the Cross is the only sacrifice acceptable by God.[56]

The desire to rebuild the Temple is nothing new. In A.D. 363, an earlier attempt was made to rebuild it. The emperor Julian, in order

---

[55] Matthew 24:1-2; Mark 13:1-2; Luke 21:5-6
[56] Acts 4:12; John 14:6

to disprove the prophecy of Christ regarding the Temple (see Matthew 24:1-2), undertook to rebuild it, but his plans were frustrated by flames that burst from the foundation. In A.D. 691, 'Abd-al-Malik built, on the site of the former Temple of Solomon, the Dome of the Rock (wrongly called the Mosque of Omar).[57] God does not want the Temple rebuilt. In fact, He has allowed the Muslims to occupy part of the former Temple location to help guarantee that it will not be rebuilt! He has already built His new Temple, as explained by Paul:

Do you not know that you are God's Temple and that God's Spirit dwells in you? If any one destroys God's Temple, God will destroy him. For God's Temple is holy, and that Temple you are.
(1 Corinthians 3:16)

Animal sacrifices have been replaced by Jesus' sacrifice, once and for all. Jesus tells us exactly when the New Covenant replaced the old system.

The law and the prophets were until John; since then the good news of the kingdom of God is preached, and every one enters it violently. But it is easier for Heaven and earth to pass away, than for one dot of the law to become void. (Luke 16:16-17)

God's law remains intact and, like the Ten Commandments, many things from the old covenant are included in the New Testament. Jesus did not come to abolish the law or the prophets, but to fulfill them.[58]

The very moment John the Baptist started preaching and baptizing people in response to their repentance, the old covenant was ended – even though animals were still being sacrificed in the Temple. Obviously, the spiritual leaders had not been listening to God because the new covenant had been prophesied in the Old Testament.

Incline your ear, and come to Me; hear, that your soul may live; and I will make with you an everlasting covenant, My steadfast, sure love for David. (Isaiah 55:3)

[57.] The Westminster Dictionary of the Bible, p. 597
[58] See Matthew 5:17

Behold, the days are coming," says the L<small>ORD</small>, *"when I will make a new covenant with the house of Israel and the house of Judah, not like the covenant which I made with their fathers ...*
(Jeremiah 31:31-32)

I will make a covenant of peace with them; it shall be an everlasting covenant with them; and I will bless them and multiply them, and will set My sanctuary in the midst of them for evermore.
(Ezekiel 37:26)

Through the prophet Zechariah, Yahweh (God's personal Name) annulled the covenant He had made with all the people and the brotherhood between Judah and Israel at the price of thirty shekels of silver.

Water Baptism as a Sign of Repentance

Never before, in the history of Israel, until the ministry of John the Baptist, had water baptism been used as a sign of repentance. Everything changed when the blood sacrifice of Jesus, followed by the baptism of the Holy Spirit, allowed every believer to have a personal relationship with God through His appointed Counselor.

I have yet many things to say to you, but you cannot bear them now. When the Spirit of Truth comes, He will guide you into all the truth; for He will not speak on His own authority, but whatever He hears He will speak, and He will declare to you the things that are to come. He will glorify Me, for He will take what is Mine and declare it to you. All that the Father has is Mine; therefore I said that He will take what is Mine and declare it to you. (John 16:12-15)

John the Baptist made it clear that he was not the Messiah:

I baptize you with water for repentance, but He who is coming after me is mightier than I, whose sandals I am not worthy to carry; He will baptize you with the Holy Spirit and with fire.
(Matthew 3:11; see also Mark 1:7–8, Luke 3:16, John 1:26–27)

Jesus' Baptism – the Baptism in the Holy Spirit

Jesus never baptized anyone with water, because His baptism would be the baptism of the Holy Spirit, after He was raised from the dead and ascended into Heaven.

Now this He said about the Spirit, which those who believed in Him were to receive; for as yet the Spirit had not been given, because Jesus was not yet glorified. (John 7:39)

Nevertheless, He did allow his disciples to baptize believers in water (see John 4:1–2).

The fulfilment of Jesus' promise, to send the Holy Spirit, was given on the Day of Pentecost, when the Holy Spirit was poured out to fulfill the prophecy of Joel.

And they were all filled with the Holy Spirit and began to speak in other tongues, as the Spirit gave them utterance. (Acts 2:4)

And it shall come to pass afterward, that I will pour out My Spirit on all flesh; your sons and your daughters shall prophesy, your old men shall dream dreams, and your young men shall see visions. Even upon the menservants and maidservants in those days, I will pour out My Spirit. And I will give portents in the Heavens and on the earth, blood and fire and columns of smoke. The sun shall be turned to darkness, and the moon to blood, before the great and terrible day of the LORD *(Yahweh) comes. And it shall come to pass that all who call upon the Name of the* LORD *(Yahweh) shall be delivered; for in Mount Zion and in Jerusalem there shall be those who escape, as the* LORD *has said, and among the survivors shall be those whom the* LORD *(Yahweh) calls.* (Joel 2:28–32)

The new covenant is the pivotal strategic move in God's plan for dealing with the enemy. Jesus provided the blood sacrifice on the Cross of Calvary. After He took a cup and gave thanks, He gave it to His disciples and commanded:

"Drink of it, all of you; for this is My blood of the covenant, which is poured out for many for the forgiveness of sins." (Matthew 26:27-28)[59]

---

[59] See also Mark 14:24; Luke 22:20; 1 Corinthians 11:25

I am the way, and the truth, and the life; no one comes to the Father, but by Me. (John 14:6)

That means (according to the Greek), that not even one person can reach the Father except through Jesus. His reference to *"the way,"* (again according to the original Greek), refers to a road or highway. He is actually saying, "I am the only road that leads to the Father," thereby negating, excluding and replacing all former covenants, sacrifices and world religions.

Defeating the Kingdom of Darkness

The Flawed Plans of Satan

Through the activities of his kingdom of darkness, Satan attempts to take over God's kingdom, both in Heaven and on earth, and throughout God's created order.

It is clear that Satan wants to be worshipped and take God's place.

I will ascend above the heights of the clouds, I will make myself like the Most High. (Isaiah 14:14)[60]

I say, "You are gods, sons of the Most High, all of you; nevertheless, you shall die like men, and fall like any prince." (Psalm 82:6)

Many people think, mistakenly, that this was said by the devil. In actual fact, it was said by the King of Babylon who built a tower which he thought could reach into Heaven. He was like many people today who consider themselves to be gods, and cannot imagine not living forever.

Evil angels and demons share Satan's desire to be exalted above the Name of Jesus.

By organizing the kingdom of darkness, Satan intended to create an army that would take over the kingdom of God. At no place in the Bible,

---

[60] See also Matthew 4:10

does it ever indicate that Satan was an archangel or the leader of the choirs of Heaven, as some have claimed. Satan was created to be the head of God's Federal Bureau of Investigation (G.F.B.I.), whose defined role, given to him by God, was to test God's people to see if they were faithful to Him. Whatever he discovered, he was to report directly back to God.

> *Now there was a day when the sons of God came to present themselves before the* LORD, *and Satan also came among them. The* LORD *said to Satan, "Whence have you come?"*
> *Satan answered the* LORD *"From going to and fro on the earth, and from walking up and down on it."* (Job 1:6-7)

What he discovered, by tempting people to sin, was that

... all have sinned and fall short of the glory of God ... (Romans 3:23)

Satan devised a scheme to gather all sinners, whether humans, angelic evildoers or spirits, into one rebellious kingdom and overthrow the kingdom of God. He made the same fatal mistake as do many military leaders, of underestimating the strength of his enemy. Not only did he underestimate God's power and the strength of God's army, but he overestimated his own power and that of his own army. He learned a hard lesson when it came to causing a war in Heaven.[61] We'll take a closer look at that battle later on.

Satan set up his kingdom with sinful angels having territorial rights over nations. Daniel identified one such evil angel:

> *The prince of the kingdom of Persia withstood me twenty-one days; but Michael, one of the chief princes, came to help me, so I left him there with the prince of the kingdom of Persia and came to make you understand what is to befall your people in the latter days. For the vision is for days yet to come.* (Daniel 10:13-14)

Each nation had a Satan-appointed angel over it. God's archangel said to Daniel:

> *"But now I will return to fight against the prince of Persia; and when I am through with him, lo, the prince of Greece will come. But*

---
[61] See Revelation 12:7-12

I will tell you what is inscribed in the book of truth: there is none who contends by my side against these except Michael, your prince." (Daniel 10:20-21)

While each nation had a rebellious angel over it, each nation also has a guardian angel. The archangel Michael, God's field-marshal, is regarded as the guardian over Israel.

How God Uses the Kingdom of Darkness for His Purposes

Although God used even evil angels to bring judgment and punishment on disobedient people, they did not occupy positions of trust, as they could attempt to thwart God's plans.[62] They are part of the devil's army.

He let loose on them his fierce anger, wrath, indignation, and distress, a company of destroying angels. (Psalm 78:49)

It was God's right, as the Commander-in-Chief of His entire army, to use both faithful and unfaithful angels to carry out His orders. He sent an evil spirit to create a problem between Abimelech and the men of Shechem so that they would turn on Abimelech and kill him, because he had had Jerubbaal's family destroyed.[63] God also used an evil spirit to deal with Saul because of his disobedience.[64]

Now the Spirit of the LORD departed from Saul, and an evil spirit from the LORD tormented him. (1 Samuel 16:14)

For those who would not listen and follow His instructions, God sent a lying spirit. Since two kings and 400 prophets would listen to neither God nor His prophet Micaiah, God gave the lying spirit permission to mislead them. The result was, that the king of Israel was killed and his army was defeated.[65] In all this, God revealed that our worst nightmare is not necessarily Satan, evil angels or evil spirits – but can be God Himself.[66]

---

[62] See Daniel 10:13
[63] Judges 9:23-24
[64] See 1 Samuel 16:14-23; 18:10; 19:9
[65] See 1 Kings 22:21–23
[66] See 2 Chronicles 18:1-36 and 1 Kings 22:1-40

Battleground Earth

God gave fair warning to all His enemies that He was going to deal with the problem of sin, evil, Satan and the kingdom of darkness. He gave prophecy after prophecy that He was going to do it once and for all, in an unusual way. He would send His Son in human form, as a baby.

For unto us a child is born, unto us a Son is given: and the government shall be upon His shoulder: and His Name shall be called "Wonderful, Counselor, Mighty God, Everlasting Father, Prince of Peace." (Isaiah 9:6)

Behold, a virgin shall conceive and bear a Son, and His Name shall be called Emmanuel (which means, God with us). (Matthew 1:23)

She will bear a son, and you shall call His Name Jesus, for He will save His people from their sins. (Matthew 1:21)

And the Word became flesh and dwelt among us, full of grace and truth; we have beheld His glory as of the only Son from the Father. (John 1:14)

What kingdom could be worried over the attack of a baby? Only one: the kingdom of darkness.

Jesus slipped into history almost unnoticed – almost – except that He caught the immediate attention of King Herod, who saw Him as a threat to his own Satan-induced desire to be worshipped. Like the devil, his spiritual father, Herod tried to kill Jesus. He commanded that all the male children in the region of Bethlehem, two years old or under, were to be killed.[67] Jesus' earthly step-father, Joseph, was warned by an Angel of the Lord (in a dream) about Herod's scheme. Joseph was to take Jesus and Mary and flee to Egypt, and stay there until the danger was passed (see Matthew 2:13).

Angels warn people of impending danger and tell them when it is safe to proceed with God's plan. They often frustrate the enemy's plans.

The war between the two kingdoms would take place in two places simultaneously. There would be two fronts. One would be on earth, and the

---
[67] See Matthew 2:16

other would be in Heaven. Most people could not see both fronts, but God could – and so could Satan. Heaven and earth are always connected, even though they do not always appear that way to the untrained, spiritual eye.

War preparations were made carefully and slowly over a thirty-three year period. First, the boy Jesus had to grow up. He did what every Jewish boy must do.

And Jesus increased in wisdom and in stature, and in favor with God and man. (Luke 2:52)

He took His place in his earthly family as the first-born among His brothers and sisters.[68] He was prepared (like any other Jewish son) to serve God. At the same time, God was preparing Jesus' cousin, John, to prepare the way for Him in a ministry of repentance.[69] The angel Gabriel, announced it to both Jesus' parents[70] and to John's parents[71] – evidence that angels can inform people of God's plans, in order to prepare them.

The war for the world began in earnest, with an event that no one recognized as the signal to commence war. They saw it only as a baptism. It happened when Jesus went to the Jordan River to be baptized by John. As He emerged from the water, the Spirit of God descended like a dove and landed on Him. He heard God's voice saying:

"This is My beloved Son, with whom I am well pleased."
(Matthew 3:17)

John pointed out the fact that Jesus was taking personal responsibility for the sins of the world, when he said of Him:

"Behold, the Lamb of God, who takes away the sin of the world!"
(John 1:29)

For our sake He made Him to be sin who knew no sin, so that in Him we might become the righteousness of God. (2 Corinthians 5:21)

Jesus took His position as the sacrificial lamb, without spot or blemish, to pay for the sins of the world. The battle lines were now set.

---

[68] See Matthew 13:55
[69] See Luke 1:13-16
[70] See Matthew 1:18-25
[71] See Luke 1:5-25

The first real battle was about to begin, in an obscure wilderness. The location was of no importance, but the combatants were.

Then Jesus was led by the Spirit into the wilderness to be tempted by the devil. (Matthew 4:1)

From the beginning of history, it has been the devil's responsibility to test and tempt people to see if they are faithful to God. Up to this point, every person whom he had tempted, had failed. Jesus looked like all the rest. His outward appearance was that of any other sinner – that of an ordinary man. Here was one time the devil could not tell the book by its cover.

How Temptation Works

Temptation is the arena of warfare, where it is seen whether a person will give in to a particular temptation and sin, or be faithful to God in whatever circumstances surround him or her. God does not tempt anybody to sin. James tells us how temptation actually works.

No one, when tempted, should say, "I am being tempted by God;" for God cannot be tempted by evil and He Himself tempts no one. But one is tempted by one's own desire, being lured and enticed by it; then, when that desire has conceived, it gives birth to sin, and that sin, when it is fully grown, gives birth to death. (James 1:13-15)

So this is how temptation works. First, we get a desire or a feeling or an idea about doing something wrong. The original idea comes from the sin within a person. We think it over, play with it in our minds, fantasize about it and then get convinced that we would like to do it. Then, when the opportunity presents itself, sometimes precipitated by the devil, but most often through our own desires, we proceed to do it.

The devil, unlike God, is not omnipresent. He can be in only one place on the whole earth at one time, dealing with one person. That does not stop him, however, from taking the credit for someone yielding to temptation that had absolutely nothing to do with him.

You are of your father the devil, *and your will is to do your father's desires. He was a murderer from the beginning, and has nothing to do with the truth, because there is no truth in him. When he lies, he speaks according to his own nature, for he is a liar and the father of lies.* (John 8:44)

Regardless of what the devil may say, we cannot blame him for our decisions. Adam tried to blame God and Eve for his sin. Eve tried to blame the serpent for her sin. They could not pass the responsibility for their sin to anybody else because they had both heard God's instructions.

And the Lord God commanded the man, saying, "You may freely eat of every tree of the garden; but of the tree of the knowledge of good and evil you shall not eat, for in the day that you eat of it you shall die." (Genesis 2:16-17)

The serpent, the devil, was cursed for his lying temptation, as were Adam and Eve. Each person is responsible for his or her own sin.

The Lord God said to the serpent, "Because you have done this, cursed are you above all cattle, and above all wild animals; upon your belly you shall go, and dust you shall eat all the days of your life. I will put enmity between you and the woman, and between your seed and her seed; he shall bruise your head, and you shall bruise his heel."
To the woman he said, "I will greatly multiply your pain in childbearing; in pain you shall bring forth children, yet your desire shall be for your husband, and he shall rule over you."
And to Adam he said, "Because you have listened to the voice of your wife, and have eaten of the tree of which I commanded you, 'You shall not eat of it,' cursed is the ground because of you; in toil you shall eat of it all the days of your life; thorns and thistles it shall bring forth to you; and you shall eat the plants of the field. In the sweat of your face you shall eat bread till you return to the ground, for out of it you were taken; you are dust, and to dust you shall return."
(Genesis 3:14-19)

While each person is responsible for his or her own sin, the devil tempts and tests them, just as he did with Jesus,[72] to prove whether

---
[72] Matthew 4:1-11; Mark 1:12-13; Luke 4:1-13

they are ready and prepared to do the ministry Jesus planned for them. When we give in to our temptations, it is made apparent to us that we have not done the right thing, but have sinned. The fallout is broken relationships, destroyed friendships, dissolved marriages and scattered families. In every case, people are hurt, resulting in guilt, condemnation, fear, hopelessness, loss of relationship with God, ruined lives, suicides, homicides and finally, death and hell. The pattern is always the same. It was set in the Garden of Eden.

The problem is that even if we say "no" to temptation, we may fall into the trap of feeling guilty for even considering or thinking about the object of our temptation. The source of this guilt may be the condemnation the devil attempts to inflict upon us – or it may be our own self-condemnation. Some people have been led to believe that they've already sinned, just by thinking about things that are contrary to God's Word. In truth, thinking about a temptation is not the same as doing it. "Vain imaginations,"[73] including sexual fantasies where there has been no fulfilment of the fantasy, is not sin unless one willingly entertains the thought to the point of acting on it. Just when people should be feeling good about resisting temptation, they allow themselves to be filled with guilt, condemnation and fear – just for thinking about a temptation that may have entered their minds.

While most people believe it is Satan/the devil who accuses them of sin, that's not always the case. As already pointed out, Satan can be in only one place in the world at one time – so he can't possibly be dealing with all the billions of people in the world at the same time. Consequently, he often gets the credit for the work of the Holy Spirit who *is* capable of being everywhere at the same time. Sometimes it's not the devil trying to make us feel guilty unjustly: sometimes it's the Holy Spirit shining a light on things that need to be changed in our lives by sensitizing our consciences to sin. It is the job of the Holy Spirit to convict the world concerning sin and righteousness and judgment.

---

[73] Acts 4:21; Romans 1:21; 2 Corinthians 10:5 (KJV)

I have yet many things to say to you, but you cannot bear them now. When the Spirit of Truth comes, He will guide you into all the truth; for He will not speak on His own authority, but whatever He hears He will speak, and He will declare to you the things that are to come. He will glorify Me, for He will take what is Mine and declare it to you. All that the Father has is Mine; therefore I said that He will take what is Mine and declare it to you. (John 16:12-15)

Blaming or giving credit to Satan/the devil for the work of the Holy Spirit amounts to blasphemy against the Holy Spirit. It is misidentifying the work of the Holy Spirit as being the work of the devil or demons. Jesus was very clear:

"Truly, I say to you, all sins will be forgiven the sons of men, and whatever blasphemies they utter; but whoever blasphemes against the Holy Spirit never has forgiveness, but is guilty of an eternal sin"— for they had said, "He has an unclean spirit." (Mark 3:28-30)

When Jesus was asked, *"Are we not right in saying that you are a Samaritan and have a demon?"* (John 8:48), the enquirers were blaspheming against the Holy Spirit – attributing the works of Jesus to the devil.

When people become preoccupied with Satan, they often miss the fact that the Holy Spirit is convicting them of their sin, prompting them to repent and receive salvation and the baptism of the Holy Spirit.

When we say "yes" to temptation and sin, our feelings of guilt, fear and condemnation are conviction from the Holy Spirit, not from Satan. The accusations of breaking God's law and falling short of His glory are a call from the Holy Spirit to repentance and forgiveness. Once we have responded, changed our ways and received forgiveness, any ongoing feelings that feel like guilt are simply reminders from the Holy Spirit to say thank you to Jesus for forgiving the sin. If anyone (including Satan) reminds us of the sin in an effort to make us feel guilty again, our response should be that we have changed our ways, been restored and received forgiveness from Jesus – and a declaration to our accusers of how wonderful He is. We can turn the attempted condemnation around and thank the person (or Satan) for reminding us about how good Jesus has been to us.

There is therefore now no condemnation for those who are in Christ Jesus. (Romans 8:1)

How to Handle Temptation

The best way to deal with the devil is to rebuke him as soon as he is recognized for trying to influence us to do something that will cause us to break God's law. We simply respond as Jesus did and say, "Be gone, Satan!"

Then the devil *left Him, and behold, angels came and ministered to Him.* (Matthew 4:11)

Then, we must not even entertain any more of his suggestions, but rather turn our attention to Jesus and start talking to Him or to our Heavenly Father – or start praying in the Spirit and spend time with Him. Singing hymns, choruses or spiritual songs, or reading some Scripture is a sure way to get past a temptation. When we put our attention on the things of God and resist Satan, we can be assured that he has been routed.

Submit yourselves therefore to God. Resist the devil and he will flee from you. (James 4:7)

We shall never be able to stand before God on Judgment Day and claim that the devil made us sin. We make the choice, no matter how strong a temptation may be.

The entertainer, Flip Wilson, used to tell a story about a preacher's wife. She went out shopping one day and bought herself a beautiful, fire-engine red, tight-fitting, expensive dress. The preacher was very upset about it. She tried passing the blame onto the devil. "Well, you see, I was walking past the store window and I saw this beautiful red dress in the window. The devil said to me, 'Sister, you should buy that beautiful dress in the window.' But, I resisted him. I said, 'No devil. It's too expensive.' But the devil said, 'Sister, it would look real good on you!' And, I said, 'Get behind me, devil.' And he did, but then he said, 'Sister, it looks real good from back here, too!' So, I bought it. The devil made me do it."

It is the devil's job to tempt us. It is our job to resist him. Then God can use us.

When we look back over our lives, recognition of all the sin and corruption we have been saved from, gives us reason to thank Jesus for His grace. We can join with the Psalmist in blessing Him.

> *"Bless the* LORD, *O my soul, and all that is within me, bless His holy Name. Bless the* LORD, *O my soul, and do not forget all His benefits – who forgives all your iniquity, who heals all your diseases, who redeems your life from the pit, who crowns you with steadfast love and mercy ..."* (Psalm 103:1-4)

When we thank Jesus for forgiving us and making us right with God, two interesting things happen. First, we have no guilt; secondly, we have the freedom to enter His courts with thanksgiving.[74] We find ourselves immediately in His presence. When we learn this trick of dealing with the devil's condemnation, we can enter into freedom without guilt and condemnation, and be released to get on with God's plans for our lives.

Having a heart of gratitude for our salvation and having confidence in our standing with God, is the most important lesson to learn in spiritual warfare. It sets us free to deal with the enemy wherever we encounter him.

We do not have to be afraid of our pasts, once our sins have been forgiven and we become born-again, Spirit-filled Christians. In fact, we can use them as weapons against sin and the devil. We become free to share our forgiven past experiences with others, so they can see what Jesus has done for us. They become part of our testimonies. Hearing about the help we've been given, gives hope to the listeners that Jesus will help them with their lives, the same way He has helped us. Our testimonies are always fresh and powerful when we tell not only how He forgave the things in our pasts, but go on to tell what He continues to do in our lives since becoming Christians. However, to have the freedom to talk about our forgiven sins, we need the power of the Holy Spirit that comes with being baptized in Him.[75] That gives us the power to be witnesses, telling what Jesus Christ has done for us.

---

[74] See Psalm 100:4
[75] See Acts 1:8

But they have conquered him by the blood of the Lamb and by the word of their testimony, for they did not cling to life even in the face of death. (Revelation 12:11)

Every time we share what Jesus has done for us, we overthrow the devil's efforts to tempt us. Every time we shrink back and do not tell people what Jesus has done for us, the devil takes ground. Those are field manoeuvres in spiritual warfare.

Some years ago, a friend, with whom I had gone to high school, became a Christian. Jesus called him into the ministry. Some time after he had been ordained and was pastoring a church, just before a Sunday morning worship service was about to start, one of our old friends from our hometown of Kirkland Lake, Ontario, turned up at his church. The old friend was not a Christian. He remembered all the sinful things he and my preacher friend had done together when they were growing up. He was sure our friend was nothing but another phony hypocrite in the ministry for money and other benefits. Since he was unable to see our friend before the start of the service, he wrote a note and sent it to him by way of one of the choir members.

My preacher friend read the note. "If you get up in that pulpit this morning and preach, I'll stand up and tell everybody here what you are really like." It was signed. He recognized his old friend's name. His stomach filled with knots. Something died inside. His past flashed before him. He remembered things he and our friend had done as young men. His temptation was to be filled with guilt and condemnation. Nevertheless, he prayed, "Lord Jesus, what shall I do? What shall I do?" He wanted to run away, but he stayed. He walked out into the sanctuary and into the pulpit.

Before starting the worship service, he pulled out the note. He announced, "Folks, I received a note this morning from an old friend with whom I grew up in Kirkland Lake. He is here this morning." He read the note to his congregation. You could have heard a pin drop.

"Well," he continued, "I want to tell you what I was like before I met Jesus and He saved me." He told them what he had been like. Then he said, "Now, I want to tell you what Jesus has done for me." After telling the whole story, before starting his worship service in the usual way, he gave an invitation for anyone who would like to receive Jesus as Savior and LORD, to come forward to the front of the church for prayer. Many, many people responded, including our old friend.

We overcome the devil by the word of our testimony, sharing with others what Jesus has done for us. That is the key to victorious spiritual warfare. It is always important, when dealing with the devil, to remember what Jesus said about him:

"When he lies, he speaks according to his own nature, for he is a liar and the father of lies." (John 8:44)

This means we must be careful not to believe him when he calls into question everything that Jesus has done in our lives. As the accuser, he will lie to us about what we have done. He will accuse us of things we haven't even done. He will distort the truth, lie to other people about us and lie to us about other people. He is often the source of gossip in our churches. His best agents, unfortunately, are rebellious, so-called Christians, or religious people willing to believe any gossip about other Christians. They find delight in passing on stories, in false hopes of gaining stature and authority over others. People who pass along such gossip are described by Dr. M. Scott Peck in his book, *People of the Lie: The Hope For Healing Human Evil.*[76]

Many pastors and church leaders have had their ministries destroyed by people who want to believe lies about them. I hate lies and gossip to the point where I have often traced back, through my churches, to find the source of gossip. Sometimes there is a human source, but most often, there is not one. I believe the devil takes great delight in using Christians to destroy other people in their churches. Jesus warns us in the parable of the wheat and tares,[77] about how the enemy continues to sow his weeds (tares) in God's fields when we're sleeping or not standing guard. He also

---

[76] ISBN 0 7126 1857 0
[77] See Matthew 13: 24-30

warns us about those who would allow themselves to be instruments of the enemy's destruction:

> *If any of you put a stumbling block before one of these little ones who believe in Me, it would be better for you if a great millstone were fastened around your neck and you were drowned in the depth of the sea. Woe to the world because of stumbling blocks! Occasions for stumbling are bound to come, but woe to the one by whom the stumbling block comes! If your hand or your foot causes you to stumble, cut it off and throw it away; it is better for you to enter life maimed or lame than to have two hands or two feet and to be thrown into the eternal fire. And if your eye causes you to stumble, tear it out and throw it away; it is better for you to enter life with one eye than to have two eyes and to be thrown into the Hell of fire.*
> (Matthew 18:6-9)

Defeating the Kingdom of Darkness

Jesus knew how the kingdom of darkness operated and systematically began to defeat it everywhere He went. He told the parable of the weeds among the wheat[78] to explain how evil is sown and why the sons of the evil one are allowed to grow in amongst the good harvest. Eventually, they will be harvested and burned with fire at the close of the age.

When John the Baptist was in prison, he heard about what Jesus was doing and sent word to Him, asking:

> *"Are You He who is to come, or shall we look for another?"*
> (Matthew 11:3)

Jesus answered by describing how He was destroying the works of the devil.

> *"Go and tell John what you hear and see: the blind receive their sight and the lame walk, lepers are cleansed and the deaf hear, and the dead are raised up, and the poor have the good news preached to them. And blessed is he who takes no offense at Me.* (Matthew 11:4-6)

---

[78] See Matthew 13:24-30

Jesus' second victory over the devil and the kingdom of darkness occurred at a wedding reception in Cana of Galilee, when He turned water into wine.[79] It was called the first of His "signs."

When Jesus healed a man on the Sabbath, He struck another blow against the devil and the kingdom of darkness. The man had been waiting at the Sheep Gate for a miracle, having been paralyzed for thirty-eight years.[80]

Every time Jesus preached, forgave sin, healed the sick, cast out a demon, or did any mighty work or miracle, He was systematically defeating the devil and destroying the kingdom of darkness. The healing of the paralytic, who walked away with his sins forgiven,[81] the healing and deliverance of the blind and dumb demoniac,[82] the healing and deliverance of the Canaanite woman's daughter[83] and other examples of healing the lame, the maimed, the blind, the dumb, and many others, were all instances of victory over the devil.[84]

A few other examples of the victories of Jesus, include the story of Him multiplying seven loaves of bread and a few fish, so that 4,000 men, plus women and children, could be fed. There were seven baskets full of leftovers.[85] The list of stories of the victories of Jesus go on and on: the healing and casting a demon out of the boy who suffered epileptic seizures and often fell into fire and water;[86] the story of the blind and the lame coming to Jesus in the Temple and Him healing them;[87] the story of Jesus delivering the man in the synagogue in Capernaum from an unclean spirit;[88] the story of Jesus healing Simon's mother-in-law who was sick with a fever;[89] stories of Jesus going throughout Galilee, preaching in the synagogue and casting out demons;[90] the story of Jesus healing

---

[79] See John 2:1-11
[80] See John 5:2-18
[81] See Matthew 9:2-6; Mark 2:1-12; Luke 5:17-26
[82] See Matthew 12:22
[83] See Matthew 15:21-28
[84] See Matthew 15:30-31
[85] See Matthew 15:32-38, Mark 8:1-9
[86] See Matthew 17:14-21; Mark 9:14-29
[87] See Matthew 21:14
[88] See Mark 1:21-28; Luke 4:31-37
[89] See Mark 1:30-31; Luke 4:38-39
[90] See Mark 1:39

the leper who knelt before Him, saying, "If you will, you can make me clean;"[91] the story of Jesus healing the paralytic who was lowered through the roof of the house on his pallet by the four men who had carried him there;[92] the story of Jesus healing the man with the withered hand on the Sabbath;[93] the story of Jesus rebuking the wind and stilling the storm by saying, "Peace! Be still!";[94] the story of Jesus casting the 6,000 unclean spirits out of the man called "Legion," setting him free so that he was clothed and in his right mind, and sending the demon-possessed swine into the sea to drown (and the demons to the abyss);[95-96] the story of Jesus inadvertently healing the woman, who had had a flow of blood for twelve years, when she touched the hem of His garment;[97] the story of Jesus raising Jairus' daughter from the dead;[98] the story of Jesus feeding 5,000 people with five loaves of bread and two fish;[99] and of course the story of Jesus walking on the water on the Sea of Galilee[100] – to name a few.

In Gennesaret, and wherever He went in villages, cities, or rural areas healing people,[101] Jesus relentlessly defeated the devil and the kingdom of darkness.

In the area of Decapolis, Jesus found a man who was deaf and had a speech impediment. He simply put his fingers into his ears, spat, touched the man's tongue and said, "Be opened."[102] Immediately, the man was able to hear and speak – striking yet another death blow to the kingdom of darkness. When Jesus healed the blind beggar, Bartimaeus, in Jericho,[103] it was all part of His mission to defeat Satan.

The battle with the devil and the kingdom of darkness became even more public when Jesus entered the Temple and drove out the buyers and sellers and overturned the table of the money changers[104] in determina-

---

[91] See Mark 1:40-44; Matthew 8:1-4; Luke 5:12-16
[92] See Mark 2:1-12; Matthew 9:1-8
[93] See Mark 3:1-6; Matthew 12:9-14; Luke 6:6-11
[94] See Mark 4:35-41; Luke 8:22-25
[95] See Mark 5:1-13
[96] See Luke 8:26-39
[97] See Mark 5:24-34; Luke 8:44-48
[98] See Mark 5:21-24, 35-43; Luke 8:41-42, 49-56
[99] See Mark 6:38-44; Matthew 14:13-21; Luke 9:10-17
[100] See Mark 6:47-51; Matthew 14:22-33
[101] See Matthew 14:35-36
[102] See Mark 7:31-37
[103] See Mark 10:46-52; Matthew 20:29-34; Luke 18:35-43
[104] See Mark 11:15-19; Luke 19:45

tion to return the Temple to His house of prayer. Satan had invaded it and turned it into a den of thieves.[105] The fact that the chief priests and scribes wanted to destroy Jesus was a sure indication to which kingdom they belonged.

In story after story, we bear witness to the defeat of the kingdom of darkness. We have the account of the unproductive fig tree withering when Jesus cursed it;[106] His feeding of the 5,000 with five barley loaves and two fish;[107] His forgiveness of the woman caught in adultery;[108] His healing of the man born blind;[109] His instructions to His disciples regarding where to let out their nets for the miraculous catch of fish;[110] His healing of the ten lepers, only one of whom returned to thank Him[111] and then His raising of Lazarus from the dead,[112] when He took authority over the devil's greatest threat – death – defeateding him and the kingdom of darkness.

Jesus' purpose is clearly expressed by John:

The reason the Son of God appeared was to destroy the works of the devil. (1 John 3:8)

Every time Jesus forgave sin, healed a sick person, multiplied food and fed hungry people, stilled a threatening storm or raised somebody from the dead, He destroyed the works of the devil. Everything He did was geared toward destroying the works of the devil and building the kingdom of God.

Every victory Jesus won over the devil and the kingdom of darkness saw people thanking Jesus and praising God for the miracles. However, there were always those who got angry. Lazarus' resurrection was the last straw as far as the chief priests and Pharisees were concerned.

So from that day on they took counsel on how to put him to death. (John 11:53)

---

[105] See Matthew 21:13; Mark 11:17; Luke 19:46
[106] See Mark 11:20-21; Matthew 21:20-22
[107] See John 6:1-13
[108] See John 8:3-11
[109] See John 9:1-12
[110] See Luke 5:1-11
[111] See Luke 17:11-19
[112] See John 11

War in Heavenly Places

On earth, Jesus was constantly provoking the enemy, sending ripple effects all the way to Heaven. People were being set free from their sins, healed and delivered from the domination of the devil and his kingdom of darkness.

> *Blessed be the God and Father of our Lord Jesus Christ, who has blessed us in Christ with every spiritual blessing in the heavenly places.* (Ephesians 1:3)

Jesus wasn't alone in His work: He prepared His disciples for ministry/war, giving them authority to do the same works as He. First, He sent out the twelve.

> *And He called the twelve together and gave them power and authority over all demons and to cure diseases, and He sent them out to preach the kingdom of God and to heal. And He said to them, "Take nothing for your journey, no staff, nor bag, nor bread, nor money; and do not have two tunics. And whatever house you enter, stay there, and from there depart. And wherever they do not receive you, when you leave that town shake off the dust from your feet as a testimony against them." And they departed and went through the villages, preaching the gospel and healing everywhere.* (Luke 9:1-6)

When they were successful, He sent out seventy more.

> *After this the LORD appointed seventy others, and sent them on ahead of Him, two by two, into every town and place where He Himself was about to come. And He said to them, "The harvest is plentiful, but the laborers are few; pray therefore the LORD of the harvest to send out laborers into His harvest. Go your way; behold, I send you out as lambs in the midst of wolves. Carry no purse, no bag, no sandals; and salute no one on the road. Whatever house you enter, first say, 'Peace be to this house!' And if a son of peace is there, your peace shall rest upon him; but if not, it shall return to you. And remain in the same house, eating and drinking what they*

provide, for the laborer deserves his wages; do not go from house to house. Whenever you enter a town and they receive you, eat what is set before you; heal the sick in it and say to them, 'The kingdom of God has come near to you.' But whenever you enter a town and they do not receive you, go into its streets and say, 'Even the dust of your town that clings to our feet, we wipe off against you; nevertheless know this, that the kingdom of God has come near.' I tell you, it shall be more tolerable on that day for Sodom than for that town."
(Luke 10:1-12,17)

These seventy came back in great excitement and reported, "Lord, even the demons are subject to us in your Name!"

In Heaven, war had been declared. The archangel Michael, the field commander of God's faithful angels, was fighting the dragon and his evil angels who had already been defeated. There was no longer any place for them in Heaven.

And the great dragon was thrown down, that ancient serpent, who is called the devil *and Satan, the deceiver of the whole world – he was thrown down to the earth, and his angels were thrown down with him.* (Revelation 12:7-9)

So effective was the coordinated attack of disciples on earth and the angels in Heaven, that the devil and his forces were defeated both on earth and in Heaven. Jesus must have smiled when He saw the devil come shooting out of the sky from Heaven like an enemy aircraft that had been shot down.

I saw Satan fall like lightning from Heaven. Behold, I have given you authority to tread upon serpents and scorpions, and over all the power of the enemy; and nothing shall hurt you. Nevertheless do not rejoice in this, that the spirits are subject to you; but rejoice that your names are written in Heaven. (Luke 10:18-20)

Yes, the devil was cast down to the earth and now he was really angry. No longer did he have access to God's throne. No longer could he report to God about the sins of His people night and day.

Rejoice then, O Heaven and you that dwell therein! But, woe to you, O earth and sea, for the devil has come down to you in great wrath, because he knows that his time is short! (Revelation 12:12)

The devil is so angry that he determines to attack the woman, the Church of Jesus Christ, and all of her offspring who bear witness to Jesus Christ.

With the defeat of the devil and his angels in Heaven, the kingdom of darkness, with its elaborate network of angels throughout the world, was dismantled. Satan was thrown down to the earth, where he continues his war today – but he does it without his angels. All the evil angels were defeated and removed from their positions of power over cities, towns, countries, and territories. They were all arrested and marched off to an eternal prison from which they will never escape, except into Hell.

*For if God did not spare the angels when they sinned, but cast them into Hell (Tartarus) and committed them to the pits of nether gloom to be kept until judgment. . . .then the L*ORD *knows how to rescue the godly from trial, and to keep the unrighteous under punishment until the Day of Judgment.* (2 Peter 2:4,9)

And the angels that did not keep their own position but left their proper dwelling have been kept by Him in eternal chains in the nether gloom of judgment until the judgment of the Great Day. (Jude 6)

All the once mighty angels who sinned; not just a few, but *all* who were a part of the kingdom of darkness and who followed the devil, are banned from roaming both earth and Heaven.

The Bible does not tell us how many angels fell in their rebellion and disobedience. Some people have tried to tell us that one-third of the angels in Heaven fell and were defeated. However, that is based upon a very questionable interpretation of a passage in the Book of Revelation, which describes what will happen when the fourth angel blows his trumpet:

> *... and a third of the sun was struck, and a third of the moon and a third of the stars, so that a third of their light was darkened; a third of the day was kept from shining, and likewise a third of the night.* (Revelation 8:12)

This describes a natural destruction of actual stars and does not talk about the stars being angels. I suspect the number of angels was far smaller than anyone would guess, because I have seen how few rebellious sinful *people* it takes to create major problems in a church. The number is usually very exaggerated and, since the devil is a liar, I suspect he would like us to believe that his army of fallen angels was much greater than it was.

> *You are of your father the devil, and your will is to do your father's desires. He was a murderer from the beginning, and has nothing to do with the truth, because there is no truth in him. When he lies, he speaks according to his own nature, for he is a liar and the father of lies.* (John 8:44)

Regardless of their actual number, they are no longer a threat to anyone. All their positions of power have been removed. Nor did these fallen angels become evil or unclean spirits or demons. They are imprisoned and they will stay in prison until Judgment Day.

The one exception, of course, is the devil who has been confined to earth.

And so, now that the rebellious angels have been dealt with, what is left of the kingdom of darkness? Well, the demons, or evil and unclean spirits, are all that are left for the devil to command. Since they have always been around in the Old Testament, it is clear that they are not the fallen angels. The Old Testament makes a clear distinction between them and angels.

As James W. Laine of Macalaster College points out, "There is not even the slightest hint of crossover or exchange of roles or of terms. Angels may take on human form, but they are never said to inhabit humans. Angels are always referred to as angels and demons are always referred to as demons or evil spirits."

Nevertheless, demons are dangerous. They still attack people and attempt to possess, harass, and kill their victims. They still take up residence in buildings and attack and victimize the occupants. That is the bad news. The good news is that any born-again, Spirit-filled Christian has authority over any evil spirit. That means that the youngest child to the oldest adult has authority to cast them out of any place they may take up residence whether it is in a person or a building.

The Greatest Battle of the War – Defeating Sin

After having dealt with the devil and his angels and capturing the forces of the kingdom of darkness, Jesus then had to deal with sin. He had to go to the Cross of Calvary in order to pay for the sin of the world. He had to buy back all those who had sinned and fallen short of the glory of God. Now was the time to fulfill God's promise of sending the Messiah. Now He was about to complete His work:

> *For God so loved the world that He gave His only Son, that whoever believes in Him should not perish but have eternal life.* (John 3:16)

> *Indeed, under the law almost everything is purified with blood, and without the shedding of blood there is no forgiveness of sins.* (Hebrews 9:22)

Jesus prepared Himself and His disciples for the greatest battle of the war. He had to be prepared to face what Paul called the sting of death, which is sin.[113] To face the greatest and last enemy, He prepared Himself by sharing the last supper with His disciples.[114] He then spent the rest of the night in prayer. Now came the greatest challenge of His ministry and life.

> *My Father, if it be possible, let this cup pass from Me; nevertheless, not as I will, but as Thou wilt.* (Matthew 26:39)

The fight was on. Never had Jesus experienced such a battle.

> *And being in agony, He prayed more earnestly; and His sweat became like great drops of blood falling down upon the ground.* (Luke 22:44)

---

[113] See 1 Corinthians 15:56
[114] See Matthew 26:26-29; Mark 14:22-25; Luke 22:15-38

Then came the betrayal by one of His own disciples, Judas Iscariot. It was no surprise. We know Jesus knew who it was because, early in His ministry, He said:

"Did I not choose you, the twelve, and one of you is a devil?" (John 6:70)

It was impossible to deceive Jesus ...

... because He knew all men and needed no one to bear witness of man; for He Himself knew what was in man. (John 2:25)

The devil tried to destroy Jesus.

And during supper, when the devil *had already put it into the heart of Judas Iscariot, Simon's son, to betray Him ...* (John 13:2)

Nevertheless, about to lay down His life for mankind, Jesus proceeded to wash His disciples' feet, to teach them, saying:

"... a servant is not greater than his master; nor is He who is sent greater than He who sent Him." (John 13:16)

Greater love (agape) *has no man than this, that a man lay down his life for his friends.* (John 15:13)

The devil and his shattered kingdom must have cheered, as the evil remnant watched Jesus being betrayed, watched Him being scourged with a whip, watched while the soldiers mocked Him and jammed the crown of thorns on His head and then watched as they wrapped Him in the purple of a king. The devil must have thought he would have the last laugh when Pilate gave consent to have Jesus crucified. Little did Satan know, for much was yet to come. Saul had not yet been transformed into Paul and had not yet shared the great lesson of God, which is this:

We know that in everything God works for good with those who love Him, who are called according to His purpose. (Romans 8:28)

Nor had the devil learned from another of his failures, in time past, in the life of Joseph:

As for you, you meant evil against me; but God meant it for good, to bring it about that many people should be kept alive, as they are today. (Genesis 50:20)

Without realizing it, the devil was cooperating with God for his own defeat.

The spiritual war was rising to a climax. The nails were being pounded into Jesus' hands and feet. The pain was inexpressible. His Cross was hoisted up between two thieves. Defeat appeared imminent. Death was in the air. Over Jesus' head was a sign:

"*This is Jesus, the King of the Jews.*" (Matthew 27:37)

But there was something happening here that even the devil could not imagine. Jesus was fighting back skillfully, in a most unusual way. While He appeared to the crowd to be the victim, He was obviously in charge, because He knew that everything happening to Him had been prophesied. Everything was running according to the battle plan, regardless of the pain.

Let's watch the battle on the Cross. First, Jesus dealt with those who crucified Him and nailed Him to the Cross to die.

Father, forgive them; for they know not what they do. (Luke 23:34)

In the most extreme circumstances, Jesus lived the words of His teachings. Peter had once asked:

"L ORD, *how often shall my brother sin against me, and I forgive him? As many as seven times?*"
Jesus said to him, "I do not say to you seven times, but seventy times seven."[115] (Matthew 18:21-22)

When Jesus taught the Beatitudes to the crowds, He said:

"*But I say to you, Love your enemies and pray for those who persecute you, so that you may be sons of your Father who is in Heaven.*" (Matthew 5:44-45)

---

[115] Greek – 490 times each day.

One of the criminals who was hanged railed at him, saying, "Are you not the Christ? Save yourself and us!"
But the other rebuked him, saying, "Do you not fear God, since you are under the same sentence of condemnation? And we indeed justly; for we are receiving the due reward of our deeds; but this man has done nothing wrong." And he said, "Jesus, remember me when You come into Your kingdom."
And He said to him, "Truly, I say to you, today you will be with Me in Paradise." (Luke 23:39-43)

Jesus promised the thief he would have eternal life. He was a saved man, plucked right out of sin and on his way to Heaven. Again, Jesus defeated the devil and his kingdom.

After Jesus was crucified, His mother Mary, His aunt Mary, Mary Magdalene, and one of His disciples, John, stood by the Cross, agonizing over the pain and injustice to their beloved Jesus. As Jesus hung there, He confirmed that God would look after His loved ones, even when He wasn't there. He turned to His mother and said:

"Woman, behold, your Son!" Then He said to the disciple, "Behold, your mother!" (John 19:27)

Despite the fact that the devil delights in trying to convince people that those whom we love, like our family, will not be taken care of by God if anything should happen to us, Jesus proved him wrong. He opened the door to God's provision. He turned His mother over to His disciple so they could look after each other. John took Mary to his home. Again, the devil and the kingdom of darkness were defeated.

About the ninth hour, Jesus cried out in a loud voice,

"My God, My God, why hast Thou forsaken Me?" (Matthew 27:46)

Jesus was not feeling abandoned here. Actually, the way this is written in Greek, Jesus is saying, "My God, My God, for just one moment, I thought You had abandoned Me." God never leaves us nor forsakes us.

... for He has said, "I will never fail you nor forsake you."
(Hebrews 13:5)

That is exactly what Jesus was proving here. He demonstrated the fact that at the very moment of our greatest crisis, even when we may be faced with our own painful death, God is with us. He was with Jesus. Jesus used Scripture skillfully to deal with this agonizing ordeal. He quoted Psalm 22, which described exactly what was happening to Him and presented the guarantee of being raised from the dead. Again, Jesus defeated the devil and his kingdom as it tried to discourage Him. He was even more encouraged.

My God, My God, why hast Thou forsaken Me? Why art Thou so far from helping Me, from the words of My groaning? O my God, I cry by day, but Thou dost not answer; and by night, but find no rest. Yet Thou art holy, enthroned on the praises of Israel. In Thee our fathers trusted; they trusted, and Thou didst deliver them. To Thee they cried, and were saved; in Thee they trusted, and were not disappointed. (Psalm 22:1-5)

Then, Jesus' human needs surfaced and He cried out in excruciating pain. He was offered some vinegar on hyssop. Echoes of His conversation with the Samaritan woman about His living water, reverberated through the universe.

... but whoever drinks of the water that I shall give him will never thirst; the water that I shall give him will become in him a spring of water welling up to eternal life. (John 4:14)

The devil promises water, but gives vinegar on hyssop – a drink of death. It takes away hope. Jesus did not need the vinegar. He had "living water" to sustain Him throughout His horrendous death on the Cross. Living water, another name for the Holy Spirit, is the only water that can take a person safely through death into eternal life. Jesus had the Holy Spirit with Him – another defeat for the devil and the kingdom of darkness.

When the sixth hour came, darkness came over the whole land and the curtain of the Temple was torn in two. The old covenant was annulled, fulfilled and completed.

> *"Behold, the days are coming," says the Lord, "when I will make a new covenant with the house of Israel and the house of Judah, not like the covenant which I made with their fathers when I took them by the hand to bring them out of the land of Egypt, My covenant which they broke, Though I was their husband," says the Lord. "But this is the covenant which I will make with the house of Israel after those days," says the Lord: "I will put My law within them, and I will write it upon their hearts; and I will be their God, and they shall be My people. And no longer shall each man teach his neighbor and each his brother, saying, 'Know the Lord,' for they shall all know Me, from the least of them to the greatest," says the Lord; "for I will forgive their iniquity, and I will remember their sin no more."*
> (Jeremiah 31:31-34)

> *So I became the shepherd of the flock doomed to be slain for those who trafficked in the sheep. And I took two staffs; one I named Grace, the other I named Union. And I tended the sheep. In one month I destroyed the three shepherds. But I became impatient with them, and they also detested me. So I said, "I will not be your shepherd. What is to die, let it die; what is to be destroyed, let it be destroyed; and let those that are left devour the flesh of one another." And I took my staff Grace, and I broke it, annulling the covenant which I had made with all the peoples. So it was annulled on that day, and the traffickers in the sheep, who were watching me, knew that it was the word of the Lord. Then I said to them, "If it seems right to you, give me my wages; but if not, keep them." And they weighed out as my wages thirty shekels of silver. Then the Lord said to me, "Cast it into the treasury" – the lordly price at which I was paid off by them. So I took the thirty shekels of silver and cast them into the treasury in the house of the Lord. Then I broke my second*

staff Union, annulling the brotherhood between Judah and Israel. (Zechariah 11:7-14)

But as it is, Christ has obtained a ministry which is as much more excellent than the old as the covenant He mediates is better, since it is enacted on better promises. For if that first covenant had been faultless, there would have been no occasion for a second. (Hebrews 8:6-7)

The new covenant was now in effect. The Lamb of God who takes away the sin of the world had been sacrificed. Jesus turned himself over to His God, demonstrating to us that we can trust the Father. This is the time for real trust. Do we believe the devil who tells us that there is nothing after death for us? Hope and truth lie only in the One who said:

"In My Father's house are many rooms; if it were not so, would I have told you that I go to prepare a place for you? And when I go and prepare a place for you, I will come again and will take you to Myself, that where I am you may be also." (John 14:2-3)

Jesus was on His way home. He knew where He was going because He had *"descended from Heaven."*[116] This was just a different way home. He hadn't traveled this way before, but in his Father's hands, He knew He would be all right. And so will we! Another defeat for the devil and the kingdom of darkness.

When Jesus said, *"It is finished"* and *"He bowed his head and gave up His Spirit"* (John 19:30), it was not the cry of a defeated man. It was the shout of victory. This is what merchants once wrote across accounts that had been completely paid off. It was Jesus' way of telling the world that the sin account had been paid in full. The debt of sin for the whole world, since its creation, was paid completely. The Cross had been dramatically changed into an altar.

For Christ, our paschal Lamb, has been sacrificed. (1 Corinthians 5:7)

---

[116] See John 3:13

Again, the devil, his work, and his kingdom of darkness had been defeated by Jesus. The crowning victory was complete!

There have been those who question the claim that Jesus laid down His life of His own accord, because He was executed by order of Pontius Pilate. How could that be so? Jesus said:

> *"For this reason the Father loves Me, because I lay down My life in order to take it up again. No one takes it from Me, but I lay it down of My own accord."* (John 10:17-18)

To answer that question, we need to understand how a person died on a Cross. Did they bleed to death? No. Pierre Barbet, in his book, *A Doctor at Calvary,*[117] explains how death happens on a Cross. It happens, he says, by asphyxiation. By hanging from one's arms for a prolonged time, one's lungs begin to fill with liquid, as they do with pneumonia. To keep from dying, a person being crucified needs to push up with his legs, despite the horrifying fact that they are supported by only a nail, piercing the feet. There were instances of men surviving on crosses for as many as three days, by pushing up in this way. That is why, when it got close to sundown on that Friday, the soldiers decided to break the legs of the three men to hasten their deaths, before the Sabbath began. As it happened,[118] they needed to break the legs of only the two thieves. When they came to Jesus, He appeared to be already dead. A spear thrust in His side, confirmed that His lungs were filled with water. Sometime during that afternoon, Jesus had stopped pushing and so had laid His life down – voluntarily. This was a pivotal battle and profound evidence of Jesus defeating the devil.

The Defeat of Death

From all earthly appearances, when Jesus died on the Cross of Calvary, it appeared that the devil and the kingdom of darkness had won.

---

[117] New York: Doubleday, 1963
[118] See John 19:31-37

But in the eyes of God, Jesus had established the kingdom of God as victorious over death.

Much to the devil's shock, Jesus was not finished yet. The worst for Satan was yet to come.

When Jesus died physically, He did not die spiritually.

For Christ also died for sins once for all, the righteous for the unrighteous, that He might bring us to God, being put to death in the flesh but made alive in the Spirit; in which He went and preached to the spirits in prison, who formerly did not obey, when God's patience waited in the days of Noah, during the building of the ark, in which a few, that is, eight persons, were saved through water. (1 Peter 3:18-20)

Jesus did not die in the ordinary sense of the word. Only His physical body ceased to function. Spiritually, He continued to carry out God's plan of spiritual warfare in every detail, doing ministry in the place of the dead during the three days that He was physically dead.

When Jesus died, he went to the place of the dead called "Sheol" in the Old Testament and "Hades" in the New Testament (Greek). He invaded it, took control of it, organized it and established His Lordship over it. It was no longer a place of unconsciousness, but a place where both the saved and the unsaved would be wide awake to both God's promises and His judgment.

First of all, He woke everybody up who was there, both the spirits (pneumati) of fallen angels and the spirits of people who had died.

For Christ also died for sins once for all, the righteous for the unrighteous, that He might bring us to God, being put to death in the flesh but made alive in the Spirit; in which He went and preached to the spirits in prison. (1 Peter 3:18-19)

Secondly, He preached salvation to the spirits of the dead people and the reason for condemnation to the fallen angels.

> *For this is why the gospel was preached even to the dead, that though judged in the flesh like men, they might live in the Spirit like God.*
> (1 Peter 3:19)

They all heard the gospel. No one could ever accuse Jesus of not giving every person who had ever lived and died, up to that time, a chance to hear the gospel and have the opportunity to be saved. However, this was a one-time-only instance of preaching to the dead. This is not something that happens today. It was a time of establishing the Saviorship and Lordship of Jesus in a one-time coup, over those who had been kept waiting for this momentous event in God's timetable.

Thirdly, Jesus organized Hades (Sheol), the place of the dead, dividing it into three sections.

The first He established was "Paradise," a place of fellowship for those who are saved, like the poor man, Lazarus.

> *There was a rich man, who was clothed in purple and fine linen and who feasted sumptuously every day. And at his gate lay a poor man named Lazarus, full of sores, who desired to be fed with what fell from the rich man's table; moreover the dogs came and licked his sores. The poor man died and was carried by the angels to Abraham's bosom. The rich man also died and was buried; and in Hades, being in torment, he lifted up his eyes, and saw Abraham far off and Lazarus in his bosom ... And He said to him, "Truly, I say to you, today you will be with Me in Paradise."* (Luke 16:19-23; 23:43)

Some people like to call this "Heaven." In fact, it is a temporary Heaven which will last until the New Heaven and the New Earth arrive and the New Jerusalem is put into place.[119] That will occur when Jesus returns and all the dead are raised.

> *Immediately after the tribulation of those days the sun will be darkened, and the moon will not give its light, and the stars will fall from Heaven, and the powers of the heavens will be shaken; then will appear the sign of the Son of Man in Heaven, and then all the tribes*

---

[119] See Revelation 21:1-3

> *of the earth will mourn, and they will see the Son of Man coming on the clouds of heaven with power and great glory; and He will send out His angels with a loud trumpet call, and they will gather His elect from the four winds, from one end of Heaven to the other.* (Matthew 24:29-31)[120]

> *Truly, truly, I say to you, the hour is coming, and now is, when the dead will hear the voice of the Son of God, and those who hear will live. For as the Father has life in Himself, so He has granted the Son also to have life in Himself, and has given Him authority to execute judgment, because He is the Son of Man. Do not marvel at this; for the hour is coming when all who are in the tombs will hear His voice and come forth, those who have done good, to the resurrection of life, and those who have done evil, to the resurrection of judgment.* (John 5:25-29)

After establishing Paradise, He established "Tartarus," a place of painful punishment and torment – a temporary Hell of punishment for those who are not saved, like the rich man.

> *There was a rich man, who was clothed in purple and fine linen and who feasted sumptuously every day. And at his gate lay a poor man named Lazarus, full of sores, who desired to be fed with what fell from the rich man's table; moreover the dogs came and licked his sores. The poor man died and was carried by the angels to Abraham's bosom. The rich man also died and was buried; and in Hades, being in torment, he lifted up his eyes, and saw Abraham far off and Lazarus in his bosom. And he called out, "Father Abraham, have mercy upon me, and send Lazarus to dip the end of his finger in water and cool my tongue; for I am in anguish in this flame." But Abraham said, "Son, remember that you in your lifetime received your good things, and Lazarus in like manner evil things; but now he is comforted here, and you are in anguish."* (Luke 16:19-25)

Tartarus, too, will last until the final lake of fire for punishment (Gehenna) is established when Jesus returns and all the dead are raised.

---

[120] See also I Thessalonians 4:13-18; 1 Corinthians 15:51-56

> *But as for the cowardly, the faithless, the polluted, as for murderers, fornicators, sorcerers, idolaters, and all liars, their lot shall be in the lake that burns with fire and sulphur, which is the second death.* (Revelation 21:8)

Jesus included, in Tartarus, a special prison for those rebellious angels who allied themselves with Satan and who were part of the kingdom of darkness.

> *For if God did not spare the angels when they sinned, but cast them into Hell and committed them to pits of nether gloom to be kept until the judgment...* (2 Peter 2:4)

> *And the angels that did not keep their own position but left their proper dwelling have been kept by Him in eternal chains in the nether gloom until the judgment of the great day; just as Sodom and Gomorrah and the surrounding cities, which likewise acted immorally and indulged in unnatural lust, serve as an example by undergoing a punishment of eternal fire.* (Jude 6,7)

The third section of Hades (Sheol) Jesus established was the abyss (Greek: abussos). It divides Paradise from Tartarus. "Abussos" is translated "abyss" in two places and "the bottomless pit" in nine places. There are eight main things to understand about the abyss.

1. It is a place where demons / evil spirits are sent for punishment. (Luke 8:31)

2. Paul warned us not to try to determine who is going to Heaven or who is going down to the abyss.[121] That decision belongs to Jesus.

3. We are told that a star, meaning an angel, will be given the key to the bottomless pit (busso) in order to open a shaft[122] from which smoke like the smoke of a great furnace will darken the sun and the air.[123]

4. From the smoke will come locusts on the earth and they will be given the power of scorpions, but will be told not to harm the

---

[121] See Romans 10:7
[122] See Revelation 9:1
[123] See Revelation 9:2

grass of the earth or any green growth or any green tree, but only those of mankind who do not have the seal of God upon their foreheads. They are going to be allowed to torture people for five months but not kill them. (Revelation 9:3-5)

5. They have as king over them the angel of the bottomless pit; his name in Hebrew is Abaddon, and in Greek he is called Apollyon (meaning "Destroyer"). (Revelation 9:11)

6. When the two witnesses, "*have finished their testimony, the beast that ascends from the bottomless pit will make war upon them and conquer them and kill them...*" (Revelation 11:7) They will be raised up to Heaven in a cloud which will result in a great earthquake. A tenth of the city will fall and 7,000 people will be killed. "*The rest were terrified and gave glory to God.*" (Revelation 11:8-13)

7. The beast that is to ascend from the bottomless pit and the people whose names are not written in the Book of Life (and who are impressed by the beast) will make war on the Lamb and the Lamb will conquer them, for He is Lord of Lords and King of Kings. (Revelation 17:8-14)

8. We are told, "*Then I saw an angel coming down from Heaven, holding in his hand the key of the bottomless pit and a great chain. And he seized the dragon, that ancient serpent, who is the* devil *and Satan, and bound him for a thousand years, and threw him into the pit, and shut it and sealed it over him, that he should deceive the nations no more, till the thousand years were ended. After that he must be loosed for a little while.*" (Revelation 20:1-3)

The conclusion follows that our God, Jesus Christ, is Lord over the whole of the three divisions in the place of the dead: Paradise, Tartarus and the Abyss. It is He who determines who will have eternal life in the New Jerusalem in the New Heaven and the New Earth. Those whose names are not written in the Book of Life will end up in the final Hell called Gehenna (the Lake of Fire and sulphur) along with the devil and the beast and the false prophet. There they will be tormented day and night for ever and ever.[124]

---
[124] See Revelation 20:10

The Place of the Dead

Now, let us take a close look at the place of the dead. In the Old Testament, in Hebrew, it was called "Sheol." It was most often translated as Hell, but it was a place to which both the righteous (saved) and the unrighteous (unsaved) went when they died. It was not a place that people looked forward to going, but everybody went there when they died. It was neither a place of reward nor a place of punishment. It was like a storage place for all who died. God placed an angel, named Abaddon, in charge of Sheol. His name was usually coupled with Sheol.[125]

The place of the dead was not a place where people were conscious.

For in death there is no remembrance of Thee; in Sheol who can give Thee praise? (Psalm 6:5)

It was a place without worship, thanksgiving, or God's truth.

For Sheol cannot thank Thee, death cannot praise Thee; those who go down to the pit cannot hope for Thy faithfulness. (Isaiah 38:18)

Death was best described as a sleep from which a person could not awaken.

Consider and answer me, O LORD my God; lighten my eyes, lest I sleep the sleep of death. (Psalm 13:3)

It was a place of total darkness. Jonah compared being in the belly of the whale to being awake in the place of the dead.

I called to the LORD, out of my distress, and He answered me; out of the belly of Sheol I cried, and Thou didst hear my voice. (Jonah 2:2)

It is clear that people could not escape God in the place of the dead.

If I ascend to Heaven, Thou art there! If I make my bed in Sheol, Thou art there! (Psalm 139:8; see also Amos 9:2)

The location of Sheol had to be down in the center of the earth, because it swallowed up those who were rebellious against God's will and

---

[125] See Job 28:22; Proverbs 15:11; 27:20

leadership ie) Korah and his followers who rebelled against Moses;[126] the Israelites who worshipped idols;[127] the Pharaoh of Egypt and his people;[128] the king of Babylon;[129] Jerusalem;[130] and all who sinned.[131] All of God's faithful were kept there, even Jacob, who said that if anything happened to his son Benjamin, he would go to Sheol himself.[132]

In Hannah's prayer for her son Samuel, she acknowledged,

> "The LORD kills and brings to life; He brings down to Sheol and raises up." (1 Samuel 2:6)

David thanked God for saving him from his enemies who wanted to kill him. He could see death with its final resting place staring him in the face. However, he said:

> "The cords of Sheol entangled me, the snares of death confronted me. In my distress I called upon the LORD; to my God I called. From His Temple He heard my voice, and my cry came to His ears."
> (2 Samuel 22:6-7)

And God rescued him.

An early or premature place in the place of the dead was guaranteed for the wicked.[133] The place of the dead can accommodate as many people as need to be kept there. Its capacity is limitless.

> Sheol and Abaddon are never satisfied, and never satisfied are the eyes of man. (Proverbs 27:20)

> They have as king over them the angel of the bottomless pit; his name in Hebrew is Abaddon, and in Greek he is called Apollyon.
> (Revelation 9:11)

> Three things are never satisfied; four never say, "Enough": Sheol ...
> (Proverbs 30:15-16)

---

[126] See Numbers 16:30-33
[127] See Deuteronomy 32:22; Isaiah 57:9
[128] See Ezekiel 31:10-17; 32:21, 27
[129] See Isaiah 14:9-15
[130] See Isaiah 28:15-18
[131] See Job 24:19
[132] See Genesis 44:29
[133] See Psalm 9:17; 55:15; Proverbs 1:12

The preacher of Ecclesiastes offered no hope for those who think they can accomplish something after death.

Whatever your hand finds to do, do it with your might; for there is no work or thought or knowledge or wisdom in Sheol, to which you are going. (Ecclesiastes 9:10)

It was a place without hope.

As the cloud fades and vanishes, so he who goes down to Sheol does not come up. (Job 7:8-9)

Although there was no hope for those who died and went to the place of the dead (Sheol) with its dreamless sleep, God Himself offered hope. David saw it:

Therefore my heart is glad, and my soul rejoices; my body also dwells secure. For Thou dost not give me up to Sheol, or let Thy godly one see the pit. (Psalm 16:9-10)

This was a promise not only for the Messiah, Jesus, but also a promise for all of God's people. God promises:

"Shall I ransom them from the power of Sheol? Shall I redeem them from Death? O Death, where are your plagues? O Sheol, where is your destruction?" (Hosea 13:14)

What Jesus Accomplished During the Three Days His Body Lay in the Grave

Jesus accomplished a great deal during the three days His body lay in the grave. He took "captivity captive,"[134] which meant He took charge of the place of the dead and woke up all those people who had died and were kept there after defeating the devil – both on earth and in Heaven. He took the devil's defeated and rebellious angels who sinned and put them in eternal chains. He established His authority over the place of the dead (Sheol/Hades) called Tartarus[135] (a temporary Hell in which people who have died would also be placed). During those three days, He also

---
[134] See Ephesians 4:8
[135] See 2 Peter 2:4

preached the Gospel to those who had died prior to the giving of the new covenant , to give them an opportunity to receive salvation[136] and give them a place in Paradise (a temporary Heaven for those who have received salvation) until Jesus returns.[137]

The final Heaven, in the New Jerusalem, is the final destination for those who have been saved. All those who have been kept in Paradise will be raised from the dead and join the rest of the believers.

There is also a final Hell, the Lake of Fire (Gehenna) prepared for Satan (the devil) and his followers. God's appointed tempter or tester cannot avoid his sentence. He will be forever punished in the Lake of Fire.[138]

What happened during the three days from Jesus' physical death on the Cross of Calvary to His resurrection, was best described by the Apostle Paul when he said,

"When he ascended up on high, He led captivity captive, and gave gifts unto men." (Ephesians 4:8 KJV)

This is also translated,

"When he ascended on high He led a host of captives, and gave gifts to men." (RSV)

Here, Paul is referring to the victory parade that every Roman general demanded, to show off his victorious army by having it march through the streets of Rome with all his prisoners and the treasure and spoil that came from defeating his enemies. This time, it's about Jesus leading a long victory parade of His saved people into Paradise, while the captives (unrepentant sinners and fallen angels) were marched into Tartarus to their respective places of punishment.

Out of that victory, rather than demanding tribute gifts (domata) from the defeated losers, Jesus gives tribute gifts to His Church in the form of what is usually called the "Five-Fold Ministry" of apostles, prophets, evangelists, pastors and teachers.

---

[136] See 1 Peter 4:6
[137] See Acts 1:11; 1 Corinthians 15:51-58
[138] See Revelation 19:20; 20:10

... to equip the saints for the work of ministry, for the building up of the body of Christ, until we all attain to the unity of faith and of the knowledge of the Son of God, to mature manhood, to the measure of the stature of the fullness of Christ; so that we may no longer be children, tossed to and fro and carried about with every wind of doctrine, by the cunning of men, by their craftiness in deceitful wiles.
(Ephesians 4:8-14)

Victory Day
Resurrection & the Coming of the Holy Spirit!

Jesus' victory over the devil and the kingdom of darkness was complete when He arose from the dead. At the moment of resurrection, He established Himself, once and for all, as Savior and Lord.

The first person to see Jesus, after He rose from the dead, was Mary Magdalene. She found the empty tomb. Jesus' body was gone. The stone used for a door had been rolled away from the entrance. Peter and John had come and gone from the tomb. All they had found was the burial cloths and an empty tomb. But Mary stayed behind crying.

> *As she wept, she bent over to look into the tomb; and she saw two angels in white, sitting where the body of Jesus had been lying, one at the head and the other at the feet. They said to her, "Woman, why are you weeping?"*
> *She said to them, "They have taken away my Lord, and I do not know where they have laid Him."*
> *When she had said this, she turned around and saw Jesus standing there, but she did not know that it was Jesus. Jesus said to her, "Woman, why are you weeping? Whom are you looking for?"*
> *Supposing Him to be the gardener, she said to Him, "Sir, if you have carried Him away, tell me where you have laid Him, and I will take*

> *Him away."*
> *Jesus said to her, "Mary!"*
> *She turned and said to Him in Hebrew, "Rabboni!" (which means Teacher).*
> *Jesus said to her, "Do not hold on to Me, because I have not yet ascended to the Father. But go to My brothers and say to them, 'I am ascending to My Father and your Father, to My God and your God.'"*
> *Mary Magdalene went and announced to the disciples, "I have seen the* Lord;*" and she told them that He had said these things to her.*
> (John 20:1-18)

Jesus was real! He had returned victorious! He had conquered death.

The comedian, Oscar Bean, was asked in a television interview by the host, Merv Griffin, if he was a religious person. He replied, "Are you asking me if I am a born-again Christian?"

Merv said, "Yes, I am. Are you?"

Mr. Bean said, "Not yet. However, I have been reading and studying about God. And, I have come to this conclusion: death must be the most exciting experience of all, because God left it to the last."

That is true; but only if a person is a born-again, Spirit-filled Christian.

Jesus' disciples were terrified when they first saw Him alive after His death on the Cross. They could wrap their heads around His reappearance, only by assuming that He must have returned as a ghost or "spirit."[139] However, Jesus came back to life as neither a ghost or spirit. He gently reassured them, saying:

> *"Look at My hands and My feet; see that it is I Myself. Touch Me and see; for a ghost does not have flesh and bones as you see that I have."*
> (Luke 24:39)

He then ate some broiled fish. He had warned,

---
[139] See Luke 24:37

"Do not fear those who kill the body but cannot kill the soul; rather fear Him who can destroy both soul and body in Hell."
(Matthew 10:28)

Jesus' war with the enemy was not just for souls. He came to save us in our entirety of being – bodies, souls, and spirits – the whole person. When He saves us, it is about us having eternal life in resurrected bodies with flesh and bones. He says,

"I am the resurrection and the life. Those who believe in Me, even though they die, will live, and everyone who lives and believes in Me will never die." (John 11:25-26)

After Jesus defeated the devil and the kingdom of darkness, His resurrection was a statement, communicating the message that He had been down this road and it was now safe to travel through death because He had died , but was now alive forevermore. Because He died and rose again, we, too, can die and be raised again for eternity.

The Purpose of Jesus' Death and Resurrection

While Jesus came to save all elements of mankind, the ultimate purpose in spiritual warfare is to win the souls of men and women – Satan to destroy and Jesus to save. The goal of Jesus' death and resurrection was to reach and save sinners. Paul says:

"He has rescued us from the power of darkness and transferred us into the kingdom of His beloved Son, in whom we have redemption, the forgiveness of sins. (Colossians 1:13-14)

After we become born-again Christians and have received the baptism of the Holy Spirit with the "signs following,"[140] Peter declares:

"But you are a chosen race, a royal priesthood, a holy nation, God's own people, in order that you may proclaim the mighty acts of Him who called you out of darkness into His marvelous light. Once you were not a people, but now you are God's people; once you had not received mercy, but now you have received mercy." (1 Peter 2:9-10)

---

[140] Mark 16:17-20

Doubt vs. Belief

The very concept of a person being able to defeat death is hard to swallow. Thomas, the disciple, had a problem accepting it. He was not with the other disciples when Jesus visited them for the first time after He was raised from the dead. Even though they all had seen Him and talked with Him, Thomas doubted their story.

> *Unless I see the mark of the nails in His hands, and put my finger in the mark of the nails and my hand in His side, I will not believe. A week later His disciples were again in the house, and Thomas was with them. Although the doors were shut, Jesus came and stood among them and said, "Peace be with you." Then He said to Thomas, "Put your finger here and see My hands. Reach out your hand and put it in My side. Do not doubt but believe."*
> *Thomas answered Him, "My Lord and my God!"*
> *Jesus said to him, "Have you believed because you have seen Me? Blessed are those who have not seen and yet have come to believe."*
> (John 20:25-29)

There are many of us who, like Thomas, have to see so that we can believe. We are doubters because it is almost impossible to accept the fact that Jesus died and then came back to life. In our experience, we have never met anyone who has died and rose again from the dead. That doubt is cleared up after we accept Jesus as our Savior and Lord and receive the baptism of the Holy Spirit, coming into a personal relationship with Him. Doubt comes from being a sinner who cannot understand the spiritual principles that govern our world. That takes spiritual discernment.

> *Those who are unspiritual do not receive the gifts of God's Spirit, for they are foolishness to them, and they are unable to understand them because they are spiritually discerned.* (1 Corinthians 2:14)

Doubt is one of the negative results of spiritual warfare in our lives. However, Jesus clears all the doubt and unbelief out of our lives when He forgives our sins and baptizes us in His Holy Spirit. We become His people, bought and paid for by Him.

Jesus had no problem with Thomas doubting. He understood his confusion. Jesus can speak for Himself today as well as He did then.

Initially, I, like Thomas, had a problem believing. After I had invited Jesus to come into my life, a friend tried to tell us that Jesus was alive and that he talked with Him every day. That sounded preposterous to me. I was determined to prove him wrong.

At that time, although I knew Jesus had forgiven me and baptized me with the Holy Spirit, I was not ready to say "yes" to His call to go into the ministry. One night, after I had climbed into bed and had started to fall asleep, I heard Somebody coming up the squeaky stairs in our house. I assumed that it was one of my brothers – until my bedroom door was opened and the light went on. Much to my surprise, I found a Stranger standing at my bedside. It was like one of those experiences when you meet someone you know, but cannot recall who it is.

The Stranger called me by name: "Gordon! Gordon! Gordon!"

As He spoke, like Mary, I recognized Him.

He said, "I want you to come and work for Me. I want you to become a fisher of men. If you will come and work for Me, I will supply all of your needs according to My riches in Glory."

I knew it was Jesus, and said, "I would be honored to work for You."

He thanked me as He turned and left the room. I heard Him go down the stairs and out the door. I got out of bed and turned the light out. Then, I sat in the darkness and thanked Jesus for remembering the Thomases of this world who need to see in order to believe.

But There's More ... the Infilling of the Holy Spirit

There was more to Jesus' death and resurrection than reaching and saving sinners. Jesus' promise of the coming of the Holy Spirit meant that His followers would be empowered to carry on His ministry on earth.

Jesus tells us how we can tell whether or not we have received the Holy Spirit, or the baptism of the Holy Spirit (the infilling of the Holy Spirit). We can tell by the signs that accompany those who believe. These He describes at the end of the Gospel of Mark.

> *"And these signs will accompany those who believe: by using My Name they will cast out demons; they will speak in new tongues; they will pick up snakes in their hands, and if they drink any deadly thing, it will not hurt them; they will lay their hands on the sick, and they will recover."* (Mark 16:17-20)

These signs provide the proof. The Greek word for "sign" (semeion)[141] means a "mark of genuineness or authenticity, directional sign, a wonder or miracle." These signs prove to others that we have experienced salvation and received the Holy Spirit. If a person does not have the signs, they do not have the Holy Spirit.

Does the Baptism of the Holy Spirit Happen at the Time of Salvation?

Today, many believers have been told they received the Holy Spirit when they believed – but that is not necessarily true. **They mistake the cleansing experience of salvation[142] for the infilling or baptism of the Holy Spirit.**

Unfortunately, most churches teach (misleadingly) that people receive the Holy Spirit when they ask Jesus to forgive their sin and give them salvation. In our experience, it's rare that people are saved and filled with the Spirit at the same time. In the *Book of Acts*, it occurs only one time out of the five times when people receive salvation.[143] The other recorded times, when people received the Holy Spirit, it occurred in a second experience, subsequent to receiving salvation.[144] More often than not,

---

[141] A *Greek-English Lexicon of the New Testament and other Early Christian Literature – Third Edition*. Revised and edited by Fredrick William Danker based on Walter Bauer's previous English Editions by W.F. Arndt, F.W. Gingrich, and F. W. Danker. The University of Chicago Press/ Chicago and London. Published 2000. Pages 920–921. Also 2nd Edition, pages 747–748. Also 4th Edition, pages 755–756.
[142] John 1:9
[143] Acts 10:44–46; Acts 4:31
[144] See Acts 2:1-4; 8:14-17; 9:10-17; 19:1-7

people experience salvation and the baptism of the Holy Spirit as two different experiences.

The Ephesian church, whose members were formerly disciples of John the Baptist, listened to Paul when he explained,

> *"John baptized with the baptism of repentance, telling the people to believe in the One who was to come after him, that is, in Jesus. On hearing this, they were baptized in the Name of the LORD Jesus. When Paul had laid his hands on them, the Holy Spirit came upon them, and they spoke in tongues and prophesied."* (Acts 19:1-7)

> *"In Him you also, when you had heard the word of truth, the gospel of your salvation, and had believed in Him, were marked with the seal of the promised Holy Spirit; this is the pledge of our inheritance toward redemption as God's own people, to the praise of His glory."* (Ephesians 1:13-14)

Although these early Christians were saved, they were not sealed with the promised Holy Spirit until after Paul had laid hands on them. Like the 120 disciples, who were in the Upper Room at Pentecost when the Holy Spirit was given, the Ephesians experienced salvation and the baptism of the Holy Spirit as two separate experiences.

When a person experiences forgiveness and salvation, he feels clean and is transformed into a new 'wineskin.' While some people receive the Holy Spirit (or new wine) at that time,[145] others require prayer, usually with the laying on of hands by a Spirit-filled person.

> *Now when the apostles at Jerusalem heard that Samaria had accepted the word of God, they sent Peter and John to them. The two went down and prayed for them that they might receive the Holy Spirit (for as yet the Spirit had not come upon any of them; they had only been baptized in the Name of the LORD Jesus). Then Peter and John laid their hands on them, and they received the Holy Spirit.* (Acts 8:14-17; see also Acts 2:4; 9:17-18; 19:6)

---

[145] See Luke 5:36-39

Because most churches teach that the Holy Spirit comes into a person's life and heart at the moment of salvation, their people are misled with a half-truth. In reality, there are only two examples of people receiving salvation and the infilling or baptism of the Holy Spirit at the same time in the Book of Acts.[146]

From my own observations, people receive the infilling of the Holy Spirit in only a minority of churches today. In the church where I was raised, most people didn't understand the further working of the Holy Spirit and so many there were frustrated. I'd hear them complaining that there was "something missing" in their lives.

The feeling of emptiness or sensing that something is missing, is the need for the infilling of the Holy Spirit. When the Holy Spirit comes into a person's life, drastic changes occur. He changes a person's character, producing His fruit: love, joy, peace, patience, kindness, generosity, faithfulness, gentleness and self-control[147] and distributing His fifteen gifts:[148]

1. The word of wisdom
2. The word of knowledge
3. The gift of faith
4. The gifts of healing
5. The gift of miracles
6. The gift of prophecy
7. The gift of discerning of spirits
8. The gift of speaking in tongues
9. The gift of interpretation of tongues
10. The gift of service
11. The gift of teaching
12. The gift of exhortation
13. The gift of giving
14. The gift of administration
15. The gift of mercy

---

[146] See Acts 4:31-33; 10
[147] Galatians 5:22-23
[148] 1 Corinthians 12:8-10 and Romans 12:6-8

Frustration is bound to develop in a person who tries to *act* as though the Holy Spirit is indwelling him or her, but truly experiences nothing of the power of the Holy Spirit ministering through him or her. These people become acutely aware of the discrepancy between what they read about the normal Christian life in the New Testament – with all the signs, wonders and miracles – and their own dry, Christian experience. Many clergy will tell these people they have to accept, by faith, that they received the Holy Spirit at the time of salvation.

Christians who have been told they received the Holy Spirit, when they did not, end up trying to fill the emptiness with good works and religious exercises. This results in defeated and disillusioned Christians. Many eventually withdraw from involvement in churches, turn to some other religion for spiritual help or believe God does not really love them. The teaching of doctrines that are not completely true has resulted in many people falling away. Paul warned:

"Now the Spirit expressly says that in later times some will renounce the faith by paying attention to deceitful spirits and teachings of demons ..." (1 Timothy 4:1)

Deceitful spirits do not want us to believe the Scriptures that teach the full Gospel. They try to explain away certain passages that describe the many ways Jesus deals with us, and that declare to us the whole purpose of God. Their 'doctrines' twist the Scriptures and selectively choose things that are in the Bible, while ignoring vital information.[149] These deceitful spirits do not want Christians, who know the whole Word of God, to spread the whole story, despite the teachings of the Bible.

Go and stand in the temple and speak to the people all the words of this Life. (Acts 5:20)

Earlier in my work as a pastor, people who knew they were missing some vital element of the Christian walk, often asked me to pray with them to receive the Holy Spirit (the baptism of the Holy Spirit). I would argue with them, trying to convince them they already "had Him," that they had received the Holy Spirit when they believed. I did this, based on

---
[149] See Acts 20:27

my belief and on my own experience. After all, I received the infilling of the Holy Spirit at the same time I invited Jesus to be my Savior and Lord – so I wrongly believed this is what all people experienced and tried to convince them they had received something, or should I say "Someone," whom they had not yet actually received.

One day, I was asked by a person whom I regarded as one of the finest Christians I knew, to help her receive the Holy Spirit. She believed Him to be missing in her life. I told her she had received the Holy Spirit when she had first invited Jesus to be her Savior. After several months of asking me to pray for her, she reluctantly said, "If you will not pray for me, I will go to another pastor and ask *him* to pray for me to receive the baptism of the Holy Spirit." That person was my wife, and I suddenly realized I'd better pay attention!

Contrary to all my teaching and understanding, I prayed for her to receive the Holy Spirit. Much to my shock she did! It was then I realized I needed to examine the Scriptures a little closer, to see what they *really* said about the Holy Spirit and how and when He fills people's lives. Finally, after examining the Book of Acts, I discovered that some people do receive the Holy Spirit when they first believe and others do not. Those who do not, need a second experience of being filled or baptized with the Holy Spirit.

Christian doctrinal statements are important as an overview of our Christian lives, but they are often incomplete, because the New Testament shows us that God the Father, Jesus Christ the Son and the Holy Spirit cannot be confined to any doctrinal box. Although God has provided only one way to be saved, He has provided flexibility in reaching those who need to know Him – probably because of the complexity of the problem of sin in people's lives and the different ways the kingdom of darkness affects everyone. Although the Book of Acts does not explain why the experience of salvation is (for some people) separated from the experience of receiving the Holy Spirit while for others the two experiences coincide, Jesus explained it when He said to Nicodemus,

"Truly, truly, I say to you, unless one is born of water and the Spirit, he cannot enter the kingdom of God." (John 3:5)

This means there are two components to receiving salvation: water (representing the baptism of repentance and forgiveness for our sin) and the Spirit (representing the baptism in the Holy Spirit which makes one a complete Christian).

At one of our services, a man said, "I want the other half."

I asked, "What do you mean?"

"I was baptized with water and now I need to be baptized with the Holy Spirit."

I said, "Yes! You are right!" We prayed and he received the other half – the Holy Spirit – and began to speak in tongues as the proof.

It doesn't matter how we receive the two; the point is that we absolutely require both, so we can have the exciting Christian life that comes from a daily relationship with God, through Jesus Christ and His Holy Spirit. That is the only way our Christian experience can look like that of the New Testament.

The Power and Danger of Human Traditions & Theologies

Some of the toughest spiritual warfare we have to wage, is against people in our churches who do not accept and believe the whole of the New Testament. They cling to man-made traditions and theologies, dismissing whatever they have not received, or experienced, by saying God no longer does those things. These doctrines of men seek to nullify the Word of God by taking the twisted word of the lying serpent, the devil, questioning truth and trying to make us doubt, as he did with Eve in the Garden of Eden so many years ago.

Jesus warned about the power of human traditions in nullifying the Word of God.

> *He said to them, "Well did Isaiah prophesy of you hypocrites, as it is written, 'This people honors me with their lips, but their heart is far from Me; in vain do they worship Me, teaching as doctrines the precepts of men.' You leave the commandment of God, and hold fast the tradition of men." And He said to them, "You have a fine way of rejecting the commandment of God, in order to keep your tradition! For Moses said, 'Honor your father and your mother;' and, 'He who speaks evil of father or mother, let him surely die;' but you say, 'If a man tells his father or his mother, What you would have gained from me is Corban' (that is, given to God) then you no longer permit him to do anything for his father or mother, thus making void the Word of God through your tradition which you hand on. And many such things you do."* (Mark 7:6-13)

This teaching, that when a person experiences salvation they always receive the Holy Spirit, is such a doctrine. It conflicts with what is described in the Book of Acts. Christians who have never received the Holy Spirit, but who, like the disciples before the Day of Pentecost, have experienced the forgiveness of their sins, usually teach it. These are the men Paul called unspiritual, or carnal, men.

Spiritual vs. Unspiritual Man

The *unspiritual* man is a person whose life is motivated by his own human spirit or soul. The Greek word for this is "psychikos." The *spiritual* man is the person whose life is motivated and directed by the Holy Spirit. The Greek word for this is "pneumatikos."

> *The unspiritual man does not receive the gifts of the Spirit of God, for they are folly to him, and he is not able to understand them because they are spiritually discerned.* (1 Corinthians 2:14)

Many people, who do not have the Holy Spirit, reject the knowledge that He distributes His gifts to people and directs them in their use. Many, who have not received the Holy Spirit in their church, dismiss the gifts of the Spirit on the basis of inexperience. They usually ignore, or are ignorant of, the history of the Church, and choose to believe Jesus stopped giving the gifts of the Holy Spirit at the end of the apostolic age. They dismiss supernatural miracles, despite eye-witness accounts or the teaching of God's Scripture. It's not uncommon for them to condemn those who have such gifts as having received them from the devil or demons – or as simply coming from the flesh. They cross the line into the most dangerous of all sins – the unforgivable sin that Jesus described as "blasphemy against the Holy Spirit."[150]

Unspiritual people expose the fact that they have not received the Holy Spirit when they refuse to accept the work and gifts of the Holy Spirit. Such people can be detrimental to the spiritual growth and welfare of those who have received the baptism of the Holy Spirit, particularly when they are involved in the same church or fellowship. In this kind of spiritual warfare, the devil uses Christians to fight against Christians, in hopes of dividing the kingdom of God. He knows that a kingdom divided against itself will not stand.[151]

Churches that allow such division to continue, will have to deal with Jesus. He calls them to repent – or else – just as He warned the church in Ephesus:

"If not, I will come to you and remove your lamp stand from its place, unless you repent." (Revelation 2:5)

This means that Jesus will close the church down. He, not the devil, closes churches down. He said,

"I will build My church, and the powers of death shall not prevail against it." (Matthew 16:18)

But the church cannot prevail against Jesus. There has been no church in Ephesus for many centuries. Today, Jesus is closing many churches which have lost or "abandoned" their first love for Him.

But I have this against you, that you have abandoned the love you had at first. (Revelation 2:4)

---

[150] See Mark 3:28-29; Luke 12:10
[151] See Mark 3:24-25

Many churches that don't listen to the Holy Spirit (regardless of size) have brought a curse upon themselves. They preach a different gospel or another gospel contrary to the gospel of Jesus Christ.

> *I am astonished that you are so quickly deserting him who called you in the grace of Christ and turning to a different gospel—not that there is another gospel, but there are some who trouble you and want to pervert the gospel of Christ. But even if we, or an angel from heaven, should preach to you a gospel contrary to that which we preached to you, let him be accursed. As we have said before, so now I say again, If any one is preaching to you a gospel contrary to that which you received, let him be accursed.* (Galatians 1:6-9)

Jesus gave the same commandment to the Seven Churches in Revelation:

> *"He who has an ear, let him hear what the Spirit says to the churches. To him who conquers I will grant to eat of the tree of life, which is in the paradise of God ... He who has an ear, let him hear what the Spirit says to the churches. He who conquers shall not be hurt by the second death ... To him who conquers I will give some of the hidden manna, and I will give him a white stone, with a new name written on the stone which no one knows except him who receives it."* (Revelation 2:7,11,17)

Over and over again, He repeated, *"He who has an ear, let him hear what the Spirit says to the churches."* The clue here is what Jesus tells not only the church in Ephesus, but all seven churches. To turn a deaf ear to the Holy Spirit is to invite Jesus to close down the church. He, Himself, will warn people to stay away from churches that don't listen to Him.

The question is, how can a person hear the Holy Spirit if he or she has not received Him? Without the baptism of the Holy Spirit and the gifts of the Holy Spirit, it is impossible to get clear direction for waging spiritual warfare and be truly victorious.

Unspiritual people reveal themselves as such by listening to Satan, a 'wannabe god' – instead of accepting the teaching of the whole Bible, regardless of their experience. They're generally unaware that demons continue to attack the New Testament, planting ideas that try to nullify the work of the Holy Spirit today. In many churches, people have unwittingly allowed the devil to usurp God's authority, declaring that God no longer does the signs and wonders reported in the Bible. We must overcome this undercover spiritual warfare by knowing and quoting the Word of God, as Jesus did when He was tempted. It was with this in mind, that Paul told Timothy to study God's Word.

> *Do your best to present yourself to God as one approved, a workman who has no need to be ashamed, rightly handling the Word of Truth.* (2 Timothy 2:15)

When we know the Scriptures (the Word of Truth) and accept them, we cannot only receive salvation, but also the baptism of Jesus (the baptism of the Holy Spirit) and prove we are authentic (spiritual) believers by performing the signs the Holy Spirit chooses to work through us.[152] To undermine the authority of the Scriptures, is to set aside our new covenant, resulting in people doing whatever seems right in their own eyes.[153] Unspiritual people can list everything in the New Testament they believe God is no longer doing, or that does not apply to them or other people. They will tell you God has stopped healing the sick and doing the miracles they read about in the Bible. They lack personal relationship with Jesus Christ and the Holy Spirit. They talk about Christianity, but their faith is limited to accepting only what their minds can grasp.

There were those who contended that Jesus was possessed by Beelzebul, by whom they claimed He cast out the demons.[154] They misidentified the Holy Spirit in Him as an evil spirit. That is exactly what people, who do not accept the Biblical work of the Holy Spirit, are doing today. It doesn't matter what doctrines our churches believe and teach if they contradict the Bible. Jesus warned,

> *"Truly, I say to you, all sins will be forgiven the sons of men, and whatever blasphemies they utter; but whoever blasphemes against*

---

[152] (Mark 16:16-20)
[153] See Judges 17:6
[154] See Mark 3:22

the Holy Spirit never has forgiveness, but is guilty of an eternal sin"— for they had said, "He has an unclean spirit." (Mark 3:28-30)

Blaspheming against the Holy Spirit means that a person attributes the works of the Holy Spirit to the devil or to demons.

People who have been saved, but have not yet received the Holy Spirit, are what I call "godly" people. They have had their sins forgiven and their names are written in Heaven,[155] but they do not have the Holy Spirit dwelling in them. They are like Jesus' first disciples who did not receive the Holy Spirit until the day of Pentecost. They do not have the "signs following" (the gifts of the Holy Spirit) that identify those who have received. Like the disciples who returned to Jesus after He had sent them out, two by two, to every town where He was about to go,[156] they do not quite understand what is going on.

The disciples were a little off center and out of focus. After being sent out, they returned with joy, saying *"Lord, even the demons are subject to us in Your Name!"* They were rejoicing about the wrong things. They couldn't see what Jesus saw, nor could they see the real importance of what had occurred, because they had not received the Holy Spirit. They missed the point of what Jesus was telling them. First, they did not report that they had had even one salvation. Like many Christians today, they were preoccupied with deliverance ministry (casting out demons). Secondly, they did not see that Satan, the devil, had just lost the war in Heaven, was cast out and limited to the earth, where he went off to make war on the rest of (the woman's) offspring, on those who keep the commandments of God and bear testimony to Jesus.

> *Now war arose in Heaven, Michael and his angels fighting against the dragon; and the dragon and his angels fought, but they were defeated and there was no longer any place for them in Heaven. And the great dragon was thrown down, that ancient serpent, who is called the* devil *and* Satan, *the deceiver of the whole world—he was thrown down to the earth, and his angels were thrown down with him.* (Revelation 12:7-9)

---
[155] See Luke 10:20
[156] See Luke 10:17-20

> *Then the dragon was angry with the woman, and went off to make war on the rest of her offspring, on those who keep the commandments of God and bear testimony to Jesus.* (Revelation 12:17)

That is why Jesus said to them,

> *"I saw Satan fall like lightning from Heaven.... Nevertheless do not rejoice in this, that the spirits are subject to you but rejoice that your names are written in Heaven."* (Luke 10:18-20)

People who have not received the baptism of the Holy Spirit get excited about the wrong things. Jude warns about the ungodly.

> *... people who long ago were designated for this condemnation as ungodly, who pervert the grace of our God into licentiousness and deny our only Master and* LORD, *Jesus Christ.* (Jude 1:4)

He reminds us of the apostles who said,

> *"It is these worldly people, devoid of the Spirit, who are causing divisions."* (Jude 1:19)

How to Tell if Someone has Been Baptized in the Holy Spirit

The leaders of the early church used the Old Testament on the day of Pentecost as their measuring stick to determine whether people had truly received the Holy Spirit.

> *Peter, standing with the eleven, lifted up his voice and addressed them, "Men of Judea and all who dwell in Jerusalem, let this be known to you, and give ear to my words. For these men are not drunk, as you suppose, since it is only the third hour of the day; but this is what was spoken by the prophet Joel: 'And in the last days it shall be, God declares, that I will pour out My Spirit upon all flesh, and your sons and your daughters shall prophesy, and your young men shall see visions, and your old men shall dream dreams; yea, and on My menservants and my maidservants in those days I will pour out My Spirit; and they shall prophesy. And I will show wonders in the Heaven above and signs on the earth beneath, blood, and fire, and vapor of smoke; the sun shall be turned into darkness and the*

moon into blood, before the day of the LORD *comes, the great and manifest day. And it shall be that whoever calls on the Name of the* LORD *shall be saved.'"* (Acts 2:14-21; see also Joel 2:28-32)

Later, Peter raised the issue of what had happened at Cornelius' house.

If then God gave the same gift to them as He gave to us when we believed in the LORD *Jesus Christ, who was I that I could withstand God?* (Acts 11:17)

Peter also addressed an early gathering of church leaders who had met to consider the inclusion of Gentiles into the church. After much debate, he stood up and said:

"Brethren, you know that in the early days God made choice among you, that by my mouth the Gentiles should hear the word of the gospel and believe. And God who knows the heart bore witness to them, giving them the Holy Spirit just as He did to us; and He made no distinction between us and them, but cleansed their hearts by faith." (Acts 15:7-9)

And, of course, what occurred on the day of Pentecost, was that they were all filled with the Holy Spirit and spoke in tongues (real languages that are either spoken in the world today, or have been spoken in the past). Jesus calls them "new languages."

And these signs will accompany those who believe: in My Name they will cast out demons; they will speak in new tongues... (Mark 16:17)

Paul calls them "other national languages."

... to another various kinds of tongues, to another the interpretation of tongues. (1 Corinthians 12:10)

The word, "tongues," is the old English word used in the King James translation of the Bible and simply means "language (tongue) or plural languages (tongues)." It is easier to understand the difference when I instruct someone who is receiving the baptism in the Holy Spirit by saying, "Don't speak your own language (whether that might be English,

Spanish, French or whatever); speak the new language the Holy Spirit will give you."

This continues to be the normal work of the Holy Spirit in believers today. It's the same thing that happened on the day of Pentecost when all 120 people, who were waiting in Jerusalem as Jesus had instructed them, began to speak in the different languages of the people who had traveled there to celebrate the feast. It continues to be the initial evidence, or proof, that a person has received the baptism of the Holy Spirit. The languages given by the Holy Spirit compose God's communication system today.

And they were all filled with the Holy Spirit and began to speak in other tongues, as the Spirit gave them utterance. (Acts 2:4)

To dismiss any of the work of the Holy Spirit, as described in the Bible, is to add or take away from the gospel. The temptation to determine which portions of the Bible are valid for today, is one of the most dangerous temptations that face us in today's spiritual warfare. In writing the *Book of Revelation*, John said:

"I warn everyone who hears the words of the prophecy of this book: if anyone adds to them, God will add to him the plagues described in this book, and if anyone takes away from the words of the book of this prophecy, God will take away his share in the tree of life and in the holy city, which are described in this book." (Revelation 22:18-19)

Giving in to the temptation to replace the teachings of the Bible with the traditions, or church doctrines of men, has done much to nullify the Word of God in our world today.

The Christian walk of an unspiritual person is pathetically lackluster in comparison with that of a truly spiritual person, who enters fully into the power available for living a life of faith in the power of the Holy Spirit. When we take our place in the kingdom of God, Jesus gives us all authority in Heaven and on earth to venture forth in the power of His Name.

Go therefore and make disciples of all nations, baptizing them in the Name of the Father and of the Son and of the Holy Spirit, teaching them to observe all that I have commanded you; and lo, I am with you always, to the close of the age. (Matthew 28:19-20)

Six

Today's Warfare

Living on Daily Alert

Today's warfare is so critical, that Paul calls us to be on daily alert. Despite the fact that the most crucial battle was fought and won by Jesus and the kingdom of God on the Cross of Calvary, the war is not finished.

During the Second World War, there was a period of time where the continent of Europe was under the control of the Axis armies. The Axis powers, Nazi Germany, Hungary and Italy, initially were united by their opposition to the Western world and the Soviet Union. The Allies (the U.S.A., Great Britain, Australia, New Zealand, Canada, Russia and France) battled it out against the Axis alliance. The Allies sent an invasion force which landed at Normandy, France, on D-Day, June 6, 1944, and started moving their armies away from their beachhead. As they began to push back the enemy armies, they knew they had won the crucial battle, and that it was just a matter of time before they would completely defeat their enemies. The Allied armies had to mop up the remaining Nazi resistance as they fought their way into Germany and ended the war.

C-Day (Calvary Day) was the turning point in the spiritual war, but there remains, still today, some resistance that needs to be mopped up. Although the devil and his kingdom of darkness were defeated that day, God's invasion force, the Church of Jesus Christ, led by Jesus Himself, remains in the process of completing the war. There will continue to be casualties until the final battle at Armageddon[157] in which the armies of the kingdom of God will completely defeat the armies of the kingdom of darkness, once and for all.

Until then, we are in combat mode. The spiritual armies of wickedness in heavenly places are here. That is why Paul instructs us to continue to battle the forces of darkness.

> *Therefore take the whole armor of God, that you may be able to withstand in the evil day, and having done all, to stand.* (Ephesians 6:13)

If we have our armor in place and use it prayerfully – the belt of truth central in our lives, the breastplate of righteousness protecting our hearts, our feet fitted with the equipment of the gospel of peace, the shield of faith placed before us, the helmet of salvation covering our minds and the sword of the Spirit (the Word of God) ready to use[158] – it can be used to defeat the devil and any of his army.

Battling Satan – the Front Line

Warning! Know How to Spot the Enemy and Shun Entanglement

Paul warns that not everything that looks like God or an angel is necessarily God or one of His angels – and not everyone who claims to be a Christian believer is one. Because some false apostles had infiltrated the Corinthian church, Paul wrote,

> *"Even Satan disguises himself as an angel of light. So it is not strange if his servants also disguise themselves as servants of righteousness. Their end will correspond to their deeds."* (2 Corinthians 11:14-15)

The enemy has invaded our churches. People masquerading as Christians have infiltrated the Body of Christ. Our enemy has an army composed of both people and evil spirits. Both will attempt to lead us

---
[157] See Revelation 16:16
[158] See Ephesians 6:14-17

away from the God and Father of our LORD Jesus Christ to the altars of the god of this world.

That is why Paul warned,

> "Therefore, my beloved, shun the worship of idols. I speak as to sensible men; judge for yourselves what I say." (1 Corinthians 10:14-15)

In the ancient world, many people continued to worship the idols of their former religions, even when claiming Christianity. This continues today. Many still want to believe the devil's great lie, that all religions worship the same god, that they are all like trains leading in the same direction. Untrue!

It's impossible to dabble in another world religion and claim to be a Christian at the same time. Trying to combine occult practices with Christianity is not Christianity. Reincarnation has no place in the teachings of Scripture. Mixing and matching beliefs that suit the whimsy of those who place their own wisdom above that of God, is fruitless. God does not tolerate it in His kingdom. He is still a jealous God[159] who will not tolerate any rivals.

> I do not want you to be partners with demons. You cannot drink the cup of the LORD and the cup of demons. You cannot partake of the table of the LORD and the table of demons. Shall we provoke the LORD to jealousy? Are we stronger than He? (1 Corinthians 10:20-22)

In the course of carrying out my pastoral duties, I went to visit a woman who had had surgery in the Toronto Western Hospital. As I was walking past the receptionist, she evidently noticed my clerical collar and asked if I were a minister or priest.

"A minister," I said.

She explained, "There's a patient in the intensive care unit who has attempted suicide. She's been calling for a minister all day long."

I went up to see the thirty-year-old patient. Her doctor had her on an intravenous drip for life support. After just a few minutes of conversation, I learned she had been involved with a psychic group that had established

---
[159] See Exodus 20:5

contact with the spirit world. Each person had received a spirit guide, who was supposed to be the spirit of a person who had once lived on earth and was waiting to be reincarnated. For the first few weeks, she said, it was exciting to have this guide inside her body, giving her advice and telling her what to do.

"But, soon I realized it would not leave me. In fact, it had possessed me and began to force me to do things I didn't want to do. I tried to stop attending the psychic group, but the spirit guide would not allow that. It forced me to go. It went from causing me to have a nice, religious experience, to hurting me and degrading me to the point that I didn't want to live. That's why I wanted to end it all and swallowed a hundred tranquilizers."

Someone had found her and called for an ambulance. She was crying as she told me what she had experienced. She begged, "Can you help me? Can you help me?"

I explained that there was only one way she could be set free; that was to ask Jesus Christ to forgive her for her involvement in this psychic group and to ask Him to be her Savior and Lord. "Then," I said, "you need to receive the baptism of the Holy Spirit. The Holy Spirit will take the place of the spirit guide, who is actually an evil spirit. If you will let Jesus be your Savior and Lord, I can cast the demon out of you and you'll be free." I then asked, "Would you like to be set free?"

She was vehement, "Yes, oh, yes!"

At that point, a nurse interrupted us and said, "I'm sorry but I have to move her out of this room and into a hallway bed, because we need this bed for a more critical patient."

I thought to myself, "Hmmm – somebody does not want this young woman to be set free – but it is not going to work."

Fifteen minutes later, without the intravenous drip, we resumed our conversation. I asked the young woman the same questions again, and again she agreed that she wanted to be set free. I then commanded the evil spirit to leave her body and to go to the abyss. There was no drama or evidence of anything changing, but knowing the authority we have, I knew the evil spirit had to leave. We prayed and the young woman received salvation and the baptism of the Holy Spirit and began to speak in tongues – the evidence that she had truly been filled with the Holy Spirit.

When she stopped speaking in tongues, she said, "It has gone! It has gone! Thank you Jesus for setting me free!"

I visited her a couple of more times in the hospital. I gave her a Bible and a book about how to live the Christian life.

Many people allow themselves to get involved in psychic groups and occult practices, totally oblivious to the dangerous consequences.

When we become Christians and are baptized with the Holy Spirit, we are empowered to love the LORD our God with all our hearts, with all our souls, with all our strength, and with all our minds; and our neighbors as ourselves.[160] We must leave behind the kingdom of darkness – along with its symbols, articles and unholy scriptures. It is important to remove these articles from our homes.

> *Many also of those who were now believers came, confessing and divulging their practices. And a number of those who practiced magic arts brought their books together and burned them in the sight of all; and they counted the value of them and found it came to fifty thousand pieces of silver.* (Acts 19:18-19)

The believers in Ephesus burned their books of magic. The fireplace is the proper place for tarot cards, ouija boards and books that explain these things.

It is important to get rid of anything that is symbolic of false religions or occult practices, because they attract the evil spirits that ruled them. Old religious practices, and serving the devil and demons in any way, must be totally rejected and the associated items disposed of, so that no

---

[160] See Luke 10:27

one else will ever be able to use them. It is wrong to give them to other people, because the enemy, through those articles, will victimize them. Repentance for engaging in these practices is a necessary step after rejecting them. That is why Paul says,

"Therefore, if any one is in Christ, he is a new creation; the old has passed away, behold, the new has come." (2 Corinthians 5:17)

In spiritual warfare, the first person we have to deal with, is the head of the spiritual host of wickedness – the devil (Satan). When he shows up, most people panic, fearing they won't be able to deal with him successfully. They remember Peter's warning and worry about being overcome.

Be sober, be watchful. Your adversary the devil prowls around like a roaring lion, seeking some one to devour. (1 Peter 5:8)

They forget James' encouragement:

Submit yourselves therefore to God. Resist the devil, and he will flee from you. (James 4:7)

When we have received the baptism of the Holy Spirit, we do not have to fear the devil because we have authority over him. With the power and guidance of the Holy Spirit we can resist him and be assured he will have to flee.

Resist him, firm in your faith, knowing that the same experience of suffering is required of your brotherhood throughout the world. (1 Peter 5:9)

In the same way, we don't have to give in to any temptations that originate from our own desires, but rather submit ourselves to God and, through the authority He gives us, experience freedom from demonic interference.

Knowing who the enemy is and being aware of his tactics, is critical in battle.

Satan's Tactics

The most effective strategy of both the devil and demons, is to convince people that evil spirits do not exist.[161] That is why they often attack vulnerable people who have little credibility. Young children or people who are sleeping are prime candidates. After the attack, they skillfully persuade their victims that the visitation was just a nightmare. They convince people, especially those who claim to be believers, that the Bible is full of myths (demonology supposedly being one), which are not to be taken literally.

Satan's tactics are basically the same today as they were in Job's time. He has always used the same approach. He questions God's Word. He lies. He sometimes kills the friends, family, or people around whomever he is tempting or testing. He may even try to kill the person. He will often send so-called "spiritual friends" who will advise the person (wrongly), as to why he or she is having problems. Jesus warned that Satan has permission to mess up our lives when He said,

"The thief comes only to steal and kill and destroy ..." (John 10:10)

Jesus had first-hand knowledge of Satan's tactics from the experience of His own temptation.

First, the tempter (the devil) questioned Jesus, to see if He knew who He was. He called into question who Jesus was, twice.

"If you are the son (daughter) of God ..."
(Matthew 4:3,6; see also Luke 4:3,9)

In a similar pattern, he will call into question who we are in Jesus Christ, whether or not we are the sons or daughters of God, whether we are really Christians, whether we are really going to Heaven, whether we have really been baptized with the Holy Spirit, et cetera ad nauseum. He will try to get us to question things like the way we witness and carry out ministry and, in fact, everything God has done in our lives. He will try to make us question the way we act and the things we do in our relationship with God.

---

[161] The Screwtape Letters by C.S. Lewis, gives profound insight into this perverse strategy.

Unless we are strong in the LORD, well-outfitted in the armor of God, these evil suggestions and questions can put us off-balance and make us second-guess things that are not in question. They are designed to undermine our confidence and disarm us so we won't be a threat to Satan or his kingdom. He wants to see if we'll be foolish enough to do what he suggests, rather than what Jesus tells us to do.

In his temptation of Jesus, the devil then appealed to the most basic, physical needs of man. He suggested that Jesus should turn stones into bread – but Jesus knew that the real problem was not bread, but sin. When sin was taken care of, food would be supplied. The deepest needs in human life are not physical needs. Sin is the problem. If sin is dealt with, a person will never starve to death.

I have been young, and now am old, yet I have not seen the righteous forsaken or their children begging bread. (Psalm 37:25)

Scripture always has the answers for the devil's temptations, and so Jesus fired back:

"Man shall not live by bread alone, but by every word that proceeds from the mouth of God." (Matthew 4:4)

The devil will suggest we should do ministry in ways God does not approve. For instance, in taunting Jesus to turn stones into loaves of bread, he didn't bother mentioning the fact that there is no place in Scripture where God ever required anyone to turn stones into bread. God supplied manna from Heaven and multiplied fishes and loaves of bread – but He never turned stones into bread.

In his third attempt, after Satan had realized physical temptation wasn't going to work with Jesus, he attacked on the level of the soul. While he purported to challenge Jesus to demonstrate the depth of His trust in God and prove who He was by letting the angels catch Him, he was really hoping that Jesus would commit suicide by jumping from the fifteen-storey Temple. His lying arrogance was unmatched in his mocking suggestion that the angels would be glad to catch Him.

God never told anyone to jump off a building; the Temple was made for worship – not circus acrobatics. Nor were the angels ever supposed to play catch with the children of God in a side-show attempt to make people believe in Jesus Christ.

This was getting serious. Jesus knew that catching people was not in the angels' job descriptions, so He countered once again with Scripture:

"You shall not tempt the LORD your God."
(Matthew 4:7; see also Luke 4:9-12)

Both Jesus and the devil knew that He was *"the Lord your God."*

The angels minister to us to help us not fail in either temptation or ministry. Again, the devil twisted Scripture.

Are they not all ministering spirits sent forth to serve, for the sake of those who are to obtain salvation? (Hebrews 1:14)

Following Jesus' victory over Satan's attempted temptations, the angels ministered to Him. That's what angels do. They minister to Jesus and to His people.

God never does, or authorizes us to do, anything that is not in the Bible. Recently a friend asked whether I thought that some weird things that were happening in a certain ministry were from God. My reply was, "No, those things are not in Scripture, nor do they reflect the character of Jesus Christ."

"But," my friend questioned further, "can't the Holy Spirit do something new that's not in the Bible?"

"Absolutely not," I replied, "because the Bible is our covenant with God. It is our protection. If something is happening that is not in the Bible, it's not from God. Even worse, it's probably from the devil."

I have applied all this to myself and Apollos for your benefit, brethren, that you may learn by us not to go beyond what is written, that none of you may be puffed up[162] *in favor of one against another.*
(1 Corinthians 4:6)

---
[162] Proud or conceited

The most dangerous temptation, for many in church leadership today, is to accept and follow the devil's suggestions for ministry. He loves to make Jesus Christ look like a fool, especially when he can get Christians to participate. That is why there are severe warnings in the Bible for people who would add to or take away from it.

> *I warn everyone who hears the words of the prophecy of this book: if anyone adds to them, God will add to him the plagues described in this book, and if any one takes away from the words of the book of this prophecy, God will take away his share in the tree of life and in the holy city, which are described in this book. He who testifies to these things says, "Surely I am coming soon." Amen. Come,* LORD *Jesus!* (Revelation 22:18-20)

In other words, if it isn't in the Bible, don't do it. We need to study the Scriptures so we cannot be deceived when the devil encourages us to do something God has not told us to do.[163]

Fourthly, the devil took the gloves off and went for his final and best shot – the one that had always worked before. He went for the jugular, the core of human life, the realm of the Spirit. He removed all his pretenses and made a naked appeal for the one thing he wanted most – to be worshipped. He showed Jesus all the kingdoms of the world and offered them to Him – if Jesus would simply bow down and worship him.

The devil's last temptation involved making the kind of offer that is routinely accepted by sinful people.

> *And the devil took him up, and showed him all the kingdoms of the world in a moment of time, and said to him, "To you I will give all this authority and their glory; for it has been delivered to me, and I give it to whom I will. If you, then, will worship me, it shall all be yours."* (Luke 4:5-7)

> *... and he said to Him, "All these I will give You, if You will fall down and worship me."* (Matthew 4:9)

---

[163] See 2 Timothy 3:15

Bribery didn't work with Jesus. He knew all the kingdoms of this world were *already* His anyway and did not even belong to the devil (who owned no property on the earth). He not only knew who He was; He knew what the Bible said. I suspect Jesus must have had a difficult time trying not to laugh out loud when the devil tried to offer Him all the kingdoms of the world.

> *Then Jesus said to him, "Begone, Satan! for it is written, 'You shall worship the Lord your God and Him only shall you serve.'"*
> (Matthew 4:10)

If the devil tried to bribe Jesus by offering Him all the kingdoms of the world, he will try to bribe us too, with bribes some might think are too good to pass up. He may promise us the world. He knows we like money, so he usually promises to make us wealthy. That certainly sounds better than a cross, but Jesus has given us the blueprint for how to respond to such temptations.

Jesus struck the devil dumb with His responses. Satan had just lost the battle. "All have sinned, *but not this One*," must have been ringing in his ears as he turned tail and slunk away. Jesus was the first person he had been unable to tempt! It must have been almost impossible for him to fathom. He learned a hard lesson in his head-on attempted temptations of Jesus. Never again would he tempt Him in a face-to-face confrontation, because he now knew Jesus couldn't be fooled by his tactics.

Jesus demonstrated the fact that any person who had been baptized with water for repentance – and had been baptized with the Holy Spirit for empowerment[164] (with the proof of the "signs following[165]") could resist any temptation to sin and carry out the ministry of Jesus Christ.

> *Jesus answered ... "Truly, truly, I say to you, unless one is born anew, he cannot see the kingdom of God.... unless one is born of water and the Spirit, he cannot enter the kingdom of God. That which is born of the flesh is flesh, and that which is born of the Spirit is spirit. Do not marvel that I said to you, 'You must be born anew.' ... he who*

---
[164] Mark 15
[165] Acts 2:4

believes in Me will also do the works that I do; and greater works than these will he do, because I go to the Father." (John 3:3,5-7; 14:12)

In his attempted temptations of Jesus, Satan's biggest mistake was to think that Jesus would ever respond to anything involving any kind of sin. Although Paul wrote that all have sinned and fall short of the glory of God, this did not apply to Jesus. Satan must have forgotten that:

We have not a high priest who is unable to sympathize with our weaknesses, but One who in every respect has been tempted as we are, yet without sin. (Hebrews 4:15)

Recognizing Satan's tactics requires discernment. Thinking the devil will be recognized by a *feeling* of fear or evil, is a huge misconception. Quite the contrary; the devil knows that if he gives people a good religious experience, he'll have them hooked and they'll do anything he suggests. He knows that people can argue with a theory, but not with a religious experience. He loves to give us good experiences. He knows that if he makes us feel good, we'll do anything he suggests, including being disobedient to God and His Word.

To this very day, the devil uses the same tactics of temptation to deal with us. His mandate is to test whether or not we are going to be faithful to God. Sin remains the biggest and most persistent problem we have to deal with in spiritual warfare.

Just a Wannabe God with a Job

When Satan shows up, he does not usually reveal himself as a threatening entity. In fact, he often comes disguised as God.[166] He wants to be acknowledged as God; not as *a* god, but *the* God.

The devil/Satan is a wannabe God who is not, nor ever will be, God. He is only a fallen angel – but he did have, and still has authority to test and tempt believers in order to see if they are being faithful to God. Satan is called the prince of the world or the ruler of this world ... but never "the God of this world." The Greek word "archon" which is translated

---
[166] See 2 Corinthians 11:13

"prince" is defined as "one who has eminence in ruling capacity, ruler, lord, prince" as with reference to demons.[167]

> *In their case the God of this world has blinded the minds of the unbelievers, to keep them from seeing the light of the gospel of the glory of Christ, who is the likeness of God."* (2 Corinthians 4:4)

Many people think, mistakenly, that Paul was referring to the devil/Satan as, *"the God of this world"* in this passage. No, he was not! Paul knew the difference between the work of God and Satan. The God of this world[168] is the LORD God of Israel whose name in Hebrew is "Yahweh" and in Greek is "Jesus".

The one place where he is called *"the prince of the power of the air, the spirit that is now at work in the sons of disobedience,"*[169] is in the context of the fact that he can travel anyplace in the lower atmosphere to tempt and test people.

Earlier, in Chapter One, we explored the two Greek words for air: "aer" and "aither." Again, "aer" refers to the lower hemisphere, which extends from the earth's surface to the top of the highest mountain on the earth. The second word for air, "aither," describes the higher hemisphere which extends from the highest mountain upwards into space and on up to Heaven. The word used here is "aer," so Paul is describing the devil/Satan as ruler of the "air-aer," the lower hemisphere. There is only one true God and he is *not* the devil. Ever since Satan lost the war in Heaven and was cast down to earth[170] he has been confined to the lower atmosphere, where it is his responsibility to test and tempt people.

> *I will no longer talk much with you, for the ruler of this world is coming. He has no power over Me...* (John 14:30)

> *Now is the judgment of this world, now shall the ruler of this world be cast out...* (John 12:31)

---

[167] Matthew 9:34; 12:24; Mark 3:22; Luke 11:15
[168] Greek - "age"
[169] Ephesians 2:2
[170] Luke 10:18

While we have seen that the *"God of this world"* (age-Greek) is the LORD God of Israel, the *"ruler of the world"* is the devil/Satan. The devil/Satan has been given some administrative responsibility in terms of tempting and testing us to see whether we are prepared and ready for God's plans for our lives. Having him show up is often a sign that God wants to use us in ministry – and so it is almost a compliment. He comes to tempt only people who God wants to use in some special way. He has to test our spiritual strength in order to see if we will be faithful to Jesus Christ, no matter how difficult he makes it for us. If we do not pass the test, we become aware of our areas of weakness and recognize in what areas we need to grow before we can be used by God in ministry. When we pass the tests, God will open the doors to new ministry.

He is also the ruler of the demons/evil spirits.[171] Because he sinned from the beginning,[172] he has been judged and will be "cast into the Lake of Fire."[173] Nevertheless, he must carry on his assigned responsibility until that time. His judgment is recorded in the Scriptures.

> *...the accuser of the brethren has been thrown down who accuses them day and night before our God. And they have conquered him by the blood of the Lamb and by the word of their testimony, for they loved not their lives even unto death.* (Revelation 12:10-11)
>
> *Now is the judgment of this world, now shall the ruler of this world be cast out...* (John 12:31)

Recognizing Who is at Work

Today, we have many people who mistake the work of the Holy Spirt which is *"to convict the world of sin and righteousness and judgement"* [174] for the work of the devil/Satan. The devil/Satan can only be in one place at any given time in the world dealing with one person at a time doing his work of "accusing the brethren of their sin, while the Holy Spirit has the quality of "omnipresence" which means that He can be in many or all places at the same time.

---

[171] Matthew 9:34; 12:24; Luke 11:15
[172] John 8:44
[173] Revelation 20:10
[174] John 16: 8

> *And I heard a loud voice in Heaven, saying, "Now the salvation and the power and the kingdom of our God and the authority of His Christ have come, for the accuser of our brethren has been thrown down, who accuses them day and night before our God.*
> (Revelation 12:10; see also Luke 10:18)

When the disciples asked, "Why do you speak to them in parables," Jesus explained that He did not want the wrong people to understand. Because of their sinful minds, they would try to use the Gospel for their own personal, wrong motives .

> *Then the disciples came and said to Him, "Why do you speak to them in parables?"*
> *And He answered them, "To you it has been given to know the secrets of the kingdom of Heaven, but to them it has not been given. For to him who has will more be given, and he will have abundance; but from him who has not, even what he has will be taken away. This is why I speak to them in parables, because seeing they do not see, and hearing they do not hear, nor do they understand. With them indeed is fulfilled the prophecy of Isaiah which says: 'You shall indeed hear but never understand and you shall indeed see but never perceive. For this people's heart has grown dull, and their ears are heavy of hearing, and their eyes they have closed, lest they should perceive with their eyes, and hear with their ears, and understand with their heart, and turn for me to heal them.' But blessed are your eyes, for they see, and your ears, for they hear. Truly, I say to you, many prophets and righteous men longed to see what you see, and did not see it, and to hear what you hear, and did not hear it.*
> (Matthew 13:10-17)[175]

In other words, Jesus did not want the wrong people to understand because they would use the kingdom of Heaven for their own sinful purposes. We can see this happening today with the rejection of the authentic baptism of the Holy Spirit[176] in many churches and the conse-

---

[175] See also Mark 4:10 and Luke 8:9-10
[176] Acts 2:4; 8:14-17; 9:17; 1 Corinthians 14:18; 10: 44-48; 19:1-7

quent loss of the preaching of the Gospel with the "signs following[177]" and ministry using the gifts of the Holy Spirit.[178] People do not want the legitimate biblical "signs, wonders and miracles."

> *How shall we escape if we neglect such a great salvation? It was declared at first by the* LORD, *and it was attested to us by those who heard him, while God also bore witness by signs and wonders and various miracles and by gifts of the Holy Spirit distributed according to His own will.* (Hebrews 2:3-4)

Preparing His disciples, Jesus said,

> *"These things I have spoken to you, while I am still with you. But the Counselor, the Holy Spirit, whom the Father will send in My Name, He will teach you all things, and bring to your remembrance all that I have said to you.... And now I have told you before it takes place, so that when it does take place, you may believe. I will no longer talk much with you, for the ruler of this world is coming. He has no power over Me; but I do as the Father has commanded Me, so that the world may know that I love the Father.* (John 14:25-26,29-31)

> *"Nevertheless I tell you the truth: it is to your advantage that I go away, for if I do not go away, the Counselor will not come to you; but if I go, I will send him to you. And when He comes, He will convince the world concerning sin and righteousness and judgment: concerning sin, because they do not believe in Me; concerning righteousness, because I go to the Father, and you will see Me no more; concerning judgment, because the ruler of this world is judged."* (John 16:7-11)

> *But if you have bitter jealousy and selfish ambition in your hearts, do not boast and be false to the truth. This wisdom is not such as comes down from above, but is earthly, unspiritual, devilish.*
> (James 3:14-15)

> *And these signs will accompany those who believe: in My Name they will cast out demons...* (Mark 16:17)

---

[177] Mark 16:17-30
[178] Romans 12:6-8; 1 Corinthians 13:8-10

Jesus continues,

"When the Spirit of Truth comes, He will guide you into all the truth; for He will not speak on His own authority, but whatever He hears He will speak, and He will declare to you the things that are to come. He will glorify Me, for He will take what is Mine and declare it to you. All that the Father has is Mine; therefore I said that He will take what is Mine and declare it to you." (John 16:13-15)

I have a friend who heard about Jesus visiting me physically in my bedroom one night and calling me into full-time ministry. My friend wanted the same experience. He wanted Jesus to show up and visit him, too. He became preoccupied with this desire. He was convinced that if Jesus would visit him, he would never doubt God again.

Well, one night, after he had gone to sleep, he was awakened to discover that his room was filled with a supernatural light. There stood a figure who looked exactly the way he had always thought Jesus would look. It was awesome. He felt so good. It was wonderful! The presence in his room was overwhelmingly beautiful.

He said to the figure, "Are you God? Is that you, Lord?"

"Yes," came the reply, in exactly the gentle voice he was sure Jesus would have.

"Lord, what do you want me to do?" he asked, full of awe and inspiration.

"I just want you to bow down and worship me. That's all, just bow down and worship me," the figure said.

"Oh yes, Lord," my friend answered eagerly. "I'll do that for You." He started to go down on one knee, when suddenly a Thought came to him.

"May I please see your hands and side?" he asked.

Later, as he recounted the incident to me, he said, "Poof! Just like that, he disappeared." He knew then, that Satan had almost deceived him. Never again did he concern himself with supernatural visitations. Instead, he looked to Jesus, the Holy Spirit and the Bible to develop an intimate, personal relationship with God.

When the devil comes to tempt us, he rarely makes himself visible. He likes to ambush us and tempt us in such a way that we won't know where the suggestions are coming from. We'll usually think the ideas are our own. He'll present us with opportunities to sin and give us alternatives to the Bible, whispering them into our minds. He'll appeal to our greed and selfishness, fan the flames of rebellion and point out the supposed advantages to breaking God's laws. He'll encourage us to engage in all the works of the flesh:

> *"... fornication, impurity, licentiousness, idolatry, sorcery, enmities, strife, jealousy, anger, quarrels, dissensions, factions, envy, drunkenness, carousing, and things like these.* (Galatians 5:19-21)

Of course, Satan never reminds us about the penalty for sin and lies about what will happen as a result of our sin. He promises the world – and gives nothing but pain, heartache and regret. As Jesus warned,

> *"The thief comes only to steal and kill and destroy; I came that they may have life and have it abundantly."* (John 10:10)

The Prosecution and Our Defense Team

The Greek word "diabolos" or "satan" comes from the Greek judicial system and refers to a prosecuting attorney for the state. Satan knows all God's laws. As a legal representative, prosecuting attorney in God's court, he presents charges against all people who have broken God's New Testament Law.

The devil is never really "mister nice guy." As *"the accuser of our brethren,"*[179] his job is to accuse us, charge us, indict us, find fault with us and blame us for any wrong doing or breaking of God's law. With a complete record of every sin we have ever committed, he loves to remind us about all the times we have failed. He tries to bury us under so much condemnation, that we can be of no service to God. He knows if he can lay a powerful enough guilt trip on us, he has a good shot at paralyzing us and rendering us ineffective as Christians. If he can rob us of hope,

---

[179] See Revelation 12:10

he stands a good chance of leading us into disobedience against God. If he can control our lives with fear, we will be unable to serve God. The mistake we make is in listening to him and accepting what he says as being absolutely true.

While Satan's record of our sins may be entirely accurate, any remembrance we have of any of our past sins is not there for the purpose of guilt and condemnation. It is there as a reminder of God's grace and all Jesus has done for us, an opportunity to thank Jesus for forgiving us and setting us free. Instead of feeling guilty when the devil reminds us of any of our past sins, we need to learn to say, "Thank you, devil, for reminding me of how good Jesus is to me. He forgave me for every sin I have ever committed. Thank You, Jesus, that there is therefore, now, no condemnation for me." When someone else reminds us of sins we have committed in the past, rather than feel guilty, we can say, "Thank you, my friend, for reminding me of how good Jesus has been to me, in setting me free from those sins." It can become an opportunity to tell that friend about Jesus and share the gospel – in hopes that he or she can find the joy of salvation from the evidence of our experience.

Thankfully, when we have repented for our sins, two defence lawyers come to our aid: Jesus and the Holy Spirit. Of Him, Jesus said,

"Blessed are those who mourn, for they shall be comforted."
(Matthew 5:4)

Unfortunately, this verse has been wrongly translated. It is should read, "Blessed are those who mourn (for their sin), for they shall receive the Comforter (parakletos - Holy Spirit). It is the Holy Spirit who comes into our lives to comfort us. Jesus gave us His job description.

Nevertheless I tell you the truth: it is to your advantage that I go away, for if I do not go away, the Counselor will not come to you; but if I go, I will send Him to you. And when He comes, He will convince the world concerning sin and righteousness and judgment: concerning sin, because they do not believe in Me; concerning righteousness, because I go to the Father, and you will see Me no more; concerning judgment, because the ruler of this world is judged. I have yet many things to say to you, but you cannot bear them now. When the Spirit of Truth comes, He will guide you into all the truth; for He will not speak on His own authority, but whatever He hears He will speak, and He will declare to you the things that are to come. He will glorify Me, for He will take what is Mine and declare it to you. All that the Father has is Mine; therefore I said that He will take what is Mine and declare it to you. (John 16:7-15)

We are supposed to consult the Holy Spirit every day and hear what He is saying to us, because He is also called "the Spirit of Christ."[180] Jesus gave the same commandment to each of the believers in the Seven Churches,

"He who has an ear, let him hear what the Spirt says to the Churches." (Revelation 2:7,11,17,29; 3:6,13,22)

Our second defense lawyer, Jesus, is our "advocate" (parakletos) with the Father (1 John 2:1).

My little children, I am writing this to you so that you may not sin; but if any one does sin, we have an advocate with the Father, Jesus Christ the righteous. (1 John 2:1)

Satan's rebellious angels who sinned were chained up in the temporary hell (Tartarus), limiting his work.

God did not spare the angels when they sinned, but cast them into Hell and committed them to pits of nether gloom to be kept until the judgment. (2 Peter 2: 4; see also Jude 6)

Paul, in his second letter to the Thessalonians, reminds us that it is not the devil/Satan who is our worst nightmare. After describing what will precede the Day of the Lord, he concludes with a warning.

Let no one deceive you in any way; for that day will not come, unless the rebellion comes first, and the man of lawlessness (sin) is revealed,, the son of perdition, who opposes and exalts himself against every

---
[180] Romans 8:9

so-called god or object of worship, so that he takes his seat in the temple of God, proclaiming himself to be God. Do you not remember that when I was still with you I told you this? And you know what is restraining him now so that he may be revealed in his time. For the mystery of the lawlessness is already at work; on he who now restrains it will do so until he is out of the way. And then the lawless one will be revealed, and the LORD Jesus will slay him with the breath of His mouth and destroy him by His appearing and His coming. The coming of the lawless one by the activity of Satan will be with all power and with pretended signs and wonders, and with all wicked deception for those who are to perish, because they refused to love the truth and so be saved. Therefore God sends upon them a strong delusion, to make them believe what is false, so that all may be condemned who did not believe the truth but had pleasure in unrighteousness. (2 Thessalonians 2:3-12)

God, has authority over the devil/Satan, demons/evil spirits and does not hesitate to use them to carry out His instructions whenever His people will not listen to Him. Such was the case when 400 prophets would not tell the truth to the kings of Israel – Ahab, Judah, and Jehoshaphat – that they were not to go to war with Syria because they would be defeated. When the kings sent for the prophet Micaiah, Micaiah told them God had shown him that He had sent a lying spirit to give the 400 prophets a false prophecy.[181] The kings sent Micaiah to prison and King Ahab was killed.

Does the Devil (Satan) Possess People?

The Devil himself does not possess people; he does not go inside them and control them. That is not his work. His work is to tempt people. The only instance in the Bible, where the devil actually took possession of a person, involved the account of Judas.

After he received the piece of bread, Satan entered into him.
(John 13:27; see also Luke 22:3)

---

[181] See 1 Kings 22 and Chronicles 17

This is the only place where we are told that Satan, himself, entered a person and took control – probably because he did not want to leave such an important task as the betrayal of Jesus, up to an evil spirit.

After Satan entered and possessed him, Judas could not bear the guilt of committing the most dastardly deed in history. He threw down the silver coins he had been paid in the Temple, bitterly rejecting the profit. Even though he repented, however, he killed himself.[182]

Learning to Deal With Satan's Tactics

If a person falls for Satan's manipulations and sins when tempted, he or she will be wracked with guilt, which may cause a turning away from God. On the other hand, if the person resists the temptation, the result will be a stronger relationship with God than ever before.

When David was king of Israel, Satan incited him to take a census. God did not want him to conduct one. While we're not told the exact reason for God's position, there is a good reason why He did not want a census taken of Israel. We don't need to know His reasoning; we need only to be obedient to His leading. Perhaps this was an issue of David's pride. (We can get pretty full of ourselves and think we are responsible for the increase when our affairs are going well, as were David's.) The temptation is to disregard, or forget, what God has done. Too often, when large numbers are involved, people want to take credit for what He has done. God doesn't need large numbers; He needs only a few people who are willing to serve Him. Gideon, with only 300 men, was able to defeat an enemy army of over 135,000, using the humble weapons of trumpets, empty jars and torches. Little becomes much in the hands of the LORD. What matters, is trust and obedience.

In any case, Satan took up a position against Israel.

Satan stood up against Israel, and incited David to number Israel.
(1 Chronicles 21:1)

---

[182] See Matthew 27:3-5

Joab, the commander of David's army, tried to persuade David not to carry out the census, because God never took notice of numbers.

*But Joab said, "May the L*ORD *add to His people a hundred times as many as they are! Are they not, my lord the king, all of them my* L*ORD's servants? Why then should my* L*ORD require this? Why should He bring guilt upon Israel?"* (1 Chronicles 21:3)

Sometimes, people will sin even when their best friends try to stop them. They ignore the advice and, as in this case, may cause other people grief through involving them. The consequences of sin can be devastating, as seen in this instance. God made a swift judgment. He gave David a choice of three things:

... either three years of famine; or three months of devastation by your foes, while the sword of your enemies overtakes you; or three days of the sword of the L*ORD, pestilence on the land, and the Angel of the* L*ORD destroying throughout all the territory of Israel.* (1 Chronicles 21:12)

David chose the three days of pestilence. 70,000 men died as a result. There are always consequences to sin.

King David learned how to make Satan work for him against his enemies. He described how his enemies were constantly spreading lies against him and were fighting against him.

Appoint a wicked man against him; let an accuser bring him to trial. When he is tried, let him come forth guilty; let his prayer be counted as sin! (Psalm 109:6,7)

He goes on to show how an enemy will be destroyed, being tempted by Satan, and his family will join him in paying the price of his sin.

This was not a new lesson for David. He had learned it a long time before and warned that neither he nor anyone else should attempt to kill one of God's anointed.

> But David said to Abishai, "Do not destroy him; for who can put forth his hand against the LORD's anointed, and be guiltless? ... As the LORD lives, the LORD will smite him; or his day shall come to die; or he shall go down into battle and perish." (1 Samuel 26:9,10)

Further, the warning resonated:

> "Touch not mine anointed, and do my prophets no harm."
> (Psalm 105:15)

This principle of spiritual warfare – turning our enemies over to Satan for discipline – was carried over from the Old Testament to the New Testament. It is something we sometimes have to do.

> ... you are to deliver this man to Satan for the destruction of the flesh, that his spirit may be saved in the day of the LORD Jesus.
> (1 Corinthians 5:5)

> ... among them Hymenaeus and Alexander, whom I have delivered to Satan that they may learn not to blaspheme. (1 Timothy 1:20)

Like David, we must learn how to make Satan work for us against our enemies.

The last place Satan was mentioned in the Old Testament, was in a vision God gave to Zechariah about the high priest standing before "the Angel of the LORD." Satan was there to resist him. He was doing his job, showing Joshua's sin to God. Joshua was clothed with filthy garments – as we all are until we repent and are washed whiter than snow and given white clothes[183] – but Zechariah heard the LORD declare Joshua forgiven.

> Behold, I have taken your iniquity away from you, and I will clothe you with rich apparel. (Zechariah 3:4b)

Satan stood rebuked by God. Once Joshua was forgiven and stood in his new garments of righteousness, God gave him a prophecy describing the Messiah, Jesus, as *"the Branch."*

> Hear now, O Joshua the high priest, you and your friends who sit before you, for they are men of good omen: behold, I will bring My Servant the Branch. (Zechariah 3:8)

---

[183] See Revelation 7:14

God did not reject Satan's contentions, because Satan was right in his accusations – but Satan, himself, was not without sin. God said simply,

*"The L*ORD *rebuke you, O Satan! The L*ORD *who has chosen Jerusalem rebuke you! Is not this a brand plucked from the fire?"*
(Zechariah 3:2)

We are all brands plucked out of the fires of Hell when we are saved. Each of us must learn to pay the same heed to Satan's accusations as we would to that of any enemy of our souls and not slip into sin by cursing, swearing or verbally abusing him.

We get a further picture of how to deal with Satan when the archangel Michael contended with him for the body of Moses.

But when the archangel Michael, contending with the devil, *disputed about the body of Moses, he did not presume to pronounce a reviling judgment upon him, but said, "The L*ORD *rebuke you."*
(Jude 1:9)

Whenever we are dealing with Satan, we must, like Michael, resist the inclination to make reviling judgments against him. If we don't resist that urge, we run the danger of falling into his hands by failing the temptation and falling into sin.

Unprotected Areas of Entry for the Enemy

Areas of sin and trauma in a person's life are like open doors with welcome mats, saying, "Come on in!" for demons.

Two years ago, I received a telephone call from a woman in her early thirties, who had been living with a man. She called, terrified, because she had begun to be raped by an incubus demon on a regular basis. She had told her mother what was happening and her mother, who had heard that this was a part of our ministry, suggested she call me to help her.

The young woman called and asked, "Do you know about something called an incubus?"

I said, "Of course, I do! Why are you asking?"

She said, "Because there is one in the house where we're living and it has raped and molested me several times. I can't find anybody to help me. My mother said you might be able to help. Can you?"

I said, "Before I can answer that question, I need to ask you a question. Are you married?"

She said, "No, my boyfriend and I don't believe it's necessary to get married."

I said, "Then, I cannot help you and I will explain why. Since you are not married, you are willfully committing fornication which is, according to God, sin."

Shun fornication! Every sin that a person commits is outside the body; but the fornicator sins against the body itself.
(1 Corinthians 6:18)

I continued, "In order to get rid of the demon, you must be willing to repent of the sin you have been committing and invite Jesus to be your Savior. You need also to receive the baptism of the Holy Spirit, with the evidence of speaking in tongues."

And they were all filled with the Holy Spirit and began to speak in other tongues, as the Spirit gave them utterance. (Acts 2:4)

I said, "Then, you will have to be willing to get married, so Jesus can guide you in your relationship. As it is now, the demon has a right to invade your house and attack you, because you are living in the kingdom of darkness, of which it is a part.[184] If I were to come and cast it out, with you willfully living in sin, it would have a right to stay – so it would simply leave and come back with seven more. Your life would then be worse than it is now. So, if you are willing to let Jesus be your Savior and Lord and get married, or separate and live separately, then I will come and get rid of it. You must decide whom you are going to serve. The choice is yours."

---

[184] See Luke 11:18

When the unclean spirit has gone out of a man, he passes through waterless places seeking rest; and finding none he says, "I will return to my house from which I came." And when he comes he finds it swept and put in order. Then he goes and brings seven other spirits more evil than himself, and they enter and dwell there; and the last state of that man becomes worse than the first. (Luke 11:24-26)

She thought about it and said, "No, I don't want to become a Christian. I'll just leave things as they are for now and put up with it."

There are people who will tolerate all kinds of abuse rather than honour God and experience the exciting life Jesus has prepared for them.

I told the woman that whenever she had had enough of living in what Jesus calls "a far country,"[185] she was welcome to call and I'd be willing to help her. The problem is that many people enjoy the pleasures of sin for a season[186] and don't understand the pain Satan will bring into their lives as a result of following his ways. Some, like the prodigal son,[187] come to their senses and turn back to Jesus for help. This particular woman, like many others, continues to enjoy her sinful life, despite the evil consequences; and therefore, has not yet called for help.

One of the most frequent doors of entry into people's homes and lives is opened when a family member has died.

While pastoring my church in Brampton, Ontario, I called a friend, who was involved in our church, about arranging a meeting on a Monday morning. She said, "Gordon, I really want to go to the meeting but the trouble is that my father comes to visit me every Monday morning, so could you set a different day?"

I agreed and hung up the telephone. I explained to my wife that we couldn't have the meeting with her on Monday morning, because her father came to visit her every Monday. My wife reminded me that I had conducted her father's funeral two years ago.

---

[185] See Luke 15:13
[186] See Hebrews 11:25
[187] See Luke 15:11-32

Then, of course, I remembered, so I called the woman back to verify that I had heard her correctly. She admitted that he visited her as a ghost.

I said, "You have a major problem. That ghost is not your father. It is an evil spirit, called a familiar spirit,[188] because it is pretending to be your father. It has come to gain your confidence and then to harm you. It wants to take your attention off Jesus and God's plans for you."

"What can I do about it?"

I said, "I'll go over to your house on Monday morning at the time the spirit usually arrives and get rid of it for you."

She agreed. When the evil spirit showed up, I cast it out and prayed with our friend to be renewed by the Holy Spirit, since she had already been baptized in the Holy Spirit.

After the death of another friend of mine, his wife called me, because she had just had a strange thing happen in her home. Her two small dogs had run into her bedroom when she was in bed, ready to go to sleep. Both of them ran into a corner of the room and stood with their backs to the wall, looking toward the door through which they had come. These were usually high-energy animals, jumping and bouncing all over the house and barking, but on this night they were whimpering with their eyes fixed on the open door. The woman looked at the door and saw two beings, shaped like giant bowling pins about six feet tall. They reminded her of the "Schmos" characters in the "Lil' Abner" comic strip.

They each had one eye in the center of their heads, as they walked into her bedroom. One of them sat on her bed. She was terrified, but was able to ask, "What do you want?"

One replied, "You know what we want." Then, it stood up and the two walked out into some other place in her house.

She asked me, "Could these be evil spirits?"

I told her, "They certainly are! I'll come over tomorrow and get rid of them for you." She heartily agreed.

---

[188] Leviticus 19:31, 20:6,27; Deuteronomy 18:11; 1 Samuel 20:3,9; 1 Chronicles 10:13; Isaiah 19:3, 29:4

When I arrived, I asked her to go outside and pray while I got rid of the demons. I went through her house and cast the evil spirits out. She did not have any more visitations. Then we prayed and asked Jesus to fill her afresh with the Holy Spirit.

A young married couple came to see me at my church in Brampton, Ontario. The husband explained that his in-laws all talked about ghost visitations from their father (his father-in-law) who had died after he and his wife got married. He had always laughed their stories off as bad jokes and thought they had been putting him on.

However, just a few days before our meeting, he had been at his mother-in-law's house, waiting for her and his wife to return from shopping, so he could drive his wife home. He was concerned about his wife, because she was pregnant and he wanted to help her home with her shopping bags. While waiting, he lay down on the living room couch and fell asleep. He was awakened when he heard footsteps coming down the hallway to the living room. He opened his eyes, expecting to see his wife and her mother, but instead, he saw a ghost that looked like his dead father-in-law. He jumped up off the couch and ran right out of the house and got into his car and drove home.

He asked me, "Is this kind of thing normal?"

I assured him that it was not and explained that her family thought it was all right because the evil spirit had told them it was. Further, I explained that this was not the spirit of his wife's father. It was an evil spirit pretending to be her father, even to the point of disguising itself to look like him. I told him about familiar spirits and warned that it is not safe to allow them to stay. The husband arranged a meeting for me with the whole family. I explained their problem and they all agreed that the evil spirit had to go. Consequently, I went through the house and cast it out and sent it on to the abyss.

The young man called me several months later, upset and crying. Their baby had been born, but the little boy was not expected to live through the night, because he had been born with many congenital physical defects. He had a cleft pallet, a hair lip and two club feet. Both of his hips were out of joint. There was also something wrong with his lungs. The new parents wanted to know if I would go to the hospital and baptize their baby with water.

I agreed, but, remembering the evil spirit that had been visiting the family, I said, "I would be honored to go to the hospital and baptize him. However, I am also going to pray for his healing."

Through his tears, he said, "Whatever you want to do is okay with us."

I went to the hospital at midnight, when I knew there would be nobody around except the nursery nurses who knew me and who were extremely helpful and compassionate. The little guy was in an oxygen tent. The first thing I did was to say, "I command any evil or unclean spirit to leave this baby and go to the abyss and stay there."[189] Then, I laid hands on him and asked Jesus to please heal the little boy. After that, I baptized him with a few drops of water, "In the Name of the Father and the Son, Jesus Christ, and of the Holy Spirit." Then I went home.

The telephone at the side of our bed began ringing at 6:30 the next morning. A frantic voice, choking with tears, said, "Reverend Williams! Reverend Williams! Come to the hospital right away! Please come right away!"

I was fully awake and said, "I'll be there as fast as I can." As I drove to the hospital, my thoughts and prayers were about how I was going to be able help this family through the painful death of their first-born baby. But when I arrived at the hospital nursery, the situation was not at all somber. The young parents proudly showed me the baby. He was completely normal! No hair lip or cleft pallet! No hips out of joint! No club feet! Lungs were normal! There were tears of joy all around!

The new father explained that when the nurse had gone to check the baby, she thought somebody had switched babies. The whole nursery went into panic mode. It was only after checking, and comparing the

---

[189] See Luke 8:31

baby's foot prints against the ones that were taken at birth, that they realized this was the same baby – but without the congenital birth defects. We thanked Jesus for a *wonderful* miracle.

Because most Christian clergy do not take the Bible's reports about Jesus, His disciples and the first Christians casting out evil spirits seriously, many children are born with demon-induced birth defects. These could have been avoided, with proper use of the gifts of the Holy Spirit.[190] Jesus said that the first sign of an authentic believer was to cast out demons. He said,

And these signs will accompany those who believe: in My Name they will cast out demons; they will speak in new tongues; they will pick up serpents, and if they drink any deadly thing, it will not hurt them; they will lay their hands on the sick, and they will recover.
(Mark 16:17-18)

I received a call from a man who lived north of Markdale, Ontario, Canada, on a farm. The man explained that ghosts were making all kinds of noise in his house. They were talking and shouting in different rooms, opening and slamming doors, moving furniture around and turning lights on and off. He didn't know what to do, so he had talked with his pastor, who was also baffled. Nevertheless, the pastor had read a newspaper article about my deliverance ministry and clearing a house of evil spirits. He suggested the man should give me a call.

I explained that these spirits were not ghosts of people who had lived there prior to his purchase of the farm. They were actually evil spirits.

He asked, "Can you get rid of them?"

I explained that I could, under certain conditions.

He asked, "What are they?"

I explained that, because he was already a Christian, the only remaining condition would be for him and his wife to receive the baptism of the Holy Spirit, enabling Jesus to be Lord over their lives.

---

[190] See Romans 12:6-10; 1 Corinthians 12:8-10

They agreed.

I went to their home and prayed with them to receive the baptism of the Holy Spirit. I knew they had received, because they began to speak in tongues – the evidence. I went through their house and barn and got rid of the evil spirits.

About two years later, the man called again and explained, "We have purchased a new farm, just northeast of here and we are not going to move in until you come and clean it out first."

I said, "I would be honored to do that." I went through the new house and barn and got rid of any evil spirits that were there. They moved into the house and have lived there for many years, without any harassment from evil spirits.

The Unforgivable Sin – Blasphemy Against the Holy Spirit

The devil strikes his coup de grâce when he is successful in convincing a Christian that he or she has committed the unpardonable sin. Sadly, too many Christians fall for this one and become guilt-ridden, to the point of depression, despair and even suicide.

The unforgivable sin is committed when someone misidentifies the work of the Holy Spirit as the work of evil spirits and accuses Spirit-filled believers of being possessed by demons.

There is a lot of blasphemy against the Holy Spirit going on today. Unfortunately, the accusations often come from people who are supposed to be able to recognize the Holy Spirit's work (like the Sadducees and Pharisees); but because they are not spiritual, baptized-in-the-Holy-Spirit people, they fall into blasphemy instead. They don't have the tools of discernment to recognize the true working of the Holy Spirit.

At an early point in Jesus' ministry, it almost looked as if people were going to recognize Him as the Messiah, Emmanuel, God in the flesh – but they didn't.

One such example happened in Capernaum, in Jesus' own house.[191] Four men carried their friend to the house, hoping Jesus would heal him.

---

[191] See Mark 2:1-12; Matthew 9:1-8; Luke 5:17-26

By the time they arrived, however, there was no room left for anybody to get in. Determined to get Jesus to pray for their friend, the men cut a hole in the roof of the house and lowered him, pallet and all, into the room where Jesus was ministering. When Jesus saw the four men's faith, He said to the paralytic,

"My son, your sins are forgiven." (Mark 2:5)

Now some of the scribes were sitting there, questioning in their hearts, "Why does this man speak thus? It is blasphemy! Who can forgive sins but God alone?" (Mark 2:6-7)

They almost knew who He was! It seemed as though the Scribes were about to get the revelation – but they missed what every demon on earth knew and what Jesus went on to explain.

And immediately Jesus, perceiving in His Spirit that they thus questioned within themselves, said to them, "Why do you question thus in your hearts? Which is easier, to say to the paralytic, 'Your sins are forgiven,' or to say, 'Rise, take up your pallet and walk?' But that you may know that the Son of Man has authority on earth to forgive sins ... I say to you, rise, take up your pallet and go home." (Mark 2:8-11)

Even Spirit-filled Christians run the risk of believing Satan's lies if they don't know their Scriptures. Knowing and understanding the written Word of God takes study, time spent in His presence and prayer for true understanding. Shallow Christians are like the Sadducees. Jesus said:

"You are wrong, because you know neither the Scriptures nor the power of God." (Matthew 22:29)

Knowing the Scriptures is of crucial importance in dealing with the devil, because he will misquote them, quote only a part of a verse, misapply them, use them out of context – or simply make something up and pretend it's Scripture. Therefore, it is of the utmost importance that we study the Scriptures, in order to know what's really in it; and further, to know the power of God, the Holy Spirit and His works.

The unforgivable sin has to do with the Holy Spirit. Jesus said:

> *"Therefore I tell you, every sin and blasphemy will be forgiven men, but the blasphemy against the Spirit will not be forgiven. And whoever says a word against the Son of Man will be forgiven; but whoever speaks against the Holy Spirit will not be forgiven, either in this age or in the age to come."*
> (Matthew 12:31-32; see also Mark 3:28-30; Luke 12:10).

Jesus gave this warning to some Pharisees who, when they observed Jesus casting out demons (something neither they nor the priests in the Temple could do), criticized Jesus and said that it was only by Beelzebul, the prince of demons, that He was casting out demons. They basically accused Jesus of being in cahoots with the devil.

> *He casts out demons by the prince of demons.*
> (Matthew 9:34; *see also* Mark 3:22 and *Luke 11:15)*

> *Are we not right in saying that you are a Samaritan and have a demon?"*(John 8:48)

Jesus answered,

> *"But if it is by the finger of God that I cast out demons, then the Kingdom of God has come upon you."* (Luke 11:20)

On another occasion,

> *... the Scribes, who came down from Jerusalem said, "He is possessed by Beelzebul, and by the prince of demons He casts out demons." And, He called them to Him, and said to them in parables, "How can Satan cast out Satan? If a kingdom is divided against itself, that kingdom cannot stand. And if a house is divided against itself, that house will not be able to stand. And if Satan has risen up against himself and is divided, he cannot stand, but is coming to an end. But no one can enter a strong man's house and plunder his goods, unless he first binds the strong man; then indeed he may plunder his house. Truly, I say to you, all sins will be forgiven the sons of men, and whatever blasphemies they utter; but whoever blasphemes against*

the Holy Spirit never has forgiveness, but is guilty of an eternal sin" – for they had said, "He has an unclean spirit."
(Mark 3:22-30; see also Luke 11:14-23)

Neither the Scribes nor the Pharisees had a clue about who Jesus was. Both groups misidentified the work of the Holy Spirit in Jesus for the work of the devil and concluded that Jesus must be possessed by a demon – yet these were the people who were sure they would be able to identify the Messiah when He would come. They assumed they would be the ones who would proudly welcome Him. Sadly, these people were spiritually blind and deaf because of their powerless religious traditions.

When the Sadducees questioned Jesus regarding the resurrection of the dead,[192] He chastised them for knowing neither the Scriptures nor the power of God. Their erroneous thinking permeated their entire approach to the issue of who He was. His response was fitting for the scribes, Pharisees, Sadducees and most of the Jewish people who listened to Him, but did not recognize who He was.

On another occasion, the Pharisees and the Scribes criticized the disciples for not observing some of the traditions of the elders. They couldn't understand how someone could be from God, yet operate apart from expected traditions. In response, Jesus quoted Isaiah:

This people honors Me with their lips, but their heart is far from Me; in vain do they worship Me, teaching as doctrines the precepts of men. You leave the commandment of God, and hold fast the tradition of men. And He said to them, 'You have a fine way of rejecting the commandment of God, in order to keep your tradition! For Moses said, 'Honor your father and your mother'; and, 'He who speaks evil of father or mother, let him surely die'; but you say, 'If a man tells his father or his mother, what you would have gained from me is Corban' (that is, given to God) – then you no longer permit him to do anything for his father or mother, thus making void the Word of God through your tradition which you hand on. And many such things you do.'" (Mark 7:6-13)

---
[192] See Matthew 22:23-33

Many clergy today are in the same dangerous situation. They are supposed to know the Scriptures and the power of the Holy Spirit, but they misidentify the work of the Holy Spirit being done through Spirit-baptized Christians. They often attribute what they see to psychological abnormalities. This error can lead them onto dangerous ground and blasphemy against the Holy Spirit, the unforgivable sin.

In several places in the Bible, we are told how to recognize the work of the Holy Spirit. We are told that there are signs that follow those who believe.[193] Paul tells us about the gifts of the Holy Spirit in Romans 12:6-8 and 1 Corinthians 12:1-15. Unspiritual, ungodly, or carnal people will not accept that these gifts and signs are active in our world today, and in so doing, identify themselves as truly unspiritual.

> *All Scripture is inspired by God and is useful for teaching, for reproof, for correction, and for training in righteousness, so that everyone who belongs to God may be proficient, equipped for every good work.* (2 Timothy 3:16-17)

The Scripture states clearly how the Holy Spirit equips people to do the ministry of Jesus. He baptizes them with the Holy Spirit, empowering them to do even greater things than He did.[194]

> *And they were all filled with the Holy Spirit and began to speak in other tongues* (Greek: other national languages), *as the Spirit gave them utterance.* (Acts 2:4)

> *Having gifts that differ according to the grace given to us, let us use them: if prophecy, in proportion to our faith; if service* (ministry), *in our serving* (ministry); *he who teaches, in his teaching; he who exhorts, in his exhortation* (encouragement); *he who contributes* (gives), *in liberality* (generosity); *he who gives aid* (leadership), *with zeal* (enthusiasm); *he who does acts of mercy, with cheerfulness.* (Romans 12:6-8)

> *To one is given through the Spirit the utterance* (word) *of wisdom, and to another the utterance* (word) *of knowledge according to the*

---

[193] See Mark 16:17–20
[194] See John 14:12-14

same Spirit, to another faith by the same Spirit, to another gifts of healing by the one Spirit, to another the working of miracles (miraculous power), *to another prophecy, to another the ability to distinguish* (discern) *between spirits, to another various kinds of tongues* (other national languages), *to another the interpretation of tongues* (other national languages). (1 Corinthians 12:8-10)

The fifteen gifts of the Holy Spirit in Greek are "charis" (singular) or "charismata" (plural). "Charis" means "grace." Thus the gifts of the Holy Spirit are gifts of grace. When they are not welcomed or encouraged to be used or received, the distribution of God's grace is cut off and the gifts of the Holy spirit cannot be used to meet people's needs.

When people don't understand these ministry gifts, they risk misidentifying the Holy Spirit as an evil spirit and falling into blaspheming against the Holy Spirit. Because this is still a problem today, Jesus warned of this potential error in His dealings with the unspiritual people of His day. The only people who can really blaspheme against the Holy Spirit are religious people who are supposed to be able to recognize and identify the presence and work of the Holy Spirit.

The New Testament tells us who the Holy Spirit is, what He is like and what He does. We need to know the Scriptures so that we can identify Him and His work.

I have ministered to many people who were convinced, by the devil's lies, that they had committed the unpardonable sin. I had to show them, through the Scriptures, that the people who have actually committed it, do not have a guilty conscience, like they had. The people who do sin against the Holy Spirit are full of arrogant pride. They see themselves as being right and Jesus being wrong. If a person had actually committed the unpardonable sin, the Holy Spirit would not be indwelling them and they would not be able to speak in tongues,[195] have the other gifts of the Holy Spirit and want to be in church services.

---

[195] See Mark 16:17

Reverse Blasphemy Against the Holy Spirit

Recently, we have been running across a new problem which I can only call "reverse blasphemy against the Holy Spirit" – people claiming the Holy Spirit *did* something that He actually *did not do*. They misidentify the works of the devil and demons as being the work of the Holy Spirit.

The confusion is a result of people not understanding the importance of receiving the baptism of the Holy Spirit and so not being able to recognize the real thing. The genuine work of the Holy Spirit, through "signs following,"[196] the ministry of the fifteen gifts of the Holy Spirit,[197] and the growth of the fruit of the Spirit[198] is indispensable for a successful Christian life. People are so anxious to have supernatural religious experiences that they think every religious experience is from Jesus Christ.

The problem has become increasingly common today, in some Christian ministries where the leadership cannot tell the difference between the work of the Holy Spirit and demons. In such meetings, counterfeit signs, wonders, miracles and so-called ministry gifts have replaced Biblical signs, wonders, miracles and the legitimate ministry gifts of the Holy Spirit. People go to these meetings to find the God of the Bible, but because the leaders have no gifts of discernment, people have received evil spirits.

I have been in meetings, most notably in Toronto, where possessed people, who were assumed to have been baptized with the Holy Spirit, were actually out of control. Rather than *"signs following,"* many people have other things happening to them. Rather than speaking in tongues as the Holy Spirit gives them utterance, they make uncontrollable animal sounds and their bodies shake uncontrollably as though they're having strange epileptic seizures or suffering from some form of palsy. They bark like dogs, oink like pigs, growl like lions and tigers and do unusual things with their bodies; hopping like rabbits, jumping like kangaroos or walking like a dog on their hands and feet. Many exhibit violent bending

---

[196] See Mark 16:17-18
[197] See Romans 12:6-8; 1 Corinthians 12:8-10
[198] See Galatians 5:22-23

motions that makes them look as though they are being punched continually in the stomach. The bottom line is that their strange behaviors are not in line with Biblical descriptions of Spirit-filled, Spirit-led Christians.

I watched a man in a church in Florida, who was on his hands and knees barking like a dog. He was wearing a dog collar on his neck, to which was attached a leash, held by a man who was singing, "Where He leads me, I will follow." These weird demonstrations and manifestations are all the work of demon-possessed people.

They get away with this demonic behavior because nobody has, or exercises, the gift of the Holy Spirit called discerning of spirits.[199] These people lack genuine peace – and obviously do not use the Bible as the standard for their spiritual lives, because their bizarre behavior does not line up with Scripture. The tragic result has been that many churches have become places that worship demons. People who go into their meetings, seeking for the God of the Bible, come out possessed by demons.

When people witness the absurd physical manifestations of possessed people, they often conclude that the people are behaving strangely to gain attention. Not at all! On the contrary: possessed people usually lose control of their bodies and voices and end up embarrassed and hurt.

In 2010, 1 was in Ecuador where I had been invited to preach, teach and do ministry in some house churches and other kinds of churches. During the eight days of ministry, we saw people of all ages – from little children to senior citizens – receive salvation, healing and deliverance. Over a thousand people received the baptism of the Holy Spirit with the evidence of the "signs following."[200] People were equipped with the authority to cast out demons, speak in new languages (tongues) and exercise the ministry of healing, with the laying on of hands.

During one of the church services in Quito, a couple in their thirties, who had already received salvation, asked to receive the baptism of the Holy Spirit. The woman explained, "I need healing for something strange tormenting me in my chest."

---

[199] See 1 Corinthians 12:10
[200] Mark 16:17-18

As I laid hands on them, they prayed for forgiveness of any sin that they might have. The man received the baptism of the Holy Spirit and began to speak in tongues. As I prayed for his wife, her body began to shake uncontrollably, as if she were having epileptic seizures. Strange sounds started coming out of her mouth. As she started to fall backwards, I grabbed her by the shoulders to keep her from falling and commanded the demon to leave her three times.

And it left her. I then prayed with her to receive the baptism of the Holy Spirit and she began to speak in tongues.

Later, she came to me and showed me a drawing she had made of the demon leaving her body. She said, "This is what came out of me!" Later, she went to her pastor and told him that a demon had gone out of her body. He was emphatic, declaring, "Christians cannot have demons!"

Unfonunately, he was wrong. The only kind of a Christian who cannot be possessed by demons/evil spirits is one who has received the real baptism of the Holy Spirit with the proof of the "signs following."[201]

If there are no signs, then there is no Holy Spirit. People mistake the forgiveness of sin for receiving the Holy Spirit because they are spiritually clean. It is a bad teaching or doctrine that leads people to believe that they received the Holy Spirit when there is no proof or evidence. Only one time in the Book of Acts, did people receive the Holy Spirit at the same time as they believed – and they had the proof of speaking in tongues.

> *While Peter was still saying this, the Holy Spirit fell on all who heard the Word. And the believers from among the circumcised who came with Peter were amazed, because the gift of the Holy Spirit had been poured out even on the Gentiles. For they heard them speaking in tongues and extolling God. Then Peter declared, "Can any one forbid water for baptizing these people who have received the Holy Spirit*

---

[201] Mark 16:17-18

just as we have?" And he commanded them to be baptized in the Name of Jesus Christ. (Acts 10:44-48)

In the four other times, people received salvation first and then the baptism of the Holy Spirit secondly.[202] Salvation makes us into new wineskins. The baptism of the Holy Spirit fills our new wineskins.

And no one puts new wine into old wineskins; if he does, the new wine will burst the skins and it will be spilled, and the skins will be destroyed. But new wine must be put into fresh wineskins. And no one after drinking old wine desires new; for he says, "The old is good." (Luke 5:37-39)

When a person receives the authentic Holy Spirit, the first gift he or she is given, is that of speaking in a language he or she has never learned – the gift of speaking in tongues[203] – the evidence that he or she has definitely been baptized in the Holy Spirit. The gift of tongues brings the tongue under the influence of the Holy Spirit.[204]

Often, when people receive the baptism of the Holy Spirit, they will fall down as they are filled with the Holy Spirit. I see this as the gift of miracles,[205] giving them salvation, the baptism of the Holy Spirit, healing of their body – or direction and instruction from the Holy Spirit. Often, there will be a temporary, minor shaking as the Holy Spirit does His work in their bodies, but He will give them peace and self-control. There will be no uncontrollable body movements.

But the fruit of the Spirit is love, joy, peace, patience, kindness, goodness, faithfulness, gentleness, self-control; against such there is no law. (Galatians 5:22-23)

Through the baptism in the Holy Spirit, people are able to hear what the Holy Spirit is saying to them – often in a still, small voice – every day. By their own choice, they can position themselves in agreement with His

---

[202] Acts 2:4; 14:14-17; 9:17, 1 Corinthians 14:18
[203] See Mark 16:17; Acts 2:4; 10:46; 19:6)
[204] See James 3:1-12
[205] See 1 Corinthians 12:10

plans and purposes for their lives. The Holy Spirit does not force people to do and say things against their will.

In contrast to the true workings of God, the leaders of 'off-kilter' ministries commit reverse blasphemy of the Holy Spirit. They misinterpret the works of demons as the work of the Holy Spirit. Jesus gave a stern warning to the scribes, who accused him of being possessed by Beelzebub.[206]

> *Whoever blasphemes against the Holy Spirit can never have forgiveness, but is guilty of an eternal sin – for they had said, "He has an unclean spirit."* (Mark 3:29-30)

Jesus also warned the Pharisees, who accused Him of casting out demons by the power of the devil.

> *Therefore I tell you, people will be forgiven for every sin and blasphemy, but blasphemy against the Spirit will not be forgiven. Whoever speaks a word against the Son of Man will be forgiven, but whoever speaks against the Holy Spirit will not be forgiven, either in this age or in the age to come.* (Matthew 12:31-32)

The scribes and Pharisees were attributing the work of the Holy Spirit to the work of demons. The problem with off-kilter ministries today, is exactly the same problem, but with a twist. These ministries interpret the work of demons who possess people and cause them to do all kinds of degrading things, as the works of the Holy Spirit. The leaders are continuously chasing after things that are not the signs, miracles and wonders described in the Bible; for example, having decayed teeth receive gold fillings, which, after testing, are not found to be genuine gold. They are supposedly sprinkled with gold flakes falling from the ceiling. Stones, reputed to be precious gemstones, appear, but upon examination, are found not to match the standards for precious stones.

People are being deceived who want these sorts of miracles. Whenever anybody goes beyond what is written in the Bible, they miss God's plan and purpose. Paul wrote,

---

[206] See Mark 3:22

"I have applied all this to myself and Apollos for your benefit, brethren, that you may learn by us not to go beyond what is written, that none of you may be puffed up in favor of one against another."
(1 Corinthians 4:6)

Paul also warned,

"The coming of the lawless one by the activity of Satan will be with all power and with pretended signs and wonders, and with all wicked deception for those who are to perish, because they refused to love the truth and so be saved. Therefore God sends upon them a strong delusion, to make them believe what is false, so that all may be condemned who did not believe the truth but had pleasure in unrighteousness." (2 Thessalonians 2:9-12)

If anything supernatural occurs, the like of which is not in the Bible, then it is not from God.

Ministries that embrace things which go beyond what is written in the Bible are not a blessing but a curse, because so many people are victimized by those of whom Jesus said,

"You are wrong, because you know neither the Scriptures nor the power of God." (Matthew 22:29)

People need to be careful where they go to seek God. They cannot take it for granted that churches and church leaders are following, and being guided by, Jesus Christ. Not all know the works of the Holy Spirit and follow the will of our Heavenly Father.

Non-biblical so-called signs, wonders and miracles are not from the only true God, Jesus Christ. God knew we were not the smartest beings in creation, so He made our relationship very simple: one God, one LORD, one Savior. Even then, sin and flesh entice people to try another choice; one which offers life, but in the end, leads only to death, Hell and hopelessness. If it isn't in the Bible, then it isn't from God. It's the KISS principle: "Keep It Simple Saints."

Some time ago, I received a phone call from a man in Denmark. An accented voice asked, "Can you help me? Can you help me?"

I asked, "What is your problem?"

The man explained that three years prior, he had gone to a meeting in Denmark, which was led by some people from a church near the Toronto Airport. He had responded to the altar call, in order to receive the baptism of the Holy Spirit, with the evidence of speaking in tongues.[207] Instead of receiving the Holy Spirit, however, something else had entered his body. Since that time, his stomach had felt like it was being continually punched, causing him to double over. This condition continued night and day. Through tears, he said, "I can't take much more of this. My stomach is very sore. Can you help me?"

I asked where he had found my phone number and he told me he had found it on our web page.

"I cannot help you," I said, "but I know Somebody who can."

He asked, "Who is it?"

"His Name is Jesus Christ." I explained that, unknowingly, he had exposed himself to a false ministry and had been possessed by a demon. I told him it would be necessary to ask Jesus to forgive him for going to that meeting, even though he had not realized what would happen to him. After that, I would command the demon to leave him and then we would pray for him to receive the baptism of the Holy Spirit, with the gift of speaking in tongues.

He agreed.

Over the phone, I commanded the demon to leave and to go to the abyss and stay there. Then the man prayed with me, asking Jesus to forgive him for exposing himself to demon possession and to give him the baptism of the Holy Spirit. Immediately, he began to speak in tongues.[208]

---
[207] See Mark 16:17
[208] See Acts 2:4; Acts 10:44-46

If you then, who are evil, know how to give good gifts to your children, how much more will the Heavenly Father give the Holy Spirit to those who ask Him! (Luke 11:13)

After a few minutes, he stopped and said, "It's gone! It's gone! My stomach's all right! Thank you."

I have heard from people from many countries who have been possessed by demons because they could not tell the difference between the work of the Holy Spirit and the work of demons.

On another occasion, I was doing a week of meetings at the Pentecostal Church in Kingsville, Ontario, Canada. During the ministry time, while I was praying with people, the pastor came to me and asked me to help a woman who was lying on her back on the floor. She was shaking and making the epileptic-like physical movements that I immediately recognized from other people who had been to the same Toronto church. I got down beside her and asked what was happening to her.

She said, "I don't know! I don't know!"

I said, "You need to receive Jesus as your Savior and Lord and receive the baptism of the Holy Spirit."

Through her uncontrollable, jerking body movement, she said, "I am saved and baptized with the Holy Spirit and I do speak in tongues."

This was a surprise to me. I then took authority over the evil spirit and commanded it to leave her immediately and to go to the abyss and stay there. Then I prayed for her to have peace and self-control.

I moved on to pray for other people. When we had finished praying for everyone, the woman came to talk with me. She asked, "Can you explain what happened to me?"

"You tell me what happened to you," I said.

She described how she had gone on a bus trip to the church in Toronto. At the end of the meeting, an invitation was given. She had walked to the front and asked for prayer. She said, "When the pastor prayed with me, this thing came onto me."

"Did it go inside of you?"

"No, but it rode on me, like a monkey on my back, forcing me to do things with my arms and legs and head that I had no control over."

Then I realized what had happened to her. Since she had already received the baptism of the Holy Spirit, the demon had not been able to go inside of her body, so it rode on her back like a monkey, forcing her to make unwanted body movements. It exhausted her.

I cautioned her to never go to that church again, or to any other meeting similar to that one, or something worse might happen to her. She agreed.

When given the opportunity, demons will attack and attempt to possess or control anybody. They take control over people's bodies, either by possession or harassment. This is an example of the kingdom of darkness exercising its lordship over people. Jesus wants us to be free from sin and the devil and evil spirits. He wants us to have self-control.

... when the true worshipers will worship the Father in spirit and truth, for such the Father seeks to worship Him. (John 4:23)

When the authentic Holy Spirit comes into a person's life, the fruit of the Holy Spirit becomes apparent – especially peace and self-control. It results in the freedom to raise our hands in worship. People who have received the genuine baptism in the Holy Spirit will not do anything to embarrass or degrade themselves.

But the fruit of the Spirit is love, joy, peace, patience, kindness, goodness, faithfulness, gentleness, self-control; against such there is no law. (Galatians 5:22-23)

People involved in reverse blasphemy have a religious experience that is *not* from God. Without knowing the Scriptures, which are our covenant with God, we are open to every wind of doctrine and can easily be led away from the truth.

For the time is coming when people will not endure sound teaching, but having itching ears they will accumulate for themselves teachers to suit their own likings, and will turn away from listening to the truth and wander into myths. (2 Timothy 4:3-4)

Deceived people sometimes resemble the possessed woman in Philippi, who warned people loudly to stay away, because the people in the church didn't see or understand what was happening. Even worse, there are people who have the gift of discerning spirits who, because of possible criticism, will not point out demon activity. Paul explains how the Holy Spirit is supposed to work in the lives of individual churches,[209] so we can immediately recognize meetings that are not carried out decently and in order.[210] When we go beyond what is written,[211] we allow demons to run our meetings and make a mockery of the working and gifts of the Holy Spirit.

In order to resist the temptation of the devil to receive his version of a convincing religious experience, we must learn to be like the Bereans:

Now these Jews were more noble than those in Thessalonica, for they received the Word with all eagerness, examining the Scriptures daily to see if these things were so. (Acts 17:11)

Our protection comes from examining the Scriptures daily, so that the devil cannot lead us astray with his false religious experiences.

When God's people don't listen to Him, they are at risk of being misled by demons who come to them as angels of light, misrepresenting themselves as faithful angels, serving the God of the Bible. They often pretend to be gods whom people will worship and serve.[212] They regularly misinterpret the Bible, suggesting people have permission to sin, just as the devil did with Adam and Eve, when he tried to manipulate them with a confusing question.

Did God say? (Genesis 3:1-7)

He tries the same approach with us today.

---

[209] See 1 Corinthians 14:26
[210] See 1 Corinthians 14:40
[211] See 1 Corinthians 4:6
[212] See Deuteronomy 32:17; Psalm 106:37; 1 Corinthians 10:19; Revelation 9:20

> For such men are false apostles, deceitful workmen, disguising themselves as apostles of Christ. And no wonder, for even Satan disguises himself as an angel of light. So it is not strange if his servants also disguise themselves as servants of righteousness. Their end will correspond to their deeds. (2 Corinthians 11:13-15)

> ... *not to go beyond what is written* ... (1 Corinthians 4:6)

Today, any believer who goes beyond what is written in the Bible can be led into sin, because instead of carefullly listening to the Holy Spirit, they go chasing after counterfeit signs. The proof of their disobedience and rebellion towards God becomes evident when God sends an evil spirit to expose them.

One of the most frightening examples of this is given in the Book of 1 Kings. The kings of Israel and Judah called together the prophets of Israel to seek God's will about going to war against Syria. They wanted to regain land that had been captured by Syria, so they assembled about 400 prophets to tell them whether or not to battle against Ramoth-Gilead. All 400 prophets told the kings to go to battle.

Not satisfied, Jehoshephat asked, "Is there not here another prophet of the Lord of whom we may inquire?"

They sent for Micaiah who, after some delay, told them, "I saw all Israel scattered upon the mountains, as sheep without a shepherd." That was a prophetic way of saying that Israel would lose if they went to war and their leader would be killed.

Micaiah then described a vision he had of God on His throne, surrounded by the host of Heaven. In the vision, the Lord said, "Who will entice Ahab, that he may go up and fall at Ramoth-Gilead?" Then a spirit volunteered, saying, "I will entice him. I will go forth and will be a lying spirit in the mouths of all his prophets." Micaiah warned the kings, knowing he would not be popular.

> *Now therefore behold, the* Lord *has put a lying spirit in the mouth of all these your prophets; the* Lord *has spoken evil concerning you.*
> (For the whole account, read 1 Kings 22:1–40 and 2 Chronicles 8:4-34.)

King Ahab disregarded Micaiah's prophecy, went to war and was killed. This happened because he preferred to believe what the four hundred false prophets were saying rather than what the only prophet who heard from God was saying. Four hundred prophets wanted to please their king rather than their God. King Ahab disregarded God's only legitimate prophet because he did not want to serve Yahweh. Knowing this, God gave the lying spirit permission to give a false prophecy to the 400 prophets – exactly what Ahab wanted to hear.

False prophets are prevalent today. They do not hear from the Holy Spirit. Nevertheless, because people like to have their ears tickled, they chase after these lying spirits.

An appalling and horrible thing has happened in the land: the prophets prophesy falsely, and the priests rule at their direction; My people love to have it so, but what will you do when the end comes? (Jeremiah 5:30–31)

There are two ways to identify false prophets. First, they'll prophesy that the Temple in Jerusalem is going to be rebuilt. When speaking to His disciples (who were impressed with the great and wonderful buildings), Jesus prophesied:

"You see all these do you not? Truly I say to you, there will not be left here, one stone upon another that will not be thrown down." (Matthew 24:1-2; Luke 21:5-6; Mark 13:1-2)

It is clear from the original Greek grammar that Jesus meant the Temple would be destroyed once for all time. An attempt to rebuild it in 373 AD failed when fire came up out of the ground and destroyed the building materials and most of the workmen. Jesus has already rebuilt His new Temple.

Do you not know that you are God's Temple and God's Spirit dwells in you? If anyone destroys God's Temple, God will destroy him. For God's Temple is holy and that Temple is you. (1 Corinthians 3:16-17)

The second sign of a false prophet is revealed through any prophecy that that involves setting dates regarding the return of Jesus. So-called date-setting prophets re-adjust their prophecies when the second coming does not coincide with their dates. They misunderstand Jesus' meaning when He said, "Truly, I say to you, this generation will not pass away till all these things take place."[213] According the Greek text, He was saying, "This *race* will not pass away till these things take place." We Christians are Jews by adoption.[214] We are members of the Tribe of Judah.[215] The generation at Jesus' time on earth has passed away. He said no one – not even the angels in Heaven – would know the day or the hour.

> *But of that day and hour no one knows, not even the angels in heaven nor the Son, but the Father only.* (Matthew 24:36)

The reason why "no one," (including Jesus) knows when He will return is that before He can return, the full number of people who are to be saved must come into the Kingdom of God.

> *... a great multitude which no man could number, from every nation, from all tribes and peoples and tongues...* (Revelation 7:9)

A friend of mine, Rodrigo Garcia, is an engineer. Using today's building standards and the dimensions of the New Jerusalem given in Scripture, he estimated the approximate number of people who could be housed in the New Jerusalem. The extraordinary number is 26,050,114,285,800,000[216] saved people. Until the full number of those who are to be saved is reached and Jesus returns, the saved who pass away will live in Paradise. Those who are not reaching out to the lost are preventing Jesus from returning because they are not doing what He commanded every believer to do.

> *Go therefore and make disciples of all nations, baptizing them in the Name of the Father and of the Son and of the Holy Spirit, teaching them to observe all that I have commanded you; and lo, I am with you always, to the close of the age.* (Matthew 28:19-20)

---

[213] Matthew 24:34
[214] Romans 8:23; Galatians 4:5
[215] Revelation 7:5
[216] 26 quadrillion, 50 trillion, 114 billion, 285 million, 800 thousand people

And these signs will accompany those who believe: in My Name they will cast out demons; they will speak in new tongues; they will pick up serpents, and if they drink any deadly thing, it will not hurt them; they will lay their hands on the sick, and they will recover.
(Mark 16:17-18)

But you shall receive power when the Holy Spirit has come upon you; and you shall be My witnesses in Jerusalem and in all Judea and Samaria and to the end of the earth. (Acts 1:8)

Jesus made it clear that He wants His house to be full.

A man once gave a great banquet, and invited many; and at the time for the banquet he sent his servant to say to those who had been invited, "Come; for all is now ready."
But they all alike began to make excuses. The first said to him, "I have bought a field, and I must go out and see it; I pray you, have me excused."
And another said, "I have bought five yoke of oxen, and I go to examine them; I pray you, have me excused."
And another said, "I have married a wife, and therefore I cannot come."
The servant came and reported this to his master.
Then the householder in anger said to his servant, "Go out quickly to the streets and lanes of the city, and bring in the poor and maimed and blind and lame."
And the servant said, "Sir, what you commanded has been done, and still there is room."
And the master said to the servant, "Go out to the highways and hedges, and compel people to come in, that my house may be filled. For I tell you, none of those men who were invited shall taste my banquet." (Luke 14:15-24)

So, it's not the number of years, months or days to be watched for Jesus to return; it's the number of salvations that are sealed.

Today, many people buy into the claims of false prophets and know their books better than they know the Bible. Peter taught about how to identify false prophets.

> *First of all you must understand this, that no prophecy of Scripture is of private interpretation, because no prophecy ever came by the impulse of man, but men moved by the Holy Spirit spoke from God.*
> (2 Peter 1:20-21)

In other words, authentic prophecy must always agree with what the Bible says. If what is being spoken is in conflict with the Scriptures, it is false.

False prophecy can come from one of three sources: the devil, evil spirits or the person speaking. The person speaking could be telling lies in hopes of controlling people or appearing to be more spiritual than others. Giving wrong direction is, in his or her mind, secondary to the potential for power, financial gain or influence.

Authentic prophecy is not dependant on an interpreter to explain its meaning. It will happen just as it was given. A thorough knowledge of the Bible is, therefore, essential before approval of any so-called prophecy. The charismatic gift of discerning of spirits[217] is invaluable as a tool used by the Holy Spirit to warn people if they are being deceived.

The worst nightmare of a prideful, non-repentant person who places his or her own agenda above that of God, is not the devil or demons: it is our God.

Regrouping – Forgiving Ourselves and Moving Ahead

It's often easier to forgive everybody else for their failures and sin, than to forgive ourselves. We constantly put ourselves down for inconsistencies, failures, and past sins *that God has already forgiven!* He doesn't keep a record of our past sins, but we do – and so does the devil. We end up battling paper tigers that serve only to hold us back and render us immobile in the kingdom of God.

I remember the first sermon our student minister, Bob Gray, preached one Sunday evening in our church in Englishtown. He called his message: "Do You Think You are Bigger Than God?" He told us God has forgiven us for all of our sins, but that many of us won't forgive ourselves for the things

---
[217] 1 Corinthians 12:10

we have done. So, that makes us bigger than God, in our own minds. The reason why so many Christians are full of guilt, is not because either God or the devil made them feel guilty, but because they will not forgive themselves. Until they do, they can love neither God, nor their neighbors as themselves. Agapé love does not keep a record of wrongs.[218] There are many who need to face themselves in a mirror and forgive themselves.

We need to look ourselves squarely in the eyes and say, "Jesus forgave you for all your sins and so I forgive you for all your sins." Having done that, we can resist the devil, who tells us that because we have sinned and failed God, we cannot forgive ourselves. Without forgiving ourselves, we can't be successful in spiritual warfare.

Paul admonished us not to think of ourselves more highly than we ought. He directed us to think with sober judgment, each according to the measure of faith that God has assigned us.[219] Thinking highly of ourselves can make us prone to not forgive ourselves. How could someone like me be so stupid? If you find it hard to answer that question, this may be your problem.

So if you think you are standing, watch out that you do not fall.
(1 Corinthians 10:12)

Comparing Ourselves to Others

When in the midst of temptation, it's totally non-productive to look around and compare our temptations with those of others. When people compare themselves with others, they usually start to feel sorry for themselves, complaining, "It isn't fair! It isn't fair!" Well, of course, it isn't fair! Whoever said Satan was fair? Quite to the contrary, he will tempt us in every way possible. He will cause us to get sick or go bankrupt. He will attack our families, try to kill us and the people we love, try to destroy our reputation – or whatever he thinks will cause us to sin – so that we will not be able to be used by God. He will make life difficult, hoping we'll blame God and turn away from Him.

---

[218] See 1 Corinthians 13:4-7
[219] See Romans 12:3

Don't think Jesus was treated any better, or with any favoritism.

For we do not have a High Priest who is unable to sympathize with our weaknesses, but we have One who in every respect has been tested as we are, yet without sin. (Hebrews 4:15)

Through His own life, Jesus demonstrated that when the Holy Spirit is with us, in the middle of our temptations,

... we may receive mercy and find grace to help in time of need.
(Hebrews 4:16)

In other words, we don't have to handle our tests or temptations alone; the Holy Spirit is available to help in all aspects of spiritual warfare.

Another reason for not comparing our temptations or tests to those of anyone else, is that the devil treats everyone the same way: badly. If you feel your temptations seem to be worse than those of most other people, take it as a compliment, because it may well be that the reason for it is that God wants to use you more than most other people. Wouldn't that be wonderful?

Instead of complaining (which is one way to fail a temptation), we need to praise Jesus, and thank God for His goodness.

Paul modelled the way we should respond to difficulties. Throughout all the years he spent in jail and all the bad treatment and persecution he suffered, he did not succumb to the temptation to complain, but encouraged his brethren (us) to rejoice in our circumstances.

Rejoice always, pray without ceasing, give thanks in all circumstances; for this is the will of God in Christ Jesus for you.
(1 Thessalonians 5:16-18)

No testing has overtaken you that is not common to everyone. God is faithful, and He will not let you be tested beyond your strength, but with the testing He will also provide the way out so that you may be able to endure it. (1 Corinthians 10:13)

In other words, we do not have to face the devil alone. Our Heavenly Father, Jesus, the Holy Spirit – God will help us. All we have to remember is that we have not been left alone. We have His promise that He will never leave us.

... I will never leave you nor forsake you. (Hebrews 13:5)

In the midst of our worst nightmare of temptation, we have Jesus' words to remind us what to do.

Ask, and it will be given you; search, and you will find; knock, and the door will be opened for you. For everyone who asks receives, and everyone who searches finds, and for everyone who knocks, the door will be opened. (Matthew 7:7-8)

In the midst of our greatest temptations, the *greatest* temptation may be to not ask for help, thereby blocking the way of escape already provided by Jesus, the only One who knows the way of escape from temptation.

The bad news is that, in order to serve Jesus Christ, we must face the devil and endure testing and temptation. The good news is that with Jesus' help and with the power of the Holy Spirit, we can defeat the devil and he will have to flee. If we can resist and defeat the head of the kingdom of darkness, we can certainly resist and defeat his soldiers.

Seven

TACTICS OF DEMONS

Understanding How to Deal with the Tactics, Characteristics, Weapons and Agendas of Demons

Being able to recognize the plans, purposes, tactics and weapons of Satan is not enough when trying to be victorious in spiritual warfare. Assisting him in his kingdom of darkness, is a whole host of demons. Understanding of the following points is essential, in order to deal effectively with them.

1. We need to be able to tell the difference, just as Jesus did, between sin, physical sickness (infirmities or disease), mental or psychological disorders and possession by demons. Evil spirits are not responsible for everything that happens, either in the world or in the lives of people, whether they are Christians or not. If they were, we would not need the gift of discerning of spirits.

The main problem we have to deal with is sin. Of course we have to be prepared to deal with evil spirits when they rear their ugly heads, but the ability to recognize what is involved, is critical.

God makes it perfectly clear that the main problem with the human race is sin. We need to be able to recognize the difference between sin and possession by evil spirits.

As it is written: "None is righteous, no, not one; no one understands, no one seeks God. All have turned aside, together they have gone wrong; no one does good, not even one." (Romans 3:10-12)

For there is no distinction; since all have sinned and fall short of the glory of God, they are all justified by His grace as a gift, through the redemption which is in Christ Jesus, whom God put forward as an expiation by His blood, to be received by faith. (Romans 3:22b-25a)

The Holy Spirit equips some people with the gift of discerning of spirits,[220] so they can easily determine the difference between sin and the work of evil spirits.

The Greek word for "to shudder" is "phrisso" which means to tremble or shake with fear. Many people do not understand that the fear they may be experiencing is a result of their sin, rather than anything to do with demonic activity. They mistake the conviction of sin, caused by the Holy Spirit's presence, for the presence of the devil or evil spirits.

This confusion happens when people think God's presence will always make them feel good. While human fellowship may make us feel good, the fellowship of the Holy Spirit involves a calling to repentance of our sin. Failure to respond to God's convicting nudges results in tension and anxiety. Repentance is the only route to the peace of God that passes all understanding.

And the peace of God, which passes all understanding, will keep your hearts and your minds in Christ Jesus. (Philippians 4:7)

Anybody who is preoccupied with demons is in sin, because we are supposed to be preoccupied with Jesus.

2. Demons try to degrade, isolate and cause illnesses in people. Some demoniacs live in deserted places like the tombs[221] or inhabit

---

[220] See 1 Corinthians 12:10
[221] See Luke 8:29

ruined cities.²²² Some live in houses.²²³ Most often, they invade the bodies of people, taking possession of them and living in them, degrading and causing illness in them.²²⁴

3. Demons may imitate various mental, emotional, psychological and physical symptoms in the people whom they possess. That is why the healing of a sick person (who is actually possessed) is described as driving or casting out malignant demonic forces.²²⁵

The most frequently copied psychological problems are schizophrenia and multiple personality disorders. Jesus had to deal with evil spirits who caused blindness, dumbness, deafness, epilepsy and the like. The demoniacs of Jesus' day, all appeared to have psychological problems. However, it's not always so obvious today. Legitimate physical and psychological problems, often resulting from people being mistreated by other people, are often hidden by the sophistication of our society. Chemical imbalances and food deficiencies can lead to legitimate physical and psychological problems. It goes without saying, that there will be physical and psychological problems, caused by sin, in the lives of those who have sinned. We have to be careful to learn how to recognize people's problems, or else we can hurt them and worsen their condition.

Because demons will mimic physical and psychological problems, people who have been possessed can run into problems with the medical community. When they attempt to explain their symptoms to their doctors, they are often regarded as suffering from delusions, or auditory and visual hallucinations. They are often diagnosed as paranoid (at the worst) and psychotic (at the least). The result is generally either hospitalization, heavy medication, or both. These people learn quickly not to be forthright with their psychiatrists, psychologists, counselors, clergy, friends or family members. They know they risk being trapped, if they dare make honest calls for help. They quickly learn to try to live with the

---

²²² See Revelation 18:2
²²³ See Luke 11:24
²²⁴ See Luke 8:30; Matthew 11:18; Luke 7:33; 8:27; John 7:20; 8:48 ff; 10:20
²²⁵ See Matthew 7:22; 9:32; 9:34; 10:8; 12:24 ff.; 17:18; Mark 1:34,39; 3:15,22; 6:13; 7:26; 7:29f. ; 9:38; 16:9,17; Luke 4:41; 8:2,33,35,38; 9:49; 11:14ff.; 13:32

thing that is controlling, tormenting, and slowly destroying their lives. They often end up locked in psychiatric wards, heavily medicated.

One Halloween, the year the movie *The Exorcist* came out, I had been receiving a lot of publicity from radio interviews, television talk show appearances and my review of the movie in the Toronto Star. Demon possession was suddenly a hot topic. Consequently, I was receiving invitations from various places to go and speak. One of those invitations came from a couples club at a church in Norval, Ontario. I knew I had been invited as a Halloween prank. The people assumed, as many did, that the topic of evil spirits and possession were just medieval superstition.

As I shared with them some of our ministry experiences, the atmosphere changed from one of laughter to dead seriousness. As I described some of the symptoms connected with possession, these people realized that they knew people who were trapped in a society that did not take them seriously and which left them at the mercy of a spirit world that they did not understand. I explained that when evil spirits or demons possess a person, they will often imitate real emotional, psychological and physical problems, such as schizophrenia. I made it clear that there is a real psychological disorder called schizophrenia, because some people want to believe that every emotional, psychological and physical problem is caused by demons, when that is not the truth. When demons are involved, they simply cause the symptoms to appear.

At the end of the meeting, the pastor's wife told me that I had described her best friend, who had been in and out of psychiatric wards for many years. Everyone at the meeting knew this woman. The pastor's wife asked me if I would be willing to see her and hopefully set her free from her problem. I agreed, but only if her friend would call me and set up an appointment herself. The woman lived in Georgetown, Ontario.

A few days later, I received a telephone call from this very troubled and upset woman. We had a long conversation, during which she told me that she had been suffering from her problem for eight years. She had not been able to sleep without medication for that whole time. Every time she tried to tell a doctor about what she saw and heard in her house, she would be put on heavier doses of drugs. She had learned not to tell any professional counselor what she had really been experiencing. After discussing her condition, I realized she was demon-possessed.

After she shared with me all that she had been going through, I asked her to come to my office. She explained that she could not go near Christian churches or she would have a total breakdown and end up spending weeks or months in a hospital ward. In fact, her doctor and husband had forbidden her to go into a Christian church. I then explained to her that, if she had the problem that I thought she had (I didn't tell her what I suspected), she would not have it after she left my office. She found that hard to believe.

"Do you mean to tell me that after suffering with this for eight years, after one visit to your office, I will no longer have the problem?" Her voice was incredulous.

"That is exactly what I mean."

She said, "But, what if you are wrong and I have a breakdown? My husband and doctors will be angry with me and put me back in the hospital. I can't risk it."

I then told her that if I were wrong, I would take personal responsibility for her and talk to both her husband and her doctor. Finally, she agreed to come.

When the woman entered my office, I saw a worn-out, very plain, unattractive person with dark circles under her eyes. She appeared to be about fifty-years-old. She was wearing no makeup and a badly fitting green dress and her hair was dishevelled. She had a club foot and limped badly with a built-up shoe on one foot. She was a pitiful sight.

She sat down, obviously nervous and uncomfortable. I asked her to share with me about when her life had fallen apart. She said it happened when she and her husband moved to Georgetown, in Ontario. As we talked, I mentally noted that she had physical reactions whenever I mentioned the name of Jesus. She became very agitated.

I then asked her two questions: Do you want to be set free – and are you willing to let Jesus Christ be your Savior and Lord and receive the Holy Spirit?

In obvious desperation, she replied, "Yes. Yes."

I then approached her and took authority over the spirits, without touching her. I said, "In the Name of Jesus Christ, I command all evil and unclean spirits to leave this woman now and go to the abyss." They left her with hardly a twitch. I then placed my hands on her head and had her follow me in prayer, "Dear Jesus, I want you to be my Savior and Lord. Please forgive me for any sin or wrong I have done. Please fill my heart with the Holy Spirit and take charge of me. Thank you, Jesus."

She could hardly believe that her nightmare was over.

I gave her a Bible and some Christian books that would help her to develop a healthy relationship with God. Unfortunately, I made the mistake of also giving her a book which described her condition. She telephoned me the next day and explained that she had no idea the problem she had was so dangerous. I told her to throw the book away because it no longer applied to her.

I had forgotten that after people are set free from demon possession, more often than not, they have no memory of the experience. Very often, they have memory blackouts coinciding with the times when the demon was in control. On the other hand, some people have clear memories and can tell of having watched themselves, under the control of the evil spirit, do and say things over which they had no control. They describe the situation like an out-of-body experience; like viewing themselves from a third party perspective, but from inside their minds.

Several months later, my secretary called on our intercom and asked if I would see a young lady who had just come into the office. I agreed and asked her to send her down to my office. I responded to the soft knock on my door by inviting whoever was there to please come in. The door opened and there was a very attractive woman in her twenties who looked as though she had just come from a hair stylist. She was well dressed in a red dress and matching red high-heeled shoes. She wore makeup that was not overdone. She smiled at me and asked, "Do you remember me?"

I said, "I'm sorry but I do not remember you. Where did we meet?"

She smiled and laughed lightly, saying, "I am the woman from Georgetown!" She sat down and explained, "I want to tell you what happened after I left your office. First, my mind was very clear. I was completely healed. As I was driving home, I felt a strange pain in my club foot. It was healed and, as you can see, it is normal."

She had been transformed, completely set free and healed of her deformed foot. I could hardly believe my eyes. What a miracle!

She had come because of a problem her six-year-old son was having. She said, "I'm wondering if the problem I had could have been transferred to my son, because he is having problems like I had."

"No," I said. I was puzzled, because I had sent those evil spirits to the abyss. Silently, I asked God for wisdom. Then, I asked how long she and her family had lived in the house she was living in.

"Oh, about eight years," she replied. That was exactly the time when she had been possessed.

I asked her if, when they moved into that house, she had noticed anything strange.

"Oh, you mean the spirits. There are the nice ones and the bad ones. I like the nice ones, but the bad ones are terrible."

"Whether they seem good or bad, they're all the same. They are all evil spirits who are playing games with you. They may seem nice at one time, but then they'll turn nasty and try to hurt, harass or possess you or your family members." I then said, "Look, with your permission, I'll follow you to your house. I'll go through the house and get rid of the evil spirits."

She agreed. Before going into the house, she asked, "Do you want me to tell you what room they live in?"

I smiled, "No. Let me tell you what room they *used* to live in – after I go through the house."

Before going inside, we prayed with her little son to invite Jesus to be his Savior and for the protection of the Holy Spirit. I asked them to remain outside while I went through it, because evil spirits will sometimes try to hurt people. Then, I went through the house, room by room, and cast out the evil spirits and asked the Holy Spirit to fill every room with His presence and to protect their family.

I heard from the woman several times, while we lived in Brampton, to let me know that everything was fine and that she was free to go to church and serve Jesus Christ.

4. When trying to determine whether a person is possessed by an evil spirit, it helps to remember that demons will react when we use the Name of Jesus frequently in conversation. If a demon is in possession of a person, the person will become highly agitated and have to run away, or the person will suddenly appear to fall asleep, just as if a light switch was turned off. This can occur in a worship service, or in any kind of fellowship group. It can be confusing, because not everyone who falls asleep in a worship service, or a fellowship meeting, is possessed with an evil spirit; they may just be bored or tired.

About five years ago, a woman who worked in the local Christian bookstore, told us about a woman shopper who had been looking for books that might help her and her husband deal with their youngest son, whom they were unable to control. The boy would fly into fits of anger, hitting his older brothers and sister. Since they couldn't protect his older eight-year-old brother, they arranged for him to take self-defense lessons.

One day, the parents were in the bookstore, telling the owner about their struggles with their son. They told about how they had taken the boy to counselors and nothing had seemed to help. They even recounted the fact that Christian friends had suggested the boy might be demon possessed; and how frustrated they were, because no one seemed to know anybody they could call on for help, should that be the case. The owner of the bookstore was unable to recommend anybody either. Our friend had been listening to the conversation and mentioned the possibility that I might be able to help. The parents wondered if she could call me, which she did.

Upon hearing about the situation, I agreed that the boy might be possessed and, if the parents agreed, I would be willing to see him. Our friend contacted the mother who lived in the small village of Holstein, Ontario, about fifty miles from our home. The mother, in turn, called me. She described how the boy reacted badly, whenever the family tried to pray with him. He would scream if they tried to tell him about Jesus or read the Bible to him.

I assured her I would be able to help if the boy was demon-possessed. When I arrived at their house, I was invited in and sat down to talk at the kitchen table so I might assess the problem. The father and three of the children were at home and the eldest, a teenager, was at school. The mother called the children out of their rooms so they could meet me. The problem child came to me, welcomed me and climbed up to sit on my lap. The eleven-year-old daughter said, "Are you here to get rid of that bad spirit that hurts him and makes him do bad things?"

Shocked, the mother asked, "What spirit are you talking about?"

The girl responded, "The one that keeps turning the lights on and off at night and opens and closes the doors so we can't sleep."

The mother pointed to the boy on my lap, "I thought he was doing those things."

The children said, "No! No! No! It's the bad spirit!"

I then explained that I could get rid of this evil spirit that was causing problems in the house and harassing the little boy. "But first," I said, "each of you need to invite Jesus to be your Savior and receive the baptism of the Holy Spirit."

The mother said, "We are all born again Christians, except our youngest boy."

I asked the little boy, "Would you like to invite Jesus to be your Savior and forgive you for all the bad things you have done?"

He enthusiastically agreed and prayed with me.

I explained that, for their protection, they all needed to receive the baptism of the Holy Spirit and speak in tongues, so that in the future, they would be able to deal with any evil spirit that tried to disturb them. They all agreed. So, all six of us joined hands in a circle and prayed. They were all baptized with the Holy Spirit and began speaking in tongues – the father and mother, daughter and two brothers. I then asked all of them to step outside so I could go through the house and get rid of the bad spirit that had been causing the problems. They did. I went through the entire house and commanded the evil spirit to go to the abyss and stay there. Then, I invited the Holy Spirit to fill the house.

Before I could say goodbye, the five-year-old boy asked, "Can I invite Jesus into my heart again?"

"That's not necessary," I told him, "because He is with you and will not leave you."[226] There is no age limit for people to receive salvation and the baptism of the Holy Spirit. The Holy Spirit is the counselor, who will guide us into the truth. We all – children, teenagers, adults, senior citizens – need His daily guidance so we can fulfill God's plans for our lives.

5. Demons react to Christians who are born-again and baptized with the Holy Spirit. They will cause the person who is possessed to become agitated and very emotional. The reason for this, of course, is that they are tormented by the presence of the Holy Spirit in the life of a Christian. The very presence of Jesus causes the demons to be in torment.

For many years, pastors and counselors, who seem unable to cast demons out, have brought people to me who they suspect of being possessed. Most often, their diagnosis has proven to be correct.

Two women on the staff of a Baptist church, brought a twenty-five-year-old woman to my office. A group of people in a Bible study and prayer meeting had spent three hours one night and four hours on

---

[226] See Hebrews 13:5

a second night, trying to cast demons out of this young woman. The demons were totally resistant to their attempts and so they brought the woman to me for help.

As the young woman and I started to talk, the demon began to react to the point where the young woman said, "I've got to get out of here." I have discovered, that people who are possessed with demons, will react very emotionally to the Name of Jesus Christ. Simply talking about Him, and using His Name frequently in a conversation, will cause the demons to react. They will get very uneasy, to the point where they will start to curse and swear and attempt to get away.

Before she had a chance to get out of her chair, I asked the young woman two questions.

The first was, "Do you want to be set free?" The reality is that not every person who is possessed by demons wants to be set free, because initially, the demons may give him or her an enjoyable religious experience. In this case, the (demonic) religious experience had already turned sour, causing her anxiety and pain.

The second question was, "Are you willing to receive Jesus Christ as your Savior and LORD and receive the baptism of the Holy Spirit?" She replied yes to both questions. I then suggested that we go into our chapel in order to deal with the problem.

The young woman said, "Oh, no! I don't want to go through all of that again! I don't want to waste a lot more time."

I explained, "We don't allow that to happen here. You will be set free so fast that you will hardly be able to believe it happened so quickly."

Reassured, she agreed and the four of us went into the chapel, where I asked the two questions again. Her answer was the same. I took authority over the woman in the Name of Jesus Christ and commanded the demons to leave her body, to go to the abyss and to stay there. Immediately, they were gone! I then prayed with her, with the laying on of hands, and she repented for her sin. She received salvation and the baptism of the Holy Spirit and fell to the floor, speaking in tongues.

The two women who accompanied her were surprised. One asked, "Is she free? Have they gone?"

I said, "Yes, she is free and they are gone." I knew they were not convinced, because the exorcism had happened so quickly. However, a few days later, one of them telephoned to say, "She is wonderfully set free – but why couldn't we cast them out?"

I explained, "The demons knew that you do not believe the whole Bible."

She reacted, "That's not true. We are a Bible-believing church."

I asked, "Tell me about the baptism of the Holy Spirit and the gifts of the Holy Spirit."

She said, "Well, that's a matter of opinion."

I said, "You're right! The demons found out that you have the wrong opinion and so they didn't have to obey you. The Bible contains God's new covenant with people, and when we decide we can pick and choose what parts of it to believe and obey, we lose our spiritual authority."

The good news is, the young woman was set free to serve Jesus Christ.

As in the story of the seven sons of Sceva,[227] the demon in the possessed man recognized who Jesus and Paul were, because they were filled with, and led by, the Holy Spirit. The same is true about anyone who has received the baptism of the Holy Spirit with signs following. The first sign of authenticity is the authority of believers to cast out demons; and the second is the ability to speak in new tongues (which should be correctly translated "in new languages"). This ability demonstrates the authority of Jesus Christ and the power of the Holy Spirit to demons. They know the words being spoken are under the guidance of the Holy Spirit. They know they must obey such believers. Unbelievers, or religious people who are not under the Lordship of Jesus, do not have the signs following. Demons know they do not have to obey them but, in fact, can resist them and attack them without fear.

---

[227] See Acts 19 – See also pages 341-343 for a fuller treatment.

6. Demons influence people to develop their own religious traditions and doctrines, far from what is written in Scripture.

So, for the sake of your tradition, you have made void the Word of God. You hypocrites! Well did Isaiah prophesy of you, when he said: "This people honors me with their lips, but their heart is far from Me; in vain do they worship Me, teaching as doctrines the precepts of men." (Matthew 15:6–20; see also Mark 7:6-13)

For this reason, Paul wrote to the Corinthians:

... that you may learn by us not to go beyond what is written, that none of you may be puffed up in favor of one against another. (1 Corinthians 4:6)

This is what we see happening today, in Christian churches where people are having all kinds of (false) revelations, by which they misinterpret the New Testament. They think it gives them permission to develop church programs which actually originate in the doctrines of demons. These people accept information from evil spirits because they do not know the voice of the Good Shepherd.

Richard Syrette, the host of the Toronto radio talk show mentioned earlier, found that in Toronto, there are many people who have been possessed and there are numerous houses and buildings that have been invaded by demons. From the the number of calls into his program, he is concerned about all the harmful things happening to those who are being victimized. He cannot understand why so few people are able to set people free from demons.

I can answer his question. The main reason so few people can set people free from demons, is that Christian clergy and so-called "believers" have been accepting doctrines of demons which teach them that the Bible is not the Word of God and that the covenant God made with man, is not accurate. These doctrines of demons claim the Bible is faulty, unreliable or not to be taken literally. Therefore, they have no power of the Holy Spirit working through them to set people free. They teach that it is not necessary for people to be, as Jesus said in John 3:5, *"born of water and of the Spirit."* Those words really mean that they must, along with salvation, be baptized with the Holy Spirit so they will have authority over the devil and be able to set people free from evil spirits.

> *You are of your father the devil, and your will is to do your father's desires. He was a murderer from the beginning, and has nothing to do with the truth, because there is no truth in him. When he lies, he speaks according to his own nature, for he is a liar and the father of lies.* (John 8:44)

The doctrine of demons I hear most often, is that God has stopped doing the things recorded in the Bible. The demons teach that, even though people have sinned and fallen short of the glory of God, they will be saved, regardless of their lifestyles. They teach that people should do whatever is right in their own minds and that there is no such thing as Heaven or Hell. One of their favourite lies is that there is no Satan and that there are no such beings as demons.

7. Demons want people to believe there are certain things in the Bible that God no longer does. For example, people may try to discredit portions of the New Testament by saying, "God no longer baptizes people with the Holy Spirit, as recorded in the Book of Acts, so it is no longer necessary to speak in tongues or to receive the gifts of the Holy Spirit."[228]

The error of relegating the baptism of the Holy Spirit to the dusty shelf of antiquity is a sure sign of demonic influence in a church. If it were true that it's not for today, God would no longer heal people through prayer or distribute the gifts of the Holy Spirit among His people. All the miraculous work described in the New Testament would have stopped with the death of the original disciples. However, the history of the church proves this to be untrue.

8. Demons tell Christians that the work of the Holy Spirit is really the work of the devil, trying to cause them to commit the unpardonable sin of blasphemy against the Holy Spirit.[229] The result is confusion and an

---
[228] See Romans 12:6-8; 1 Corinthians 12:8-10
[229] See Mark 3:27-29; Luke 12:9-11

inability of many people to identify the authentic work of the Holy Spirit. Even worse, demons misidentify the work of evil spirits and people's sin as the work of the Holy Spirit.

9. Demons are especially effective in misleading Christians regarding the baptism in the Holy Spirit. Through the years, since the amazing coming of the Holy Spirit at Pentecost,[230] the devil and his followers have been chipping away at the fundamental truth Jesus taught, just prior to His ascension. They have been very successful in drawing the church away from recognition of the baptism in the Holy Spirit as a tenet of the Christian faith. Jesus said,

"John baptized with water, but before many days you shall be baptized with the Holy Spirit." (Acts 1:5b)

This is a brilliant ploy, because it is only through receiving the Holy Spirit, that people have the power and authority to expel demons and send them to the abyss.

It is not uncommon for demons to attempt to bluff their way around Christians, hoping Spirit-baptized believers will not have the boldness or knowledge to deal with them head-on. They lie to escape embarrassing defeat at the hands of informed and knowledgeable Christians.

10. Demons try to deceive us concerning the coming of our LORD Jesus Christ (see 2 Thessalonians 2:1). Paul warns:

"The coming of the lawless one by the activity of Satan will be with all power and pretended signs and wonders, and with all wicked deception for those who are to perish, because they refused to love the truth and so be saved. Therefore God sends upon them a strong delusion, to make them believe what is false, so that all may be condemned who did not believe the truth but had pleasure in unrighteousness." (2 Thessalonians 2:9-12)

11. The devil and demons have diluted authentic Christian theology with their own demonic theology, which essentially dispenses

---
[230] See Acts 2

with the necessity of following the terms of the New Testament. Jesus referred to this corrupted theology as the "traditions of men."

> ... the traditions of men which make void the word of God. (Mark 7:13)

> ... holding the form of religion but denying the power of it. Avoid such people. (2 Timothy 3:5)

Paul warned of this theology from Hell – or should I call it this theology that *leads to* Hell.

> Now the Spirit expressly says that in later times some will depart from the faith by giving heed to deceitful spirits and doctrines of demons, through the pretensions of liars whose consciences are seared, who forbid marriage and enjoin abstinence from foods which God created to be received with thanksgiving by those who believe and know the truth. (1 Timothy 4:1-3)

12. Demons facilitate the drifting away from sound doctrine through the newer Bible paraphrases, which rewrite the Scriptures, to make the demands of the New Covenant optional and which fail to take seriously the work of either the Holy Spirit or the devil and his evil spirits. Today, it's clear that, in most church circles, the clergy do not recognize the seriousness of sin, the devil or demons. This has resulted in believers becoming as vulnerable as unbelievers. Believers who have been victimized by the devil and demons, through false doctrines and sin in the churches, are leaving the churches because they have to find a place of safety.

13. Demons try to make people believe they are gods who can perform false wonders such as making what appears to be gold, flutter down from the ceiling in the midst of a spiritual meeting. What people see, in fact, is fool's gold and what they are experiencing is a delusion, similar to a performance of a professional magician who gives a convincing impression of reality. All other so-called gods are demons.

> ...what pagans sacrifice they offer to demons and not to God. I do not want you to be partners with demons. You cannot drink the cup

of the Lord and the cup of demons. You cannot partake of the table of the Lord and the table of demons. Shall we provoke the Lord to jealousy? Are we stronger than He? (1 Corinthians 10:20-24)

14. Demons pretend to be angels sent from Jesus Christ. Since the devil is known as the prince of the power of the air, he likes people to worship him and his messengers, the demons. People believe they are from God. They swallow their false prophecies and revelations instead of believing the Bible. Such people place themselves under the same judgment that the devil and the demons receive in the Lake of Fire.

...even Satan disguises himself as an angel of light. So it is not strange if his servants also disguise themselves as servants of righteousness. Their end will correspond to their deeds. (2 Corinthians 11:14-15)

And the beast was captured, and with it the false prophet who in its presence had worked the signs by which he deceived those who had received the mark of the beast and those who worshiped its image. These two were thrown alive into the Lake of Fire that burns with sulphur. (Revelation 19:20; see also 20:10, 14)

... and if any one's name was not found written in the Book of Life, he was thrown into the Lake of Fire. (Revelation 20:15)

But as for the cowardly, the faithless, the polluted, as for murderers, fornicators, sorcerers, idolaters, and all liars, their lot shall be in the lake that burns with fire and sulphur, which is the second death. (Revelation 21:8)

This is why John warned believers to test the spirits.

Beloved, do not believe every spirit, but test the spirits to see whether they are from God; for many false prophets have gone out into the world....Whoever knows God listens to us, and he who is not of God does not listen to us. By this we know the Spirit of Truth and the spirit of error. (1 John 4:1,6)

15. Demons have made it unfashionable to believe they exist. In the interim between the coming of the Holy Spirit at Pentecost and the evolution of our sophisticated western society, the devil and his demons have gradually gained success in making the understanding of the spiritual problems of sin, demon possession, and the works of the devil, not only unfashionable, but subject to mocking – despite the fact that in all other societies, they are recognized and taken seriously, even though their misinformed leaders cannot deal with them.

In his book, *The Screwtape Letters* (instructions from a professional devil/demon named Screwtape, to his nephew Wormwood, a junior tempter),[231] C.S. Lewis writes, "My dear Wormwood, I wonder you should ask me whether it is essential to keep the patient in ignorance of your own existence. That question, at least for the moment, has been answered for us by the High Command. Our policy, for the moment, is to conceal ourselves."

16. Demons use occult practices as substitute worship, to make people believe that, once demons have possessed houses or people, there is no higher authority that can make them leave. They, themselves, however, are very aware of who Jesus is and the fact that Christians, who have the power of the Holy Spirit, have full authority over them.

Then he goes and brings seven other spirits more evil than himself, and they enter and dwell there; and the last state of that man becomes worse than the first. (Luke 11:26)

17. Demons appeal to the greed in people who want the rewards and benefits of the Christian gospel but, like the rich young man who wanted eternal life, do not want to do what is necessary to obtain it.[232] The demons discourage Christians from tithing as a means of leading them into financial problems.[233]

18. Demons often hook people by giving them a warm religious experience, accepting them just as they are, making them as comfortable as possible and definitely not requiring them to deal with their sin. According to Paul, demons encourage people to make idols that represent them and then to direct their worship to these idols.

---

[231] HarperCollins, March 6, 2001, p.32
[232] See Matthew 19:16-22; Luke 10:25; 18:18
[233] For further study, see Acts 10:4; 2 Corinthians 9:7; Hebrews 7:1-19 and Malachi 3:6-12

Claiming to be wise, they became fools, and exchanged the glory of the immortal God for images resembling mortal man or birds or animals or reptiles. (Romans 1:22)

19. Demons have their best success when they pick on children, the sick, people running away from God and anyone else who is vulnerable.

20. Demons or evil spirits will move into houses or buildings and occupy them. They are often called ghosts, or mistakenly thought to be somebody who once lived in, worked at, or frequented the place. They will harass and bother those who live or work there. They will attempt to possess the people who live in a house and turn them into demoniacs. Many people, when they move into a new house, discover there are either unseen, or sometimes visible, spirits living there. Some stay and attempt to live with the spirits. Others will evacuate the premises and sell the house to some other unsuspecting family.

Whenever I cast evil spirits out of any building, house, apartment, or church building, I call the procedure "blessing out the building."

A few years ago, I received a telephone call from a friend in Toronto, Ontario. He was shopping for a new house. A real estate agent had shown him one that was listed at $50,000., a price well below the other houses in the neighborhood. It was in excellent condition, but it had a resident ghost. He wanted to know if there was any way the spirit could be removed. I told him how to do it. He followed my instructions and made an excellent purchase.

Today, in Canada, if a house has some kind of a problem, the owners and the realtors who are attempting to sell the building, must make potential buyers aware of the problem. If they do not disclose that they are selling a stigmatized property, they can be held liable for any problems or damages that might occur because of the problem. "Stigmas fall under three categories: pure or psychological stigma, physical stigma and neighborhood conditions. Pure stigma includes properties that have been the scene of murders, suicides, deaths and haunting. These spooky issues are referred to as pure stigmas, because there is no physical harm to the property itself."[234] Here is tacit acknowledgement from the business world that demons exist and cause problems.

My son Karl's new neighbor told him how happy he and his wife were to have moved into their new house because of the problems they had endured in their previous home. They often discovered their furniture had been moved around and everything was in a mess when they came home from work. This continued to happen almost every day. They concluded that teenagers were breaking in and doing damage while they were away. Hoping to shed some light on the mystery and catch the culprits, they purchased some security cameras and installed them. Much to their astonishment, the cameras captured the image of a dark, cloudy spirit moving from room to room, dishevelling the furniture, pictures and contents of each room. Terrified, they called a realtor and sold the house. Fortunately, for them, the evil spirit did not follow them to their new house.

A few years ago, I was asked by the mother of a five-year-old boy in Southampton, Ontario, to go to their home, because their son was complaining about a bad boy who was hitting him and hurting him. The boy was afraid to go into a couple of rooms and did not want to sleep in the dark. Consequently, they had to leave light on in his room. Although the parents could not see any other child, it was evident there were bruises on their son.

When I went to their house, the little boy and his father were home. His father told me that what his wife had said was true, but added that they knew there was a spirit in the house, because they had taken pictures on their digital camera. The photos showed not only the demon that looked like a boy, but some others that looked like circles moving around their house.

Since the boy's mother was at work and had the camera with her, I went to where she worked to see the pictures. When I got there, I explained that, although they were Christians, they needed to receive the baptism of the Holy Spirit so they would be protected from the evil spirits

---
[234] The Realtor Edge Newsletter, July & August 2005

and would have the authority to get rid of any that came to their house in the future. She agreed, received the baptism of the Holy Spirit and spoke in tongues right there.

I returned to their home and prayed with their son and his father and they, too, received the baptism of the Holy Spirit with the evidence of speaking in tongues.

That done, driving the demons from their home and into the abyss was an uneventful matter. When they took pictures of the rooms, there was not a demon to be seen.

Jesus warned us about what happens when an unclean spirit is sent out of a man and searches for a new place in which to live. If he cannot find a new place, he will return, to see if his old house has a new resident or whether it's still available. If there's no new resident, he goes out and gets seven other spirits to return and share his house. The same principle applies to people and buildings. It is a wise policy to have a newly-acquired house blessed out by a Spirit-filled Christian so that you and your family will not inherit spirit problems.

Jesus' warning about the returning demon is not meant to worry us.[235] Rather, it is given to teach us to do ministry biblically and effectively. If we minister correctly, people will be set free and receive the ministry of salvation and the baptism of the Holy Spirit so they will be protected. Through this teaching, Jesus is telling us that, when we get rid of an evil spirit, it is necessary to replace the evil spirit with the Holy Spirit. Only then can Jesus be LORD over that person, leaving no room for an evil spirit to re-possess the person and make his or her life eight time worse. After going through a house and casting out any demons, it is vital to ask the Holy Spirit to come in and make His presence known.

Shortly after I appeared on national television to discuss the movie, *The Exorcist*, I was invited to share about deliverance ministry with the Western Toronto Ministerial Association on a Saturday morning. The membership is composed of clergy from most Christian churches in the area. My topic was "Deliverance Ministry Today." I shared the problem of

---
[235] See Luke 11:24-26

people being possessed, harassed, degraded and made sick by evil spirits. Among those who came, was a Baptist pastor who believed neither in the existence of demons nor in their ability to possess people or invade homes, houses or buildings. For him, possession was an old wives' tale. He assumed demons were simply the products of over-active imaginations or hallucinations. He let it be known in the meeting that he did not believe in evil spirits and questioned my theological education.

That same afternoon, I received a telephone call from the Baptist minister. He explained that when he listened to me share that morning about spiritual warfare and dealing with evil spirits, he thought I was somewhat misled, if not crazy; but early that afternoon, something had occurred to change his mind.

A niece, who was attending the University of Waterloo, Ontario, had packed up her belongings and left the college residence where she was living and had gone to her uncle for help. She was terrified, crying and almost incoherent as she described what had been happening in the Conrad Grebel Mennonite College where she lived. She told him that a black shadowy spirit had taken up residence in the college chapel. It could be observed moving around the chapel and was distracting to anybody who tried to worship or pray as it flew around. It made distracting sounds and threatened anybody who went into the chapel. From a window in the entrance door, it could be seen moving around the chapel, like a buzzard looking for prey. None of the students were willing to go into the chapel and the services were cancelled. The girl did not want to return to the college and had determined to drop out of university and return home.

After listening to his niece, the minister realized that perhaps my report about spiritual warfare was not as crazy as he had thought. He asked me to speak with her. After telling me her story about what had been happening in the college chapel, she said, "If you don't believe me, you can talk with the president of our Christian college group."

Just to confirm her story, I called the young man and he described the same strange occurrences. Then he asked, "Can you get rid of it?"

I confirmed that I could and would. I arranged to go over to the college chapel a few days later at midnight, the best time to cast the demon out of the chapel, because there would be fewer students around and it would attract the least attention. I met with the I.V.C.F. President and some other Christian students, and asked them to stay outside the chapel praying. One young woman, who had a Mennonite background and who was terrified by the demon explained, "What happened one night, is that a witch wind came into the college chapel. My parents told me about this kind of a spirit. There isn't anything we can do about it. I'm all packed to go home tomorrow."

"After tonight," I explained, "the demon will be gone." I then instructed the Christian students to stay outside, in the hall, and pray while I went into the chapel. I emphasized, "No matter what happens, do not come into the chapel." Also, I asked them not to allow anyone else to enter the chapel while I was exorcising the demon.

Before entering the chapel, I looked through the small window and could see this black spirit floating, like the Goodyear blimp, and circling around the chapel like a bird of prey. I went inside and, taking authority, I said, "Evil spirit, I command you in the Name of Jesus Christ to leave this chapel." It began to swoop around the chapel like a wind, making a howling noise and causing the lights, which hung from the ceiling, to spin around as it swooped threateningly towards me, but without touching me. I shouted again, "In the Name of Jesus Christ, I command you, evil spirit, to leave this chapel and to go to the abyss and stay there." It made one final circle around the chapel and departed to the abyss.

Then, I asked the Holy Spirit to fill the chapel with His presence and to allow the peace of God, that passes all understanding, to fall upon the chapel. I then went out into the hallway and invited the praying students to come inside. "The evil spirit is gone! Jesus is Lord in this place again." We prayed, thanking Jesus that He has given us all authority in Heaven and on earth to cast out demons in His Name.

And these signs will accompany those who believe: in My Name they will cast out demons ... (Mark 16:17)

Several weeks later, I received a telephone call to let me know that every thing was fine in the chapel.

In another situation of evil spirits occupying a dwelling, I received a referral from one of my nieces with regard to a house where one of her friends lived with her family. It was in the village of Shallow Lake, Ontario. For over 100 years, this house had been haunted by evil spirits which victimized the inhabitants.

The young couple who were living there, had a six-year-old son. The evil spirit had appeared to the little boy one night and had brought along other evil spirits. The child told his mom, "Last night the little boy came to visit me and he brought his friends with him who live in the ground, but they're not like dead people."

His mother knew about that so-called "little boy," because she had grown up with his visitations, during which he brought those "friends of his" who lived in the ground, but were not like dead people. She remembered, vividly, the torment she had lived with as a child, growing up in the house. She did not want her son to have to grow up with the antics and torturous experiences that she and her brothers and sisters, parents, grandparents and great grandparents had suffered, but she didn't know what to do.

One day, when she went to pick up her mail, she told our niece, who worked in the small post office, what had happened. That was when my niece called and asked me to do something about getting rid of the demons.

I met the woman and my niece at the house. I assured the mother that the Holy Spirit could get rid of those evil spirits. I explained that, for their protection, both she and her little boy would need to invite Jesus to be their Savior and Lord and receive the baptism in the Holy Spirit.

"I'll do anything to protect my family from those spirits," the woman replied. So, we prayed together and both she and her son received Jesus and the baptism of the Holy Spirit and began to speak in tongues.

I asked them to stay outside, while I went through the house to get rid of the demons. I cautioned them not to come inside, no matter what noise they might hear from inside the house.

I started with the upstairs and then went through the rooms on the main floor, commanding the evil spirits to leave. Expecting one door to open into a closet, I discovered it actually led to a stairway down into an unfinished basement. As I walked down the stairs, an evil spirit grabbed me by both of my legs, through the unfinished stairs, and tripped me so that I went flying, head-first toward the rocks jutting out of the unfinished floor. I threw my arms out in front of me to cushion my fall. My hands, wrists and forearms were scratched and bleeding. I got very angry and said, "That is enough! I command every evil and unclean spirit to leave this basement and this house and go to the abyss and stay there – in the Name of Jesus Christ!"

A loud crash ensued, like the sound of a door being slammed behind them, as the evil spirits left – after a hundred years of residence.

So if the Son makes you free, you will be free indeed. (John 8:36)

I cannot overemphasize how dangerous the ministry of casting out demons can be, if a person attempts to cast them out without the authority of salvation and having received the baptism of the Holy Spirit.

Home invasions are often a way demons will suddenly appear in a house or building. Some time ago, I received a frantic call from a friend, who had just had a weird occurrence in her home. Two strange women, whom she did not know, arrived at her door and rang her doorbell. When she opened the door, one of them said, "We are here to pray for you. May we come in?"

Since she did not know them, my friend asked them who they were and what church they were from. They would not tell her. Remembering what John had written, she refused to allow them to enter her house.

If any one comes to you and does not bring this doctrine, do not receive him into the house or give him any greeting; for he who greets him shares his wicked work. (2 John 1:10-11)

As my friend shut the door, one of the women began to pray. When my friend turned around, she saw mice running all over her house. One of her granddaughters was staying with her and, afraid they might hurt her, she carried her into her bedroom, shut the door and placed a towel in the space under door – but when she turned around, she saw mice coming out of her clothes closet. She scooped up her granddaughter, carried her outside, put her in her car and drove her to her mother's home.

She prayed about what to do and realized that the appearance of the mice had something to do with the two women who had come to her door. She called me and asked if this could be some kind of a curse or a spiritual attack. I agreed that it sounded like one and offered to drive to her home.

When I arrived, I have to admit that I have never seen so many mice running around anyone's house. I asked my friend to go outside and pray, while I dealt with the problem.

As I prayed about the problem, the Holy Spirit told me that these mice were evil spirits that needed to be cast out of the house. So, taking authority over the house, I commanded every evil and unclean spirit to leave each room in the Name of Jesus Christ and to go to the abyss and stay there. The so-called mice all disappeared. As usual, I then invited the Holy Spirit to fill every room with His presence and to protect my friend who lived there.

The mice have never returned. Evil spirits often take the tangible physical forms of animals and people.

The fact that demons can invade places of worship and discourage the preaching and ministry of the gospel of Jesus Christ, is generally not even considered when churches seem stuck in a rut, or encounter problems of various sorts.

While pastoring the United Church in Harriston, Ontario, I was puzzled by the fact that, during the Sunday worship services, there seemed to be something wrong; the people were not responding to our ministry, as I had formerly experienced. While the choir was singing, I began to pray about what was wrong.

I said, "Jesus, what is wrong here? Why are these people not free to worship and praise you and respond to the gospel?"

The Holy Spirit said, "They cannot respond, because there is an evil spirit in this place."

I was surprised, so I asked Him for confirmation from a third party. At the conclusion of the service, as people were leaving the building, a woman whispered cautiously to me, "Gordon, could there be an evil spirit hindering worship in this church?"

"I don't know," I answered, "but I am going to find out." That night, at midnight, I went down to the church building and turned on all the lights. I locked all the doors, so that I would not be interrupted as I went through the building to get rid of any evil spirits that might be there.

I started in the Christian Education building, moved through the church basement, went through the sanctuary and then went on into one of the two entrance towers, at the front of the church. In each of the rooms, I had commanded, "Every evil or unclean spirit, I command you, in the Name of Jesus Christ, to leave this room and this building and go to the abyss and stay there."

When I said this in the first entrance tower, I heard a loud crash, like someone slamming a big door. I moved on to the second tower, firmly repeating my instructions, to complete the blessing out of the entire church. Then, I ran quickly back through the building, checking each door to make certain they were locked and that no one had come in while I was blessing out the building. All doors remained locked. No one had come in. Then it dawned on me; I realized what the noise had been. It was the evil spirit, unhappily leaving, under protest, as it made its way to its designated place in the abyss. I then asked the Holy Spirit to fill the church with His presence, so that we could minister without hindrance.

At the next worship service, we saw people respond to an invitation for prayer for the first time in that church. A retired couple, Jack and Georgia Martin, both received Jesus Christ as their Savior and Lord, and both received the baptism of the Holy Spirit. Not only that, but Georgia was healed of a kidney problem. Later, Jack shared that he had been a church elder for fifty years and had never had the assurance of his salvation. Furthermore, he had never understood that he could receive the Holy Spirit and speak in tongues. The knowledge that he could hear God speaking to him and could pray for other people's needs transformed his life. He became an effective witness with the signs following.

On another occasion, I was asked by a friend, the pastor of a Methodist Church in Buffalo, New York, to visit his church building. An evil spirit had been manifesting itself, in the form of a woman, in the church. People were seeing it and it was disrupting the ministry of the church. Many thought it was the ghost of a woman who had been a faithful member of the church. She would often walk down the aisle and distract people from worshipping Jesus Christ. Although some laughed about the spirit's presence, it caused many to be filled with fear, to the extent that they stopped attending.

My friend asked if I would go through the church and cast it out. Although he had as much authority as I did to get rid of the evil spirit, because of inexperience, he asked me to do it. Of course I agreed.

I went room by room, through the entire big, old church and cast the evil spirit out of the building, sending it to the abyss. Afterwards, my friend and I prayed and asked the Holy Spirit to fill every room with His presence.

My friend immediately saw a difference in the response to his ministry, as he preached and prayed with people for their needs; both during the worship services and in other meetings. The membership began to grow as people received salvation, the baptism of the Holy Spirit, healing, deliverance and equipping to do ministry.

I learned, many years ago, that wherever we are doing the ministry of Jesus, whether in church buildings or in our home, evil spirits will often attempt to invade the premises and attack and bother people who have come. The evil spirits are often brought in by people coming to receive ministry. It seems they come into meetings riding on people, like monkeys on their backs or shoulders, and drop off to create problems for others. Fortunately, one of the gifts of the Holy Spirit, provided by God, is the gift of "discerning of spirits," by which we can identify evil spirits and cast them out.

Sometimes, when there are demons in a house or building, you can see them with peripheral vision. Occasionally I will see movements out of the corner of my eye, or I will see someone standing off to the side; but when I look directly at the place, the person is not there. We have heard sounds in our attic like mice or rats or some small animal, but when we examine the attic, there is no sign of the presence of any creatures. Whatever the indications, whenever anything peculiar happens, I immediately go through the house, room by room, and cast out any evil or unclean spirit. I then ask the Holy Spirit to fill the house with His presence. Immediately, there will be peace throughout the house. Whenever this occurs, I take it as a compliment to our ministry.

House invasions by evil spirits are a fairly common occurrence in homes of both Christians and non-Christians. Demons count on ignorance of their existence to give them the upper hand when they move in.

One day, I received a telephone call from an old friend, whose granddaughter lives in our town, Orangeville, Ontario. I knew the young woman and her parents. She and her husband had been married only a few years, when one morning, at three a.m., she woke up with something she couldn't see, sitting on her chest. She felt paralyzed and could not speak. Terrified, she watched the clock's hour hand on the dresser at the foot of their bed, move from three to four. Finally, she thought of Jesus and was able to speak His Name. Whatever was on her chest, left.

But that wasn't the end of it. She became aware of something she couldn't see, moving around her house. She didn't know what was happening to her, so she called her grandmother, who referred her to me.

I went to visit the young woman and she described what had happened to her.

I explained that her house had been invaded by an evil spirit that was now trying to control her and the house. Since she was already a Spirit-filled Christian, she was not in danger of being possessed, but as she had already discovered, she could be physically abused and even hurt by the evil spirit. So, before I cast it out of the house, we prayed, asking Jesus to forgive her for any sin in her life and to fill her afresh with the Holy Spirit. We then prayed in tongues.

Before blessing out the house, as usual, I asked her to leave while I dealt with the evil spirit, so she went for a drive. As I took authority over the house in Jesus' Name, there suddenly appeared what looked like a huge bat, with a wingspan of about three feet, that swooped down from the second floor towards me and then flew around me in a circle.

I said, "So, there you are! I command you, in the Name of Jesus Christ, to leave this house and to go to the abyss and to stay there."

It flew through the closed door and went to its appointed place in the abyss. I then went through all of the rooms and commanded any other evil spirits that might be lingering there, to go to the abyss. That done, I asked the Holy Spirit to fill every room in the house with His presence – and then there was peace in the house.

A frightening attack by an evil spirit is not uncommon. Many people have had this happen in their own homes or in a hotel or when visiting someone else's home.

It happened to my wife, Ruth, while staying in a motel in Boston. She was taking an afternoon nap when she was awakened by something in the room. She saw a dark, shadowy, cloud-like figure moving through the room. It landed on top of her. She was unable to move. After a few minutes, she was able to think and then say the Name of Jesus. The spirit backed away from her and she took authority over it, commanding it to leave and go to the abyss – and it did. It is a good practice, when staying in a motel, or hotel, to do what I call a "spiritual cleaning," by commanding any evil or unclean spirit to leave your room, or rooms, and send any that are there into the abyss; then asking the Holy Spirit to fill the room or rooms with His presence. There will be immediate peace so you can have a restful and uninterrupted stay.

In another situation, I received a call from a woman in Toronto who asked, "Could an evil spirit do damage to my walls?"

I asked what she meant.

"During the night, I could hear scratching sounds in our living room. When I went in to look the next morning, there were big scratch marks all over the upper portion of the walls. When I go out shopping and return home, there are more and more of these scratches. They look like they've been put there by a great big hand. My husband is accusing *me* of doing this damage. I can't even reach to the top of the walls – and we don't even own a ladder. I can't understand what is happening to me. Could this be caused by evil spirits?"

"It sounds likely," I said. So, I went to her house and saw all the damage on the walls. As usual, I asked her to step outside, while I went through the house, to rid it of any evil spirits. I went through every room and, as often happens, they left without any fuss.

The lady called a week later and explained that the scratching had stopped and a repair man had fixed the damage. Evil spirits or demons can cause great damage to houses and furniture.

While preaching in a church in Grande Prairie, Manitoba, one of my messages was about deliverance. After the service, a man approached me and explained that his family had been experiencing some strange things in their home. For example, their van was parked in a separate garage and somehow, the engine had started without the ignition key. It had not only started, but was put into gear and driven through the garage doors, smashing them. This had happened not just once, but twice. "Could this be caused by evil spirits?" he asked.

I asked if they had experienced any other strange things.

The children had heard noises in the walls and ceilings and seen dark figures.

"It sounds like you have evil spirits in your house," I said.

At the man's request, I went to their home and cast out the evil spirits from their house, garage and van. They have never since been troubled by strange happenings.

After I had preached a Sunday evening service at a church west of Shelburne, Ontario, the pastor asked me to talk with a young couple who were having some strange things happening in their house.

They explained, "We have a wrought iron stove we purchased and placed in our living room. Banging noises began to come from inside the stove and the pipes. Then we noticed that both the stove and the pipes had dents poking out. The banging noise would go on sometimes for only a few minutes, but sometimes for several hours." They asked, "Could our stove be haunted?"

I agreed that was a possibility. So, I went to their house after the service and heard the banging noises coming from inside the stove and saw the dents. I concluded there must be an evil spirit living in the stove. For safety's sake, I asked the family to step outside while I dealt with the evil spirit, because I could not predict how it was going to act. Then, I commanded any evil or unclean spirit to leave the stove and go to the abyss. It made its last bang and left the stove and the house. Afterwards, I prayed with the family to receive Jesus as their Savior and LORD and they were baptized with the Holy Spirit.

That's not the only situation I've encountered with a stove. I'm not sure what it is about stoves, but maybe the demons are just 'warming up' for their eternity.

Several years after the first incident, while I was the senior pastor at the Good Samaritan Church in Kitchener, Ontario, a young mother in her thirties called me, because something strange had started to happen in her home.

"Could it be," she asked, "that there's an evil spirit in my wrought iron stove in our family room? Recently, it started making banging noises. Now there are dents punched out from inside the stove and the pipes."

I told her that it was, indeed, possible and related the previous story to her. When she requested that I go to her home and deal with her situation, I agreed, with the same results I had previously had. I have to wonder if these "stove spirits" may be warming up for their eternity! At any rate, I cast the evil spirits out of her stove and invited the Holy Spirit to fill her house with His peace – and He did.

20. When demons are being cast out of a house or building they will often react violently because they do not want to be removed from the place in which they are residing. That was the reason why I asked the students to wait outside. As a rule, everyone in a demonized building should be removed for their safety, and also to prevent any misunderstanding of what method or procedures are being followed. Evil spirits will try to intimidate those who are there, when they are being removed, by becoming violent; pushing people, hitting them or throwing things at them. I have found the best method is to do it alone or with one other Christian who has been prepared.

Shortly after arriving in Kitchener, Ontario, as the pastor of Zion United Church, I was asked to visit a woman whose children were under the care of the Children's Aid Society. She had a history of alcohol, drug and sexual abuse. When I went to her apartment, her two daughters were visiting her. As we talked, I recognized that her problem was more than sin. It was evident that she needed to have her sins forgiven and come into a saved relationship with Jesus Christ, but it was also evident to me that an evil spirit possessed her. She shared with me about the thing that lived inside of her and talked to her. It often demanded that she do things to hurt and abuse her children and herself. The girls told me about a problem in one of the bedrooms where some spirits were causing them distress. The mother's boyfriend confirmed that what they were telling me was true.

First of all, I cast the evil spirit out of the mother. Then I prayed with the mother and the girls to invite Jesus into their lives as their Savior and Lord. They were all baptized with the Holy Spirit. Then, I asked them all to go outside while I went through the apartment and blessed it out.

A couple of weeks later, I received a telephone call from the woman's lawyer, to ask me if I would be willing to give evidence in court on behalf of the woman; she was asking for custody of her daughters. The woman had told her social worker about what had happened when I visited them. The lawyer could see there was a remarkable change for the better in her behavior; however, he explained that the court would want to hear about the exorcism. I agreed, but reluctantly, because I know the kind of misunderstandings that can happen when the subject of demons and demon possession is raised in a public setting like a courtroom.

Before I entered the courtroom, the woman's lawyer discussed the proceedings with me. He assured me he was a Christian and that I would not have a problem with him. Moreover, he assured me that the Crown Attorney was also a Christian and we would not have a problem with him either. However, they did not know where the judge stood spiritually. We needed to pray for him to be given understanding when the testimony was given.

After I entered the witness box and took the oath, I was asked by the Crown Attorney to describe the events that took place when I went to visit the woman and her children. I explained that, after I had prayed with them to become Christians, I had asked them all to leave the apartment so that I could bless out the apartment and get rid of any evil spirits that might be residing there.

The Crown Attorney then asked me whether I had walked through the apartment carrying one of the girls on my shoulder. I laughed out loud at the thought of it and told him I had not done so. I was alone when I blessed out the apartment. He laughed, because one of the girls had told a story she had made up about going through the apartment and doing some weird things. She obviously had an over-active imagination and had given it too much rein.

Finally, the judge gave his decision, "It would appear this case has already been decided in a higher court than mine. I approve and concur, with the agreement of the Children's Aid Society, that the girls be placed back in their mother's custody." The judge, it turned out, was also a Christian.

Another time, I was preaching for a week's crusade in the town of Chelmsford, near Sudbury, Ontario. The meetings were held in a school auditorium. I was preaching on a stage, with doors on each side opening into a hallway. Every night, the meetings were well attended and the altar ministry was exciting as we saw people receive salvation, the baptism of the Holy Spirit, healing and answers to other needs.

I noticed a young man, who was over seven feet tall, sitting in the front row every night of the meetings. As soon as I would begin to preach, his head would nod. Almost as though he were controlled by a light switch, his eyes would close and he would appear to fall to sleep immediately. When I would finish preaching and give the invitation for people who wanted prayer to come forward – again, like a light switch – the man would wake up, stand up and leave the auditorium via the exit door on my right. This happened on all seven nights.

However, on the last night, as I was praying individually with the people who had responded to the altar call, the exit doors on the left side of the auditorium suddenly burst open and this giant of a man came striding towards me. He held up his big right hand, now made into a fist poised to strike me, as he shouted, "I'm going to kill you!" As I turned to face him, he attempted to punch me in the face. However, I stepped aside as his fist went by my head. Led by the Holy Spirit, I reached out and gently touched him on the end of his nose and said, "In the Name of Jesus Christ, I command you to come out of this man." As if I had hit him with an upper cut punch, he went flying backwards through the doors into the hallway. He landed flat on his back as if he were paralyzed. I followed him quickly into the hallway and, just to be sure, commanded the evil spirit to leave him immediately and to go to the abyss and to stay there. It left him and he regained control of himself. He prayed with me to ask Jesus to forgive him for his sin and to receive the baptism of the Holy Spirit. He immediately burst into tongues. I then helped him get up off the floor. He was set free.

Six months later, the man came to see me. He explained, "When I was a little boy, this thing came inside me and, if I didn't do what it told me to do, it would hurt me. So, I did a lot of bad things to a lot of people and I was always in trouble. I've talked to many counselors and pastors, but nobody could help me; but that night in the school, Jesus set me free. I'm a new man."

He became a new creature in Christ.

Therefore, if any one is in Christ, he is a new creation; the old has passed away, behold, the new has come. (2 Corinthians 5:17)

Evil spirits, like the devil, are all thieves who come "only to steal and to kill and destroy."

The thief comes only to steal and kill and destroy. I came that they may have life, and have it abundantly. (John 10:10)

No matter how much superhuman strength the devil may give to people, no one is any match for the power of the Holy Spirit.

21. Demons love to dehumanize people by causing them to do things they ordinarily would not do. They like to humiliate the people whom they possess. The demoniac whom Jesus set free lived in the tombs and ran around completely naked.[236] The demons caused the man to live a lonely isolated life hiding from people.

22. Demons can give the people whom they possess super-human strength. The demoniac named "Legion," was so strong that he could break the chains that were put on him to restrain him.

Recently, I received a telephone call from a man whose son was possessed with a demon/evil spirit. The man had just received a frightening call from the son who was hiding in his closet when he called, because the demon in him had told him that it wanted him to kill some people. The demon, whose name was "Prosatanis," threatened to kill the

---
[236] See Luke 8:27

young man if he would not do what it commanded. The boy had been seeing a doctor, who had put him on the drug Prozac, in an attempt to control his behavior. Although he weighed only about 150 pounds, he had super-human strength. He could lift up the back end of a transport trailer without any effort. The father was worried and had called his pastor friend, Rev. David Black, who had referred him to me.

I met with the father and son in my friend's church sanctuary. The son was sitting in the front pew growling like a dog. I asked him two questions: "Do you want to be set free from this demon?" and "Are you willing to let Jesus Christ be your Savior and LORD and be baptized with the Holy Spirit?"

He growled at me and said, "Yes, sir!"

I then asked him to stand up in front of the communion table, which he did without a word or a growl. I repeated the same two questions.

He growled again and asked, "Does that mean I will have to speak in tongues?"[237]

I had not mentioned "speaking in tongues," but every demon/evil spirit knows that anybody who speaks in tongues is someone they must obey. I took authority over the demon in him, without touching him, and commanded it to leave him in the Name of Jesus Christ and go to the abyss.[238] It left without any arguing or physical reaction – except that when it left the son, it brushed by the father, pushing him aside and startling him. Nevertheless, it was gone and the young man was set completely free.

I laid hands on him and led him in prayer, during which he asked Jesus to forgive him for any sin or wrong he had done. I then prayed with him to receive the baptism of the Holy Spirit. Immediately, he began to speak in tongues.[239] His tongue language was biblical Hebrew. Having studied Hebrew in both university and seminary, I could tell he was praising God and thanking Jesus for setting him free and becoming his Savior and LORD.

---
[237] Acts 2:4; Mark 16:17
[238] Luke 8:31
[239] See Acts 19:1-6

Just to make certain he was really speaking in tongues given by the Holy Spirit, I asked the father, "Has your son ever studied a biblical language?"

He laughed and said, "No! He never finished high school because of the evil spirit in him."

I then explained, to both of them, that the tongues language the Holy Spirit had given to John was Hebrew and that I had heard him praising God in that language.

The father, who had been standing behind his son when I cast the spirit out said, "That was a powerful demon, wasn't it?"

I asked him why he would say that and he replied, "Because, it pushed me aside when it came out of my son."

The young man was completely set free. As we are told by Jesus,

So if the Son makes you free, you will be free indeed. (John 8:36)

The young man thanked me for helping him. As we were about to leave the church, the father said, "Oh, by the way, David asked me to remind you to clean up the church before you left it, but, I can't see any mess that needs to be cleaned up."

I laughed and explained that David had not been talking about a physical mess, but about a spiritual mess. He wanted me to make certain there were no evil spirits left lurking around the church before I left. Taking that cue, I went through the building, room by room, and blessed it out in the Name of Jesus Christ.

I then gave John some instructions about studying the New Testament and about how to listen to the Holy Spirit, praying both in English and in tongues every day, so he could receive wisdom from God.

A couple of months later, my wife and I had lunch with Rev. David Black and his wife. He said, "That young man from whom you cast out the demon is growing well as a Christian. He is doing everything you instructed him to do." He was completely free and growing spiritually and had the normal strength of a young man his age and weight. His doctor had taken him off his medication.

23. **The most commonly used weapons of evil spirits are lies, accusations, deception and masquerades** that (once recognized for what they really are) are often more laughable than frightening.

24. **Demons often give erroneous instructions to people**, which the people accept mistakenly as being some new teaching from God. This is especially prevalent among those involved in the leadership of churches.

> *Now the Spirit expressly says that in later times some will depart from the faith by giving heed to deceitful spirits and the doctrines of demons, through the pretensions of liars who consciences are seared, who forbid marriage and enjoin abstinence from foods which God created to be received with thanksgiving by those who believe and know the truth.* (1 Timothy 4:1-3)

25. **Demons attract rebellious people to false religions and the occult world through deception,** false Christs, false prophets, counterfeit signs and wonders, counterfeit and powerless gifts in order to deceive, *"if possible, even the elect."*

> *For false Christs and false prophets will arise and show great signs and wonders, so as to lead astray, if possible, even the elect.* (Matthew 24:24)

26. **Demons like to frighten people.** Putting fear in people is part of demons' defense strategy when they meet Christians who can cast them out. They will often run around frantically; shouting, cursing, swearing or giving bloodcurdling screams, trying to intimidate anyone who has authority over them. It's not unlike the strategy of any small child who tries to get his or her way over parents in public. Any mother who has had her child throw a tantrum in a busy shopping mall will know what I mean. Evil spirits love to throw tantrums and they need to be treated with the same firmness one would use with a small child: spiritually speaking, we have to take control, command it to be quiet, leave the person and go to the abyss in the Name of Jesus. The demon will have to obey and leave.

It is not out of the scope of demons, to frighten or harass people through today's technology.

One time I received a panic call from a woman in Etobicoke, Ontario. She explained fearfully that her daughter and granddaughter were visiting her apartment. While she and her daughter were chatting in the kitchen, the sixteen-month-old granddaughter was playing in another room. Suddenly, the little girl began to scream. The woman and her daughter ran down the hall to the little girl. They found her terrified. The young mother noticed that the little girl had been playing with a cell phone that had a video recorder in it. She looked at the recording her daughter had somehow turned on and saw the reason for the screaming. On the screen, a black figure was standing in front of the little girl, with its hand over the little girl's face. The grandmother called a friend, who happened to be one of my song leaders. The friend told the grandmother to call me. I went immediately to the address and cast the demon out of the apartment, into the abyss. Then, I prayed with the mother and grandmother to receive Christ as their Savior and Lord. Both received the baptism of the Holy Spirit and the peace of God that passes understanding, as they spoke in tongues. I also prayed with the little girl so she would have no fear.

Naive or inexperienced Christians can be unpleasantly surprised when they discover that evil spirits don't always leave without a fight. Naiveté can place them in danger. Ignorance of what the Bible says, can also place them in danger. When demons resist, it's not an indication of superior power, or a sign that they have the right to stay and possess people or buildings; it's just an impressive display of the depth of their rebellion against Jesus Christ. Seeing a demon-possessed adult having a demon-produced tantrum – falling to the floor screaming, kicking, flailing, shouting, crying, cursing and grabbing attention – can be intimidating for a Christian who isn't confident of where he or she stands in terms of the authority he or she has in Christ. On the surface, it could look as though deliverance is an impossible task. When challenged by bully-type evil spirits, it is easy for inexperienced Christians to lose confidence in their authority and feel like spiritual failures. The reality is, that the weakest voice, empowered by the Holy Spirit can strike a death blow to the enemy. Any suggestion that a Christian does not have authority over the enemy is a lie. While it can happen that a Christian may get kicked, punched, pushed, bruised, or hit by objects hurled by a demon possessed person, once they stand in the authentic authority given in the Name of Jesus Christ, human inadequacy will give way to the power of God.

I often suggest that people who have had their egos and bodies bruised in deliverance ministry, need to watch the *Rocky Two* movie. It's about a man who had just won a boxing match for the heavy-weight boxing championship of the world. Both he and the former world champion are in the hospital. Rocky, the winner, hobbles down to his opponent, who is lying in a hospital bed. Rocky is not crying over the fact that he was he was injured while winning the bout. He just wants assurance of his superior power. He says to the former champ, "I just want to ask you one question, 'Did you give me your best?'"

The answer was, of course, "Yes!"

It is not always easy to defeat the enemy, but it will be wonderful to hear Jesus say,

> *"Well done, good and faithful servant; you have been faithful over a little, I will set you over much; enter into the joy of your Master."* (Matthew 25:21)

In the course of doing the ministry of Jesus, we can be mistreated and even killed.[240] It is normal, when in the process of casting out stubborn demons who are protesting their removal, to have doubts about whether or not we'll eventually be successful. It is normal to have doubts about whether or not we really have the authority to cast them out. Fear and insecurity can rise up and say, "He who is in the world is greater than He who is in you," when the truth is just the opposite.

> *Little children, you are of God, and have overcome them; for He who is in you is greater than he who is in the world.* (1 John 4:4)

Perseverance,[241] empowered by the Holy Spirit, always wins.[242]

---
[240] See Revelation 12:11
[241] See Ephesians 6:18; Hebrews 12:1
[242] See Revelation 2:7,11,17,26; 3:5,12,21

27. Demons have names. If questioned and asked to name themselves, demons will usually lie; because as long as we do not know their real names, and call them by a wrong name, they won't have to leave the person they have possessed. Their aliases usually are something like the spirit of hate, the spirit of lust, or the spirit of murder. They will most often call themselves by one of the works of the flesh, because they cause the people whom they control to commit those sins.

The list of aliases demon use is very limited in both the Old and the New Testaments: evil spirit,[243] unclean spirit,[244] spirit of slavery,[245] spirit of the world,[246] spirit of cowardice, timidity or fear,[247] spirit of the antichrist,[248] spirit of error,[249] spirit of harlotry or whoredom,[250] spirit of infirmity or disability,[251] spirit of divination,[252] deaf and dumb spirit,[253] spirit of jealousy[254] and spirit of deceit.[255] The names describe what they do rather than who they are.

The more well-known names of demons, who were worshipped as gods in the Old Testament are: Dagon, a god of the Philistines;[256] Molech, a god of the Ammonites[257] and Baal, a god of the Moabites.[258] These are just a few of many. It is interesting to note that Jesus never called the demons by their names, even after the one demoniac told Him his name was Legion.[259]

Because Jesus asked the demons their names, many Christians think they must ask demons to tell them their names. This has resulted in a lot of Christians losing their authority to cast out demons.

---

[243] See Acts 19:15
[244] See Matthew 12:43; Mark 1:23; Mark 5:2; Mark 9:25; Luke 4:33
[245] See Romans 8:15
[246] See 1 Corinthians 2:12
[247] See 2 Timothy 1:7
[248] See 1 John 4:3
[249] See 1 John 4:6
[250] See Hosea 4:12
[251] See Luke 13:11
[252] See Acts 16:16
[253] See Mark 9:25
[254] See Numbers 5:14
[255] See 1 Timothy 4:1
[256] See Judges 16:23
[257] See 1 Kings 11:7
[258] See Numbers 25:1-3
[259] See Mark 5:9; Luke 8:30

Because Jesus is the Son of the Most High and more than that – Emmanuel, God in the flesh – demons cannot lie to Jesus. When asked, they must tell Him their true names. However, that is not the case with Christians. Demons will lie to us, because they know that if they give their real names, we can command them to leave the person they have been afflicting, or the building they have been haunting. They know they are under the authority we have been given by Jesus Christ to cast them out.[260] Therefore, in order to prevent us from commanding them to leave, they will make up names so that they will not have to obey when we command them to leave. They may identify themselves as the spirit of hate, or the spirit of Jezebel, or the spirit of one of the works of the flesh[261] – indicating what they do, but hiding who they are. Sometimes, they may identify themselves as one of the ancient spirits; such as Baal, Molech or Dagon, who were worshipped as gods. Today, all other modern religions have different demons who are worshipped as gods. When Christians try, foolishly, to cast out the demons by using one of these pseudonyms, the demons become quiet and pretend to have left the person or building.

After a failed exorcism, the demons will quickly resume the activities associated with their possession. The victim may later be accused of not wanting to be set free, or of harbouring some sin that brought the demons back, or of having some supposed generational curse that allows the demons to return to them.

We do not need to know the names of demons in order to cast them out of a person. We can simply command any evil or unclean spirit to leave in the Name of Jesus Christ.

Early in my ministry, I read a foolish book that taught it was necessary to have the demons name themselves, before they could be expelled. Around that same time, I was called to the home of a woman, who had been told that she was possessed with demons. I took authority over her and commanded the demons to name themselves. I made a list of thirty-two names and proceeded to command each of them to leave, using the

---

[260] See Mark 16:17
[261] See Galatians 5:19-21

names I had received. After commanding them all to leave, I asked the woman, "How do you feel now?"

She answered quietly, "Fine. I'm fine."

But the Holy Spirit said to me, "They have not gone. They are quiet because they are pretending to have gone." I then prayed with the woman to repent and asked the Holy Spirit to fill her and drive out the demons. A number of different voices began to scream, as the demons left her on their way to the abyss. She began to speak in tongues and was set free. She is now serving Jesus Christ in the power of the Holy Spirit with the signs following.[262] The demons are liars like their father, the devil.[263]

Obviously, we must be able to distinguish between behavior caused by sin and behavior caused by demons. Sin is the major problem. Regardless of whether they have names or not, evil spirits or demons are under a Christian's authority – which means that they have to leave when commanded to do so in the Name of Jesus Christ.

28. Although it takes only one demon to possess a person, demons usually cluster in groups.

Then Jesus asked him, "What is your name?" He replied, 'My name is Legion; for we are many.'" (Mark 5:9)

Legion had between 3,000 and 6,000 evil spirits. Misery seems to love company. They like to gang up and swarm a person, but regardless of their number, when commanded to leave a possessed person, they have to leave.

29. Demons have intelligence and can recognize people and talk to them. Demons recognized Jesus' true identity, when people did not. Unlike Jesus' human critics, the demons always knew who Jesus was. They immediately recognized Him and shouted out to Him:

"What have we to do with you, Jesus of Nazareth? Have You come to destroy us? I know who you are, the Holy One of God!"
(Mark 1:24; Luke 4:34)

---

[262] See Mark 16:17-18
[263] See John 8:44

> *And whenever the unclean spirits beheld him, they fell down before him and cried out, "You are the Son of God."* (Mark 3:11)

They also recognize Christians. A prime example is the one that beat up the seven sons of Sceva.[264] This story illustrates the difference between those who have no authority over evil spirits and those who do.

> *But the evil spirit said to them in reply, "Jesus I know, and Paul I know; but who are you?"* (Acts 19:15)

The evil spirit proceeded to beat and overpower them and the seven sons ran out of the house naked and wounded.

Evil spirits know their enemies and can identify us.

30. Demons are tormented when they are in the presence of Jesus Christ or a Spirit-filled Christian. This means we torture them simply by our presence; causing them excruciating pain, anguish, suffering, annoyance and agony when they know that they are going to be cast out and sent to the abyss. Legion, speaking in behalf of the evil spirits in him, was in great pain when he beseeched Jesus not to torment him.[265]

Rarely do we, as Spirit-filled Christians, know the problems we are creating for the devil and the demons.

About twenty years ago, one of my brothers was attempting to start up a business with a friend, in which they expected to become very wealthy. During the process, they had a problem with one of the trucks they were going to use. Neither of them knew how to fix the problem. They got frustrated to the point of being beside themselves with anger; cursing, swearing and even kicking the vehicle. Totally frustrated, they sat down, not knowing what to do next.

That was when a man in a black suit drove up in a limousine, got out of his car and told them how to repair the problem. This happened on two different occasions. The man claimed to represent God and told them that if they would do what he told them, he would make them rich. He gave them a demonstration of his power by showing them how

---

[264] See Acts 19 – also see pages 341-343 for a fuller treatment.
[265] See Matthew 8:29; Mark 5:7; Luke 8:28

he controlled the world through, what looked like, strings of lightening coming down from the sky. It was an awesome and convincing display. They were impressed. My brother agreed to cooperate with this 'god.'

The business was developing nicely and, one day, this god told my brother that he wanted him to deliver a message to his brother, Gordon. My brother agreed, but the message didn't make any sense to him. In fact, he thought I would think he was crazy. He delayed – until they had yet another problem with their truck and the man turned up again in his limousine, unannounced. He told them he would not help anymore and that they would not succeed in making the money they expected if my brother did not give me the message.

My brother telephoned and asked me to meet with him. I agreed, and my wife Ruth and I went to visit him. He wanted to talk to me alone because, to him, the message didn't make sense. I encouraged him to go ahead. He explained that I was to take this message seriously, because god, who was very powerful, had given it to him. He said, "This is the message: 'Stop tormenting my creatures.'" He went on to explain what he thought to be the meaning of the message.

I told him *he* didn't understand and said, "No! That is not what the message is about. I knew we were causing some damage to the kingdom of darkness, but I never realized we were being so successful."

I continued, "You are in big trouble. You have been dealing with the devil. This is about our ministry, which is often referred to as 'deliverance ministry' or 'casting out of demons.' The person you were dealing with is described in the Bible and is a god all right; he is called the '*prince of the power of the air*;'[266] but he is not the real God of the whole world. You have been visited by the devil himself. I did not know I was doing so much harm to his creatures."

Then I opened up my New Testament and read:

And behold, they cried out, "What have you to do with us, O Son of God? Have you come here to torment us before the time?"
(Matthew 8:29)

---
[266] Ephesians 2:2

I explained to my brother that the creatures referred to in his message, were what we call evil spirits or demons. I said, "You can tell him that the answer is, 'No, I will not stop tormenting his creatures.'"

My brother was astonished and dismayed, but he left that business and got into a different kind of work.

The same thing can happen today, whenever someone acts impetuously; without the legal authority of Jesus Christ, without the power of the Holy Spirit or without the permission of the possessed person.

31. Evil spirits will attempt to persuade a Christian to leave them alone and not cast them out. They will suggest other solutions than casting them out; or, if you persist, they will try to convince you to allow them to go to some place other than the abyss of punishment. As with Jesus,[267] they will suggest alternatives, such as allowing them to go into some animal. They may even beg to be allowed to stay. It's imperative to remember that we are at war with them. Human inclinations to be tolerant, compassionate or accommodating have no place in dealing with evil spirits. Their goal is to destroy the person whom they are possessing. We can't risk being tricked into feeling sorry for an enemy that wants only to steal from, destroy or kill the person in whom they reside.

Jesus left us with only a few examples of how He dealt with demons. The most complete conversation recorded to teach us, was with the man called "Legion."[268] Through that conversation, we learn that demons will try to convince us not to send them to the abyss. They like to negotiate by offering other alternatives. Legion's alternative suggestion, that they be allowed to go into the pigs, sounded reasonable. The story sounds as though Jesus was cooperating. There are those readers who have concluded that the demons outsmarted Jesus by drowning the pigs, leaving the demons free to find another place. Not so. The demons ended up in the abyss,[269] whether they wanted to go or not. They knew Jesus must be obeyed. That is why they asked,

---
[267] See Luke 8:31
[268] See Matthew 8:28-34; Mark 5:1-20; Luke 8:26-39
[269] Luke 8:31

"Have you come to torment us before the time?" (Matthew 8:29)

The way this is written in Greek reads, "Have you come (once and for all) to torment or torture us (once and forever) before the appointed time (chairos)?" Demons know their eschatology better than most people, because they know they have been judged already. They knew it was the appointed time whenever Jesus, the most high God,[270] confronted them.

Even the demons believe – and shudder. (James 2:19)

No grace period exists for demons since Jesus came and they know it. Because of the great numbers of swine drowned, it's obvious why the people of that area begged Jesus to leave their neighborhood.[271] Since demons, by their own sinful nature, cannot repent and receive salvation, all they can do is believe, tremble and receive a one-way trip to the abyss, the bottomless pit into which Satan will be sent for a thousand years; the place from which the beast will be let loose.[272]

And they begged him not to command them to depart into the abyss. (Luke 8:31)

And He seized the dragon, that ancient serpent, who is the Devil and Satan, and bound him for a thousand years, and threw him into the pit, and shut it and sealed it over him, that he should deceive the nations no more, till the thousand years were ended. After that he must be loosed for a little while. (Revelation 20:2-3)

On a Saturday morning, while serving St. Paul's Church, Brampton, Ontario, our home telephone rang.

"Hello?"

A woman's voice said, "I need your help."

When I asked who she was, she hung up. After this happened another ten times, I asked my wife, Ruth, to listen to the woman's voice. We agreed that it sounded like the voice of a friend, Betty (not her real name), a member of our church.

---

[270] See Acts 16:17
[271] See Matthew 8:34
[272] See Revelation 11:7; 17:8

So, I tried to phone her a few times and received a busy signal. Finally, her husband answered and I asked him if his wife was home. He told me she was home all right, but had been sick in bed all morning. I asked if there was a telephone in their bedroom and he said there was. I then explained to him, that we had received several telephone calls from a woman who either would not, or could not, identify herself and that it sounded like his wife. I suggested that my wife Ruth and I would like to go over to see her and he agreed.

When we arrived at our friends' home, Ruth went upstairs to see Betty. After a few minutes, she came back downstairs and said, "Gordon, there is something wrong. I think you need to go up there."

So all three of us went upstairs to Betty's room. I asked Ruth and her husband to wait outside the room in the hallway. When I went in, our friend was lying in her bed with the bed covers pulled up around her head. Her eyes were closed and she appeared to be fast asleep. I went over to the bed and gently shook her shoulder. I said, "Hi Betty, it's Gordon Williams."

With her eyes closed she said, "That's not my name."

Since she had a sense of humor, I thought she was trying to be funny; so I went along with the game and said, "Then, what is your name?"

She replied, "My name is Mary."

I asked, "What are you doing here?

Very serious, she said, "You know what I'm here for."

I said, "I don't know why you are here."

Her eyes glared at me as she answered, "I'm here to kill her."

I realized there was another entity, an evil spirit speaking through her. I said, "I'm sorry Mary, but you cannot do that. You are going to have to leave her."

The angry voice within her said, "I don't have to leave because you tell me to."

I agreed and said, "You are right. You do not have to leave because I tell you to leave – but you do have to leave because I tell you to leave in the Name of Jesus Christ. So, now I command you, evil spirit, to leave Betty in the Name of Jesus Christ and go to the abyss and stay there."

It left without any further argument. Our friend opened her eyes. With a surprised look on her face, she exclaimed, "Gordon, what are you doing in my bedroom?"

I explained that her husband and my wife were in the hall and quickly asked them to join us in the bedroom. I explained that Betty had been possessed with an evil spirit that had tried to kill her by causing her to drink two-and-a-half, twenty-six-ounce bottles of Scotch whiskey. Further, I explained that, for health and safety, she needed to receive the baptism of the Holy Spirit. She agreed and as I prayed with her, she began to speak in tongues. The effects of the alcohol totally left her body. The after effects were nullified and replaced with the life-giving New Wine[273] of the Holy Spirit's power.

> *And when Paul had laid his hands upon them, the Holy Spirit came down on them; and they spoke with tongues and prophesied.*
> (Acts 19:6)

Later, I asked Betty if she had any idea when, or where, she might have been invaded and possessed by the evil spirit.

She explained that she had gone to a meeting at another church, where, at the conclusion of the meeting, the pastor had gone from person to person, laying hands on people as he prayed for them. After he touched her and began to pray for her, she felt as though something strange was happening to her, but she just shrugged it off.

By her description, it sounded as though the pastor, without enough experience, and without realizing it, was causing what is known as a "transference of spirits." When he laid hands on people to pray for their needs, he may not have discerned that some of them were actually possessed by evil spirits. The demons could have moved out of a possessed person, onto the pastor's hands. When he laid his hand on

---

[273] See Luke 5:37-38

the next person, an evil spirit would move from his hands on to the new person. From there, it would go inside his or her body and possess the person.

The cardinal rule in casting out of evil spirits is not to lay hands on a possessed person until after the evil spirits have been cast out of the person and sent to the abyss. If evil spirits are not commanded to go to the place of their punishment, they will try to return to the person from whom they have been expelled, and bring back seven more evil spirits;[274] or, they may just go to another person to possess him. Another possibility is that the evil spirit will react and cause the possessed person to hurt the person who is trying to cast them out. This occurs when people attempt, unsuccessfully, to cast out demons without proper instruction and training.

I suggested that our friend stay away from those meetings, because they were dangerous. Obviously, the pastor didn't know what he was doing.

About a year after this, there was a scandal in that church when it was discovered that the senior pastor was carrying on an adulterous affair with a woman in his church. In addition, the associate pastor was involved in a homosexual relationship with a man in the same church. Both were threatening each other with exposing the sins of the other to the church.

Because of the sexual sins of these pastors, evil spirits were immune to any exorcism they might have attempted. Both of the pastors had lost their authority to cast them out. Both pastors were later removed from their positions in that church.

The devil and evil spirits can immediately recognize those Christians who have authority over them and those who do not. So when we are casting them out of people and out of houses and buildings and sending them to the abyss, they attempt, regularly, to convince us to stop our deliverance ministry.

---

[274] See Matthew 12:43-45

32. Evil spirits will leave a person immediately when commanded by any Christian who exercises his or her authority. All we have to do is follow Jesus' example.

> *For He had said to him, "Come out of the man, you unclean spirit!"* (Mark 5:8)

> *And He said to them, "Go." So they came out and went into the swine; and behold, the whole herd rushed down the steep bank into the sea, and perished in the waters.* (Matthew 8:32)

> *And when Jesus saw that a crowd came running together, He rebuked the unclean spirit, saying to it, "You dumb and deaf spirit, I command you, come out of him, and never enter him again."* (Mark 9:25)

> *But Jesus rebuked him, saying, "Be silent, and come out of him!" And when the demon had thrown him down in the midst, he came out of him, having done him no harm.* (Luke 4:35)

In every case, Jesus used the imperative and it happened immediately.

If it takes longer than a few seconds or minutes to cast out an evil spirit, then either there are no demons there, or the person or people attempting to cast them out have lost their authority. I often hear of people spending two, three, four, ten hours – or more – trying to cast out a demon. There is something very wrong when this happens if, in fact, there are even any there.

The longest I can remember it taking to cast out an evil spirit was seven minutes, but that was early in my ministry when I made the mistake of asking the evil spirits to name themselves. They lied to me so that I wouldn't have their right names and therefore, would not be able to command them to leave. At the time, I didn't realize that we don't need to have names to tell them to leave.

Evil spirits know every Christian who has authority over them. That is why the demon said to the seven sons of Sceva,[275]

---
[275] See Acts 19 – also see pages 341-343 for a fuller treatment.

"Jesus I know, and Paul I know; but who are you?" (Acts 19:15)

After one of my guest interviews on the Richard Syrette radio talk show, I received a call from a woman who explained that she and her family were afraid for their lives. They had been living in a house in Toronto. After some strange things had begun to happen, they realized that a demon had moved into their house. It began to harass her family, particularly her son and two daughters. Night after night, they were wakened by noises in their house. In order to escape the nights of terror, they sold their house and moved to the woman's dream house in the country, just south of Barrie, Ontario, where they were sure they'd be safe. They were horrified to discover that their nightmare followed them to their new home. Things became even worse. The evil spirit dragged her children – eighteen, twenty and twenty-two-year-olds – out of their beds at night and pushed them under their beds.

She called her Roman Catholic priest who went to their house to exorcise the spirit. After failing to get rid it, the priest ran out of the house, terrified, and told the woman he would not come back. He could do nothing about the demon.

In another desperate attempt to escape the evil spirit, the family moved to Port Hope, Ontario – but it followed them there, too.

The woman was frantic. One day, however, she happened to be listening to the Richard Syrette radio program when we were discussing the problem of clergy who had no authority to cast out demons, with reference to the priest in the movie, *The Exorcist*. She called in to the program and asked for help. I explained that, in order to deal with this evil spirit safely, it would be necessary for all members of her family to receive salvation and the baptism of the Holy Spirit. She would know she had received the Holy Spirit when she began to exercise the gift of speaking in tongues – the sure evidence. I asked if her family would be prepared to receive salvation and the baptism of the Holy Spirit.

She discussed the requirement with her family and they all agreed. Then she called and asked me to go over. To shorten the story, I cast the evil spirit out of their house and they all received Christ and the baptism of the Holy Spirit. They were never bothered again.

On another occasion, I received a telephone call from friends who owned a Christian book and church supplies store on Yonge Street, Toronto, Ontario.

The owners, Maureen and Paul, explained that there were some peculiar things happening in the building where the business was located – like the heating system stopping without any apparent reason and various items of merchandise being mysteriously moved and broken after hours. The final straw came when a water pipe, located in a wall, broke – flooding the store and pouring out into the street. An inspector, after examining the damage, could not find any reason why the pipe should have broken. It was a mystery.

She explained, "We think there must be demons in the building. We have sensed something evil there. Could you go through the building to see if there is something demonic at work here?"

I agreed to go and went down to the store late at night. I wanted to go through their building alone. I asked that they remain outside and pray for me, while I went through the five-storey building. There was a main floor, in which the store was located; a second storey that was used for ministry and special services, called the "Upper Room;" and three storeys above which were used for inventory. I took authority over the building in the Name of Jesus Christ and proceeded through the store level and the second floor. Although there was a freight elevator, I walked up the stairs, on the left side of the building, blessing out each level as I went.

As I was ascending the stairs to the fifth level, I saw a dark figure, standing at the top of the stairway with his arms crossed over his chest. As I drew closer to him, I could see that he was dressed in a black robe with a pointed hood covering his head. I could not make out any facial features, except two dull eyes, glaring menacingly at me. I said to it, "So, there you are. I have been looking for you. You are going to have to leave this building right now. I command you to leave this building in the name of Jesus Christ and go to the abyss." Without a word, it disintegrated as it went through the wall.

I then asked the Holy Spirit to fill the whole building with the peace of God which passes all understanding, and to bless the owners of the business and all customers.

33. Demons should always be sent to the abyss – their place of punishment. When Jesus dealt with the demons in Legion, they begged him not to send them to the abyss.[276] Nevertheless, that's where they landed, in spite of their attempt to escape by going into the swine. There is a place of punishment prepared for evil spirits. We need to send them there or else they will just possess another person or re-possess and torment a former victim.

34. Demons were afraid of Jesus, as they are of any born-again, Spirit-filled Christian. Demons are more afraid of us than we are of them. While they may try to frighten us off with screaming, shouting or weird behavior, all we have to do is to command them to be quiet and leave and they will.

35. It is important not to touch a person, or lay hands on a person who has been possessed by evil spirits. First, because they will react, often by attempting to hit or beat up the person who is trying to get rid of them. The seven sons of Sceva learned a hard lesson when they tried to exorcise a demon. They were severely beaten up and had their clothes torn off.[277]

When I was on staff with *100 Huntley Street,* I made an appointment to see a forty-five-year-old man, whose family thought he might be possessed with an evil spirit, because of his weird behavior, growling and making animal noises at other people. The man arrived and my secretary asked him to sit on one of the chairs in the hallway and wait for me there.

Whenever somebody walked pass him, he would growl. As more people passed him, he would get louder and louder, to the point where

---
[276] See Luke 8:31
[277] See Acts 19:16 – also see pages 343-344 for a fuller treatment.

people were being frightened and upset. Four of the men on our staff decided that they should take the matter into their own hands and they escorted him into an empty office. They made the mistake of putting their hands on his head and shoulders and holding his hands as they tried to cast out the evil spirit. He went wild on them. They tried to hold him down on the floor, but he threw them all over the room – punching, hitting, kicking and tearing their clothes, growling while they struggled with him. Finally, they decided they had better leave him alone and ran out of the room.

The man got up off the floor, straightened his clothes, left the office and sat down, once again, on the same chair in the hallway, growling at anybody who walked by.

I finally arrived, knowing nothing about this. I went over to the man and asked, "Is your name John?"[278]

He growled at me and said, "Yes."

I invited him into my office. We talked for a short while so that I could determine his problem. It did not take long for me to determine that he was, indeed, possessed. I asked him the two questions: "Do you want to be set free?" and "Are you willing to receive Jesus Christ as your Savior and LORD and the baptism of the Holy Spirit?"

He growled again, but said, "Yes, sir."

I then took authority over him in Jesus' Name and commanded the demon to leave him and to go to the abyss and stay there.

It left without a squeak.

Then I laid hands on the man and he prayed with me to ask Jesus to forgive him for all of his sins and baptize him with the Holy Spirit. We asked the Holy Spirit to give him springs of Living Water,[279] flowing out of his heart, into his mouth so he could speak in tongues. He opened his mouth and began to speak in the promised new language. He was set free. We then went into the cafeteria to have a coffee. He was completely normal.

---

[278] Not his real name.
[279] John 4:10-15

One of the men who had tried to deal with him, came over to our table and called me aside, saying, "That man is very dangerous."

I told him, "Not now! He has been set free. He's saved and baptized with the Holy Spirit." Then I noticed that the fellow to whom I was speaking, had a black eye and his shirt and sports jacket had been torn. I asked, "What in the world happened to you?"

He explained later, after the man had gone home, what had happened before I arrived. I had thought he and his companions knew better than to lay hands upon a possessed person without their permission. Anyone who does so, without a possessed person's permission and without authority of the Holy Spirit, will discover – as did the seven sons of Sceva[280] and these four men – that demons will attack any unauthorized person and attempt to hurt and even kill them.

36. Occasionally, demon possessed people will have a friend who is also possessed;[281] but most often, they are loners. Nevertheless, it should be no problem for a Spirit-filled Christian to set as many people free from demons as is necessary.

I received a call from a woman who lives in Walkerton, Ontario. She and her husband had traveled with an evangelist for sixteen years, hoping to receive the baptism of the Holy Spirit – which they knew was crucially important, in order to have a full and exciting Christian life. Unfortunately, her husband had died without having this desire satisfied. Not wanting that to be her experience, she asked, "Where can I go to receive the baptism of the Holy Spirit, with the evidence of speaking in tongues?"

"You can receive the baptism of the Holy Spirit at any of our meetings," I replied. However, since she was unable to drive to a meeting, I offered to go to her home and pray with her there, the next time I was traveling in her area.

She said that would be excellent, but then mentioned she was having a problem in her home. She could hear voices coming from the spare

---
[280] See Acts 19 – also see pages 341-343 for a fuller treatment.
[281] See Matthew 8:34

bedroom. Her door bell would ring but, when she would go to answer the door, there would be nobody there.

I said it sounded as though her house had been invaded by some evil spirits.

The lady then told me about her elder sister, who was living on a farm near Goderich, Ontario. After this sister and her husband had moved into their farmhouse, some peculiar things had started happening. Before taking a shower, the sister would lay the clothes she planned to wear that day, out on her bed. After her shower, she would find them mysteriously gone. At first, she thought her husband, who had a sense of humor, had come in and taken her clothes. However, whenever she looked out the window, he would be riding his tractor in the field, doing his chores. Her clothes would turn up a week or two later; filthy, wrinkled and sometimes torn.

In an attempt not to get caught without clothes, if she knew she would have to change later on, the sister began to wear two sets of clothing. She would remove the first set so she could go on to her appointments. This had gone on for more than twenty years. She was frustrated, helpless and felt defeated. Her family and friends treated her as an eccentric at best, and mentally disturbed at worst.

The Walkerton woman wanted to know if I would visit her sister and her sister's husband. I said I would and asked her to call her sister and find out when we could set a date.

A week after they had sold their farm and moved into the town of Goderich, I took the afternoon to visit the two sisters. I went to see the sister in Walkerton first. When I arrived, I explained that before praying with her to receive the baptism of the Holy Spirit, I would go through her house and get rid of any evil spirits that were there. As usual, I asked her to please, for her safety, step outside the house. She went out to pray in the yard while I took authority over the house in the Name of Jesus Christ. I went room by room, commanding any unclean spirit to leave and to go to the abyss. The evil spirits tried to push me out of the house, but I reiterated my command and they left. Then, I asked the Holy Spirit to fill every room with His presence.

I called the lady back into her house and told her, "They have all gone!" I gently laid hands on her and asked her to pray with me as we asked Jesus to forgive her for any sin in her life and to baptize her with the Holy Spirit. The Holy Spirit filled her heart and she spoke in tongues.

Thereupon, she announced, "I have not been a very good hostess today. I have't even asked you if you would like a cup of tea."

"That would be very nice," I said.

She served the tea with cookies and we were talking when suddenly, her door bell began to ring furiously. She exclaimed, "Oh, no. The demons haven't left!"

"Go and open the door," I said.

She opened the door hesitantly and there stood the mailman, with a parcel for her.

Relieved and laughing she said, "I thought the demons were not gone."

I explained, "Jesus always likes to do some follow up on His own, to assure us that the enemy has gone."

I then drove the half hour to her sister's new home in Goderich. When I arrived, the furniture was still not in place and the couple was living out of boxes. She explained that her husband was in the hospital, where he had had unsuccessful surgery for cancer. He was dying. On top of that, the demon had followed them to their new house. (Demons will often follow people from one house to another.)

I said, "This is the last day you are going have to put up with that demon. For your own safety, please step outside while I get rid of the evil spirit. Then we will pray for you to receive the baptism of the Holy Spirit." She agreed and everything went quietly and without incident.

When she came back inside, she said, "Something is different."

"Yes, the evil spirit has spent its last day at your expense." We prayed with the laying on of hands.[282] She asked forgiveness for her sins and

---
[282] See Acts 8:17

received the baptism of the Holy Spirit with signs following. She said, "This is a new experience for me. Is this what my sister received?"

"Yes, it is. Now, why don't I go to the hospital to visit and pray with your husband?"

She agreed, "He would like that!"

Whenever demons invade and occupy a house, they can cause bad health. I suspected her husband's cancer was the result of such a situation. When we arrived in her husband's hospital room, a friend was visiting. Her husband was awake and hooked up to several intravenous support systems.

I asked him, "Are you a Christian?"

"Yes, I'm a Baptist."

"Have you received the baptism of the Holy Spirit yet?"

"No, but I have always wanted to."

"Then, I would like to pray with you for that – and also for healing."

He smiled.

I laid hands on him and prayed. He was baptized with the Holy Spirit and easily began to speak in tongues. I saw tears of joy on his cheeks. Then, I asked Jesus to heal him of this incurable cancer. They thanked me for coming.

Two weeks later, I telephoned to see how they were. The lady said, "My husband is home because Jesus healed him of the cancer, just like you asked!" Later, I visited and prayed with them, thanking God for what He had done.

37. When evil spirits leave a person they will not always leave quietly. Sometimes, they will scream and yell under protest. Occasionally, but very rarely, they may cause the person from whom they are being forced to leave to begin choking, coughing, and even to vomit; but this will happen only occasionally. If a Christian expects these physical reactions, as the sign that an evil spirits is leaving, the evil spirits will perform for them and usually not leave. Sometimes, when so-called exorcists have not realized there are no evil spirits in a person, they have been known to try to induce vomiting and the like.

The proof that demons have left a person and the person has received God's protection is that he or she will have the initial evidence of speaking in a new tongues language.

So those who received his word were baptized, and there were added that day about three thousand souls. (Acts 2:41)

Recently, I counselled a young woman who had been put through an ordeal by a woman who was supposed to have a deliverance ministry. This so-called exorcist punched her in the stomach and hit her physically for about six hours, trying to expel the demons whom she perceived to be in the woman. The young woman was hit and pummeled so much that she got sick to her stomach. The exorcist told her not to be alarmed, because her vomiting proved the demons were finally leaving. The young woman told me that she got sick to her stomach because she had been punched so often. She did not have a demon. She was baptized in the Holy Spirit and this woman with her so-called deliverance ministry could not tell the difference between the Holy Spirit and an evil spirit. The victim had been physically abused and could have had the exorcist charged with assault. There is a lot of this physical abuse going on in church circles, all under the banner of casting out demons – where there are none.

A woman in her mid-thirties came to me for help. She had attended a meeting where someone determined that she needed to have demons cast out of her because she had a facial twitch and a peculiar mannerism. Several people had forced her to the floor and held her there against her will. They then began to attempt to cast out various non-existent spirits. She became exasperated and angry and, when she realized they were looking for her to exhibit certain manifestations, she simply acted out what they expected of her so they would let her go free. These people had been unable to recognize the presence of the Holy Spirit in her and did not want to accept the legitimate signs following, by which Jesus tells us we can identify a born-again, Spirit-filled Christian. This woman was emotionally hurt from the experience. It took some counselling and encouragement to help her to forgive the people who had abused her.

Unfortunately, such people have just enough knowledge to make them dangerous to other people, Christians and non-Christians alike.

Such was not the case at *100 Huntley Street* Christian ministry some years ago, following a particular telecast. Father Bob MacDougall, a priest on staff, sent a volunteer counselor to ask me to come to the chapel where he wanted me to join him in setting a woman free from evil spirits. When I entered the chapel, the woman was lying on the floor. A man's voice was coming out of her mouth. Father Bob was gently kicking the sole of her shoe saying, "Come out in the Name of Jesus." The evil spirit was trying to argue with him. Father Bob was ignoring it and persistently saying, "Come out in the Name of Jesus."

I walked over to the woman and joined Father Bob. I said, "Yes, come out of this woman in the Name of Jesus Christ."

The woman turned her eyes on me and the voice said, "And you, you're stupid too."

I replied, "Well, you don't have to be very smart to know that. But, nevertheless, you have to leave, now, in the Name of Jesus Christ."

The demon left. The woman started to talk in her normal voice. Father Bob and I prayed with her to receive Jesus as her Savior and LORD and she began to speak in her new tongues language.[283] She walked out a free woman. There was no weirdness.

38. There will always be reactions to deliverance ministry. First, there will be those who will give thanksgiving and praise to God for setting the person free. Second, there will be criticism from those who do not believe that anybody can be possessed by evil spirits and who will, therefore, ridicule such ministry as a fraud or emotionalism. Third, there

---
[283] See Acts 2:4

will be criticism from some people in spiritual leadership who cannot tell the difference between the Holy Spirit and an evil spirit; these people will be in danger of committing the unpardonable sin.[284]

39. After an evil spirit leaves a person, a new tenant is required to take up residence in the formerly possessed person, or, if the evil spirit has not been properly sent to the abyss, the person will be in danger of having it return. The only safe tenant is the Holy Spirit. Therefore, it is of the utmost importance, for the person's future safety, to explain candidly what is going on in his or her life and to offer salvation and the baptism of the Holy Spirit, so that Jesus can be their Savior, Lord and Protector.

40. Any individual, or people whom you think need to have an evil spirit or spirits cast out of them, should be asked the following two questions:

1. Do you want to be set free?
2. Are you willing to invite Jesus Christ to be your Savior and Lord and be baptized with the Holy Spirit?

If the person agrees, you can proceed to take authority over the demon or demons in the person and command them to leave. Normally, there will be no physical reactions. If the person says "No" to either question, let him or her go on his or her way with the encouragement that, when they decide they want to be set free, they're welcome to return to see you.

One of my relatives has been harassed by a demon for many years. Early in his marriage, a man who lived next door to him in Niagara Falls, Canada, was murdered. From that day on, strange things began to happen in my relative's house. The lights in his house would go on and off at all times of the day or night. While he would be watching television, the electrical cord would be pulled suddenly out of the wall plug by unseen hands, rolled up and tied in a knot. There would be knocking on the walls and on an outside door – but no one would be there when the door was opened.

---
[284] See Matthew 12:22-37

My relative was not a religious person. In fact, he claimed to be an atheist with no belief in God or a spiritual world. He blamed the strange phenomena on the hydro electric power lines that went past his house. He finally became so frustrated that he built a second house behind his first one and moved into it. He then burned down the first house, believing the problem in it would disappear. However, he was wrong. The problem moved with him into his new house.

Eventually, the problem manifested as the ghost of a strange little old lady, who could be seen moving from room to room. The strange phenomena continued to happen. After several more years of irritation, my relative built a third house behind the second house and moved into it. He gave the second house to one of his sons and his family. One day, his son asked him, "Did you see any strange things in the house while you were living in it?" My relative would not admit that he had seen the spirit and been harassed by it for many years. Since he made me promise not to discuss this with anybody, including his son, until after his death I was unable to cast the demon out of the house. Despite the fact that I told him I could get rid of the evil spirit and give peace to the family, he remained unwilling to allow it to happen. They have since both died.

41. After an evil spirit has been cast out of a person, it is not wise to counsel the person about the problem they had and go into a lot of detail. Most people, after they have had evil spirits cast out of them, will have no memory, or very little memory, of the possession. Those who do, will soon lose the memory of it – if they have been led to invite Jesus to be their Savior and Lord and have been baptized with the Holy Spirit. The Holy Spirit will quickly do a healing of memories and the people will be in their right minds.[285]

The wisest thing to do is to encourage the person to develop a healthy relationship with Jesus Christ through studying the Bible, developing a healthy prayer life (including praying with their new tongues language every day),[286] participating in fellowship groups in the church, worship-

---
[285] See Luke 8:35
[286] See Ephesians 6:18

ping faithfully on Sunday and finding ways to serve Jesus Christ daily. If people become preoccupied with demons, they will live in constant fear. Conversely, if they are preoccupied with Jesus, they will live in power, love, and a sound mind.[287] They must be warned not to open themselves up again to evil spirits by participating in occult practices or going to places where they could be in danger of being attacked. Once filled with the Holy Spirit, however, they will belong to Jesus and, while they may occasionally harassed, they will not be able to be possessed.

42. Occasionally, after people have had evil spirits cast out of them, some may experience what I call a "bell echo effect." This means that, like a bell has an echo effect after it has stopped ringing, some people may think they continue to hear the evil spirit still talking or whispering to them – even after it has gone. It is similar to what happens after a person, who has been very close to someone else, dies, and the surviving person thinks that he or she hears the deceased person's voice, or even imagines seeing them in familiar surroundings. Such people will require frequent assurance that they are, indeed, free until the echo effect passes. The most effective assurance will come when the person has been baptized with the Holy Spirit and speaks in tongues.

43. We must be careful not to lay hands on a person when we are casting out demons, not so much for our own safety, but for the safety of other people. If we lay hands on a demon-possessed person when we command the evil spirits to leave, they may slither onto us, temporarily, until we place our hands on another person. The evil spirit will then transfer onto the next person we touch, and attempt to possess that person. I have seen this occur in prayer meetings or at the altar, when an invitation has been given to people to go to the front of the church service for prayer and ministry. This phenomenon is called the "transference of spirits." By not being careful, a person, who is praying for people, can unwittingly spread evil spirits among those who have come for prayer. The transferred demons will go home with the person and invade his or her home, possibly possessing the person or someone else in the home.

---

[287] See 2 Timothy 1:7

Also, it's important to never lay hands on a demon-possessed person, or one whom you suspect to be possessed, because the demon may react and cause injury in its attempt to prevent its exorcism.

44. It is not always necessary to minister deliverance in pairs. Because Jesus sent the seventy[288] out to do ministry in pairs, it is often thought it is necessary to send Christians out in twos to do ministry – especially to engage in spiritual warfare where evil spirits may have to be cast out. While this is a good suggestion when possible and appropriate, it is not always a necessity. When Jesus sent the seventy out, none of them had been baptized with the Holy Spirit. Although they had authority, they did not have the power to withstand warfare alone. While it is encouraging to have another Christian along (if it is someone who will not be frightened at the prospect of having to deal with evil spirits), it is optional, not compulsory. So, whether you go alone or with some other Christian, it is comforting to know, if you have been baptized with the Holy Spirit, that you are not alone, because the Comforter is always with you and will protect you. The same is true regarding fasting.

45. The devil will use vain imaginations, such as the concept of generational sin and curses, to sidetrack Christians, when they are trying to minister to the needs of other people. Because many Christians know neither the Scriptures nor the power of God,[289] this has been an easy thing for him to do. After confusing them with false understanding, he will sidetrack them by encouraging them to develop phantom ministries, illegitimate ministries or ministries geared to non-existent sin or problems.

For example, if we know neither the Scriptures nor the power of God, we may attempt to do ministry in an area that was mentioned in the Old Testament, but that was taken care of by Jesus at the Cross – and is, therefore, no longer a valid ministry. A case in point, is so-called "generational sin." We have whole ministries built on God's warning to Israel that He would visit the iniquity of the fathers upon the children unto the third

---

[288] See Luke 10:1
[289] See Matthew 22:29; Mark 12:24

and fourth generation of them that hate Him.[290] This means God said that He would make the children pay for the sins of their parents for three and four generations.

The truth is that God got rid of generational curses or generational sin in preparation for the New Covenant (see Jeremiah 31:27-34; Ezekiel 18:1-32). Now, everyone is responsible for his or her own sin.

The son shall not suffer for the iniquity of the father, nor the father suffer for the iniquity of the son; the righteousness of the righteous shall be upon himself, and the wickedness of the wicked shall be upon himself. (Ezekiel 18:20)

Nevertheless, demons like to challenge Christians by telling us generational sin gives them the right to remain in the person whom they have possessed.[291] Jesus' disciples tried to connect the blind man's blindness to generational curses when they questioned the cause of it.

"Rabbi, who sinned, this man or his parents, that he was born blind?"
Jesus answered, "It was not that this man sinned, or his parents, but that the works of God might be made manifest in him." (John 9:2-3)

Since the coming of the new covenant, each person is responsible for only his or her own sin. However, unless we're knowledgeable about what Jesus accomplished on the Cross, through studying the Scriptures, we can unwittingly, and unnecessarily, give demons permission to stay and defeat us. Every time a Christian speaks or prays in tongues, he or she is encouraged in the Spirit, regarding authority to deal with the devil and demons.

There have been many books written about the need to have this so-called generational sin dealt with today. Many ministries have been built upon this Old Testament curse. **Whatever reality exists in these ministries comes from the sin of the fathers being passed on through the transference of evil spirits, instead of through punishment by God.** This is another way the devil has tempted Christians to become pre-occupied with demons rather than Jesus Christ.

---

[290] See Exodus 20:5; 34:7; Deuteronomy 5:9
[291] See Exodus 20:5, 34:7; Numbers 14:18

The sad thing about such a so-called ministry is that, as far as God is concerned, the Bible tells us quite clearly that he no longer passes the sins of the fathers on to their children.

> *The word of the Lord came to me again: "What do you mean by repeating this proverb concerning the land of Israel, 'The fathers have eaten sour grapes, and the children's teeth are set on edge?' As I live, says the Lord God, this proverb shall no more be used by you in Israel. Behold, all souls are Mine; the soul of the father as well as the soul of the son is Mine: the soul that sins shall die. If a man is righteous and does what is lawful and right ... he shall surely live says the Lord God.... The soul that sins shall die. The son shall not suffer for the iniquity of the father, nor the father suffer for the iniquity of the son; the righteousness of the righteous shall be upon himself, and the wickedness of the wicked shall be upon himself."* (Ezekiel 18:1-20)

Notice that the revocation of generational sin came from Ezekiel, before the advent of Jesus. Paul reminds us that if we are in Christ, everything is new.

> *If we confess our sins, He is faithful and just, and will forgive our sins and cleanse us from all unrighteousness. If we say we have not sinned, we make Him a liar, and His Word is not in us.*
> (1 John 1:9-10)

> *So if anyone is in Christ, there is a new creation: everything old has passed away; see, everything has become new!* (2 Corinthians 5:17)

By getting Christians to focus on something that God changed under the new covenant, people can be hurt and spiritually abused. The enemy laughs at those who do not study to show themselves approved,

> *Do your best to present yourself to God as one approved, a workman who has no need to be ashamed, rightly handling the word of truth.*
> (2 Timothy 2:15)

46. Evil spirits will encourage people to believe that God is doing a "new thing" that replaces the new covenant of the Bible. The "new thing" *was* the new covenant.

47. Demons can disrupt church services, church meetings, prayer meetings, Bible study meetings or any meetings which have the purpose of *"equipping the saints for the work of ministry,"*[292] by encouraging people to go to sleep or to stay away from the meetings. They can disrupt any kind of a meeting; whether at work, school, university or home at unexpected times.

It's not unusual for people to tolerate disruptions which may be mistakenly assumed to be physical problems – when they are actually spiritual problems of demon possession.

48. Demons will try to convince people not to preach the gospel of Jesus Christ, supposedly because it will turn people off. They manipulate them into thinking they should develop a new paradigm to replace the New Testament paradigm (i.e. replace God's plan with something ineffective which will be so-called "seeker friendly" rather than Holy Spirit-friendly). Consequently, churches try to develop programs that won't offend anyone. They refuse to pay attention to God's Scriptures which state clearly that the gospel has a built-in offense which confronts people with the truth of their sin.[293] Demons will always provide the alternatives to the genuine gospel of Jesus Christ.

---

[292] See Ephesians 4:12
[293] See Matthew 6:1; 11:6; 13:57; John 6:61; 14:6-7; Mark 6:3; Luke 7:23

Hand to Hand Combat With the Enemy Forces

Tactical Operations

For though we live in the world we are not carrying on a worldly war, for the weapons of our warfare are not worldly but have divine power to destroy strongholds. We destroy arguments and every proud obstacle to the knowledge of God, and take every thought captive to obey Christ, being ready to punish every disobedience, when your obedience is complete. (2 Corinthians 10:3-6)

The Main Stronghold

The main stronghold we have to overcome, in our spiritual warfare, is sin – the result of disobedience to God and falling prey to the temptations of Satan and his demons.

...but each person is tempted when he is lured and enticed by his own desire. Then desire when it has conceived gives birth to sin; and sin when it is full-grown brings forth death. (James 1:14-15)

Since the devil is not omnipresent, he can be in only one place at one time to tempt people to sin; therefore, most of our temptation comes from within ourselves. Many people mistake the work of the Holy Spirit for the work of the devil. It is the responsibility of the Holy Spirit to convict the world concerning sin and righteousness and judgement.

And when He comes, He will convince the world concerning sin and righteousness and judgment. (John 16:8)

It's not a battle we can win through our own strength, strategies or fortunate breaks in life. It's foundational to understand that we are all held captive by sin, and that the only way to be set free, is to put our faith in Jesus Christ and the knowledge that He came to give His life as payment for the ransom demanded by sin. Only through His provision and plan, can we be victorious.

For the Son of Man came not to be served but to serve, and to give His life as a ransom for many. (Mark 10:45)

The major work of spiritual warfare, lies in dealing with sin. Some people sin outrageously, others more moderately, resulting in feelings of guilt. No matter how great or small the sin may seem to us, any sin at all cuts us off from God and prevents us from having a relationship with Him. It is receiving His forgiveness that establishes, or reestablishes, a relationship with God. The seriousness of sin has to be seen from God's viewpoint, not ours. However, when He forgives us, He forgives us for everything. That is why John's words are so encouraging and reassuring:

If we confess our sins, He is faithful and just, and will forgive our sins and cleanse us from all unrighteousness. (1 John 1:9)

Whether we know what all our sins have been or not, God forgives them all, when we go to Him for cleansing.

When God forgives us, we are "justified," which means He treats us just-as-if we had never sinned! Not only that, but He forgets it. We are then in a talking relationship with God.

And such were some of you. But you were washed, you were sanctified, you were justified in the Name of the LORD Jesus Christ and in the Spirit of our God. (1 Corinthians 6:11)

The cost of the ransom, demanded by sin, is rarely pointed out to us. I've had many people ask about the price Jesus had to pay for us. They wonder about the price of one soul – the worth of one person. Over and over again, I've had people ask, "What did it cost Jesus to save me? If my ransom were paid in dollars and cents, what would He have paid for my salvation?"

Rev. Melvin B. Tolson, a Methodist minister and professor at Wiley College in Marshall, Texas, recently became recognized in the movie, *The Great Debators*. He wrote: "The wickedness of the heart is beyond human understanding; so much so that Jesus attempted to get us to understand its damage to people and the whole earth itself, by putting a monetary value on the cost of one man's sin in the parable of the unforgiving servant.

In that parable, Jesus answered those questions in dollars and cents. The unforgiving servant owed the king 10,000 talents.[294] A talent was a measurement of gold. According to today's gold price, that servant (representing you or me) owed the king (God), $32,380,042,000.00 (32 billion, 380 million, 42 thousand dollars). Even if a person had that much money, he or she could not pay for his or her own sin because only a human who has not sinned can pay for our sin debt. The only Person who has not sinned is Jesus Christ.[295] It was He who paid for our sin on the Cross of Calvary.

When Jesus had received the vinegar, He said, "It is finished;" and He bowed His head and gave up His Spirit. (John 19:30)

"It is finished," meant "paid in full." We owed a huge debt and that's why we need a Savior. Even though the value of Jesus sacrifice of Himself, for us, far exceeded any monetary consideration, this story demonstrates the serious cost of our sin and underlines the fact that it would be impossible for any of us to pay the enormous ransom demanded by sin ourselves.

---

[294] See Matthew 18:21-35
[295] See Hebrews 4:15

The Fallout From Sin

Many people shrug their shoulders at the contention that they are sinners, saying they have never really committed any serious sin or wrongdoing. They have been, according to their own understanding, good moral people – good citizens. They have paid their taxes, have never been in trouble with the law, take pride in being good neighbors and are generally nice people. They have never been drug-addicts or alcoholics or abused their spouses or their children. They may have gone to church and worked hard all of their lives, perhaps establishing enviable reputations or standing in the community. However, they are still sinners, because they have broken God's laws, whether they recognize it or not. They may be 'gentle sinners,' as opposed to 'vicious sinners,' who have hurt others; but sadly, 'gentle sinners' are often blind to the reality that they cannot get to Heaven because of their good deeds and moral lives. They're under the dangerous illusion that being a 'good person' is their ticket.

Knowing God and having a personal relationship with Him, is key. Only when a person repents and invites Jesus to be Savior and Lord, can he or she have the right to go to Heaven. Once we have been forgiven, all our sin is forgiven and in God's eyes, we are washed whiter than snow.

By today's standards, the first sin didn't *seem* all that bad, either. Eve and Adam simply disobeyed God's command not to eat from one tree in the middle of the garden, by succumbing to the serpent's temptation to eat its fruit. The problem is that most of us do not understand the damage caused by even the most innocuous appearing sin. In order to catch a glimpse of the magnitude of the fallout, we need to look at the results of the first sin recorded in the Garden of Eden.[296] That one act of disobedience brought in sin, sickness and death – not just to the planet, but also to the whole of creation.

Consequently, every time a person sins, the effects are felt throughout the whole of creation. We are like tuning forks; when we sin, we send discordant notes throughout the world, affecting people and nature, causing immeasurable damage. God knew that the only way to get us to understand the damage caused by our sinning, and to deal with it, was

---
[296] See Genesis 3:1-24

to send Jesus to suffer and die on the Cross. That alone demonstrates the measure of our ignorance and disobedience.

A Preemptive Strike Against Sin: Spiritual Rebirth

Although we examined the meaning of spiritual rebirth and the baptism in the Holy Spirit in Chapter Five, because it is key to victory over the kingdom of darkness, it merits review here.

Jesus told the Pharisee, Nicodemus (a leader of the Jews), that he must be born again in order to enter the kingdom of God.

Jesus answered him, "Truly, truly, I say to you, unless one is born anew, he cannot see the kingdom of God." (John 3:3)

When Nicodemus questioned how that could happen, Jesus explained that he had to be born twice; once with water for repentance, and once of the Spirit, with the baptism of the Holy Spirit.

There are two components to being born again. The first is to be baptized with water for the forgiveness of sin. The second is the baptism of the Holy Spirit. When John the Baptist was asked if he was the Messiah, he said:

"I baptize you with water for repentance, but He who is coming after me is mightier than I, whose sandals I am not worthy to carry; He will baptize you with the Holy Spirit and with fire." (Matthew 3:11)

Because the "great commission" given to us by Jesus involves telling other people the message of the gospel so that they, too, can be saved, Jesus said He was sending the Holy Spirit to give us the necessary power to be witnesses.

And He said to them, "Go into all the world and preach the gospel to the whole creation. He who believes and is baptized will be saved; but he who does not believe will be condemned. (Mark 16:15-16)

But you will receive power when the Holy Spirit has come upon you; and you will be My witnesses in Jerusalem, in all Judea and Samaria, and to the ends of the earth. (Acts 1:8)

Going on the Offensive

An important aspect of the ministry of Jesus, was to introduce us to the person and personality of the Holy Spirit. It is the Holy Spirit who empowers us to take the offensive position in spiritual warfare. It is He who gives us the ability to tell others about Jesus Christ and demonstrate our own personal relationship with Him. Through His enabling, we have the gentle boldness to introduce people to Jesus personally, so they can know him as friend, Lord, Savior and God. He empowers us to reassure people that we do not have to be afraid of God anymore, like the slave with the one talent,[297] because Jesus paid for our sin. Now it's all about knowing God's love and finding His plan for our lives. It's important for people to understand that God will supply all of their needs *"according to His riches in glory in Christ Jesus"* (Philippians 4:19).

Holding our Positions

Being filled with the Spirit of God gives us access to His guidance and direction for the rest of our lives. Being baptized with the Holy Spirit empowers us to maintain our relationship with Jesus, once we have been saved.

When we are baptized with the Holy Spirit and allow Jesus to be Lord over our lives, certain signs will be evident in us. These signs are given to us so we'll always know, without any doubt (and regardless of what the devil may tell us), that Jesus has not abandoned us and the Holy Spirit has not left us. Jesus was very clear about what these signs are.

> *And these signs will accompany those who believe: in My Name they will cast out demons; they will speak in new tongues; they will pick up serpents, and if they drink any deadly thing, it will not hurt them; they will lay their hands on the sick, and they will recover.*
> (Mark 16:17-18)

The Holy Spirit gives us His gifts,[298] and His fruit,[299] identifying us as Christians.

---
[297] See Matthew 25:25
[298] See Romans 12:6-8; 1 Corinthians 12:8-10
[299] See Galatians 5:22-23

As encouragement for discouraging times when the enemy and other people try to tell us we're not saved and God has left us, Paul says,

"For the gifts and call of God are irrevocable." (Romans 11:29)

This means God does not take back the new life, nor any of the gifts He has given us, as His people. Whenever we need reassurance, we can read the Bible and use whatever gifts He has given us.

Every time we thank God for saving us, we stand our ground and defeat the devil and the kingdom of darkness. Every time we reject discouragement, and witness to someone about what Jesus has done in our lives, use a gift of the Holy Spirit, or acknowledge the fruit of the Holy Spirit, we take ground from the devil and the kingdom of darkness. Every time we allow the signs that identify us as Christians to be evident in our lives, we defeat him. Every time we cast out a demon, speak in tongues or pray for healing for someone with the laying on of hands, as directed by Jesus, we destroy the works of the devil. Every time God protects us when we pick up snakes or drink any deadly thing, we are defeating evil. Setting people free from the control of the kingdom of darkness is the goal of spiritual warfare.

Tactical Procedures Against Enemy Forces

It would be nice if the entire Christian realm would take a unified, coherent stand against the enemy forces, exhibiting the strength and authority we really have. Sadly, there's been so much confusion and fear surrounding the issue, that the tactical procedures have been less than valiant. Thence this book.

As it now stands, in an attempt to at least *pretend* that they believe the devil and evil spirits exist, many clergy give foolish advice to their church members about how to deal with the enemy. Some tell them to hang Bibles on the doors of their homes, hang religious medals dedicated to various saints in windows and on doors, prescribe "holy oil" to be smeared on the doors and windows of their homes, sprinkle "holy water" through their houses (hoping to keep the demons out), or pray that

God will intervene and drive out the evil spirits from their homes. The problem is that God has given us the authority to deal with these evil spirits and expects us to do it in the Name of Jesus and so it's unlikely that He will intervene – and even more unlikely that any of these other powerless ploys will work. God already won the war. The residual skirmishes are ours to battle.

All such advice from well-meaning pastors may sound spiritual, but it does nothing to fix the problem. Evil spirits leave only when commanded to leave by people who have received the authority of Jesus Christ, following salvation and the baptism of the Holy Spirit (with the evidence of the "signs following" in accordance with Mark 16:17-18). When we are ignorant of our spiritual enemies, of the Scripture, or of the power of God, we are left with a powerless, pathetic remnant of religion.[300] In order to have any hope of prevailing in this life, we must be people with a powerful faith, infused with the power of God. Paul reminded the Corinthian Church (and us) of the importance of demonstrating the power of God in our lives.

> *And my speech and my message were not in plausible words of wisdom, but in demonstration of the Spirit and of power, that your faith might not rest in the wisdom of men but in the power of God.*
> (1 Corinthians 2:4-5)

While I was the senior pastor of the Good Samaritan Church, Kitchener, Ontario, I received a visit from a woman, whose wedding ceremony I had conducted twenty years before. She was visibly upset and said, "I want you to tell me what has been happening to my family. I know you'll think we're all crazy, but I have to talk to somebody – so I came to you."

"Well," I said, "I have heard a lot of strange stories in my ministry, so please don't be afraid to tell yours."

"Well, all right! We have been living in our house for sixteen years. It has been terrible. After the first night we spent there, at six o'clock in the morning, we heard someone walking down the hall towards our bedroom. We thought it was one of our three children (they had two

---
[300] See 2 Timothy 3:5

girls and one boy). Our bedroom door opened and a short elderly man, who was *transparent*, a *ghost*, walked over to our bed and shook my arm. Then, he walked down to my oldest daughter's room and shook her arm to wake her up. He has been doing this every morning since we've lived here. It drives me crazy.

"I have spoken with several clergymen and they all tell me it's just my imagination. There are no such things as ghosts that would do that. I talked to my doctor and he said it was my imagination. I have talked with mediums, fortune tellers and other spiritualists and they all told me we are stuck with this ghost. Apparently, it has a right to be there, because it's the spirit of the man who used to live here. What can we do?"

"First of all," I said, as I looked over my calendar, "it's not the spirit of anyone who lived there. It is, what the Bible calls a 'familiar spirit,'[301] a type of evil spirit. However, I can go around to your house tomorrow morning and get rid of it, if you want me to."

She looked shocked, "Do you mean to tell me that, after sixteen years, you are going to walk into my house and get rid of it just like that?" She snapped her fingers.

"Yes, no problem! We Christians, who have been baptized with the Holy Spirit and speak in tongues, have authority over evil spirits. One thing I should mention; it will be necessary for me to be alone in the in the house when I go there. No one can be inside with me, for the safety of you and your family."

She agreed.

The next morning, I went to the house at the same time the evil spirit usually showed up – at six o'clock in the morning. It was a raised bungalow. I went through the basement rooms first, commanding any evil spirits to leave the house in the Name of Jesus Christ. As I went upstairs and into the hallway, I saw the little old man come walking through the front door. He had the features of a person, but I could see through his body in different places. He looked at me. I said to him, "I have been

---

[301] Leviticus 20:6,27; Deuteronomy 18:11; 1 Samuel 28:7-9; 2 Kings 21:6; 23:24; 1 Chronicles 10:13; 2 Chronicles 33:6; Isaiah 8:19; 19:3; 29:4

looking for you. I command you, in the Name of Jesus Christ, to leave this house and to go to the abyss and never come back here again." Without a word, the demon turned around, walked back down the hall and through the closed door. It never returned.

About five years later, the couple celebrated their twenty-fifth wedding anniversary. At the party, I was greeted by their son. I said, "I haven't seen you for a few years."

He smiled. "Not since you got rid of that spirit in our house."

No Neutral Territory

Some people are under the erroneous understanding that certain people cannot be possessed with demons. In truth, demons can attack and possess anybody who is not a Christian and who has not received the baptism of the Holy Spirit. Conversely, they can attack and harass, but *not* possess, any Christian who has the Holy Spirit living in them. They can invade any house or building, church or place of worship, without the permission of the people who live or work in the buildings.

The Question of Children

Many think babies and children, under a certain age, are exempted from being attacked or possessed by demons. This is based upon a wrong teaching, that babies and children are innocent and have never sinned. This is completely untrue.

> *But now the righteousness of God has been manifested apart from law, although the law and the prophets bear witness to it, the righteousness of God through faith in Jesus Christ for all who believe. For there is no distinction; since all have sinned and fall short of the glory of God, they are justified by His grace as a gift, through the redemption which is in Christ Jesus, whom God put forward as an expiation by His blood, to be received by faith.* (Romans 3:21-25a)

We are all born with sinful natures. The only person who was born without sin, and who never sinned, was Jesus Christ.[302] He came to forgive our sins. John the Baptist was speaking of Jesus when he said,

---
[302] See Hebrews 4:15

> *"I baptize you with water for repentance, but He who is coming after me is mightier than I, whose sandals I am not worthy to carry; He will baptize you with the Holy Spirit and with fire."* (Matthew 3:11)

The baptism of the Holy Spirit is our only protection against being possessed by demons. This is why I suggest to parents that it is important for little children, usually about three-years-old, to have prayer to receive salvation and the baptism of the Holy Spirit. In so doing, they receive God's protection against possession by evil spirits.

The first child from whom I cast out demons, was the little three-year-old girl who bounced up and down in her crib like a basketball, without moving a muscle.

While preaching at the Crossroads Christian Assembly, Newcastle, Ontario, I was asked by a friend, Rev. David Black (who pastored a church in the neighboring town of Newtonville, Ontario), to go to his home to meet a married couple. The woman was studying for the Presbyterian ministry and she was in her final year of seminary in Toronto, Ontario. They explained that, although they were born-again Christians, they had never received the baptism of the Holy Spirit. They had a six-month-old baby. At their request, I prayed with them, with the laying on of hands, to receive the baptism of the Holy Spirit. They both fell to the floor speaking in tongues. We then prayed together with both the mind and with the Spirit, for God's plan for their lives. They were now prepared for her ordination and the ministry that Jesus had planned for them.

> *What am I to do? I will pray with the spirit and I will pray with the mind also; I will sing with the spirit and I will sing with the mind also.* (1 Corinthians 14:15)

They added that they had another problem – a serious spiritual problem. While nursing her baby at three o'clock in the morning, the woman had been sitting on a couch in their living room in the dark, when she began to pray out loud. A voice in the darkness shouted at her, "That is not going to do you any good." Startled, she jumped off the couch and turned on the lights. She could see no one, but this was nothing new to her. She and her husband had heard voices from time to time, in different rooms in their house. There was never anyone to be seen. They were worried, especially for the safety of their baby girl.

When I explained that it sounded as though they had some evil spirits living in their house, they didn't want to go home. However, I told them that, with their permission, I could go through the house on my way to the church service, and cast them out. They gave me permission. So, on my way to the service, I went to their house to cast the demons out or, as I prefer to call it, to bless out the house.

They returned to their house two days later and gave me a call. The woman asked, "Did you go through every room in our house to get rid of the evil spirits? We can still hear voices in two rooms."

Since it had been dark when I went through it, I asked her to describe the floor plan of her house to me. As she did, I realized I had missed two rooms.

"No problem!" I said. "Since you have received the baptism of the Holy Spirit, you now have the authority to cast the evil spirits out of your house yourself." I explained what she needed to do to cast them out. Then, I said, "Tell your husband to take your daughter outside while you bless the rooms out, because sometimes the evil spirits will resist being sent to the abyss. In such cases, they will attack anybody in the house."

She agreed. Her husband took their daughter outside to the driveway. As he was holding the little girl, he thought he should pray for his daughter's protection. Not knowing what was about to happen, he said, "I command anything that is not of Jesus Christ to leave my daughter." A demon came out of the girl and attacked him. It attempted to go into his mouth. He coughed, choked and began to speak in tongues. The demon backed away from him, growled and took another run at him, in an attempt to go into his mouth. He ran into his house, handed his daughter over to his wife and fell on his knees on the kitchen floor. The demon growled and attacked him. He choked, spoke in tongues, and the demon backed away. But again, the demon growled and attacked him. Again he choked, coughed, spoke in tongues – and the demon backed away. Every time it attempted to go into his mouth, a clear white liquid called "ectoplasm" poured out of the demon. It continued attacking him. Every time it attempted to go into his mouth, the ectoplasm would pour out onto the floor.

The wife took a drain board from her kitchen sink to catch it and dump it into the sink. After two hours of these attacks, she called our pastor friend, who said, "I have never had any experience with anything like this. Call the Pentecostal pastor." She called the Pentecostal pastor and explained what was happening to her husband. He responded, "I have never had experience with anything like this. Call Gordon Williams."

She called me and described the situation. I asked her to hold the phone where I could hear what was going on. I could hear the demon growling and the squish, as the ectoplasm flowed out and the evil spirit tried to go into the man's mouth and possess him. Then, I heard the man choke and cough and begin to speak in tongues and then the growling of the demon as it backed away from him.

"I'll get there as soon as possible." It took me two and a quarter hours to drive back to their home. However, I instructed the wife to take their baby out of the house so she wouldn't have to watch what was going on.

She objected, "But, what will happen to my husband?"

"Your husband is being attacked by a stupid demon who doesn't know that it cannot enter him – but it's continuing to try."

When I arrived, their kitchen floor was completely covered with ectoplasm that had squirted out from the evil spirit every time it attempted to go inside the man. I watched as the demon growled at him and attempted to enter his body through his mouth. The ectoplasm came pouring out from his mouth, as the demon made each fruitless attempt and backed away for yet another try. I commanded the evil spirit, "In the Name of Jesus Christ, I command you, evil unclean spirit, to leave this man and this house and go to the abyss and stay there." It obeyed.

I pulled my friend up off his knees. He asked, "Are you sure it's gone? I think it's stuck in my throat."

I got a flashlight and asked him to open his mouth. I could see that the uvula, the small piece of flesh that hangs down from the middle of the soft palate above the back of the tongue, was swollen up as big as my small finger. It was also pushed forward, because of the evil spirit trying repetitively to go inside, but coming back out, for over four hours. I pushed the uvula back in place with my finger and said, "It is gone!"

Because he is a singer, I told the man, "Now, I am going through this house for the last time and I'm going to get rid of any more evil spirits that might be here. I want you to stand up and sing praises to Jesus Christ." While he sang, I went through every room in the house driving out every evil spirit that remained. Then, I cleaned up the ectoplasm that had covered the kitchen floor and any place I could determine had been touched with it with paper towels and detergent. I put the contents in a plastic garbage bag and took it home with me, hoping to take a sample to a laboratory for testing. However, before I could do so, my wife put it into the garbage collection.

A couple of weeks later, the woman called and asked, "When evil spirits live in a house, do they leave behind residue that can cause allergies?"

"I have never been asked that question before. But, no doubt they leave some kind of residue behind when they can and it strikes me that the ectoplasm I cleaned up might be responsible in this case. Whatever the case, there is a good possibility that they could cause allergies."

She explained, "I have just had our house tested for allergies. The two rooms, where the evil spirits seemed to have stayed most, tested positive for allergies. However, the tests could not determine what it was that was causing them."

We must conclude that demons can, and do, leave behind toxic residue which can cause various sicknesses or allergies and which will victimize the people who reside there.

Since this couple had been baptized with the Holy Spirit for only two days, and had no experience casting out evil spirits, they were easily victimized by an evil spirit who was not very bright. What an introduction to spiritual warfare!

I received a telephone call, one afternoon, from a woman who explained, "You do not know me, but I know you from seeing you on television. I have a problem, of which I have just become aware. My daughter's best friend stayed overnight with our family. Last night, I put the girls in the bathtub together and came downstairs while they were playing and washing. I was shocked when I heard an elderly woman's voice talking to the two girls upstairs. I couldn't make out her words, but I knew nobody was in our house except the two girls and myself. I went up stairs, where I found the two girls alone, and asked who they were talking to. They exchanged looks at each other, but wouldn't say anything. I insisted they tell me who they were talking to, because I was the mommy and they had to tell me. Finally, my daughter said, 'We were talking to the green lady with the long green fingernails and black clothes. She lives upstairs in the attic. She told us we weren't to tell anybody, especially you, that she was here.' I was startled and suspected the green woman might be a demon. Could this be possible?"

I told her that the green lady was probably a demon who was trying to be friendly with the children, to win their favor, before hurting them and perhaps possessing them. Demons have only one purpose, like the devil. It is to "steal, kill and destroy."

The thief comes only to steal and kill and destroy. I came that they may have life, and have it abundantly. (John 10:10)

The mother asked, "What can we do about it?"

I asked, "Are you a Christian?"

"Yes, I am and I have received the baptism of the Holy Spirit and have spoken in tongues."

"Then, you have the authority to deal with the green demon. It will probably not show itself to you, but if you follow my instructions, you can get rid of it and send it to the abyss. Here's what to do: go from room to room, commanding this and any other evil spirits to leave your house, in the Name of Jesus Christ. Then tell them to go to the abyss. That done, invite the Holy Spirit to fill your home with His presence. Also, for the children's protection, they both need to ask Jesus to be their Savior."

She interjected, "They have both done that."

"Then, they also both need to receive the baptism of the Holy Spirit, with the evidence of speaking in tongues."

She said, "They are only eight and nine years old. Can they be baptized with the Holy Spirit and speak in tongues at those ages?"

I said, "Anybody who can call on the Name of the LORD, especially children, can receive the Holy Spirit and have an exciting relationship with Jesus Christ, just like adults." I also told her that if she had any problem getting rid of this demon, she should call me back and I would travel to her home in St. Catharine's.

Later, she called me back and explained, "I did everything you told me to do. The demon is gone. The girls are baptized with the Holy Spirit and they are speaking in tongues."

I am often asked, "What sinful or wrong thing have we done to have our house invaded by demons?"

I have tried to find the answer to that question. First of all, demons seem to possess – indiscriminately – anyone who is not a born again, Spirit-baptized Christian. All people are vulnerable to possession until they have the Christian experience of Pentecost.

There does not seem to be any requirement for possession by demons except that a person cannot be born again and baptized with the Holy Spirit. Even believers are possessable if they have not received the baptism of the Holy Spirit, with the evidence of speaking in tongues and the signs Jesus described.

At this point, I need to add a further caveat. Anyone who is involved in any kind of occult practice or spiritual exercises associated with eastern religions, is practically guaranteed to be possessed by a demon. Occult practices are listed in Deuteronomy 18:9-14.

No one shall be found among you who makes a son or daughter pass through fire, or who practices divination, or is a soothsayer, or an augur, or a sorcerer, or one who casts spells, or who consults ghosts or spirits, or who seeks oracles from the dead. For whoever does these things is abhorrent to the Lord*; it is because of such abhorrent practices that the* Lord *your God is driving them out before you. You must remain completely loyal to the* Lord *your God. Although these nations that you are about to dispossess do give heed to soothsayers and diviners, as for you, the* Lord *your God does not permit you to do so. They include going to fortune-tellers and séances; playing with Ouija boards; consulting witches and wizards and the like. Anyone who has done these sorts of things needs to confess it to God and to reject the spirit associated with it.* (Deuteronomy 18:10-14)

Demons will invade the homes of Christians who are doing ministry to try to prevent them from being faithful to Jesus Christ.

On the flip side, they will also invade the homes of people who are *not* believers – to frighten them, so that they will not become believers. They will indiscriminately invade non-Christian homes because the people who live there are sinners, who do not know and believe in the most high God, who is Jesus Christ.

The bottom line is that evil spirits will invade homes, regardless of whether the people living in them are Christian believers or not. If they invade Christian homes, I tell the people that it is because they are being faithful to Jesus and the demons are trying to trip them up. While it can be viewed as a compliment from that perspective, it's important not to get discouraged; but to take authority over the evil spirits, cast them out and invite the Holy Spirit to fill the house with His presence. While evil spirits try to intimidate people into thinking that they cannot be driven away or cast out of possessed people, Jesus Christ has given Spirit-filled Christian believers authority over them, regardless of their visible displays of power. The experience of casting evil spirits out, gives a Christian more confidence in carrying out his or her ministry.

In the course of my research, I learned that many books and teachings available today carry incorrect teaching, and can victimize and spiritually abuse Christians. Many, if not most, of the books on so-called deliverance are really manuals on how to teach Christians to worship demons. Self-accredited experts have even invented a term which they think is a better translation of the Greek word which means to be possessed with an evil spirit or a demon, and that word is "demonized."

Everywhere we see the devastation of Christians who have been damaged and left floundering, feeling that they have failed Jesus Christ. These Christians have been victimized – or should I say "demonized" – by so-called experts in deliverance ministry. Many have been accused of not cooperating in their deliverances. Such nonsense! It is not they who failed Jesus Christ; it was their pastors and counselors who did not know what they were doing.

Unfortunately, many such pastors and counselors have picked up just enough knowledge to make them extremely dangerous. They are like ambulance medics who, because they know first-aid and may have saved a few lives at the scene of a car accident, imagine themselves to be fully qualified, even ranking right up there with medical doctors, and think they can begin doing major surgery. The result is that they may kill, hurt, or lose fragile patients, but they excuse themselves by saying, "Oh, she didn't have enough faith," "He wouldn't cooperate," "They didn't really want to be set free," "He wouldn't release the demon" or "They wouldn't receive their deliverance."

Such people may make a great show of casting out demons. In fact, they'll see them in everybody. It's common for them to misidentify sin as the work of demons. Such are those of whom Jesus spoke:

> *"Not every one who says to me, 'LORD, LORD,' shall enter the kingdom of Heaven, but he who does the will of my Father who is in Heaven. On that day many will say to me, 'LORD, LORD, did we not prophesy in Your Name, and cast out demons in Your Name, and do many mighty works in Your Name?' And then will I declare to them, 'I never knew you; depart from Me, you evildoers.'"* (Matthew 7:21-23)

It's important to be wary of anyone whose main claim to fame is that they have a deliverance ministry. Those people are usually preoccupied with demons and know just enough to make themselves dangerous. When they look at people who have problems, they will always see demons. The best response to someone like that is to do what Joseph did when Potiphar's wife wanted to take him to bed: run for your life in the opposite direction.

On the other hand, a balanced Christian counselor will bring healing. He or she will be able to tell the difference between sin, evil spirits and the Holy Spirit.

Every Christian, according to Jesus, has a deliverance ministry,[303] but it's critical for each one to learn how to differentiate between sin and the activity of demons and, where demons are involved, to learn how to deal with them carefully. In actual fact, there are very few people who truly require deliverance ministry.

---

[303] See Mark 16:17

Skilled Warfare

Sending Demons to the Abyss

Demon possession refers to the process whereby an evil spirit actually enters a person and controls his or her thinking, actions and bodily functions; and causes that person to do things he or she would not ordinarily want to do. If the possessed person does not cooperate, they are often tormented, injured and sometimes even killed. So intense can the torment be, that possessed people will often, in an attempt to escape the evil spirit or spirits who possess them, either commit, or attempt to commit, suicide.

Symptoms of Demon Possession

We need to look at the symptoms of demon possession observed in the man called "Legion."[304]

- He was acting weird.
- He was living in degraded and dehumanized conditions.
- He was not wearing any clothes.
- He was not living in a house, but among the tombs.
- He had superhuman strength (he had broken the chains and fetters that bound him)

---
[304] See Mark 5:1-15; Luke 8:26-39

- Nobody could control him.
- His behavior was frightening to people.
- He appeared to be out of control of his own body. (He self-mutilated.)
- He appeared to have epileptic-type seizures.

Night and day among the tombs and on the mountains he was always crying out and bruising himself with stones. (Mark 5:5)

Luke tells us the demons drove him into the desert.

For he had commanded the unclean spirit to come out of the man. (For many a time it had seized him; he was kept under guard, and bound with chains and fetters, but he broke the bonds and was driven by the demon into the desert.) (Luke 8:29)

Casting Out (Evicting, Exorcising or Removing) Demons

The casting out of demons, which is commonly called deliverance, is one of the most controversial aspects of Christian ministry today.

This controversy and the unwillingness of most churches to recognize the problem, has left many people who are affected by demons; whether they may be suffering from demon possession, living in a house that has been invaded by demons or struggling under some other aspect of demonization, trapped and without hope – living in fear and torment. The good news is that we Christians, who have been baptized with the Holy Spirit, have the spiritual authority to deal with this problem.

And these signs will accompany those who believe: in My Name they will cast out demons; they will speak in new tongues; they will pick up serpents, and if they drink any deadly thing, it will not hurt them; they will lay their hands on the sick, and they will recover. (Mark 16:17-18)

When demons are in torment, the possessed person is also in pain. Demons cannot tolerate the presence of the Holy Spirit. It puts them in agony because they know He gives Spirit-filled Christians the authority to deal with them, sending them to the abyss for their punishment as Jesus did. They'll try anything to keep from being sent there.

Any presence of evil spirits is a direct hindrance to God's plans to save and baptize people with the Holy Spirit. When they possess people, they are taking the Holy Spirit's rightful place.

Laying the Groundwork for Deliverance

Before trying to cast evil spirits out of anyone, it is vitally important to warn them about what will happen if they are not willing to allow Jesus Christ to be their Savior and Lord. If the person does not want to be set free from the evil spirit, it is unwise to cast it out, because it will return with others and the person will end up in much worse condition.

In spite of the demonic control, inevitably, the time will come when a possessed person will call out for help. This is what happened when the possessed man ran and fell down at the feet of Jesus and worshipped Him.

Obviously, it is always important to ask for, and receive, a possessed person's permission to cast out the demon.[305] If we go ahead, arrogantly, without the possessed person's permission, we can make a bad situation worse.

When the Gerasene demoniac saw Jesus, he cried out and fell down before him, and said with a loud voice,

> "What have You to do with me, Jesus, Son of the Most High God? I beseech You, do not torment me." (Luke 8:28)

This was this possessed man's strange way of asking for help.

There are situations where people enjoy being possessed – for a period of time – because demons sometimes give people (who are not grounded in the Scriptures) a counterfeit religious experience. Later on, however, these people discover they have lost control of themselves. As the demon or demons gain progressive control over them, the people may lack the ability to speak for themselves.

Surprisingly, not everyone wants to be set free. An evil spirit can provide a person with a religious experience that can be addictive. For

---

[305] Although Paul did not follow this procedure with the slave-girl who had a spirit of divination (Acts 16), it is advisable.

example, demons can use a possessed person as a medium, to deceive people into believing they can communicate with loved ones who have died. Of course, they cannot, but people, who are not knowledgeable about what Scripture says, are vulnerable to being controlled by deception and kept in the kingdom of darkness. Many people do not want to serve God and have chosen to serve the devil in the kingdom of darkness.

> *Enter by the narrow gate; for the gate is wide and the way is easy, that leads to destruction, and those who enter by it are many. For the gate is narrow and the way is hard, that leads to life, and those who find it are few.* (Matthew 7:13-14)

The road that leads to life is hard, but not for those who have been saved and baptized with the Holy Spirit, and who have the power of the Holy Spirit to walk on it. It is, of course, the most exciting way.

"This Kind Never Comes Out Except by Prayer and Fasting"[306]

In gaining confidence to step forward and continue the ministry of Jesus, it's critical to understand what kind of preparation needs to be made. Most Christians have been led to believe that prayer and fasting from eating food is necessary before they can cast out demons/evil spirits. This comes from a misunderstanding based on Jesus' admonition in Matthew 17:21:

> *"This kind never comes out except by prayer and fasting."*
> (Matthew 17:21)

One time I fasted from food for a whole month in an attempt to get the Holy Spirit to show me the next kind of ministry Jesus wanted me to do. At the end of the fast, He told me nothing. It was only later, in a prayer meeting, that He spoke to me and told me I was going to begin the work of an evangelist.[307] Fasting from food does not move Jesus to tell us what we want to hear.

---

[306] Matthew 17:21
[307] Ephesians 4:11

It's important to understand that this admonition came before Jesus' followers had received the baptism of the Holy Spirit with the *"signs following,"*[308] on the Day of Pentecost. The first of these *"signs"* is the authority to cast our demons. This authority is with us at all times when we have received the baptism of the Holy Spirit.

When the disciples were unsuccessful casting the demons out of people before they had received the baptism of the Holy Spirit, their only recourse was to "pray and fast."

There has been widespread misunderstanding stemming from a misinterpretation of Jesus' words when He appeared to His disciples after being raised from the dead.

"He who believes in Me, as the Scripture has said, 'Out of his heart shall flow rivers of living water.'" Now this He said about the Spirit, which those who believed in Him were to receive; for as yet the Spirit had not been given, because Jesus was not yet glorified." (John. 7:38-9)

Jesus said to them again, "Peace be with you. As the Father has sent Me, even so I send you." And when He had said this, He breathed on them, and said to them, "Receive the Holy Spirit. If you forgive the sins of any, they are forgiven; if you retain the sins of any, they are retained." (John 20:21-23)

According to the Greek grammar, He was saying, "In the future, you will receive the Holy Spirit. When that happens, if you forgive the sins of any, they are forgiven; if you retain the sins of any, they are retained."

That would happen after Jesus ascended into Heaven.

And while staying with them He charged them not to depart from Jerusalem, but to wait for the promise of the Father, which, He said, "you heard from Me, for John baptized with water, but before many days you shall be baptized with the Holy Spirit." (Acts 1:4-5)

As we know, the disciples were amongst the first 120 people to receive the Holy Spirit.[309]

---

[308] Acts 2: 4; Mark 16:17-18
[309] Acts 2:4

After receiving the baptism of the Holy Spirit, while it is not necessary to fast in terms of refusing food, there is another kind of fasting that is required. Today it is no longer about abstinence from food, because that would make it a 'works righteousness,' or an attempt to influence Jesus to show us an earned favour.

Today's fasting is all about doing the will of our Heavenly Father. It was explained clearly by God through the prophet Isaiah.

> *"Is not this the fast that I choose: to loose the bonds of wickedness, to undo the thongs of the yoke, to let the oppressed go free and to break every yoke? Is it not to share your bread with the hungry, and bring the homeless poor into your house; when you see the naked, to cover him and not hide yourself from your own flesh. Then shall your light break forth like the dawn, and your healing shall spring up speedily; your righteousness shall go before you, the glory of your LORD shall be your rear guard. Then you shall call, and the LORD will answer; you shall cry, and He will say, Here am I."* (Isaiah 58: 6-9)

This is the kind of "fasting" which will remain the measurement of faithfulness by which we shall all be judged when Jesus returns.

> *Not every one who says to Me, "LORD, LORD," shall enter the kingdom of Heaven, but he who does the will of My Father who is in Heaven.* (Matthew 7:21)

> *When the Son of Man comes in His glory, and all the angels with Him, then He will sit on His glorious throne. Before Him will be gathered all the nations, and He will separate them one from another as a shepherd separates the sheep from the goats, and He will place the sheep at His right hand, but the goats at the left. Then the King will say to those at His right hand, "Come, O blessed of My Father, inherit the kingdom prepared for you from the foundation of the world; for I was hungry and you gave Me food, I was thirsty and you gave Me drink, I was a stranger and you welcomed Me, I was naked and you clothed Me, I was sick and you visited Me, I was in prison and you came to Me."*

Then the righteous will answer him, "Lord, when did we see Thee hungry and feed Thee, or thirsty and give Thee drink? And when did we see Thee a stranger and welcome Thee, or naked and clothe Thee? And when did we see Thee sick or in prison and visit Thee?'
And the King will answer them, "Truly, I say to you, as you did it to one of the least of these My brethren, you did it to me." Then He will say to those at His left hand, "Depart from Me, you cursed, into the eternal fire prepared for the devil and his angels; for I was hungry and you gave Me no food, I was thirsty and you gave Me no drink, I was a stranger and you did not welcome Me, naked and you did not clothe Me, sick and in prison and you did not visit Me."
Then they also will answer, "Lord, when did we see Thee hungry or thirsty or a stranger or naked or sick or in prison, and did not minister to Thee?"
Then He will answer them, "Truly, I say to you, as you did it not to one of the least of these, you did it not to Me."
And they will go away into eternal punishment, but the righteous into eternal life. (Matthew 25:31-46)

This is the daily fast that we are called to perform as we serve Jesus in the power and baptism of the Holy Spirit.

When confronted by a situation where demons/evil spirits need to be cast out of people, there is most often no time to prepare in any human way. But once we receive forgiveness, salvation and the baptism of the Holy Spirit, the preparation has already been accomplished and we are ready to cast out any kind of demon/evil spirit. We need to be in constant communication with the Holy Spirit everyday, always ready to do His will. He is our Jesus-appointed Counselor. When we receive Him, He never leaves us.

The gifts and call of God are irrevocable. (Romans 11:29)

As the King James Version translates it, *"The gifts and calling of God are without repentance."* (Romans 11:29)

This means that when we receive the baptism (gift) of the Holy Spirit and His ministry gifts, the gifts with which He has equipped us for His service will never be taken from us. This means we have full equipping, preparation and authority to do what Jesus has called us to do – which includes casting out demons whenever it is required. In other words, the Holy Spirit does not come and go from our hearts as long as we live.

Once we have been prepared for dealing with evil spirits by receiving the baptism of the Holy Spirit, the only further preparation that may be needed is to confess any outstanding sin and ask Jesus to forgive us for anything that may stand between Him and ourselves, and fill us afresh with the Holy Spirit.

If we confess our sins, He is faithful and just to forgive us our sins and to cleanse us from all unrighteousness. (1 John 1:9)

And do not be drunk with wine, in which is dissipation; but be filled with the Spirit. (Ephesians 5:18)

It doesn't matter how powerful or threatening the demons/evil spirits act towards us, what kind of tantrums they throw or how dangerous they may try to appear, they must obey anyone who has received the baptism of the Holy Spirit. These people have been prepared with the *"signs"* following to carry out the ministry of Jesus.

Evil spirits may come up with all kinds of accusations to make Christians think they may have lost authority – like the fact that their children are not serving God or their spouse is backslidden. They'll taunt them with things like, "You aren't tithing, so I don't have to do what you tell me," even when the person is actually tithing. They'll try anything to convince believers not to cast them out and send them to the abyss.

Demons love to remind us about past sin (that has already been confessed and forgiven) in an effort to persuade us that we really do not have either the right or the authority to cast them out. Whenever they try that sort of attack, we can simply thank them for reminding us of how good Jesus has been to forgive us all our sin and cleanse us from all unrighteousness – and thank Jesus for forgiving us and baptizing us with the Holy Spirit, giving us authority over the demons! With that, we can command the arguing demons to leave in Jesus' Name and go to the abyss.

Watching Jesus as the Expert in Deliverance Ministry

Jesus is the real expert in this area of ministry. If we observe closely how He set people free from possession, we can, with compassion and guidance of the Holy Spirit, learn lessons that will prevent us from victimizing people who need our help. Many people have suffered at the hands of well-meaning Christians who haven't had a clue about how to minister deliverance properly and effectively. Following the way Jesus did things eliminates all kinds of difficulties.

When dealing with evil spirits, it does not matter what so-called kind or class of demons they are; they are all dealt with in basically the same way. An evil spirit is just an evil spirit. Any kind of demon can be cast out in the same way. So, regardless of how we have to deal with them, the same principles apply, as evidenced through the ministry of Jesus.

> *And He went about all Galilee, teaching in their synagogues and preaching the gospel of the kingdom and healing every disease and every infirmity among the people. So His fame spread throughout all Syria, and they brought Him all the sick, those afflicted with various diseases and pains, demoniacs, epileptics, and paralytics, and He healed them.* (Matthew 4:23-24)

Casting out demons was seen as a form of healing. Now let's get down to specific cases with which Jesus dealt so we can understand how to minister correctly. Just as there were people who were possessed with demons then, there are people who have been possessed with them today.

The first case of Jesus dealing with a person who was possessed with an evil spirit, was a man who lived in the area of Gadara, and who is described as having an unclean spirit.

> *They came to the other side of the sea, to the country of the Gerasenes. And when He had come out of the boat, there met Him*

out of the tombs a man with an unclean spirit, who lived among the tombs; and no one could bind him any more, even with a chain; for he had often been bound with fetters and chains, but the chains he wrenched apart, and the fetters he broke in pieces; and no one had the strength to subdue him. Night and day among the tombs and on the mountains he was always crying out, and bruising himself with stones. And when he saw Jesus from afar, he ran and worshiped Him; and crying out with a loud voice, he said, "What have you to do with me, Jesus, Son of the Most High God? I adjure you by God, do not torment me."
For He had said to him, "Come out of the man, you unclean spirit!" And Jesus asked him, "What is your name?"
He replied, "My name is Legion; for we are many." And he begged Him eagerly not to send them out of the country.
Now a great herd of swine was feeding there on the hillside; and they begged him, "Send us to the swine, let us enter them."
So He gave them leave. And the unclean spirits came out, and entered the swine; and the herd, numbering about two thousand, rushed down the steep bank into the sea, and were drowned in the sea. The herdsmen fled, and told it in the city and in the country. And people came to see what it was that had happened. And they came to Jesus, and saw the demoniac sitting there, clothed and in his right mind, the man who had had the legion; and they were afraid.
(Mark 5:1-15; see also Luke 8:26-39*)*

This is the classic teaching example of how to exorcise a person who is clearly possessed with evil spirits, as evidenced by many of the symptoms or characteristics.

This man had been dehumanized by the demons inside which controlled him. He was not in his right mind. He was wearing no clothes and lived alone under strange circumstances in a cemetery amongst the tombs. Having broken the chains which people had put on him to subdue and control him, and having escaped from his guards, he had superhuman strength. His life was marked by frantic hyperactivity. The demon had driven him into the desert, so he was traveling throughout the area, frightening people with his wild, uncontrollable behavior, crying out loud and cutting himself.

The demon in this story had a name; it was "Legion." Demons have actual names. They are not called, "the spirit of hate" or "the spirit of lust"; they have names. The name of the most mentioned demon in the Bible is "Baal." In this particular case, there was more than one demon possessing the man. The name, Legion, indicates that there were probably between 3,000 and 6,000 demons, because their spokesperson said, "for we are many."

When the man came face to face with Jesus, the demons recognized Jesus right away. Obviously, being in His presence caused them pain and torment, because they caused the man to fall down before Jesus.

What have you to do with me, Jesus, Son of the Most High God? I beseech You, do not torment me. (Luke 8:28)

How did Jesus handle the demoniac? He was frightened by neither the man's behavior, nor his appearance. In fact, it was the other way around. The demons in him were frightened by Jesus.

The demons, like a lot of people, thought they could talk Jesus into changing his mind. They tried to offer an alternative and outsmart Him, so they wouldn't have to go to the abyss, their place of punishment. They wanted Him to allow them to go into a herd of 2,000 swine that was feeding on the hillside so they could continue their rebellion against God. Any person or demon who thinks Jesus is a fool, will discover that He deals with people and demons with perfect justice.

Far be it from Thee to do such a thing, to slay the righteous with the wicked, so that the righteous fare as the wicked! Far be that from Thee! Shall not the Judge of all the earth do right? (Genesis 18:25)

Jesus cast them out of the demoniac by simply commanding them to leave, despite the fact that they didn't want to go. He did not touch the man; nor did he yell, scream or argue with them. He simply exercised

His authority over them. Although He gave them permission to enter the swine, once they left the demoniac and went into the herd, the swine stampeded into the lake and drowned. Without living bodies to possess, the demons had to go headlong into the abyss – as Jesus knew they would. It takes more than a few thousand demons to talk their way around Jesus. Demons could never have fooled Him.

Once the demons left, the man was immediately normal. He put on clothes and was in his right mind.[310]

When we are confronted by someone who is possessed with a demon, we have to remember that, as born-again, Spirit-filled Christians, we are sons and daughters of God. Demons will recognize who we are, but, like Jesus, we have authority to cast them out of people and send them to the abyss. They may try to argue with us, suggest solutions and try to convince us to leave them alone and to not to make them go, but negotiations aren't on the table.

There's no point asking a demon to name itself, because it will lie. Normally, demons will not reveal their real names, although they sometimes will if they think an exorcist will be impressed by demons that seem very powerful; but essentially they are liars. If we attempt to cast them out using a false name they may have given, they will be silent and let us think they have left. They could not fool Jesus, but they can often fool His disciples – you and me – so it's not smart to engage them in conversation.

When a Christian is faced with the need to expel a demon, there is no need to know what type or class of demon is involved. Authority is given to deal with every demon, regardless of its type. Nevertheless, the kind of demon is usually obvious by the way they affect people, buildings or political decisions.

Some assume that, because Jesus talked with the demons in the man called Legion, we should follow His example. Nothing could be the further from the truth. This is the only known incident where Jesus got

---

[310] See Mark 5:15; Luke 8:35

into a conversation with demons and I believe it was to demonstrate their predictable efforts to persuade Christians not to cast them out and send them to eternal torment in the abyss.

The best rule of thumb is to not talk with them at all. Just tell them politely to leave in the Name of Jesus Christ, and they will.

It's important to tell them where to go – to the abyss. They will be tormented just by talking to us, but they will be in even greater torment in the abyss.

If we do not command demons to go to the abyss when we cast them out of a person or building, they will be free to go and look for another person or building in which to live.[311] If they don't find one, they will return to the original person, or building, hoping to reoccupy their former home. Unless the former refuge has been cleaned out and made inaccessible, the demons will return with at least seven more spirits, worse than the first. The result will be that the person or building will end up being eight times worse off than at the beginning. Obviously, it is critical that we pray for any person from whom demons have been expelled, so they can be filled with the Holy Spirit, making their habitation inaccessible to evil.

After Jesus had cast the demons out and the swine all drowned in the lake, the people asked him to leave. He was no longer welcome in that area. When we do deliverance ministry, it's not uncommon for people to ask us to leave, as well. People, for various reasons, become uncomfortable around us, regardless of the results. Whenever we fight the kingdom of darkness, those who are still under its dominion are fearful and don't like us to be around.

Exercising our authority to cast out demons is not a key to popularity in any group – except the kingdom of Heaven. Jesus was no longer welcome in Gedara. But popularity is never the issue in a situation where deliverance is needed. The demons didn't need Jesus to be popular for Him to have authority over them. They knew who Jesus was and that it

---
[311] See Luke 11:24–26

was their time to go to the abyss. The Greek word for time (kairos) means "a definite fixed time," or "the appointed time." When Jesus came into the world, began his ministry and died for our sins, everything He did was at "the right time."

> *For He has made known to us in all wisdom and insight the mystery of His will, according to His purpose which He set forth in Christ as a plan for the fullness of time, to unite all things in Him, things in Heaven and things on earth.* (Ephesians 1:10; see also Galatians 4:9)

Whenever somebody, who needs to be set free, calls for help, the time has come for the demons involved to be sent to the abyss. Today is the time to cast out demons and set the captives free. There can be no negotiations with the devil or demons.

> *Behold, now is the acceptable time; behold, now is the day of salvation.* (2 Corinthians 6:2)

Two thousand swine were destroyed in this story. The loss in the value of the pork, alone, would have been cause to ask Jesus to leave. Besides being a recipe for devilled ham (sorry, I couldn't resist), this story of Jesus setting the demon-possessed man free is also a demonstration of the fact that the results of ministry can be very costly – in other ways than that of our comfort. According to my research, the cost of losing 2,000 swine, at today's prices, would be about $225,000.00. It's not much wonder the farmers wanted Jesus to leave!

The next person Jesus dealt with was a mute demoniac.

> *As they were going away, behold, a dumb demoniac was brought to Him. And when the demon had been cast out, the dumb man spoke; and the crowds marveled, saying, "Never was anything like this seen in Israel."*
> *But the Pharisees said, "He casts out demons by the prince of demons."* (Matthew 9:32-34)

This meant that the demon inside of the mute man prevented him from talking. We are not told exactly what Jesus did, just that He cast the demon out. The man then began to talk. The people who witnessed this marveled, saying, *"Never was anything like this seen in Israel."*

At this point, a different problem surfaced. The Pharisees mistook the authority Jesus used to cast out the evil spirit. They said, *"He casts out demons by the prince of demons."* This was not the first time, nor would it be the last, that Jesus was accused of serving the devil and the kingdom of darkness. Modern-day Pharisees in church leadership will accuse any Christian, who casts out evil spirits, of working for the devil.

In the district of Tyre and Sidon, Jesus was asked by a Canaanite woman to help her daughter.

And Jesus went away from there and withdrew to the district of Tyre and Sidon.
And behold, a Canaanite woman from that region came out and cried, "Have mercy on me, O Lord, Son of David; my daughter is severely possessed by a demon."
But He did not answer her a word.
And His disciples came and begged Him, saying, "Send her away, for she is crying after us."
He answered, "I was sent only to the lost sheep of the house of Israel."
But she came and knelt before Him, saying, "Lord, help me."
And He answered, "It is not fair to take the children's bread and throw it to the dogs."
She said, "Yes, Lord, yet even the dogs eat the crumbs that fall from their masters' table."
Then Jesus answered her, "O woman, great is your faith! Be it done for you as you desire."
And her daughter was healed instantly.
(Matthew 15:21-28; see also Mark 7:24-30)

When He wouldn't talk to the woman, it appeared that He was ignoring her – but she wouldn't take "no" for an answer. When He said it was not fair to take the children's bread and throw it to the dogs, she knew there were two kinds of dogs in the Greek language: the wild mongrels and the household pets. Jesus had mentioned the household pet. She agreed, but reasoned that even the dogs eat the crumbs that fall from their master's table. She knew her place in the kingdom of God, and Jesus could not say "no" to her. Her daughter was instantly set free from the demon.

Jesus is the bread of life.[312] It requires only one crumb of His bread to heal a person. It takes only one crumb of a phrase, to drive out an evil spirit and set the possessed person free. That phrase is, "Go to the abyss in the Name of Jesus." It's that easy.

The next experience recorded in which Jesus dealt with an evil spirit, involved His disciples.

> *And when they came to the disciples, they saw a great crowd about them, and scribes arguing with them. And immediately all the crowd, when they saw Him, were greatly amazed, and ran up to Him and greeted Him.*
> *And He asked them, "What are you discussing with them?"*
> *And one of the crowd answered Him, "Teacher, I brought my son to You, for he has a dumb spirit; and wherever it seizes him, it dashes him down; and he foams and grinds his teeth and becomes rigid; and I asked Your disciples to cast it out, and they were not able."*
> *And He answered them, "O faithless generation, how long am I to be with you? How long am I to bear with you? Bring him to Me."*
> *And they brought the boy to Him; and when the spirit saw Him, immediately it convulsed the boy, and he fell on the ground and rolled about, foaming at the mouth.*
> *And Jesus asked his father, "How long has he had this?"*
> *And he said, "From childhood. And it has often cast him into the fire and into the water, to destroy him; but if You can do anything, have pity on us and help us."*
> *And Jesus said to him, "If you can! All things are possible to him who believes."*
> *Immediately the father of the child cried out and said, "I believe; help my unbelief!"*
> *And when Jesus saw that a crowd came running together, He*

---

[312] See John 6:48

> *rebuked the unclean spirit, saying to it, "You dumb and deaf spirit, I command you, come out of him, and never enter him again." And after crying out and convulsing him terribly, it came out, and the boy was like a corpse; so that most of them said, "He is dead." But Jesus took him by the hand and lifted him up, and he arose. And when He had entered the house, His disciples asked Him privately, "Why could we not cast it out?" And He said to them, "This kind cannot be driven out by anything but prayer."*

(Mark 9:14-29; see also Matthew 17:14-21; Luke 9:37-43)

First of all, it is important to understand that, when a demon possesses a person, its purpose is more than to simply control the person. Its purpose is to steal and kill and destroy.[313] This demon was trying to kill the boy by throwing him into fire or water. Our purpose, as Christians and disciples of Jesus Christ, is to cast out the evil spirit and give the person abundant life.

The problem that faced the disciples, was that they did not understand how to exercise the authority that had been given to them. It's one thing to have spiritual authority, but another thing to know how to use it.

Jesus was disturbed that His disciples had not been able to deal with this demon and expressed His frustration with them. We need to pay attention to this lesson because we could find ourselves faced with exactly the same situation as they encountered. The disciples, since they had not yet received the Holy Spirit, did not have the power or authority to cast out demons without prayer and fasting.

> *He who believes in Me, as the Scripture has said, "Out of his heart shall flow rivers of living water." Now this He said about the Spirit, which those who believed in Him were to receive; for as yet the Spirit had not been given, because Jesus was not yet glorified.* (John 7:38-39)

Jesus rebuked the unclean spirit and the demon came out of the boy. It was that easy, when the person administering deliverance had the power

---
[313] See John 10:10

and knew how to deal with the demon. When the disciples went to Jesus privately and asked "Why could we not cast it out?" Jesus answered them.

> *He said to them, "Because of your little faith. For truly, I say to you, if you have faith as a grain of mustard seed, you will say to this mountain, 'Move from here to there,' and it will move; and nothing will be impossible to you."* (Matthew 17:20-21)

Demons are spiritual mountains. It takes faith and discernment to recognize those that require special handling.

Jesus responded rather strongly to their apparent lack of faith when He chastised the disciples. *"You faithless generation, how much longer must I be among you? How much longer must I bear with you?"* Faith requires a relationship with God. To exercise faith requires us to talk with Him. When we run into a problem like this one, we are supposed to ask God how to solve the problem. Then, when He tells us what to do, we are responsible to follow His leading and do what we are supposed to do. The disciples had obviously forgotten what Jesus had taught them. Again He made reference to the mustard seed.

> *The apostles said to the LORD, "Increase our faith!"*
> *And the LORD said, "If you had faith as a grain of mustard seed, you could say to this sycamine tree, 'Be rooted up, and be planted in the sea,' and it would obey you. Will any one of you, who has a servant plowing or keeping sheep, say to him when he has come in from the field, 'Come at once and sit down at table'? Will he not rather say to him, 'Prepare supper for me, and gird yourself and serve me, till I eat and drink; and afterward you shall eat and drink'? Does he thank the servant because he did what was commanded? So you also, when you have done all that is commanded you, say, 'We are unworthy servants; we have only done what was our duty.'"* (Luke 17:5-10)

The disciples had not done what Jesus had told them to do, when they needed to increase their faith.

From this story, we learn that whenever we are face to face with an evil spirit, we need to be prepared for its resistance. Evil spirits do not want to leave. Obviously, we have to be prepared for spiritual warfare, as Jesus was. Believing in Him and receiving the baptism in the Holy Spirit is our preparation. When we've been born again and are filled with the Holy Spirit, He can do His work through us. Even when we don't know that we're going to have to deal with an evil spirit, we should pray continuously and listen for His leading. When we're prepared, like Jesus, the demons come out instantly.

Jesus met the next person, whom He was to set free, while teaching in a synagogue on the Sabbath.[314] There was a woman there who had had a spirit of infirmity for eighteen years; she was bent over and could not fully straighten herself. The original Greek text says she had "a spirit which caused an infirmity or sickness" causing her to be "bent double." Jesus called to her, *"Woman, you are freed from your infirmity."* At that point, the demon left her. Jesus then laid His hands on her; immediately she was made straight and she praised God.

The demon that possessed this woman for eighteen years was not asked to name itself. It was recognized as a spirit that caused an infirmity or sickness. The lesson for us here, is that a Christian must not lay hands on a demon-possessed person before casting it out. After the demon has left, a Christian should lay hands on the person and pray for the residual sickness or infirmity to be gone. When handled properly, the demon leaves and the person is healed immediately. If it does not leave immediately, the person who is trying to cast it out, needs to examine himself or herself in order to see what needs to be corrected.

The next person we need to consider was a man described as a blind and dumb demoniac.[315] This meant that the man could neither see nor talk. What a life he must have lived! Prior to his affliction, he had been able to see clearly and talk plainly with those around him. Suddenly, an evil spirit had come upon him, gotten inside and captured him without any warning, rendering him totally blind and unable to talk. He was tormented and driven half-crazy by the demon taunting him. It must

---
[314] See Luke 13:10-17
[315] See Matthew 12:22-37; Mark 3:20-22

have been terrifying. He had no hope except from Jesus. Thankfully, some friends or family members took him to Jesus, and he was healed and set free from the demon.

But, once again, Jesus received criticism from the Pharisees. They accused him of working for Satan. The very people who were supposed to be able to recognize the Holy Spirit in Jesus as the Messiah, were blind to His presence. Because their own eyes were darkened, they could not see who Jesus really was. They crossed over the safety line into blasphemy when they accused Jesus of being an agent of the devil. This same accusation is often made against anyone who has this Holy Spirit authority.

> *And the scribes who came down from Jerusalem said, "He is possessed by Be-elzebul, and by the prince of demons He casts out the demons."* (Mark 3:22)

When these Pharisees looked at Jesus, they didn't see the Holy Spirit; they saw an evil spirit. That is the reason why Jesus warned them about the unforgivable sin – blasphemy against the Holy Spirit. He told them it was silly to think that a house divided against itself would stand. Even Satan isn't that stupid. Jesus warned,

> *"But if it is by the finger of God that I cast out the demons, then the kingdom of God has come to you."* (Luke 11:20)

And it *has* come. Jesus also explains that the only way that one can enter a "strong man's house," and plunder it, is after the strong man has been bound up. In this case, the devil is the strong man who must be bound up by a stronger man – who is Jesus – so that He can plunder a house by casting out the evil spirit. The house, of course, is the person who has been possessed, which means that after the demon has been evicted, the house becomes the property of the kingdom of God. The principle involved here, is that:

> *No one can serve two masters; for either he will hate the one and love the other, or he will be devoted to the one and despise the other. You cannot serve God and mammon.* (Matthew 6:24)

As Christians, we are the stronger people who can bind up the strong man, Satan, and plunder his houses; we can free possessed people by casting out the evil spirits and taking possession of the houses for the kingdom of God.

Another incident occurred in Capernaum, when Jesus was teaching in the synagogue, on the Sabbath.[316] Through this incident, Jesus showed us the best way to deal with demons who challenge and try to embarrass us.

In the congregation, was a man who had the spirit of an unclean demon. The demon could not tolerate Jesus' teaching, *"for His word had authority."* The possessed man shouted out,

"Ah! What have You to do with us, Jesus of Nazareth? Have You come to destroy us? I know who You are, the Holy One of God." (Luke 4:34)

Jesus simply rebuked the demon. *"Be silent, and come out of him."* It initially tried to resist Jesus' command, throwing the man to the floor and convulsing him, but quickly came out of him, albeit with a loud shout. In Greek, it literally says, *"The evil spirit shook the man violently and came out with a very loud shout."* This was the evil spirit's way of protesting. If the people were astonished at Jesus' teaching (for He taught them as one who had authority, and not like the scribes) they were even more surprised at what happened, because they questioned the incident amongst themselves.

And they were all amazed and said to one another, "What is this word? For with authority and power He commands the unclean spirits, and they come out." (Luke 4:36)

Demons reacted to the presence of Jesus, and they will react to the presence of any born-again Christian who is filled with the Holy Spirit and is in a public situation, teaching with authority.

Notice how Jesus handled the demons. He did not answer any of its questions. He did not talk with it. He simply commanded it to, *"Be quiet."* That was enough to stop it from shouting and making a public spectacle,

---
[316] See Mark 1:21-28; Luke 4:31-37

trying to embarrass Jesus. Jesus was not embarrassed. He exercised His authority, exorcising the evil spirit and setting the man free.

This is the same authority Jesus gives us when we receive Him as our Savior and receive His baptism of the Holy Spirit, with the signs that prove our authority.

And these signs will accompany (follow) *those who believe, in My Name, they will* (continually) *cast out demons.... And they went forth and preached everywhere, while the Lord worked with them and confirmed the message by the signs that attended it. Amen.* (Mark 16:17,20)

We must learn to use the same authority, especially when evil spirits react loudly in public places, hoping to embarrass us. They hope that if we become embarrassed and intimidated by the reactions of those around us, we'll retreat and won't force them to leave and set the people free who are being possessed by them. All we have to do is follow Jesus' model and say, *"Be silent, and come out of him (or her)."*

Jesus' first rule, when confronted with an evil spirit, is to command it to be quiet. His second rule, is to command it to go to its designated place – the abyss. Whenever we cast a demon or demons out of a person we must tell them where to go.

It is not appropriate to pray demons out of people. We must command them to leave. The demons knew what their destiny was when Jesus commanded them to go.

Notice that Jesus never cursed demons, because they are cursed already. It is important for anyone, doing deliverance ministry, not to swear and curse at demons because – for one thing, such a person is sinning by doing such a thing – and for another thing, sin gives the evil spirits a good reason not to obey. It's not necessary to scream and ridicule demons. Their hearing is excellent, to the point that yelling at evil spirits in a meeting will frighten only the other people who are there. It will get even worse when the demons start screaming and yelling back at a Christian who has no authority, or has lost his authority because of sin. The simple response is to say, "I command you, evil spirit, in the Name of Jesus Christ, to be quiet; leave this person and go to the abyss and stay there."

Another way to command them to leave, without frightening other people who may be watching and listening, is to say quietly, "In the Name of Jesus Christ, I command anything that is not of Jesus Christ, to leave this person and go to the abyss and stay there."

Then, you have to pray with the person for salvation and the baptism of the Holy Spirit and make certain they begin to speak in tongues, so you and the person involved will know (have the evidence) that the evil spirit has gone and the Holy Spirit has filled the person. Any onlookers do not need to know what kind of ministry was necessary, but they will see that a person has received salvation and the baptism of the Holy Spirit. James said,

"From the same mouth come blessing and cursing. My brethren, this ought not to be so." (James 3:10)

Jesus said,

"You brood of vipers! how can you speak good, when you are evil? For out of the abundance of the heart the mouth speaks."
(Matthew 12:34)

We should never engage in a conversation with evil spirits because they will not tell the truth. They are like their master, the devil.

You are of your father the devil, and your will is to do your father's desires. He was a murderer from the beginning, and has nothing to do with the truth, because there is no truth in him. When he lies, he speaks according to his own nature, for he is a liar and the father of lies. (John 8:44)

Review of Foundational Principles for Casting out Demons

1. Anyone attempting to expel an evil spirit or "bless out a house" (my term for driving demons out of a house and into the abyss) must be baptized with the Holy Spirit, as evidenced by the signs following (some gift of the Holy Spirit).

2. Any individual, or people whom you think need to have an evil spirit or spirits cast out of them, should be asked the following two questions:
   • Do you want to be set free? (A person must want to be set free – not everybody wants to be set free.)
   • Are you willing to invite Jesus to be your LORD and Savior and receive the baptism in the Holy Spirit, with the evidence (proof) of speaking in tongues?
3. Do not have demons name themselves. They lie!
4. Do not talk with demons any more than is necessary. They will try to talk you out of casting them out. Jesus talked with demons because of who He is.
5. Demons must be commanded to leave. Praying or singing does not get rid of them. Only taking authority over them in the Name of Jesus Christ and commanding them to go to the abyss, gets rid of them.
6. You must command them to go to the abyss specifically, or they will gather some more spirits and try to return into the person or building from which they have been sent.
7. Be strong and authoritative with demons, but do not be rude or curse and swear or yell at them. Their hearing is very good.
8. It is always wise to pray before doing an exorcism.
9. Anointing people or houses of any kind of buildings does not get rid of evil spirits.

The Two Predictable Reactions to Deliverance Ministry

1. Criticism:

Now He was teaching in one of the synagogues on the sabbath. And there was a woman who had had a spirit of infirmity for eighteen years; she was bent over and could not fully straighten herself. And when Jesus saw her, He called her and said to her, "Woman, you are

> *freed from your infirmity." And He laid His hands upon her, and immediately she was made straight, and she praised God.*
>
> *But the ruler of the synagogue, indignant because Jesus had healed on the sabbath, said to the people, "There are six days on which work ought to be done; come on those days and be healed, and not on the sabbath day."*
>
> *Then the Lord answered him, "You hypocrites! Does not each of you on the sabbath untie his ox or his ass from the manger, and lead it away to water it? And ought not this woman, a daughter of Abraham whom Satan bound for eighteen years, be loosed from this bond on the sabbath day?" As He said this, all His adversaries were put to shame; and all the people rejoiced at all the glorious things that were done by Him.* (Luke 13:10-17)

Instead of praising God that the woman was set free, the ruler of the synagogue got angry and critical. He got legalistic, losing sight of God's promises of healing. There is no better time or place for somebody to be healed than during a worship service, but those who are still under the bondage of Satan and the kingdom of darkness will always be critical of the ministry of those who deliver people from evil spirits. Criticism is sure to come when we win our engagements with the enemy. So don't be surprised if you get criticized for setting people free. When criticism does come, remember to deal with it Jesus' way:

> *Blessed are you when men revile you and persecute you and utter all kinds of evil against you falsely on My account. Rejoice and be glad, for your reward is great in Heaven, for so men persecuted the prophets who were before you.* (Matthew 5:11-12)

2. Affirmation: There are those who will respond positively and who thank God for setting free a son or daughter of Abraham.

Jesus continuously set people free throughout His ministry.

> *That evening they brought to Him many who were possessed with demons; and He cast out the spirits with a word, and healed all who were sick. This was to fulfil what was spoken by the prophet Isaiah, "He took our infirmities and bore our diseases."* (Matthew 8:16-17)

In the Classroom With Jesus

Each of the cited scenarios gives us insight into how to deal with demons in our own lives and ministries.

Jesus cast the demons out with just a word. There was no long ordeal of a half hour – or two, or four, or ten hours. He did it simply with a word. In our ministry, when dealing with evil spirits, it is done quickly. Those who attempt to administer deliverance, but fail to get the spirit to leave, need to examine themselves and their faith, and not blame the person who is possessed.

Matthew tells us why it is supposed to be so easily done. It is because what Jesus did on the Cross of Calvary was the fulfillment of Isaiah's prophecy: *"He took our infirmities and bore our diseases."*[317] When we cast out demons and heal people, it is because Jesus took them to the Cross and paid for the right to heal them by being a ransom. This should give us confident assurance when we are dealing with the kingdom of darkness.

As they did with Jesus, people will wonder what anyone is doing, who steps out in spiritual boldness, exercising the authority given in the Name of Jesus. As soon as people learn that Jesus uses normal, Spirit-filled people to set people (who are possessed by evil spirits) free, they take the possessed people to them so they can be set free. Jesus gave us all authority to act in His Name.

> *Go therefore and make disciples of all nations, baptizing them in the Name of the Father and of the Son and of the Holy Spirit, teaching them to observe all that I have commanded you; and lo, I am with you always, to the close of the age.* (Matthew 28:19-20)

During the process of discipling people, we often have to cast out the evil spirits who have possessed them and prevented them from serving Jesus Christ.

Jesus equipped His twelve disciples and then sent them out.[318] He gave them *"power and authority over all demons and to cure diseases, and*

---
[317] Matthew 8:17; Isaiah 53:4
[318] Luke 9:1-6

He sent them out to preach the kingdom of God and to heal." They had a successful trip. They preached the gospel but there was no report of any salvations. Their work was not able to be completed because they had not yet received the Holy Spirit.[319]

After preparing His disciples, Jesus appointed seventy others, whom He sent out in pairs to do ministry.[320] The devil did not know what hit him and his kingdom of darkness. He ignored the first twelve, but he couldn't ignore this company of God's soldiers. They did not understand the kind of spiritual warfare in which they were involved. It was a combined attack, involving God's army of angels, who were at war in Heaven led by the archangel Michael,[321] and this earthly army led by Jesus Christ. The attack was so successful that Jesus said to them,

"I saw Satan fall like lightning from Heaven." (Luke 10:18)

Satan must have been shocked beyond his imagination. The first attack was all it took to defeat him and his army.

The seventy were amazed. They exclaimed,

*"*Lord*, even the demons are subject to us in Your Name!"* (Luke 10:17)

Indeed they are! But they were excited about the wrong things. Jesus reminded them of the authority He had given them:

"Behold, I have given you authority to tread upon serpents and scorpions, and over all the power of the enemy; and nothing shall hurt you. Nevertheless do not rejoice in this, that the spirits are subject to you; but rejoice that your names are written in Heaven. (Luke 10:19-20)

Sometimes it is not easy to keep our focus. The whole purpose of our ministry is to lead people to salvation for Jesus Christ. Our focus must always be kept on people's need to know Him as their personal Savior, Lord, Healer, Deliverer and God. The casting out of demons is just a means to that end, so we must be careful not to become preoccupied with

---
[319] John 7:39
[320] Luke 10:1-22
[321] Revelation 12:7-9

deliverance ministry. We set people free so that they can be open to a relationship with God that will bring them into the kingdom of God and give them eternal life.

Part of the preparation Jesus gave us for deliverance ministry involved teaching on the importance of the maintenance of freedom, post-deliverance. He told us what happens when an unclean or an evil spirit is cast out of a person.

> *When the unclean spirit has gone out of a man, he passes through waterless places seeking rest, but he finds none. Then he says, "I will return to my house from which I came." And when he comes he finds it empty, swept, and put in order. Then he goes and brings with him seven other spirits more evil than himself, and they enter and dwell there; and the last state of that man becomes worse than the first. So shall it be also with this evil generation.* (Matthew 12:43-45)

As mentioned previously, the person is a 'house' in which the evil spirit lives. When the spirit has been cast out, it travels around, looking for a new place in which to live. It travels over waterless places, trying to find rest, but there is no rest for a disembodied spirit. So, it says, *"I will return to my house from which I came."* When it returns, it finds the house empty, swept, and put in order, so it recruits seven other spirits and they all enter the person. That person is then eight times worse than he was in the beginning, before the spirit was cast out.

The point is, if you are going to cast out an evil spirit from someone, you had better make certain that person fills his or her "house" with a new resident who will look after him or her. The only safe resident to allow in, is the Holy Spirit.

Unity With Those of Like Minds

There were many people who followed Jesus from a distance. They listened to Him, watched Him and followed His example. They imitated Him and even cast out demons in His Name. The disciples caught some of them in the act. John caught one such man and reported him to Jesus.

"Teacher, we saw someone casting out demons in Your Name, and we forbade him, because he was not following us." (Mark 9:38)

Jesus' answer must have shocked John:

"Do not forbid him; for no one who does a mighty work in My Name will be able soon after to speak evil of Me. For he that is not against us is for us. For truly, I say to you, whoever gives you a cup of water to drink because you bear the Name of Christ, will by no means lose his reward." (Mark 9:39-41)

We need to learn who our friends are. They are not always the people who walk with us. There may be people who, for various reasons, may not want to, or may not know how to, join our group or circle. They may stand at the edge of the crowd or sit quietly in our churches, without building relationships. They may be members of another church and come and go without drawing attention to themselves; but these may be people who see the power that is in the Name of Jesus. Just because they may appear to be different from us, or do things differently than we do, does not necessarily mean we are on different sides of the fence. People should not be discouraged because of surface differences.

Jesus tells us to look out for such people and encourage them. It may not be very long until they are with us. So, let's pray for them and encourage them to serve Jesus Christ where they are and in His Name.

Imitation is said to be the greatest form of flattery. While ministry has more to do with bringing praise and honour than flattery to Jesus, I can think of no greater honor than to imitate Him. Anyone who uses His Name to cast out evil spirits and set people free to follow Jesus, must certainly have great confidence in Him and a depth of unity with those of us who minister out of sincere hearts and His calling.

Those of us who are engaged in spiritual warfare, need all the friends we can get. Jesus may connect us with people whom we did not know were watching us and following our example, using His powerful Name.

You believe that God is one; you do well. Even the demons believe – and shudder. (James 2:19)

We would be wise to learn to do the same: believe and tremble at the Name of Jesus!

Watching Other Christians do Spiritual Warfare

Opportunities for ministry and spiritual warfare can present themselves when we least expect them. For instance, Paul and his companion, Silas, were going to the place of prayer when they met a slave girl who had a spirit of divination.[322] This young woman made money for her owners by soothsaying (predicting other people's futures). The evil spirit in her began to react to Paul and Silas, causing the girl to start following them, shouting, *"These men are servants of the Most High God, who proclaim to you the way of salvation."* This was the demon's way of trying to warn people to stay away from them. The girl followed them wherever they went in the city of Philippi. Finally, Paul had enough. He said to the spirit, *"I charge you in the Name of Jesus Christ to come out of her." And it came out that very hour.*

We can tolerate spiritual harassment for days, weeks, months, and years – or, like Paul, we can take authority over the spirits, set people free and put an end to the harassment. It's important to understand, however, that not everyone will be happy with us for dealing with the issue, as was the situation surrounding this slave girl. Her owners, who had a financial interest in her soothsaying, were angry. They didn't care about the girl, but they cared about the money they would not receive as a result of the evil spirit leaving her. They complained and had Paul and Silas arrested. Paul and Silas were then taken before the magistrates, who had them beaten, thrown into prison and put into stocks for interfering with the business of the city. Not to be sidetracked, this became their place of prayer.

God always has a purpose. The slave girl was set free from the kingdom of darkness and came to know Jesus as her Savior and LORD. Through the process of the incident, the owners and the magistrates heard about the gospel of Jesus Christ. That night, the prison's jailer and

---

[322] See Acts 16:16-26

his whole family believed in Jesus and were baptized. After Paul and Silas accomplished their ministry, they were released – with an apology!

In this same way, every time we cast out evil spirits, the door is opened for ministry so that people can be saved and be set free to serve Jesus Christ. It's no wonder that Paul was able to say with great confidence:

"We know that in everything God works for good with those who love him, who are called according to His purpose." (Romans 8:28)

Many people make the mistake of thinking that everyone with religious faith has the same power. Well, they don't. Evil spirits and the devil recognize that there is one true God and that Jesus Christ is LORD. They know that Spirit-filled believers have authority over them.

The story about the seven sons of the Jewish high priest[323] is a good example of powerless attempts to deal with demons. Sceva's sons were itinerant Jewish exorcists who had watched Paul casting out evil spirits and thought, like a lot of people, that if they could get the right formula or the right words to say, they could do what Christians do in ministry. They didn't realize just how wrong they could be. They watched and listened to Paul, but didn't realize that demons are not afraid of human words. Our words have power to set people free only if we have the faith in Jesus Christ that gives our words authority – as these men discovered. There is no "formula" or magic stringing together of words.

Nevertheless, these men attempted to cast out an evil spirit from a man, using the Name of the LORD Jesus.

Then some of the itinerant Jewish exorcists undertook to pronounce the Name of the Lord Jesus over those who had evil spirits, saying, "I adjure you by the Jesus whom Paul preaches." Seven sons of a Jewish high priest named Sceva were doing this.
But the evil spirit answered them, "Jesus I know, and Paul I know; but who are you?"
And the man in whom the evil spirit was leaped on them, mastered

---

[323] See Acts 19

all of them, and overpowered them, so that they fled out of that house naked and wounded. (Acts 19:13-16)

The demon-possessed man attacked the seven sons of Sceva, ripped off all of their clothes and beat them up. The brothers ran down the street without a stitch of clothing left on them.

What an embarrassing attempt to cast out a demon! People who have not received the baptism of the Holy Spirit, do not have the authority to cast evil spirits out of people or houses. If a person without the authority of Jesus Christ attempts to cast out demons, he or she could be badly embarrassed, hurt or even killed when the evil spirits turns on them and attacks. Fortunately, none of the sons of Sceva were killed.

When Paul and his companions were in Philippi, they had a strange encounter with a woman who was obviously operating out of a different spirit.

One day, as we were going to the place of prayer, we met a slave-girl who had a spirit of divination and brought her owners a great deal of money by fortune-telling. While she followed Paul and us, she would cry out, "These men are slaves of the Most High God, who proclaim to you a way of salvation." (Acts 16:16-17)

It might appear to modern ears that she was encouraging people to listen to them. But, in fact, she was warning people that they did not serve any of the lesser gods that the listeners might think were the greater gods. They were, in fact, servants of the only God who alone had the authority and was to be distinguished from all lesser objects of cultic devotion. He was the "Number One God" who was above all so-called gods, which Paul calls "demons."[324]

Jesus, Yahweh, is "the Most High God" (tou hupsistou theou). All demons that encountered Jesus knew this to be true, because He had authority to cast all of them out of people.

In spiritual warfare, we are powerless nobodies without Jesus as our Savior and LORD. Only when we have been saved and baptized with the

---
[324] 1 Corinthians 12:20; Revelation 9:20-21

Holy Spirit, can we safely carry on spiritual warfare, knowing that the evil spirits have to obey us.

Today, just like the people in Paul's time, we live in a world where people are well aware that there is a spiritual dimension to life. People are seeking God in other religions, in the occult world, and in private ways that allow them to be influenced by the devil and the kingdom of darkness. They need to be given more than words. As Paul said,

> *"And I was with you in weakness and in much fear and trembling; and my speech and my message were not in plausible words of wisdom, but in demonstration of the Spirit and of power, that your faith might not rest in the wisdom of men but in the power of God."*
> (1 Corinthians 2:3-5)

When we use our authority as Christians to cast out evil spirits and set people free, we give convincing demonstration of the reality of the Spirit. Such demonstrations draw attention to the power of God, hopefully leading onlookers to believe in Jesus Christ and be saved.

The story of the seven sons of Sceva exists as a warning to those who would attempt to deal with evil spirits without the proper credentials. However, when confronted with a person who needs to have a demon cast out, those who are saved and filled with the power of the Holy Spirit have full authority to command the demon to leave without any personal danger. Such people are like policemen, whose authority does not rest in themselves, but in the law. In the same way, we can arrest the so-called "strong man" and send him off to jail, which in this case, is the abyss.

The War Comes Home

The Battles Within

What could be more immediate than a battle fought in the mind? No human on earth escapes the efforts of Satan to separate man from God by influencing his thoughts.

It is critical to realize that evil spirits are not behind every instance of the breaking of God's laws or every wrong act or every flawed decision we make. Recognition of the source of the problem, is foundational to dealing effectively with it. The one thing that is certain is that the decision to act in disobedience to God is always sin. It's a choice we make personally – nothing we can blame on anyone but ourselves. Recently, I heard about some people who had the naiveté to believe that when someone has a sinful sexual relationship outside of marriage, demons are transferred from one person to another. That is not true. Trying to blame demonic activity where there is none, is worse than fruitless.

It is a measure of the awesomeness of Christ's suffering on the Cross and His glorious resurrection, that this applies to *all* people, Christians and non-Christians alike.

End-of-the-War Skirmishes

Despite the fact that the army of the kingdom of darkness, along with its leader, the devil, suffered its crushing defeat at the Cross of Calvary, it is allowed to continue to dog us with skirmishes to test our allegiance, until the end.

> *A bowl full of vinegar stood there; so they put a sponge full of the vinegar on hyssop and held it to his mouth. When Jesus had received the vinegar, He said, "It is finished;" and He bowed His head and gave up His Spirit.* (John 19:29-30)

While the war to prove the authority of God has been won, Satan's beat-up army is still very active, despite the fact that his angels who sinned are presently chained in a temporary hell (Tartarus).[325] Aware of its limitations, this so-called army of evil spirits (demons) has learned to be more careful. They have learned that wherever the Spirit of God is engaged, the kingdom of darkness loses in head-to-head battles. Consequently, they have become more sneaky and more subtle.

Paul warns that the battle lines remain drawn and we still have to contend with the remaining elements of the devil's army – the principalities, powers and world rulers. They appear to be strong, but with the power and guidance of the Holy Spirit, we are stronger.

For the most part, Christians will have little interaction with evil spirits, although they are faced with temptations from the devil and sin in response to their own evil desires.

> *Let no one say when he is tempted, "I am tempted by God"; for God cannot be tempted with evil and He Himself tempts no one; but each person is tempted when he is lured and enticed by his own desire. Then desire when it has conceived gives birth to sin; and sin when it is full-grown brings forth death.* (James 1:13-15)

Sadly, many are so guilt-ridden with the devil's reminders of their pasts, that they are rendered ineffective to the Kingdom of God. They don't understand that, when God brings them through difficult circum-

---

[325] 2 Peter 2:4; Jude 1:6

stances, the troubles should be seen as reminders of God's goodness to them. Recognition of His goodness leads to praise and worship that defeats the enemy.

Weapon of Worship – Praying in Tongues

When the Holy Spirit has been given permission to take control of the tongue and give the gift of speaking in other languages,[326] believers have the extra dimension of being able to pray in the Spirit. Prayer becomes no longer a guessing game, but an interaction with God, where the voice of the Holy Spirit becomes recognizable and we can keep focused on the kingdom of Heaven. Only then, can we find assurance that we are worshipping the right God.

James tells us[327] that our tongues are the rudders of our lives, and reminds us that very small rudders guide large ships.

> *So the tongue is a little member and boasts of great things. How great a forest is set ablaze by a small fire!* (James 3:5)

> *For every kind of beast and bird, of reptile and sea creature, can be tamed and has been tamed by humankind, but no human being can tame the tongue—a restless evil, full of deadly poison.*
> (James 3:7,8)

The more time we spend praying in tongues, the less time our tongues can be employed in evil.

Turf Wars

While not often admitted by home owners (for resale and reputation purposes), it is not uncommon for evil spirits to move into houses to harass people. This can happen even to homes of Spirit-filled believers.

When Christians discover themselves suddenly under attack, or experiencing harassment in their own homes, they wonder what they may have done wrong, to find themselves in such a situation. Instead, they should be asking themselves what they have done *right*. We are the

---
[326] See Mark 16:17; 1 Corinthians 12:10
[327] James 3:1-12

enemies of the kingdom of darkness. Evil spirits are supposed to attack those who are faithfully serving Jesus Christ.

When it happens, it can be very scary, sometimes with pieces of furniture or other household items being thrown around rooms, or even at those who live in the house. Evil spirits often make noises in the walls, attics, basements or unoccupied rooms. They speak, sing or make music to frighten the occupants. Sometimes they become violent and hit or trip people, causing them to fall down stairs or somehow be injured. They have been known to hit people with their bodies. When they do this, it most often feels like an exceptionally humid cloud has surrounded the person. When they move into a house or building, they often cause an odor like sewage.

The year I was ordained by the United Church of Canada, I was sent to Maxwell, Ontario, Canada, as the pastor of four churches. From the moment we arrived, everything began to go wrong. The manse, (a clergy residence) which was provided for us, was in such a filthy condition that we couldn't move into it until some cleaning, painting and wall papering had been done. However, in spite of all the cleaning and renovating, a terrible sewage smell remained throughout the house. Three of our four children became sick. Despite all we did, we could never discover the source of the problem. Our twins, who were only a few weeks old at the time, became so ill that they had to be hospitalized during the last two months that we lived in that house. The hospital tested them for many possible ailments, but could not diagnose their problem.

We lived in Maxwell for only one year, before I accepted the invitation to become the pastor of the church in Englishtown, New Jersey. We made an appointment with the pediatrician in Princeton, New Jersey, where they had been born, and drove them directly from the Owen Sound, Ontario hospital, to him. After examining them for a few minutes, he determined they were suffering from a food allergy.

Looking back, from what we have learned in the intervening years, we realize we were victimized by demons. The sewage smell, with no apparent reason, was one symptom of the presence of demons. Another symptom was the onset of an undiagnosable illness in the children. Demons will often cause or imitate actual physical allergies and diseases.

We were doubly victimized, because teaching about demons was overlooked in our university and theological studies. Because it was humanly impossible to study all areas of Christian beliefs, it was assumed we would find the answers to any questions about evil spirits in the Scripture, as all spiritual problems were addressed the Bible.

While preparing for a ministry trip to Saskatchewan, I received a telephone call at eight o'clock in the evening, the night before I was to leave. My flight was leaving at six o'clock in the morning, so I had planned to go to bed early.

The call was from a man who had heard me at a Full Gospel Business Men's meeting in Drayton, Ontario. His six-year-old daughter was suffering from a problem that his doctor could not diagnose. She had been tested at a hospital, but the doctors there had been unable to find any medical reason for her problem. Every evening, at ten-thirty, she would begin to vomit up the entire contents of her stomach. She was losing weight and their family doctor had explained the seriousness of her condition. If they couldn't find the reason for her sickness, she was going to die. Time was growing short.

"Well," I explained, "I'm on my way to Saskatchewan and I have to catch a flight at six a.m., but I'll be happy to see your daughter when I get back."

"She might die before you get back." Desperation was in his voice. "I called, because my mother-in-law was at one of your meetings. She told us how you had shared about casting demons out of a child, and suggested our daughter might have a problem with demons, because she talked about a little girl who came to visit her every night."

Their house was over an hour away, south of Arthur, Ontario, but I decided to drive there and talk to the little girl. So much for going to bed early! When I arrived, I took the child aside for a brief chat. She confirmed that this 'little girl,' whom she thought was an angel, came to see her every night.

I gathered the whole family and explained that, to deal with this problem, they would all need to invite Jesus to be their Savior and Lord and receive the baptism of the Holy Spirit, so that they would have authority over any demons. They agreed; but first, I took authority over the little girl. In the Name of Jesus Christ, I cast out anything that was not of Jesus and commanded it to go to the abyss and stay there. Then, I prayed with the parents and their three children and they all began to speak in tongues.

After I returned from Saskatchewan, the father called me. He said, "After you left our house, we were uncertain that our daughter had been helped. We watched the clock move from ten to ten-fifteen, to ten-twenty-five and finally to ten-thirty, expecting her to start vomiting. Next, we watched the clock move from ten-thirty-one to eleven. Nothing happened! Every night since then, she has not vomited. She is healed! Thank you so much and may Jesus be praised!"

Children are easy victims of possession. Many people, who are not knowledgeable about spiritual matters, believe that children, who have been baptized with water or dedicated to God, are protected from being possessed by evil spirits. Unfortunately, such is not the case. Most often, when evil spirits attack, harass or possess children, adults chalk it up to the children's wild imaginations or their efforts to get attention. Demons can cause children to behave with peculiar, and often bad, manners and behavior.

I have discovered that, occasionally, when I am away from home doing ministry of almost any kind, my home and family will be attacked and my family members will be harassed. When this first started happening, we didn't understand what was going on. First, we thought we had rats in the walls and attic of our house. We could hear noises that sounded like rodents. Then our young children started having nightmares. They would sometimes get out of bed and sleepwalk in terror. When wakened, they would have absolutely no memory of what had happened. We finally realized this was the enemy's counter-attack against us because, in our service to Christ, people were receiving Jesus as their Savior and Lord, being baptized with the Holy Spirit and being healed.

When we started to recognize what was happening, we could see that the devil had redirected some of his spirit-forces to our home; so we simply took authority over them and cast them out of our house. Getting rid of evil spirits in a house requires a Spirit-filled Christian to go from room to room, speaking aloud the Name of Jesus Christ and commanding all unclean and/or evil spirits to leave the house and go to the abyss. He or she must then ask the Holy Spirit to fill the whole house with His presence. It is wonderful to realize we have caught the enemy's attention to the point where he finds it necessary to attack us. Take it as a compliment when the devil has to send his soldiers to attack you, your house, your family, your business or your church. It means you are being an effective soldier in God's army.

Most people whose homes are invaded by demons, however, are not Christians. This makes sense, but for a different reason; for the kingdom of darkness, it's always open season on non-believers. They're easy prey as trophies of the spiritual war. They don't recognize where the troubles are coming from and they don't have the weapons to defend themselves. Anyone who is not saved can be attacked and possessed by the devil's forces. However, there's no standard to predict who will have his or her home invaded by an evil spirit, or be possessed by an evil spirit or spirits. The other issue is that there are probably not enough demons to get to everybody – which is fine, as far as they're concerned, because sin is all that is required to place a person outside of the kingdom of God and on their way to Hell. It doesn't take the efforts of an evil spirit to get them there.

But now the righteousness of God has been manifested apart from law, although the law and the prophets bear witness to it, the righteousness of God through faith in Jesus Christ for all who believe. For there is no distinction; since all have sinned and fall short of the glory of God, they are justified by His grace as a gift, through the redemption which is in Christ Jesus. (Romans 3:21-24)

The Inconsistency of the Enemy

Demons don't follow consistent rules or laws. Their inconsistency, impatience and lack of reliability appear to be their mode of operation. They are liars, manipulators and tricksters and care only about themselves.

I have not been able to discover any common denominator, among those who have been attacked in their homes, to predict what evil spirits will do. They are inconsistent and will attack and attempt to possess anybody, regardless of who they are – whether born-again believers or non-believers. They will invade the homes of anyone, whether Christian or not. In war, everyone is vulnerable to falling victim to a dictator and his army. Obviously, everyone is subject to the kind of misfortunes of those who are under the domination of the devil and the kingdom of darkness.

Similarly, there is no standard or law which says that anyone who gets involved in the occult (such as witchcraft, ouija boards, tarot cards or medium-led séances) or in some false religion, will automatically become possessed by an evil spirit or have terrible things happen to them. The devil and the kingdom of darkness are not consistent. They do not operate according to any standards or laws. At best, we can say only that they operate randomly. Sometimes our apprehensions are borne out, but sometimes nothing happens. Sometimes they will attack and invade, possess and harass, but sometimes they won't.

Neither the devil nor his so-called angels or messengers of light (evil spirits) have any predictability in terms of long-term consistency and faithfulness. Only God is in for the long term – for eternity. As we give our lives to Him as born-again, Spirit-filled believers, His kindness to us is immeasurable. He promises that we will have the presence of the Holy Spirit with us forever. Jesus, not the devil, promises that He will never leave us.

> *Keep your life free from love of money, and be content with what you have; for He has said, "I will never fail you nor forsake you."* (Hebrews 13:5)

The devil will always, eventually, leave and forsake us. Evil spirits can be counted upon to desert those whom they destroy. Jesus alone is faithful to His promises. He gives us a personal, long-term warranty on eternal life, by giving us the down payment of the Holy Spirit.

Question: Can a Christian be Possessed by an Evil Spirit?

The question remains: "Can a Christian be possessed by an evil spirit?" There are two answers to this question:

1. Yes
2. No

First of all, the only kind of a Christian who can be possessed by an evil spirit, is one who has repented of their sins, been forgiven and experienced the cleansing that comes with salvation – but has not received the infilling of the Holy Spirit that comes with the baptism in the Holy Spirit.

If we confess our sins, He is faithful and just, and will forgive our sins and cleanse us from all unrighteousness. (1 John 1:9)

I baptize you with water for repentance, but He who is coming after me is mightier than I, whose sandals I am not worthy to carry; He will baptize you with the Holy Spirit and with fire. (Matthew 3:11)

... for John baptized with water, but before many days you shall be baptized with the Holy Spirit. (Acts 1:5)

While many dispute the necessity of speaking in tongues, the reality is that it serves as evidence of having received the Holy Spirit.

And these signs will accompany those who believe: in My Name they will cast out demons; they will speak in new tongues ... (Mark 16:17)

The signs that are evident in the life of a Spirit-filled believer, confirm the message of the Gospel.

*And they went forth and preached everywhere, while the L*ord *worked with them and confirmed the message by the signs that attended it.* (Mark 16:20)

The Apostle Paul in writing to the Thessalonians says,

"May the God of Peace Himself sanctify you wholly; and may your spirit and soul and body be kept sound and blameless at the coming of our Lord Jesus Christ." (1 Thessalonians 5:23)

Here Paul describes a person who is complete in Jesus Christ. Until we are baptized in the Holy Spirit, we have only the two component parts with which we are born: the "human spirit/ soul" (psyche) and the human body (soma). Until we receive the third component, the Holy Spirit or spirit or Holy Ghost, who fills us when we receive the baptism in the Holy Spirit, we are incomplete persons.

A complete person is comprised of three components:

1. Holy Spirit (pneuma)
2. Soul/spirit (psyche)
3. Body (soma)

Jesus is the only person who was born with all three components. Anyone who has not received the Holy Spirit is unprotected and vulnerable to being possessed, harassed, injured or killed by a demon/evil spirit. As previously stated, but stated again for clarity, the proof of having received the Holy Spirit or the baptism of the Holy Spirit through a personal day of Pentecost[328] was outlined clearly by Jesus.

These signs will accompany those who believe:

In My Name they will cast out demons; they will speak in new tongues (languages), *they will pick up serpents, and if they drink any deadly thing it will not hurt them* (protection); *they will lay hands on the sick, and they will be healed.* (Mark 16:17-18)

The Greek word for signs (semeion: singular; semeia: plural) is defined as 1. "a sign or distinguishing mark, whereby something is known, sign, token, indication; 2. an event that is an indication or confirmation of intervention by transcendent powers, miracle, portent."[329]

---

[328] See Acts 2:1-3
[329] "A Greek-English Lexicon of the New Testament and Other Early Christian Literature," Third Edition, revised and edited by Fredrick William Danker, 2000; p. 920-921.

While demons can land on true believers, they can stay for only as long as we allow them to do so. We are not immune to being bullied by them – sometimes even to the extent of being shoved or hit, as though by a boxer. They have been known to try to wrestle us down to the floor, if given the opportunity, in a vain attempt to control us. It is not uncommon to have them attempt to sit on us, especially when we are asleep. I've had many Christians tell me about waking up, startled to feel something invisible sitting on them, or covering them with its demonic presence, to the point where they cannot move or even speak. Thankfully, these evil spirits have to leave as soon as we speak the Name of Jesus.

It's not unusual for people to begin to be harassed by demons when they occupy their thoughts with the devil and evil spirits – when they should be preoccupied with the Father, Jesus Christ, and the Holy Spirit; the kingdom of God and His righteousness. Whenever anyone sees only evil spirits/demons, the devil and sin, then he or she is worshipping the kingdom of darkness. When people get absorbed with the devil, they need to repent and start spending more time with Jesus Christ in prayer and Bible study and fellowship with other Christians. They need to learn to listen to the still voice of the Holy Spirit.[330]

While Spirit-filled Christians cannot be possessed by evil spirits, Christians who have not received the baptism of the Holy Spirit, those the apostle Paul refers to as "unspiritual people," *are* vulnerable to possession.

The unspiritual man does not receive the gifts of the Spirit of God, for they are folly to him, and he is not able to understand them because they are spiritually discerned. (1 Corinthians 2:14)

"Spiritually discerned" means they are explained by the Holy Spirit. These people have religious structures but reject the spiritual power of true godliness.

... holding the form of religion but denying the power of it. Avoid such people. (2 Timothy 3:5)

---

[330] See Revelation 2:7,11,17,29; 3:6,13,22

Paul pointed out that there were three groups of people[331] in the church:
1. Unbelievers (apistoi)
2. Outsiders/ungifted (idiotes: singular; idiotai: plural)
3. Believer/believers (pisteuousin: plural; pistos: singular

The "outsiders/ungifted," (idiotai), are those who do not belong to the community, though they join in its gatherings. They are characterized as such by the fact that they do not understand speaking with tongues and then by the fact that they are not members.[332] In each case, the context demands a reference to non-Christians. Here, then, the "idiotes" is the unbeliever who does not possess the charisma of speaking with tongues or interpretation of tongues. That the "idiotai" are not a middle group between "apistoi" (believers) and "pistoi" (unbelievers) is clearly understood by the fact that the context does not demand such a distinction, and that there is no grounds for it."[333]

This means then, that any person who claims to be a born-again Christian, but who has not received the baptism of the Holy Spirit with the proof of the "signs" is not a complete Christian; if in fact, he or she is one at all. These people belong to the other group of "idiotai" who may attend church meetings but are not born-again Christians. They reject the baptism of the Holy Spirit and the gifts of the Holy Spirit.

I have discovered over the years that such people can be possessed by demons/evil spirits. While true believers, who have had their personal day of Pentecost,[334] cannot actually be *possessed* by demons/evil spirits; many times I have seen evil spirits attach themselves to unwary believers and subject them to various forms of physical and uncontrollable bodily shaking. This is blamed mistakenly on the Holy Spirit, who gives self-control[335] to those who receive Him.

---

[331] See 1 Corinthians 14:1
[332] See 1 Corinthians 14:24
[333] "Theological Dictionary of the New Testament", Vol. 3, 1967, Edited by G. Kittel; p. 216-217
[334] Acts 2:4
[335] See the list of the fruit of the Spirit in Galatians 5:23

In a church in Sudbury, Ontario, a couple who responded to my invitation were standing waiting for prayer. Both were trembling in a way that reminded me of epilepsy. I asked them, "What is going on here?"

The man said, "I don't know. We cannot stop shaking. This started when we were at a church in Toronto, after they laid hands on us and prayed. They said it was the Holy Spirit. We need prayer for the shaking to stop."

I explained that they had been possessed by demons. They wanted to be set free. I commanded the demons to leave their bodies and they did. The couple repented for going to a meeting that exposed them to the works of demons. I then laid hands on them and they received the authentic baptism of the Holy Spirit with the evidence of speaking in tongues. They now had the peace and self-control described as part of the fruit of the Spirit.

> *But the fruit of the Spirit is love, joy, peace, patience, kindness, goodness, faithfulness, gentleness, self-control; against such there is no law.* (Galatians 5:22-23)

Many people today have been told that they received the Holy Spirit when they have not. Such was the case when, in Philip's ministry, Peter and John were sent to Samaria to see if any of the new believers had received the Holy Spirit. The record proves that, although the believers had been baptized in the name of Jesus, they had not yet received the Holy Spirit.

> *"for He* (Holy Spirit) *had not yet fallen on any of them* (Greek: not one), *but they had only been baptized in the Name of Jesus. Then they laid their hands on them and they received the Holy Spirit."* (Acts 8:16-17)

From all the years in my ministry, I have discovered that most people in the churches have never received the baptism of the Holy Spirit, and so have not been equipped or able to do the ministry of Jesus. With neither the signs of proof nor the gifts of the Holy Spirit,[336] nor the ability to pray

---
[336] See Romans 12:6-8; 1 Corinthians 12:8-10

in the Spirit (tongues language) they live in constant insecurity, knowing "something is missing" which does not allow them to fulfill Paul's admonition in Ephesians 6:18.

> *Pray at all times in the Spirit, with all prayer and supplication. To that end keep alert with all perseverance, making supplication for all the saints.* (Ephesians 6:18)

They are lacking assurance of the marvellous "sealing," of which Paul writes:

> *"In Him you also, who have heard the word of truth, the gospel of your salvation, and have believed in Him, were sealed with the promised Holy Spirit, which is the guarantee of our inheritance until we acquire possession of it, to the praise of His glory."*
> (Ephesians 1:13-14)

Consequently, they don"t have the confidence to move forward effectively in the spiritual warfare to which we are called.

The second answer, "No," refers to the only kind of Christian who cannot be possessed, and that is one who has repented of their sins, been forgiven and experienced the cleansing that comes with salvation[337] and received the baptism of the Holy Spirit confirmed with the evidence of speaking in tongues.[338] The Holy Spirit fills the human body like a hand fills a glove, leaving no room for any evil spirit to enter the person.

When preparing his disciples for his departure, Jesus said,

> *"And I will pray the Father, and He will give you another Counselor, to be with you for ever, even the Spirit of Truth, whom the world cannot receive, because it neither sees Him nor knows Him; you know Him, for he dwells with you, and will be in you."* (John 14:16,17)

The Greek word for counselor is "parakletos," and is used as a title of the Holy Spirit. The word comes from the ancient Greek judicial system,

---

[337] See John 1:9
[338] See Mark 16:17 and 1 Corinthians 12:10

where it referred to the defense attorney, the advocate who appears in another's behalf. The Holy Spirit knows the whole law of God,[339] the law of Christ[340] and the royal law.[341] We need such a Helper to guide us and keep us secure in our salvation.

> *But the Counselor* (parakletos), *the Holy Spirit, whom the Father will send in My Name, He will teach you all things, and bring to your remembrance all that I have said to you.* (John 14:26)

> *Nevertheless I tell you the truth: it is to your advantage that I go away, for if I do not go away, the Counselor* (parakletos) *will not come to you; but if I go, I will send Him to you. And when He comes, He will convince the world concerning sin and righteousness and judgment: concerning sin, because they do not believe in Me; concerning righteousness, because I go to the Father, and you will see Me no more; concerning judgment, because the ruler of this world is judged.* (John 16:7-11)

> *When the Spirit of Truth comes, He will guide you into all the truth; for He will not speak on his own authority, but whatever He hears He will speak, and He will declare to you the things that are to come. He will glorify Me, for He will take what is Mine and declare it to you. All that the Father has is Mine. Therefore I said that He will take what is Mine and declare it to you.* (John 16:13-15)

> *In Him you also, who have heard the word of truth, the gospel of your salvation, and have believed in Him, were sealed with the promised Holy Spirit ...* (Ephesians 1:13)

Happily, we have one other attorney.

> *My little children, I am writing this to you so that you may not sin; but if any one does sin, we have an advocate with the Father, Jesus Christ the righteous; and He is the expiation for our sins, and not for ours only but also for the sins of the whole world.* (1 John 2:1-2)

---

[339] See Romans 7:25
[340] See Galatians 6:2
[341] See James 2:8

William Barclay writes, "The word 'parakletos' has a great background in Greek law. The parakletos was the prisoner's friend, the advocate and counsel for the defense, the man who bore witness to his friend's character when he most needed it, and when others wished to condemn him; therefore when we describe the glorified as our parakletos, we mean that He is there to speak for us before God."[342]

What a job description! In the Old Testament, whenever a person sinned, the Holy Spirit would leave, as in the story of Samson, who did not know that the LORD had left him.[343] However, ever since the Day of Pentecost, the Holy Spirit stays with us through thick and thin. Jesus said,

"I will not leave you orphaned; I will come to you." (John 14:18)

The Holy Spirit fulfills Jesus' promise:

"... and lo, I am with you always, to the close of the age."
(Matthew 28:20)

This means that, when Spirit-filled Christians sin, the Holy Spirit does not leave, but instead, convicts them of their sin, calling them to repent and to serve Jesus anew.

And when He comes, He will convince the world concerning sin and righteousness and judgment ... (John 16:8)

While God has permitted Satan to be active in the minds of men to test the degree of their devotion to Him, there are boundaries beyond which he cannot go and conditions regarding his ability to dominate people and situations.

No place in the New Testament says a faithful, born-again, Spirit-filled Christian can be possessed by an evil spirit. It says clearly we can be attacked and harassed, but not possessed.

Some people would call this harassment, being "demonized," but there is no indication in the Bible that every time a person sins, an evil spirit

---

[342] "New Testament Words" William Barclay, page 222
[343] See Judges 16:20

moves into that person. When we have received the baptism of the Holy Spirit, the Holy Spirit is our protection from the devil and from any kind of possession by evil spirits/demons. Just as the Israelites put the lamb's blood on their door posts and lintels to stop the angel of death from entering their houses and killing their first-born children, so the blood of Jesus prevents any evil spirit from entering us. He was the Lamb who was slain for our protection from evil. This protection, in the form of the Holy Spirit, covers us after receiving Jesus and being baptized by the Holy Spirit with the proof of the "signs following"[344] that identify true believers.[345]

While evil spirits/demons cannot go inside the flesh of a true believer, neither can they inhabit our human soul/spirit[346] because we have the protection of the Holy Spirit. Occasionally, an evil spirit may suggest we do something sinful, but it has no power to force us to do it.

Cooperating with the Holy Spirit, Through Use of His Gifts, to Avoid Possession

The Holy Spirit becomes a constant aggravation to the unrepentant believer. For instance, when a person does not cooperate with Him by not using the gift of speaking in tongues (which is God's communication system), he or she will begin to feel that something is not right. Things will begin to happen which indicate that he or she has not been listening to the Holy Spirit for guidance in ministry and witnessing. Cooperating with the Holy Spirit requires one to pray in the Spirit (tongues) every day so he or she will know what to do. Timothy had this problem. He developed a fear that caused him to lose confidence in his ministry. Other symptoms I have observed are heart palpitations, a full chest, a funny tickle in the throat, continuous tears for no apparent reason, and burning mouth. Paul encouraged Timothy to pray in tongues every day.[347] He addressed the problem again, in his second letter to Timothy.

---

[344] Mark 16:17

[345] While some may think this is overly repeated throughout this book, it has been done with purpose in hopes that no one who reads it will be able to walk away without the understanding of what characterizes a "true believer."

[346] "Soul" and "spirit" are two words translated from the Greek which both refer to the human spirit (psyche).

[347] See 1 Timothy 4:14 and 1 Corinthians 14:2,15

Hence I remind you to rekindle (Greek: every day) *the gift of God that is within you through the laying on of my hands; for God did not give us a spirit of timidity but a spirit of power and love and self-control.* (2 Timothy 1:6-7 RSV)

The King James version says it a little differently.

Wherefore I put Thee in remembrance that Thou stir up the gift of God, which is in Thee by the putting on of my hands. For God hath not given us the spirit of fear; but of power, and of love, and of a sound mind. (2 Timothy 1:6-7 KJV)

The gift that comes with receiving the Holy Spirit is the gift of speaking in tongues (the evidence), a new language that is unknown to the person.[348]

And the believers from among the circumcised who came with Peter were amazed, because the gift of the Holy Spirit had been poured out even on the Gentiles. For they heard them speaking in tongues and extolling God. (Acts 10:45-46)

And when Paul had laid his hands upon them, the Holy Spirit came on them; and they spoke with tongues and prophesied. (Acts 19:6)

When Timothy was not praying daily with his Spirit-given language, he was troubled with fear. When he did pray in the Spirit, he experienced love, power and a sound mind.[349]

Speaking and singing in tongues also brings good health and healing.[350] Paul used the word "edification" ('oikodomeo), which is a construction term for building or renovating a structure. When applied to the human body, it means that healing occurs when a Christian prays in tongues for himself or for other people.[351]

Being baptized with the Holy Spirit does not guarantee faithfulness, but it does prevent a person from being possessed by an evil spirit.

That being said, it does *not* prevent *harassment* by evil spirits.

---

[348] See Mark 16:17; Acts 2:4; 1 Corinthians 14:18
[349] See 2 Timothy 1:7
[350] See 1 Corinthians 14:4
[351] See Mark 16:18

The Consequences of Turning One's Back on the Holy Spirit

We can grieve the Holy Spirit by not listening to Him. He does not force us to do what Jesus wants us to do, but His desire is to equip and assist us to be effective witnesses for Jesus Christ.[352] Besides warning us not to grieve the Holy Spirit,[353] we are also told not to quench the Spirit.[354] Further, the Scriptures warn that it is possible to outrage the Spirit of grace.

> *How much worse punishment do you think will be deserved by those who have spurned the Son of God, profaned the blood of the covenant by which they were sanctified, and outraged the Spirit of grace?* (Hebrews 10:29)

Walking on such dangerous ground, can lead to blasphemy against the Holy Spirit – which will not be forgiven.[355] Once a conscience has been seared,[356] the worst possible fate must be faced: the blotting out of such a person's name from the Book of Life.[357]

Christians who have experienced salvation and the baptism of the Holy Spirit, who think they can sin with impunity, are making the biggest mistake of their lives.[358] The gifts of the Holy Spirit are meant to bring spiritual and physical health to the body of believers. Failure to use them, results in sickness and premature death.

The ultimate consequence will occur when standing before Jesus at the Final Judgment, with our defense lawyer, the Holy Spirit. The devil, the prosecuting attorney for the kingdom of God (the legitimate accuser of the brethren – Greek: "kategoros"), will bring charges against anyone who has broken God's laws. He will have a complete list of all the sins they have committed (unless the person has already repented and received forgiveness from God). The defense attorney, the Holy Spirit,

---

[352] See Acts 2:4
[353] See Ephesians 4:30
[354] See 1 Thessalonians 5:19
[355] See Matthew 12:31
[356] See 1 Timothy 4:2
[357] See Revelation 3:5
[358] See Acts 17:30

will not be able to defend them by saying, "Washed clean by the Blood of the Lamb," but will have to agree with the prosecuting attorney, that His client is guilty. This is the picture of Satan's role as described in the Book of Job.[359] The difference today, is that since the devil was cast out of Heaven down to earth,[360] he can no longer travel back and forth from earth to Heaven to report to God about all the sins being committed. The judgment will be to serve eternity in the Lake of Fire – where the prosecuting attorney himself will end up.[361]

Peter gives a warning:

> ... then the LORD knows how to rescue the godly from trial, and to keep the unrighteous under punishment until the day of judgment, and especially those who indulge in the lust of defiling passion and despise authority. Bold and wilful, they are not afraid to revile the glorious ones, ... For if, after they have escaped the defilements of the world through the knowledge of our LORD and Savior Jesus Christ, they are again entangled in them and overpowered, the last state has become worse for them than the first. For it would have been better for them never to have known the way of righteousness than after knowing it to turn back from the holy commandment delivered to them. It has happened to them according to the true proverb, "The dog turns back to his own vomit, and the sow is washed only to wallow in the mire." (2 Peter 2:9-10, 20-22)

The writer of Hebrews gives a similar warning:

> For it is impossible to restore again to repentance those who have once been enlightened, who have tasted the heavenly gift, and have become partakers of the Holy Spirit, and have tasted the goodness of the Word of God and the powers of the age to come, if they then commit apostasy, since they crucify the Son of God on their own account and hold him up to contempt. For land which has drunk the rain that often falls upon it, and brings forth vegetation useful to

---

[359] See Job 1:12
[360] See Revelation 12:10
[361] See Revelation 19:20; 20:10

those for whose sake it is cultivated, receives a blessing from God. But if it bears thorns and thistles, it is worthless and near to being cursed; its end is to be burned. (Hebrews 6:4-8)

To the Church in Sardis, Jesus said,

"He who conquers shall be clad thus in white garments, and I will not blot his name out of the Book of Life; I will confess his name before My Father and before His angels. He who has an ear, let him hear what the Spirit says to the churches." (Revelation 3:5-6)

In other words, there are people who have known Jesus as Savior and Lord, and been baptized with the Holy Spirit, who can turn their backs on Jesus and be in a worse state than they were before they became Christians. A severe warning is given to those who think they can sin without serious consequences.[362]

So, when we receive the baptism of the Holy Spirit, with the proof of the signs following, we cannot be possessed; the Holy Spirit does not leave us or revoke our calling and His gifts, but those gifts will be used as evidence against those who arrogantly disregard them. Often, because such people, in their rebellion, turn away from Jesus, their behavior may appear to have many of the symptoms of being possessed by demons, because they are similar, but these people are not possessed. To mistake sin for possession, has been one of the biggest mistakes that Christians who *"know neither the Scriptures nor the power of God"* make, in their efforts to get rid of the symptoms.

But Jesus answered them, "You are wrong, because you know neither the Scriptures nor the power of God." (Matthew 22:29)

Sin cannot be cast out of a person. The person exhibiting the symptoms, has to repent to be set free from sin. On the flip side of the coin, demon-possessed people need to have demons cast out of them by a Spirit-filled believer before they can repent, receive salvation and the baptism of the Holy Spirit and be witnesses for Jesus Christ.[363]

---

[362] See Matthew 7:15-29; 18:21-35; 25:1-46
[363] See Acts 1:8

The warning to Saul applies to us today.

For rebellion is as the sin of divination (witchcraft), *and stubbornness is as iniquity and idolatry. Because you have rejected the word of the* LORD, *He has also rejected you from being king.* (1 Samuel 15:23)

While Jesus said that no man can pluck his sheep out of His hand, they can apparently jump out of His hand and leave behind everything He gave them.

My sheep hear My voice, and I know them, and they follow Me; and I give them eternal life, and they shall never perish, and no one shall snatch them out of My hand. (John 10:27-28)

It is not impossible to walk away from our salvation. Some think such a thing would be inconsistent with God's grace, but it's not necessarily so. God's law is still in operation and conditions apply in the new covenant. Nobody can sin with immunity or impunity. God still hates sin. Anybody who thinks he or she can get away with it, is fooling him or herself.

If a person turns away from Jesus, forsakes the new life in Christ and gets re-entangled in sin, then his or her condition will be worse in the end than it was in the beginning. However, it does not mean that an evil spirit will automatically move into and possess the person who has lost eternal life. It means the person is in sin, which, in itself, is extremely serious. If we do not want to keep the terms of the new covenant, then we get its penalties.

The more common danger, is for people to add to the Scriptures by putting an evil spirit behind every sin, or to ignore what the Scriptures say about demon possession. Neither is there wisdom in writing the symptoms off as figments of somebody's imagination, hallucinations, or the result of wrongful use of drugs.

We must be careful not to give the devil and the kingdom of darkness more credit than they are due. The Bible defines their spheres of operation and their authority. The greatest danger is not the devil or 10,000 demons; our greatest danger is *giving in* to our own sinful desires when we are tempted. That is something that all the demons in the world cannot make us do. Only we can give in to sin, thereby placing our own lives in danger. It would be like any first-born Jew, who would have been foolish enough to have left the safety of his home, after the lamb's blood had been placed on the door posts and the lintel of his house.[364]

> *The blood shall be a sign for you, upon the houses where you are; and when I see the blood, I will pass over you, and no plague shall fall upon you to destroy you, when I smite the land of Egypt.* (Exodus 12:13)

The same can be said of any person who leaves the safety and covering of the blood of Jesus to expose him or herself foolishly to sin and the kingdom of darkness.[365]

> *The next day he saw Jesus coming toward him, and said, "Behold, the Lamb of God, who takes away the sin of the world!"* (John 1:29)

The Armour

We need to be ready at all times. Paul, in his letter to the Ephesians, gives precise instructions regarding the weapons which will enable us to overcome all circumstances.

> *Therefore take the whole armor of God, that you may be able to withstand in the evil day, and having done all, to stand. Stand therefore, having girded your loins with truth, and having put on the breastplate of righteousness, and having shod your feet with the equipment of the gospel of peace; besides all these, taking the shield of faith, with which you can quench all the flaming darts of the evil one. And take the helmet of salvation, and the sword of the Spirit, which is the Word of God.* (Ephesians 6:13-17)

> *For the word of God*[366] *is living and active, sharper than any two-edged sword, piercing to the division of soul* (psyche-human soul/spirit) *and spirit* (pneuma - Holy Spirit), *of joints and marrow,*

---

[364] See Exodus 12:1-13
[365] See 1 Corinthians 5:7; Revelation 1:5-6
[366] See John 1:1,14,17

> *and discerning the thoughts and intentions of the heart. And before Him* (Jesus) *no creature is hidden, but all are open and laid bare to the eyes of Him with whom we have to do.* (Hebrews 4:12-14)

Paul explains how the weapons, that are effective in waging spiritual warfare, are not like human weapons.

> *... for the weapons of our warfare are not worldly but have divine power to destroy strongholds. We destroy arguments and every proud obstacle to the knowledge of God, and take every Thought captive to obey Christ.* (2 Corinthians 10:4-5)

The weapons of our warfare are the "signs following"[367] by which our preaching and ministry is confirmed,[368] meaning proven and verified. So, if there are no signs, then there has been no proof of what is preached. The weapons of our warfare include the ministry gifts of the Holy Spirit[369] by which all of our needs can be met.[370]

Many Christians disregard Paul's instructions and description of the weapons we must use, because they approach spiritual warfare with the same mind set they have for fighting human battles. They look for things they can *do* to fight the devil and the kingdom of darkness, even trying to turn the use of the whole armor of God into an offensive tactic against the enemy. But that's not it at all! The whole armor of God, is the protection we are given by Jesus Christ – the key to successful warfare. The whole armor of God describes a daily relationship with Jesus Christ, a lifestyle for walking with the Holy Spirit. It describes a relationship with our Heavenly Father. An authentic relationship with God, listening and obeying His instructions, is our real armor. We are safe when we walk in relationship with God. Our protection is relationship with the Holy Spirit.

The amazing thing about fighting spiritual warfare, is that we don't actually have to do very much except be in personal relationship with Jesus Christ. We simply "do whatever he says to do."[371] We operate, not

---

[367] See Mark 16:17-20
[368] Means to put something beyond doubt, confirmed
[369] See Romans 12:6-8; 1 Corinthians 15:8-12
[370] See Philippians 4: 19
[371] See John 2:5

in our own strength, but in the power of the Holy Spirit. We conduct the warfare, not with our own understanding, but with the wisdom of God, given – moment by moment – each day.

This is why Paul advised us to pray continuously.

Pray at all times in the Spirit, with all prayer and supplication. (Ephesians 6:18)

Trust in the LORD with all your heart, and do not rely on your own insight. In all your ways acknowledge Him, and He will make straight your paths. (Proverbs 3:5-6)

Let's do a breakdown on the whole armor of God, as described in Ephesians 6:13-17.

- **"Stand therefore, having girded your loins with truth"** describes the daily personal relationship Jesus Christ.

And Jesus said to him, "I am the way, and the truth, and the life. No one comes to the Father but by Me." (John 14:6)

- **The "breastplate of righteousness"** describes the right-relationship with God, which Jesus bought, paying the price so that we could become "the righteousness of God."

For our sake He made Him to be sin who knew no sin, so that in Him we might become the righteousness of God. (2 Corinthians 5:21)

As such, we can recognize His voice and talk with Him, and He with us, moment by moment, every day – so that the roar of the lion will not frighten us.

My sheep hear My voice. I know them, and they follow Me. (John 10:27)

He who has an ear, let him hear what the Spirit says to the churches. He who conquers shall not be hurt by the second death … He who has an ear, let him hear what the Spirit says to the churches. To him who conquers I will give some of the hidden manna, and I will give him a white stone, with a new name written on the stone which no one knows except him who receives it ... (Revelation 2:11,17; see also Revelation 2:7,29; 3:6,13,22)

Be sober, be watchful. Your adversary the devil prowls around like a roaring lion, seeking some one to devour. (1 Peter 5:8)

- **"... having shod your feet with the equipment of the gospel of peace"** refers to the peace of God, which guards our hearts and minds, and is reinforced by our daily walking and talking with Him.

And the peace of God, which passes all understanding, will keep your hearts and your minds in Christ Jesus. (Philippians 4:7)

- **The "shield of faith, with which you can quench all the flaming darts of the evil one"** describes our daily relationship with Jesus in which we do whatever He says[372] so that, like Paul, we can know, beyond a shadow of doubt, that God can be trusted to look after us.

... and therefore I suffer as I do. But I am not ashamed, for I know whom I have believed, and I am sure that He is able to guard until that Day what has been entrusted to me. (2 Timothy 1:12)

It is in that relationship that all the fiery attacks of the enemy are absorbed, giving us the assurance nothing in all of creation can separate us from the love of God.

For I am sure that neither death, nor life, nor angels, nor principalities, nor things present, nor things to come, nor powers, nor height, nor depth, nor anything else in all creation, will be able to separate us from the love of God in Christ Jesus our LORD. (Romans 8:38-39)

- **The "helmet of salvation,"** refers to the absolute assurance that our sins are forgiven.

If we confess our sins, He is faithful and just, and will forgive our sins and cleanse us from all unrighteousness. (1 John 1:9)

We no longer carry any guilt, but we have eternal life.

---

[372] See John 2:5

And this is the testimony, that God gave us eternal life, and this life is in His Son. He who has the Son has life; he who has not the Son of God has not life. (1 John 5:11-12)

With this assurance of salvation, Satan, the accuser of the brethren, cannot condemn us.

But they have conquered him by the blood of the Lamb and by the word of their testimony ... (Revelation 12:11)

- **The "Sword of the Spirit,"** is the Word of God and refers to the daily food for our souls, provided by Jesus Christ, who *is* the Word of God and who strengthens us to follow the leading of the Holy Spirit.

For the Word of God is living and active, sharper than any two-edged sword, piercing to the division of soul and spirit, of joints and marrow, and discerning the thoughts and intentions of the heart. (Hebrews 4:12)

For all who are led by the Spirit of God are sons of God. (Romans 8:14)

But you are not in the flesh, you are in the Spirit, if in fact the Spirit of God dwells in you. Any one who does not have the Spirit of Christ does not belong to Him. (Romans 8:9)

But you shall receive power when the Holy Spirit has come upon you; and you shall be My witnesses in Jerusalem and in all Judea and Samaria and to the end of the earth. (Acts 1:8)

- The final piece of armor is **"praying always with all prayer and supplication in the Spirit."** This describes our communication system with Jesus Christ through the Holy Spirit. It includes praying in tongues, our spiritual language. This weapon is activated by the Holy Spirit so that we can pray not only with the mind, but also with the Spirit.

What am I to do? I will pray with the spirit and I will pray with the mind also; I will sing with the spirit and I will sing with the mind also. (1 Corinthians 14:15)

It is through this amazing method of prayer, enabled by the baptism in the Holy Spirit, that Jesus gives us daily instruction and wisdom through His Holy Spirit.

> *When the Spirit of Truth comes, He will guide you into all the truth; for He will not speak on His own authority, but whatever He hears He will speak, and He will declare to you the things that are to come.*
> (John 16:13)

Praying in the Spirit means more than simply praying in one's normal language as he or she feels guided. When we pray in tongues (praying in the Spirit), we speak mysteries to Jesus through the Holy Spirit, enabling us to bypass our own intellect and be in constant relationship with Him.

> *For one who speaks in a tongue speaks not to men but to God; for no one understands him, but he utters mysteries in the Spirit.*
> (1 Corinthians 14:2)

When we learn to release the words of the Holy Spirit by praying in tongues, prayer becomes no longer a guessing game; it is direct communication with God, as we hear the voice of His Holy Spirit explaining things He will tell us only when we are praying in tongues.

"The one who speaks in tongues (Greek: pneumati lalei musteria) utters secret truths in the Spirit which he alone shares with God, and which his fellow-man, even a Christian, does not understand."[373] The exception, of course, comes when someone who has the gift of interpretation of tongues, gives the interpretation – or when someone who understands the language being spoken, gives the translation.

> *... to another the working of miracles, to another prophecy, to another the ability to distinguish between spirits, to another various kinds of tongues, to another the interpretation of tongues.*
> (1 Corinthians 12:10)

The full armor of God refers not to what we wear, but to whom we relate. Except for the sword of the Spirit and prayer, it is defensive armor;

---

[373] A Greek-English Lexicon of the New Testament and Other Early Christian Literature, by William F. Arndt and F. Wilbur Gingrich, p. 532

so our protection in spiritual warfare comes as we develop an intimate personal relationship with God. This is why the modern versions of Scribes, Pharisees, Sadducees, and the kingdom of darkness are easily defeated today. Like their ancient predecessors, they do not understand Jesus. They, like a lot of people today, think that eternal life is a reward for following laws, going to church and trying to do things that are written in the Bible. They have not grasped the point, or the essence, of the kingdom of God: God wants to have a daily personal relationship with us, just like He had with Adam and Eve. That is the reason why Jesus came. That is the reason why the Holy Spirit was sent. That is the reason why we have a Heavenly Father and not an impersonal judge.

Spending time with Jesus – every day – prepares us to fight.

You search the Scriptures, because you think that in them you have eternal life; and it is they that bear witness to Me; yet you refuse to come to Me that you may have life. (John 5:39-40)

To be prepared to do battle with the devil, we must go to Jesus every day – spending time with Him, discussing our lives and circumstances and getting direction and guidance.

When we are in the midst of warfare and are getting discouraged, we can take heart from the encouragement of the apostle Paul.

Therefore do not be foolish, but understand what the will of the LORD is. And do not get drunk with wine, for that is debauchery; but be filled with the Spirit, addressing one another in psalms and hymns and spiritual songs, singing and making melody to the LORD with all your heart, always and for everything giving thanks in the Name of our LORD Jesus Christ to God the Father. (Ephesians 5:17-20)

In other words, Paul learned, as we all must, the critical nature of being renewed by the Holy Spirit each day. We do not have to fight the devil and the kingdom of darkness alone; neither do we have to face temptation or evil spirits by ourselves. The Holy Spirit is always with us to guide and instruct us – if He dwells within us.

But you are not in the flesh, you are in the Spirit, if in fact the Spirit of God dwells in you. Anyone who does not have the Spirit of Christ does not belong to Him. (Romans 8:9)

Alone, we get beat up, defeated and discouraged. Together with the Holy Spirit, we beat up and defeat the enemy.

The Gifts of the Spirit...
Our Practical Weapons in Spiritual Warfare

We need to learn how to cooperate with the Holy Spirit, because walking with Him is our only hope of defeating the kingdom of darkness. Learning to operate skillfully in the gifts He gives, is the key to effective use of the weapons of our warfare.

Besides having the full armour of God in place, as outlined above, we need to be skilled in using the mighty weapons, the gifts of the Holy Spirit, that are most often overlooked, but are so effective in tearing down the enemy strongholds in people's minds. These are charismatic gifts, designed for the church to use to destroy the enemy and his kingdom. They are outlined in Romans 12:6-8 and 1 Corinthians 12:4-11.

Having gifts that differ according to the grace given to us, let us use them: if prophecy, in proportion to our faith; if service, in our serving; he who teaches, in his teaching; he who exhorts, in his exhortation; he who contributes, in liberality; he who gives aid, with zeal; he who does acts of mercy, with cheerfulness. (Romans 12:6-8)

Now there are varieties of gifts, but the same Spirit; and there are varieties of service, but the same Lord*; and there are varieties of working, but it is the same God who inspires them all in every one. To each is given the manifestation of the Spirit for the common good. To one is given through the Spirit the utterance of wisdom, and to another the utterance of knowledge according to the same Spirit, to another faith by the same Spirit, to another gifts of healing by the one*

Spirit, to another the working of miracles, to another prophecy, to another the ability to distinguish between spirits, to another various kinds of tongues, to another the interpretation of tongues. All these are inspired by one and the same Spirit, who apportions to each one individually as He wills. For just as the body is one and has many members, and all the members of the body, though many, are one body, so it is with Christ. (1 Corinthians 12:4-12)

The only people who can have these gifts, are those who have been born-again and baptized with the Holy Spirit.

Jesus answered him, "Truly, truly, I say to you, unless one is born anew, he cannot see the kingdom of God." ... "Truly, truly, I say to you, unless one is born of water and the Spirit, he cannot enter the kingdom of God.... Do not marvel that I said to you, 'You must be born anew.'" (John 3:3,5,7)

But you shall receive power when the Holy Spirit has come upon you; and you shall be My witnesses in Jerusalem and in all Judea and Samaria and to the end of the earth. (Acts 1:8)

Each of the fifteen gifts of the Holy Spirit has an evangelistic thrust that catches people's attention. They are to be used to meet the needs of people and are given for the purpose of breaking through the darkness and bringing people into the light. They assist in transforming us through the renewal of our minds (so we can know the will of God) and strengthen us to resist being conformed to this world.

I appeal to you therefore, brethren, by the mercies of God, to present your bodies as a living sacrifice, holy and acceptable to God, which is your spiritual worship. Do not be conformed to this world but be transformed by the renewal of your mind, that you may prove what is the will of God, what is good and acceptable and perfect. (Romans 12:1-2)

- **Prophecy** – The Holy Spirit uses prophecy to tell us ahead of time where Jesus wants to guide us, what problems we will face, how to solve them and how to deal with the attacks of the enemy, successfully defeating him according to the Holy Spirit's direction.

- *Teaching* – This gift explains the gospel to other people so they can understand how to move out of the oppressive kingdom of darkness into the freedom of the kingdom of God.

- *Exhortation* – This gift is used by the Holy Spirit to encourage people to follow God's wonderful plan for them to give them a future and a hope.

- *Giving* – This gift supplies everything people need, in terms of money and material, so they can follow and complete God's plan for their lives. In stark contrast, the kingdom of darkness seeks only to discourage and bankrupt them.

- *Administration* – This gift provides leadership, organization, equipping, to enable God's army, the church, to defeat the kingdom of darkness.

- *Mercy* – This gift enables us to experience God's *seventy times seventy* (490) forgiveness daily, freeing people from the condemnation of the kingdom of darkness.

- *Wisdom* – The Holy Spirit gives us wisdom to solve our problems. The kingdom of darkness gives us only problems.

- *Knowledge* – This gift is used to tell us what Jesus wants to do in meetings – usually with regard to healing physical or mental conditions, injuries or diseases; such as cancer, heart problems or broken bones.

- *Faith* – This gift enables us to know God will keep all his biblical promises when we allow Jesus to be our Savior and Lord.

- *Gifts of healing* – This gift confirms the fact that Jesus Christ is still in the healing business and will heal people as they come out of the kingdom of darkness – where they are often inflicted with pain, sickness and death.

- *Miracles* – Jesus uses miracles to demonstrate that God will use extraordinary means to meet His people's needs in His kingdom.

- ***Discerning of Spirits*** – is used to spot and identify the enemy before, or when, they attack God's people. This gift provides protection for those in the kingdom of God.
- ***Tongues*** – let people know that God can control their tongues by giving them, supernaturally, a legitimate language they have never learned (whether one in current use or one spoken in the past) – and don't understand – to communicate with God.
- ***Interpretation of tongues (languages)*** – explains what God says to people through the gift of tongues. Through this gift, He guides His people both individually and in groups.

All the gifts of the Holy Spirit are powerful. They are used by the Holy Spirit to make us inter-dependent on each other, enabling us to work together as an army directed by Jesus Christ. As we work together in fellowship, we defeat the devil and the kingdom of darkness. No one can have all the gifts of the Holy Spirit.[374]

All these are inspired by one and the same Spirit, who apportions to each one individually as He wills. For just as the body is one and has many members, and all the members of the body, though many, are one body, so it is with Christ. (1 Corinthians 12:11-12)

In his book, *Charisma,* Philip Rief explains that when the churches stopped using the fifteen gifts of the Holy Spirit, they removed God's grace from their ministries and replaced it with their own forms of, what Jesus calls, "traditions of men." These made void the Word of God.

The Greek word for gift is "charisma" (singular); the plural being "charismata." "Charis" means "grace." Therefore, the gifts of the Holy Spirit should properly be called "gifts of grace," but because they are distributed by the Holy Spirit, they are translated and named "gifts of the Holy Spirit."

By using all fifteen gifts of the Holy Spirit in our churches, God is able to meet the needs of all of His people; but where the gifts of the Holy Spirit have been disallowed, forbidden or discouraged, the needs of people are not able to be met.

---

[374] 1 Corinthians 12:6-13

Many churches have developed substitutes which can only be described as "works righteousness." Through the use of these, people are told to do certain things to earn their salvation. This is impossible, according to the New Testament. No amount of good works can get anyone into Heaven or replace God's tools for meeting the needs of His people. When used as directed by the Holy Spirit, churches become places where signs, wonders and miracles reflect what should be the normal life of every church.

On the other hand, churches that try to teach about the gifts of the Holy Spirit without teaching that the prerequisite to receiving them is receiving the baptism in the Holy Spirit, will only frustrate their people.

Spiritual warfare can be a growing and exciting experience as we see the enemy defeated and captives set free.

People who have been born again and baptized with the Holy Spirit are recognizable by the signs that accompany them. These are signs of authenticity which mark a real and complete Christian. Born again, Holy Spirit baptized Christians are walking advertisements of God's love and power. Branded and bearing the seal of God's ownership, they are today's mighty men and women of valor.

> *And these signs will accompany those who believe: in My Name they will cast out demons; they will speak in new tongues; they will pick up serpents, and if they drink any deadly thing, it will not hurt them; they will lay their hands on the sick, and they will recover.*
> (Mark 16:17-18)

This is an exciting time to be a Christian. Everything we read in the Bible, is available to us today and Jesus will never tell us to do anything that is not in the Bible. That is our protection. We have a covenant with God, where we find instructions about how His kingdom works. The devil will always encourage us to go beyond the Bible and question God's Word – but the more we read the Bible and study it, the more we will understand it. It was written simply.

In *Parables of Life,* J. Edgar Park, shows us clearly in his parable, "The Man and the Demon," what happens when we are under attack:

"Every evening as the man was going asleep, a huge demon came and threw him down a steep place into the mire. The demon was so large that it darkened all the sky. It lifted him bodily off his feet like a great wind. Now it was very pleasant so to be carried along, but the mire in which he was always landed was filthy.

"One day he resolved to resist the demon. He set his feet in the earth and refused to be moved. To his surprise, he found himself able to keep his ground. After a terrible struggle, he was left in peace. He slept on the high ground all that night. So he continued to do with constant vigilance for many nights.

"After a long time, he was one day going asleep when he noticed a tiny insect buzzing around in the grass near him and blundering against his feet. When he slept, he asked the angel who visited him in his dreams, what the curious little creature was.

"The angel answered, 'It is the dragon which used to hurl you down the cliff.'

"'But how small it has grown!' cried he in astonishment.

"Then the angel answered, 'Nay, it has always been that size, it is you who have grown.'"[375]

No Need to Fear

So, there's no need to be afraid of the devil and his kingdom of darkness with its evil spirits/demons. They are more afraid of us, than we are of them. Any born-again, Spirit-filled Christian of any age, has the power and authority to defeat the enemy. We grow every time we are obedient and do as we are commanded. When we work willingly under the guidance of the Holy Spirit, one day we'll hear Jesus say,

> *"Well done, good and faithful servant; you have been faithful over a little, I will set you over much; enter into the joy of your Master."* (Matthew 25:21)

---

[375] Excerpted from *Parables of Life* by J. Edgar Park

Our protection from the devil and the kingdom of darkness is the same today as it always has been; it lies in a simple, personal relationship with Jesus Christ. Little children can have it. There are no qualifications regarding anyone's degree of intelligence, financial status, ethnic origins, age or abilities.

Anyone wanting to find such a relationship can simply call on Jesus by Name. Even though He usually cannot be seen, He is there. Anyone who asks Him to please forgive him or her for any sin and invites Him into his or her heart and life will be immediately forgiven and put in a right relationship with God – and given eternal life.

But that's not all. God also wants to give everyone who comes to Him the power of the Holy Spirit so he or she can live a fulfilled life, according to God's plan. To receive this power, simply asking Jesus for the baptism with the Holy Spirit – or finding someone who has the ministry of baptizing people in the Holy Spirit and asking him or her for prayer to receive, will result in the infilling of the power of the Holy Spirit. His power and presence will be recognized as the gifts He gives become evident in the life of the new believer.

We are equipped for battle when Jesus saves us, becomes Lord of our lives and baptizes us in the Holy Spirit. When we're not clear on what to do, we can ask Jesus to show us. If we do whatever He tells us, we cannot be defeated. Above all, we must enjoy our relationship with Jesus Christ each day and get to know the Holy Spirit intimately.

Through spiritual warfare we can grow in our relationship with Jesus Christ. Through one battle after another, we not only defeat the enemy but, with each victory we become stronger and more confident in serving Jesus Christ. Paul said,

> *"I have learned to be content with whatever I have ... I can do all things through Him who strengthens me."* (Philippians 4:11,13)

In closing, it is important to put spiritual warfare in perspective. The Bible gives us the balanced view we need, if only we will look for it. Using a concordance, I have discovered there are approximately 13,648 direct references to God as God, Lord, Father, Son, Jesus, Christ, Spirit, Holy Spirit and Holy Ghost. There are only 115 direct references to the devil or Satan. God's Names are mentioned 99.9999 percent as opposed to the devil's 0.00009 percent. The angels are referred to 293 times while evil spirits/demons are referred to only 130 times. The total references to the kingdom of God number 14,041 as opposed to the kingdom of darkness' 489. That means that when kingdoms are mentioned – using just these names – the kingdom of God is mentioned 99.99952 percent of the time, while the kingdom of darkness is mentioned just .00048 of one percent of the time. The angels are mentioned more times than the devil and evil spirits together. How embarrassing for the kingdom of darkness! There is no comparison. Perhaps now we can see why we need to be preoccupied with Jesus and keep our eyes focused on Him. Out of the corners of our eyes, we can catch the enemy when he tries to attack and be ready, instantaneously, to oust him.

To experience the greatest victory over the kingdom of darkness, we must allow Jesus to occupy our attention to the extent that we'll respond the same way as did Martin Luther, when confronted by the devil. When the devil woke Luther up one night, he opened his eyes, saw who it was, and said, "Oh, it's just you," then rolled over and went back to sleep. Our attention must be so filled with Jesus, that it can be said of us,

Blessed are the pure in heart, for they shall see God. (Matthew 5:8)

... and we shall.

Appendix

Where Do Demons Come From?

While writing this book, I have pondered the origin of demons. Regardless of what people want to believe, they are entities which cannot be ignored. They are a reality which can harass and torment people in their homes, at work and even possess people by actually entering their bodies to control and destroy them.

The difference between the devil and demons is that the devil comes to tempt people while demons come to attack, harass, occupy and possess people, buildings, automobiles, trucks, airplanes and ships for the kingdom of darkness.

The plural for demons in Hebrew is "mazzikin," which means "one who does harm." So the demons were malignant beings, intermediate between God and man, who were out to work harm.

Whatever their claims of origin, most people realize demons are real entities that can appear or materialize into various forms: some pretending to be people who have died; such as family members, friends, enemies or famous people. As counterfeits, their appearance duplicates or copies those people. Often, they will pretend to be Jesus, God or angels.

> *And no wonder, for even Satan disguises himself as an angel of light. So it is not strange if his servants also disguise themselves as servants of righteousness. Their end will correspond to their deeds.*
> (2 Corinthians 11:14–15)

When demons pretend to be deceased relatives or friends, they visit people to gain their confidence. At first, their visitations may appear friendly but they get progressively more abusive. They may offer advice which seems initially to be reliable and helpful – but proves to be destructive in the end. These kind of evil spirits are what the scriptures call "familiar spirits."[376] They often make themselves visible to gain trust but generally remain invisible; attacking people in their homes, breaking or moving furniture or throwing dishes, lamps, cutlery or other objects around the house. Poltergeists (so-called playful ghosts) like to throw articles around a room, move and upset furniture, cause damage to the house and physically abuse and hurt people. Their invisibility gives them a distinctive advantage in making people think they are imagining things; like seeing objects move or hearing voices talking, yelling or screaming. When evil spirits possess people, they take control of the person's body and imitate the symptoms of physical, mental and emotional disorders; such as schizophrenia or epilepsy, causing people to be captives in their own bodies. Demons can appear as people, animals, birds – or as something totally out of its element or unrecognizable – like fish floating in the air or peculiar looking people or weird objects.

Some evil spirits will sexually abuse children and adults. Some will injure and even kill people. They will often harass people to the point of suicide. They have the same purpose as the devil, who comes to kill, steal and destroy.[377] They have been known to start up vehicles and drive them away; doing damage to the vehicle, buildings, property and people.

Errors Regarding the Origin of Demons

Are They Fallen Angels?

First of all, they are not the fallen angels who sinned against God. We read:

> *Now war arose in Heaven, Michael and his angels fighting against the dragon; and the dragon and his angels fought, but they were defeated and there was no longer any place for them in Heaven. And the great dragon was thrown down, that ancient serpent, who is called the devil and Satan, the deceiver of the whole world – he was*

---
[376] See Leviticus 20:27; 1 Samuel 28:7-8; 1 Chronicles 10:13; 2 Chronicles 33:6; Isaiah 19:3
[377] John 10:10

thrown down to the earth, and his angels were thrown down with him." (Revelation 12:7-9)

The seventy returned with joy, saying, "Lord, even the demons are subject to us in Your Name!" And He said to them, "I saw Satan fall like lightning from Heaven. (Luke 10:17-18)

Since many biblical interpreters do not know their Scriptures, they misinterpret what happened to the defeated angels. Someone came up with the theory that when the great red dragon's tail swept down a third of the stars of Heaven and cast them to the earth,[378] the stars were the angels who were cast out of Heaven and were turned into demons which continue their war against Heaven in a different form. This is an error.

The Bible tells us where the rebellious angels were sent for punishment.

For if God did not spare the angels when they sinned, but cast them into Hell (Greek: Tartarus) *and committed them to pits of nether gloom to be kept until the judgment ... then the Lord knows how to rescue the godly from trial and to keep the unrighteous under punishment until the day of judgment and especially those who indulge in the lust of defiling passion and despise authority.* (2 Peter 2:4, 9-10)

And the angels that did not keep their own position but left their proper dwelling have been kept by Him in eternal chains in the nether gloom until the judgment of the great day. (Jude 6)

All such angels have been imprisoned with only one exception, that being Satan/the devil. The conclusion has to be that the fallen angels were not turned into evil spirits/demons, so evil spirits/demons must come from somewhere else.

If the fallen angels had simply been renamed as demons, we could not deal with them because they would be too powerful. Dealing with demons, however, is another story. After we have received the authentic baptism of the Holy Spirit from Jesus, we have the authority and power to cast them out, regardless of how strong they appear to be.

---

[378] Revelation 12:4

> *And these signs will accompany those who believe: in My Name they will cast out demons; they will speak in new tongues...* (Mark 16:17)
>
> *But you shall receive power when the Holy Spirit has come upon you; and you shall be My witnesses in Jerusalem and in all Judea and Samaria and to the end of the earth.* (Acts 1:8)

Although the devil is called *"the prince[379] of the power of the air,[380]* as powerful as he is, any person who has received the baptism of the Holy Spirit with the "signs following" has authority over him. We can endure his temptation for forty days, as Jesus did, or we can simply command him to leave by saying,

"*The Lord rebuke you.*" (Jude 9; Zechariah. 3:2)

Are They A Primitive Response to the Unknown?

William Barclay, who did extensive biblical teaching, dismissed the idea of demons as a primitive attempt to diagnose physical, mental and/or emotional sicknesses which were not understood at the time. Barclay, like many other Christian interpreters of Scripture, claim that the supposed existence of demons is simply a handy way of explaining real physical, mental, psychological sicknesses that people don't understand. He explained the origins of demons in the same way as did the ancient world:

- Some believed they were as old as creation itself.

- Some believed they were the spirits of wicked men who had died and were still carrying on their malignant work.

- Most people connected the demons with the old story in Genesis about the sons of God and the daughters of men.[381] The Jews elaborated on the story by saying there were two angels who forsook God and came to earth because they were attracted through lust for the beauty of mortal women. Their names were

---
[379] See Ephesians 2:2
[380] In Greek, there are two words for air: one is "aer" which refers to the space which extends from the earth's surface to the highest mountain top. The other is "aither" which refers to the space that extends from the mountain tops out into the endless space of Heaven.
[381] Genesis 6:1-8 (Compare 2 Peter 2:4-5)

Assael and Shemachsai. One of them returned to God, while the other remained on earth and gratified his lust. According to them, the demons are the children of that liaison.

The naysayers claim that primitive people would prefer to call their ailments evil spirits/demons, than deal with all the unknown elements of something like mental illness. Barclay concludes by saying, "In the end we come to the conclusion that there are some answers that we do not know."

Regardless of anyone's opinion, it is quite evident that Jesus believed in their existence and had the power to cast them out of people.

Are They Products of Jewish Lore?

According to Jewish belief, demons could eat and drink and beget children. According to some Jewish scholars, there were 7,500,000 of them. A man had 10,000 on his right hand and 10,000 on his left. They lived in unclean places where there was no cleansing water, in the desert where their howling could be heard; hence the phrase, "a howling desert." They were imagined to be especially dangerous to the lonely traveller, to the woman in child-birth, to the bride and bridegroom, to children who were out after dark and to those who voyaged at night. They were said to be especially active in the midday heat and between sunset and sunrise. There was a demon of blindness, a demon of leprosy and a demon of heart-disease; as well as a demon of any other thing that was seen to be causing problems. It was believed they could transfer their maligning gifts to men; for instance, the "evil eye" could turn good fortune into bad. They believed demons worked with certain animals: the serpent, the bull, the donkey and the mosquito. In Hebrew, male demons were known as "shedim" and the female as "lilin," after Lilith.[382] The female demons had long hair and were the enemies of children. With the prevalence of such beliefs, the appreciation for guardian angels for children was wide

---

[382] In Jewish folklore, from Alphabet of Ben Sira onwards, Lilith was Adam's first wife, who was created at the same time and from the same earth as Adam, as contrasted with Eve, who was created from one of Adam's ribs.. When Lilith supposedly rebelled and abandoned Adam, God create Eve. There is no evidence of the truth of this in the Bible.

spread.[383] So ingrained were these beliefs that by AD 340, ordinary Jewish and pagan exorcists used elaborate incantations, spells and magical rites in trying to deal with these evil spirits. There is no scriptural support for any of the Jewish lore regarding the origin of demons, except that they did exist and their exorcists failed in their attempts to get rid of them. Some people still use the phrase, "Poor devil!" Even that is a relic of the old belief.

It does not matter whether any of the lore is true or false. What matters is that, with one word of clear, simple authority, Jesus cast out demons. No one had ever seen anything like that before. The power was not in the spell, the formula, the incantation or the elaborate rite; the power was in Jesus and men were astonished.[384]

Are They Shadow People?

Today, there are many who believe demons are the ghosts of dead people. Sometimes they are called "shadow people." These are said to have come from some other planet in our universe. Others are sure they are the spirits of people from some bygone time who have lost their way and traveled into our dimension. Others claim they are people from the future who are more intelligent than we and have discovered time travel.

Are They Creatures From the Abyss?

Some people believe wrongly that demons come from the abyss; that is the prison *into which* they are sent when they are cast out of people, houses or other buildings. They are kept there until they are cast into the Lake of Fire.

And they begged him not to command them to depart into the abyss. (Luke 8:31)

The abyss has a God appointed angel who rules over the bottomless pit (Greek abusso) whose name in Hebrew is "Abaddon." In Greek he is called "Apollyon."[385] The abyss is mentioned eight times[386] in the Greek New Testament and means "bottomless pit" and "pit."[387]

---

[383] See Matthew 18:10
[384] The Gospel of Mark, The Daily Bible Study, p. 26, 27
[385] Revelation 9:11
[386] Luke 8:31; Revelation 9:1,2,11; 11:7; 17:8; 20:1-3; Romans 10:7
[387] In the New Testament this word in the Greek is "abyssos."

The Origin of Demons

For some time now, I have had a theory for which I could not find scriptural support. My first Greek professor, Dr. Arthur Little, always told us the solution to every problem is to be found in the Greek grammar. Until recently, I had a problem finding proof that my idea was accurate. Thanks to my son, Karl Williams, who provided an extra-biblical source and thanks to closer examination to the Greek grammar in the New Testament, my theory was verified. I am now convinced the Scriptures do tell us the source of demons. This has been missed or overlooked because of the sceptical view of their existence held by many church writers. For me, as has been the case for many people, it was a question of overlooking the obvious. Let's go back a bit.

First of all, we are told in the Bible,

The heart is deceitful above all things, and desperately corrupt; who can understand it? (Jeremiah 17:9-10)

Or, as the King James Version renders it,

The heart is deceitful above all things, and desperately wicked: who can know it? I the Lord *(Yahweh) search the heart, I try the reins, even to give to every man according to his ways, and according to the fruit of his doings.* (Jeremiah 17:9-10)

The Bible's description of the heart is not very complimentary.

The Lord *(Yahweh) saw that the wickedness of man was great in the earth, and that every imagination of the thoughts of his heart was only evil continually. And the* Lord *(Yahweh) was sorry that He had made man on earth, and it grieved Him to His heart. So the Lord said, "I will blot out man whom I have created from the face of the ground, man and beast and creeping things and birds of the air, for I am sorry that I have made them.* (Genesis 6:5-7)

It was so evil that God wanted to destroy the people whom he had created.

In the Bible, the "heart" is described as unregenerate, loving evil, a fountain of evil, blind spiritually, unstable, stubborn, full of pride, subtle, having hypocrisy, sensual, worldly, judicially hardened, malicious, unrepentant, diabolical, lascivious, encouraging of lustful desires, covetous, foolish, the seat of emotions, the source of vain imaginations and the source of all evil things such as the "works of the flesh."[388]

> *For out of the abundance of the heart the mouth speaks.* (Matthew 12:34)

> *And the tongue is a fire. The tongue is an unrighteous world among our members, staining the whole body, setting on fire the cycle of nature, and set on fire by Hell* (Greek "Gehenna") *... but no human being can tame the tongue–a restless evil, full of deadly poison. With it we bless the* LORD *and Father, and with it we curse men who are made in the likeness of God. From the same mouth come blessing and cursing. My brethren, this ought not to be so. Does a spring pour forth from the same opening fresh water and brackish? Can a fig tree, my brethren, yield olives, or a grape vine figs? No more than salt water yields fresh.* (James 3:6-12)

The effect of sin on our hearts was so great that God decided the only solution to the evil heart problem was a New Covenant.[389]

> *And I will give them one heart, and put a new spirit within them; I will take the stony heart out of their flesh and give them a heart of flesh, that they may walk in My statutes and keep My ordinances and obey them; and they shall be My people, and I will be their God.* (Ezekiel 11:19-20)

> *Cast away from you all the transgressions which you have committed against Me, and get yourselves a new heart and a new spirit!* (Ezekiel 18:31)

> *A new heart I will give you, and a new spirit I will put within you; and I will take out of your flesh the heart of stone and give you a heart of flesh. And I will put My Spirit within you, and cause you to walk in My statutes and be careful to observe My ordinances.* (Ezekiel 36:26-27)

---

[388] Galatians 5:19-21
[389] Jeremiah 31:31; Hebrews 8:8,13; 12:24

In the Old Testament we can see that people's hearts are so contaminated with sin that some radical spiritual heart transplanting was going to be necessary.

> *But now the righteousness of God has been manifested apart from law, although the law and the prophets bear witness to it, the righteousness of God through faith in Jesus Christ for all who believe. For there is no distinction; since all have sinned and fall short of the glory of God, they are justified by His grace as a gift, through the redemption which is in Christ Jesus, whom God put forward as an expiation by His blood, to be received by faith. This was to show God's righteousness, because in His divine forbearance He had passed over former sins; it was to prove at the present time that He Himself is righteous and that He justifies him who has faith in Jesus.* (Romans 3:21–26)

A heart corrupted by sin is a universal problem. The problem was first identified in the Garden of Eden when Adam and Eve disobeyed God. God had told Adam not to eat of the tree of the knowledge of good and evil. When the serpent spoke to Eve, he tempted her with the idea that she could be like God, knowing good and evil.

> *For God knows that when you eat of it your eyes will be opened, and you will be like God, knowing good and evil.* (Genesis 3:5)

Because Adam and Eve ate of that tree, sin makes it impossible for us to be either entirely good or entirely evil. It continually makes us want to be gods, whether in rebellion to Him as Yahweh or in rebellion to Him as our Savior and LORD, Jesus Christ.

Moses recognized the problem of rebellion.

> *For I know how rebellious and stubborn you are; behold, while I am yet alive with you, today you have been rebellious against the Lord; how much more after my death!* (Deuteronomy 31:27)

Joshua, Samuel, Ezra, Nehemiah and David all recognized the problems of rebellion.[390]

---

[390] Joshua 22:22; 1 Samuel 15:23; Ezra 4:19; Nehemiah 9:17

An evil man seeks only rebellion: therefore a cruel messenger shall be sent against him. (Proverbs 17:11)

Therefore thus says the LORD: "Behold, I will remove you from the face of the earth. This very year you shall die, because you have uttered rebellion against the Lord." ... Send to all the exiles, saying, "Thus says the LORD concerning Shemaiah of Nehelam: Because Shemaiah had prophesied to you when I did not send him, and has made you trust in a lie, therefore thus says the LORD: Behold, I will punish Shemaiah of Nehelam and his descendants; he shall not have any one living among this people to see the good that I will do to My people, says the Lord, for he has talked rebellion against the Lord." (Jeremiah 28:16; 29:31-32)

David writes sarcastically about rebellious people.

You are gods, sons of the Most High, all of you; nevertheless, you shall die like men, and fall like any prince. (Psalms 82:6-8)

Because of our rebellion, we are tempted to think we can be gods. This is obvious when people question His judgment, as did Abraham when God told him He was going to destroy the cities of Sodom and Gomorrah. *"Shall not the Judge of all the earth do right?"*[391] The Hebrew translates more accurately as, *"Will the Judge of the whole earth judge correctly with justice?"* God does more than judge correctly with justice; through Jesus Christ, He offers mercy and forgiveness.

Because the first temptation was to be gods (despite the fact that we cannot *be* gods, no matter how deeply we may try to realize that primary temptation), we create, knowingly or unknowingly, demons in our own sinful image to worship and serve. Like us, they become uncontrollable and strive to possess, harass, control, dominate and destroy all those whom they lyingly pretend to be special entities or gods sent by "god" – who is not the one real God.

This is why Paul commands us:

"Therefore, my beloved, shun[392] *the worship of idols ... What do I imply then? That food offered to idols is anything, or that an idol is*

---
[391] Genesis 18:25
[392] Greek: flee, avoid, run away from

anything? No, I imply that what pagans sacrifice they offer to demons and not to God. I do not want you to be partners with demons. You cannot drink the cup of the LORD *and the cup of demons. You cannot partake of the table of the* LORD *and the table of demons. Shall we provoke the* LORD *to jealousy? Are we stronger than He?"* (1 Corinthians 10:14, 19-22)

To avoid any question regarding the authenticity of the one true God (Yahweh), Peter explained on the Day of Pentecost,

"And there is salvation in no one else, for there is no other name under Heaven given among men by which we must be saved." (Acts 4:12)

That Name in Greek is Jesus Christ[393] and in Hebrew it is Yahweh.[394] Jesus said,

"For no good tree bears bad fruit, nor again does a bad tree bear good fruit; for each tree is known by its own fruit. For figs are not gathered from thorns, nor are grapes picked from a bramble bush. The good man out of the good treasure of his heart produces good, and the evil man out of his evil treasure produces evil; for out of the abundance of the heart his mouth speaks."
(Luke 6:43-45; Matthew 12:33-35)

So, our hearts are capable of inventing evil things. We usually think of the "evil things" that we develop in terms of what Jesus said:

"What comes out of a man is what defiles a man. For from within, out of the heart of man, come evil thoughts, fornication, theft, murder, adultery, coveting, wickedness, deceit, licentiousness, envy, slander, pride, foolishness. All these evil things come from within, and they defile a man." (Mark 7:20-23)

And what Paul describes as *"works of the flesh."*

Now the works of the flesh are plain: fornication, impurity, licentiousness, idolatry, sorcery, enmity, strife, jealousy, anger, selfishness,

---
[393] Acts 4:10
[394] Joel 2:32, Acts 2:21

dissension, party spirit, envy, murder, drunkenness, carousing and the like. I warn you as I warned you before, that those who do such things shall not inherit the kingdom of God. (Galatians 5:19-21)

We usually think of evil things as being caused by a sinful character. However, Paul says,

"And since they did not see fit to acknowledge God, God gave them up to a base mind and improper conduct. They were filled with all manner of wickedness, evil covetousness, malice. Full of envy, murder, strife, deceit, malignity, they are gossips, slanderers, haters of God, insolent, haughty, boastful, <u>inventors of evil,</u> disobedient to parents, foolish, faithless, heartless, ruthless. Though they know God's decree that those who do such things deserve to die, they will not only do them but approve of those who practice them." (Romans 1:28-32)

The translations should read *"inventors of evil things"* (Greek: epheuretos kakon), meaning the evil heart can "think out or produce (a new device, process) etc.; originate, as by experiment; devise for the first time."

This means that an evil heart can invent and produce evil beings or demons. Evil spirits are some of the "bad fruit"[395] and some of the evil treasure of the heart.[396] They are produced from "vain imaginations" (Greek emataiothesan – aorist passive of mataio; meaning vain, empty headed in their reasoning, speculation, thinking (dialogismos).

So they are without excuse for although they knew God they did not honor Him as God or give thanks to Him, but they became futile in their thinking and their senseless minds were darkened. Claiming to be wise, they became fools, and exchanged the glory of the immortal God for images resembling mortal man or birds or animals or reptiles. Therefore God gave them up in the lusts of their hearts to impurity, to the dishonoring of their bodies among themselves, because they exchanged the truth about God for a lie and worshiped and served the creature rather than the Creator, who is blessed for ever! Amen. (Romans 1:21-25)

---
[395] See Luke 6:43
[396] See Luke 6:45

The King James Version speaks more clearly of the vain imaginations.

Because that, when they knew God, they glorified him not as God, neither were thankful; but became vain in their imaginations, and their foolish heart was darkened. (Romans 1:21)

As to worshiping idols, Paul wrote,

What do I imply then? That food offered to idols is anything, or that an idol is anything? No, I imply that what pagans sacrifice they offer to demons and not to God. I do not want you to be partners with demons. You cannot drink the cup of the Lord *and the cup of demons. You cannot partake of the table of the* Lord *and the table of demons. Shall we provoke the* Lord *to jealousy? Are we stronger than He?* (1 Corinthians 10:19-22)

Paul reminds us of what God told Israel:

"I am the Lord (Yahweh) *your God, who brought you out of the land of Egypt, out of the house of bondage. You shall have no other gods before* (besides) *Me. You shall not make for yourself a graven image, or any likeness of anything that is in Heaven above, or that is in the earth beneath, or that is in the water under the earth; you shall not bow down to them or serve them; for I the* Lord (Yahweh) *your God am a jealous God, visiting the iniquity of the fathers upon the children to the third and the fourth generation of those who hate Me, but showing steadfast love to thousands of those who love Me and keep My commandments."* (Exodus 20:2-6; Deuteronomy 5:6-10)

The God of Israel, in preparation for a New Covenant, rescinded the penalty of passing the sins of the fathers on to the children (generational sin).[397] Under God's New Covenant with Jesus Christ, each person is responsible for his or her own sin and it is not passed on to the children.[398]

Paul explains something that has been overlooked in today's world; that all the other so-called "gods" represented by idols were simply demons/evil spirits.

---

[397] Jeremiah 31:29-34; Ezekiel 18:1-32
[398] John 9:1-3

Since there is only one legitimate God, the other so-called gods of other religions are inventions of the people who claim to be their prophets or leaders.

Paul also points out that every demon/evil spirit that is mistaken for a "god" has the same character flaws as its inventors. Therefore, any claim that all religions worship and serve the same God as we Christians worship is sincerely wrong. All other religions have different names for their gods reflecting the character and sinful flaws of their inventors. Paul described these as the *"works of the flesh."*

> *The works of the flesh are plain: fornication, impurity, licentiousness, idolatry, sorcery, enmity, strife, jealously, anger, selfishness, dissension, party spirit, envy, murder, drunkenness, carousing and the like. I warn you, as I warned you before, that those who do such things shall not inherit the kingdom of God.* (Galatians 5:19-20)

In the same way, Jesus exhibits the character of God which is described as the *"fruit of the Spirit."*

> *The fruit of the Spirit is love, joy, peace, patience, kindness, goodness, faithfulness, gentleness, self-control; against such there is no law.* (Galatians 5:22-23)

It is God's Holy Spirit who effects the changes in a believer, transforming our character to reflect the nature of our God. As the Holy Spirit weaves the fruit of the Spirit into the fabric of our flesh and blood and spirit, we act more and more like Jesus Christ and do the same works as did He, whose name means "Yahweh is salvation."

Peter made it perfectly clear, when on the Day of Pentecost he explained:

> *And, there is Salvation in no one else, for there is no other name under Heaven given among men by which we must be saved.* (Acts 4:12)

God made it simple and easy; that name is Jesus.

If all these different religions with their different gods, different names, different teachings and different beliefs served the same god, that god would be a schizophrenic god and we would be schizophrenic believers who would end up confused by all the different gods, heading not toward Heaven, but towards Hell.

For there is one God, and there is one mediator between God and men, the man Christ Jesus, who gave Himself a ransom for all, the testimony to which was borne at the proper time. (1 Timothy 2:5)

After being a guest on "The Conspiracy Show" hosted by Richard Syrette, I received a call from a Muslim man.

He asked, "Can you help me?" and went on to explain, "My family moved into a new house. We were shocked to discover that there were demons in our house. We are being harassed and one of my two sons is now possessed." He then asked, "Can we come to meet with you?"

I agreed.

A week later, the man arrived with his wife and his possessed son who had the signs of being possessed. He asked, "Can you help us? We went to the Mosque but they could not help us. Can you help us?"

I explained that the only way that I could do so was if they were to become Christians because their help would be coming from Jesus.

The man said, "The Koran speaks of Jesus as a great prophet."

I explained further, "He is more than a prophet; He is the Most High God who gives us authority to cast out demons from people and houses. It would be very dangerous for me to cast the demons out of your house if you weren't Christians because you wouldn't have the protection of the Holy Spirit, so they would be able to return, bringing seven times their number." I suggested they should go home and think about our conversation.

They agreed. Two weeks later, the man called again. He asked, "Will you please come to our home?"

When I arrived, the man and his wife and their two sons were there. I explained that for their safety it would be necessary for all of them to ask Jesus to forgive their sin and to receive God's Holy Spirit into their hearts. Further, I explained that the Holy Spirit would give each of them a special new language to speak and pray with, to prove that no demon could enter their bodies.

The possessed boy spoke up and said, "No! We go to the Mosque!"

His father said, "We went to the Mosque and we could find no help there. Now we are going to Jesus, the Most High God!"

First, I cast the demons out of the possessed boy. Then, I asked all four family members to pray with me as they invited Jesus to be their Savior, LORD and God. Each of them began to speak in the new tongues language that the Holy Spirit gave them.[399]

Then I asked the whole family to step outside while I went through their house, casting out the demons that were in the rooms. Before I left, the father said, "Now I hope this is the beginning of a long friendship!"

I responded, "Yes, and it will last forever when we all go to Heaven!"

People who worship demons are worshiping the demons that evil minds invent and let loose in the world. Evil people worship evil demons invented by inventors of evil things.

The first example of the inventiveness of sinful people, involved the events surrounding Moses' forty days on Mount Sinai when he received God's Ten Commandments.[400]

> When the people saw that Moses delayed to come down out of the mount, the people gathered themselves together to Aaron, and said unto him, "Get up, make us gods, which shall go before us; as for this Moses, the man that brought us up out of the land of Egypt, we do not know what is become of him."
> And Aaron said to them, "Take off the rings of gold which are in the

---
[399] Mark 16:17-18; Acts 2:4
[400] Exodus 20-31

ears of your wives, your sons, and your daughters, and bring them to me." ... And he received the gold at their hand, and fashioned it with a graving tool, and made a molten calf; and they said, "These are your gods, O Israel, who brought you up out of the land of Egypt!" When Aaron saw this, he built an altar before it; and Aaron made proclamation, and said, "Tomorrow shall be a feast to the Lord*" ... And the* Lord *said to Moses, "Go down; for your people, whom you brought up out of the land of Egypt, have corrupted themselves; they have turned aside quickly out of the way which I commanded them; they have made for themselves a molten calf, and have worshiped it and sacrificed to it, and said, 'These are your gods, O Israel, who brought you up out of the land of Egypt!'"* (Exodus 32:1,2,4,5,7,8)

Aaron attempted to explain and excuse his actions:

Let not the anger of my Lord *burn hot; you know the people, that they are set on evil. ... And I said to them, "Let any who have gold take it off," so they gave it to me, and I threw it into the fire, and there came out this calf.* (Exodus 32:22,24)

David refers to this incident when he wrote,

And a fire was kindled in their company; the flame burned up the wicked. They made a calf in Horeb, and worshipped the molten image. Thus they changed their glory into the similitude of an ox that eateth grass. They forgot God their Savior, which had done great things in Egypt. (Psalm 106:18-21 KJV)

And further...

They joined themselves also unto Baalpeor, and ate the sacrifices of the dead. Thus they provoked him to anger with their **inventions***: and the plague brake in upon them. Then stood up Phinehas, and executed judgment: and so the plague was stayed.*
(Psalm 106:28-30 KJV)

They did not destroy the nations, concerning whom the Lord *commanded them: But were mingled among the heathen, and learned their works. And they served their idols: which were a snare* unto them. Yea, they sacrificed their sons and their daughters unto devils, and shed innocent blood, even the blood of their sons and of their daughters, whom they sacrificed unto the idols of Canaan: and the land was polluted with blood. Thus were they defiled with their own works, and went a whoring with their own **inventions**. Therefore was the wrath of the LORD kindled against His people, insomuch that He abhorred His own inheritance. And He gave them into the hand of the heathen; and they that hated them ruled over them. Their enemies also oppressed them, and they were brought into subjection under their hand. Many times did He deliver them; but they provoked Him with their counsel, and were brought low for their iniquity. (Psalm 106:34-43)

David referred to this rebellion of Israel and their sinful inventions in Psalm 99.

Moses and Aaron among His priests, and Samuel among them that call upon His Name; they called upon the LORD (YAHWEH), and He answered them. He spake unto them in the cloudy pillar: they kept His testimonies, and the ordinance that He gave them. Thou answeredst them, O LORD our God: Thou wast a God that forgavest them, though Thou tookest vengeance of their **inventions**. Exalt the LORD our God, and worship at His holy hill; for the LORD our God is holy! (Psalm 99:6-9 KJV)

Even the Preacher of Ecclesiastes warned of these evil inventions.

Behold, this have I found, saith the preacher, counting one by one, to find out the account: Which yet my soul seeketh, but I find not: one man among a thousand have I found; but a woman among all those have I not found. Lo, this only have I found, that God hath made man upright; but they have sought out many **inventions**. (Ecclesiastes 7:27-29 KJV)

David was referring, of course, to the invention of demons or evil spirits or, in the KJV, devils or false gods. God makes it clear what these man-invented-created gods are. Referring to Israel, Scripture reads,

> *But Jesh'urun waxed fat, and kicked; you waxed fat, you grew thick, you became sleek; then he forsook God who made him, and scoffed at the Rock of his Salvation. They stirred him to jealousy with strange gods; with abominable practices they provoked him to anger. They sacrificed to demons which were no gods, to gods they had never known, to new gods that had come in of late, whom your fathers had never dreaded. You were unmindful of the Rock that begot you, and you forgot the God who gave you birth.* (Deuteronomy 32:15-18)

First Kings recorded an instance where King Jeroboam devised (invented) idols out of his own heart.

> *And Jerobo'am appointed a feast on the fifteenth day of the eighth month like the feast that was in Judah, and he offered sacrifices upon the altar; so he did in Bethel, sacrificing to the calves that he had made. And he placed in Bethel the priests of the high places that he had made. He went up to the altar which he had made in Bethel on the fifteenth day in the eighth month, in the month which he had devised of his own heart; and he ordained a feast for the people of Israel, and went up to the altar to burn incense.* (1 Kings 12:32-33)

In other words, he devised two idols out of his own heart in the form of calves for people to worship. Idols are physical images of the demons who pretend to be gods. When talking to Moses, God said,

> *"Arise, go down quickly from here; for your people whom you have brought from Egypt have acted corruptly; they have turned aside quickly out of the way which I commanded them; they have made themselves a molten image."* (Deuteronomy 9:12)

The word "image" is defined as "an imitation or representation of a person or thing, drawn, painted etc; especially a statute; a sculptured figure used as an idol; a person or thing very much like another, a copy, counterpart, likeness."[401] In other words, an idol is the image of a false god which is a demon/evil spirit invented/created by a wickedly sinful mind and let loose in the world to attract people to worship and serve it.

---

[401] Dictionary.com

It is the sinful attempt by people to replace the only real God with one of their own vain imaginations.[402]

It is written of Jesus,

> "He is the image of the invisible God ..." (Colossians 1:15)

> In the beginning was the Word, and the Word was with (the) God, and the Word was God ... And the word became flesh and dwelt among us full of grace and truth; we have beheld his glory, glory as the only Son from the Father. (John 1:1,14)

As Jesus is the visible image of the invisible God, so idols are the visible images of demons/evil spirits. They can resemble people (men, women, children), be called gods, come as angels of light, animals, birds, snakes, fish, scarey beings, dead people (familiar spirits), space travelers or shadow people. They, like the devil/Satan, like to be worshiped and served as gods. They encourage people to break God's Covenant and "to go beyond what is written"[403] in the Christian Scriptures. All other religions in the world worship idols which are the images of demons/evil spirits.[404] There is only one God. His Name in Hebrew is "Yahweh" and "Jesus" in Greek (which means Yahweh is Salvation). Our God does not change His Name as He moves from nation to nation nor does He change His Covenant as He moves from nation to nation around the world.

> ... one LORD, one faith, one baptism, one God and Father of us all, who is above all and through all and in all. (Ephesians 4:5-6)

Only a certain kind of Christian has the authority to resist the devil and experience James 4:7, which says he will flee if we resist him. This kind of Christian will cast demons/evil spirits from people and buildings, sending them to the abyss, ignoring their pleas not to send them there.[405] That Christian is simply a person who has received salvation[406] and the baptism of the Holy Spirit[407] with the evidence of the "signs" following to prove his or her authority.

---

[402] See Romans 1:21
[403] 1 Corinthians. 4:6; 2 Timothy 3:16-17
[404] 1 Corinthians 10:20-21
[405] Luke 8:31
[406] John 3:3,5,7
[407] Acts 2:4; Mark. 16:17-20

In an article called "Mind Creatures" from a book entitled, *Mysteries of the Unexplained*,[408] there is a description of an entity called a "tulpa" which fits the description of a demon. "The word "tulpa" is from the Tibetan language and refers to any entity that attains reality solely by the act of imagination. The entity is created solely within the confines of one's own mind; not drawn out, written down or even verbally described. If its creator continues, this 'tulpa creation' may become a physical reality through intense concentration and visualization. However, care must be taken to bring to reality only what is beneficial to the world, lest its destruction becomes more problematic than its creation."[409]

"A tulpa is a living spiritual being created by humans. "The essence of a Tibetan tulpa lies in the human ability to actualize thought. Through focus and concentration, that which is only spiritual or invisible can manifest itself in a physical form. Tibetans believe that a tulpa is a ghost or apparition of a living person, existing in the etheric or spiritual world. As a person wills the tupla to exist, it has a possibility to be seen by other persons. Tulpas can be in forms of animals, mythical creatures, and also humans. There are accounts of people who practice this actualization, and have been able to take digital photos of themselves with their tulpas."[410]

"In Tibet, where such things are practiced, a ghost of this kind is called a tulpa. A tulpa is usually produced by a skilled magician or yogi. A tulpa can often recreate itself. Some are able to produce ten different kinds of tulpa. These include animate beings – whether human, animal, or supernatural. Few westerners have had an opportunity to investigate the Tibetan claims outlined above."[411]

A French scholar and traveler, Alexandra David Neel, who spent fourteen years in Tibet, published a description of her own tulpa. She wrote that she went into a meditative seclusion and performed the prescribed concentration and rites. She was able to produce a phantom monk who became a kind of guest. At first it cooperated with her and

---

[408] The Readers' Digest Association, Inc.
[409] www.tulpa.com/explain
[410] www.unknown-creatures.com
[411] Mysteries of the Unexplained, p. 176

then began touching her body. "The fat, chubby cheeked fellow grew leaner; his face assumed a vaguely mocking, sly, malignant look. He became more troublesome and bold. In brief, he escaped my control. The presence of the unwanted companion began to prove trying to my nerves; it turned into a 'day-nightmare.' I decided to dissolve the phantom. I succeeded, but only after six months of hard struggle. My mind-creature was tenacious of life."

Alexandra David Neel didn't really understand the seriousness of what she had let loose into the world. Demons are called, or should I say "mistakenly" called, by various names that make people believe they are gods (or at least angels) to give people ungodly, demonic and unscriptural advice. Their anonymity is their strength and the fact they will not reveal their true identity gives the people they visit and attack no defense. This leaves them vulnerable to being abused – whether mentally, spiritually or physically – and causes them to be sick or to die as the result of the presence of these evil spirits.

After years of dealing with demons/evil spirits, I have come to the conclusion that they are produced, created or birthed either, as in the case of the Tibetan tuplas, as a conscious or unconscious act of the mind motivated by an evil heart. No matter by what name they are called, they are still demons created to harass, possess and cause people trouble. All the descriptions of tuplas are exactly the same as those of demons/evil spirits. I have discovered demons can be photographed with digital cameras. A demon by any other name is still a demon!

This leads me to other conclusions. First, since they are invented or created in the evil human heart with the cooperation of an evil mind (as demonstrated in the cases of the Tibetan tuplas), once birthed, they become uncontrollable. They can re-create themselves and multiply in numbers. Their first instinct seems to be to attack their creators and attempt to possess them. If they are unsuccessful, they will attempt to find a new place of residence, either in another person or in a house where they can attack, possess and torment the occupants.

As Jesus points out clearly:

"When an unclean spirit has gone out of a man, he passes through waterless places seeking rest; and finding none he says, 'I will return to my house from which I came.' And when he comes he finds it swept and put in order. Then he goes and brings seven other spirits more evil than himself, and they enter and dwell there; and the last state of that man becomes worse than the first." (Luke 11:24-26)

The good news is that when a person receives his or her new heart and new Spirit, that person can no longer create evil spirits. He or she is now capable of serving God and producing the fruit of the Holy Spirit and fulfilling God's plan for his or her life. This brings the freedom to do as Jesus directed:

"You shall love (agape) *the L*ord *your God with all your heart (kardia), and with all your soul* (psyche: human spirit) *and with all your mind* (dianoia) *and your neighbour as yourself."*
(Matthew 22:37,39; Mark 12:29-31)

Since demons/evil spirits are the fruit of wicked hearts, they are, from the moment of their creation, automatically part of the kingdom of darkness and ruled by Satan. They "disguise themselves as servants of righteousness.[412]" However, just like the whole of creation is under the authority of our God, evil spirits must obey Jesus and anybody who has authority to cast them out.

And they begged Him not to command them to depart into the abyss.
(Luke 8:31)

And these signs will accompany those who believe: in My Name they will cast out demons; they will speak in new tongues ... (Mark 16:17)

The fact that evil spirits must obey God is why God, Yahweh, was able to use a *"lying spirit"* to give a false prophecy to the kings of Judah and Israel when the 400 prophets would not prophesy what God wanted them to know. As was revealed to Micaiah, God was trying to warn the kings if they went to war, Ahab, the king of Israel, would be killed. The kings did not listen to God's prophet Micaiah, so they went to war, were defeated

---
[412] 2 Corinthians 11:15

and the king of Israel was killed.[413] This may sound strange, but God can use evil spirit/demon to carry out his commands, as evidenced by Paul in his second letter to the Thessalonians.

> *Therefore God sends upon them a strong delusion, to make them believe what is false, so that all may be condemned who did not believe the truth but had pleasure in unrighteousness.*
> (2 Thessalonians 2:11-12)

In the kingdom of darkness, no spirit has allegiance to another. The demons know exactly who Jesus is: "the Son of the Most High God."[414] They know they must obey Him, as well as those to whom He has given authority over them.[415] This is also true with Satan.[416]

Most people think, mistakenly, that their minds are in charge of their hearts. No, it is the other way around; the heart is in control and motivates the body to respond. The heart is known as the subconscious mind. The only way we can gain self-control[417] is by asking Jesus to forgive our sin and ask Him to baptize us in the Holy Spirit, so that the Holy Spirit replaces the self-willed heart and replaces it with the heart of Jesus. This is what is meant by the old phrase, "give your heart to Jesus." Jesus said,

> *"And these signs will accompany those who believe: in My name they will cast out demons; they will speak in new tongues; they will pick up serpents, and if they drink any deadly thing, it will not hurt them; they will lay their hands on the sick, and they will recover."*
> (Mark 16:17-18)

These signs prove there is "good fruit" and "good treasure" in a person's heart." This kind of heart is far from the unredeemed hearts of people who do not have Jesus Christ as their Savior and LORD.[418]

---

[413] 1 Kings 21; 2 Chronicles 18
[414] Luke 8:28-31
[415] Acts 19:13-17
[416] James 4:7; 1 Peter 5:7-9; Jude 9
[417] Galatians 5:23; 2 Timothy 1:7
[418] Matthew 12:34

And this is eternal life, that they know Thee, the only true God, and Jesus Christ whom Thou hast sent. (John 17:3)

Jesus said, *"You brood of vipers! How can you speak good, when you are evil? For out of the abundance of the heart the mouth speaks."* (Matthew 12:34)

The good man, out of the good treasure of his heart produces good, and the evil man, out of his evil treasure produces evil; for out of the abundance of the heart his mouth speaks. (Luke. 6:45)

From the same mouth come blessing and cursing. My brethren, this ought not to be so. (James 3:10)

Once a person has been baptized in the Holy Spirit, no longer do blessings and curses come out of his or her mouth: only blessings.

When a person has been baptized in the Holy Spirit, he or she cannot be possessed by an evil spirit, but has authority to safely cast demons out of people, houses and buildings and send them to the abyss[419] from which they cannot escape.

Demons are under the authority of every Christian who has received the authentic baptism of the Holy Spirit. James tells us,

Even the demons believe – and shudder. (James 2:19)

Because of our sinful nature, our wickedly deceptive minds attempt to replace God with uncontrollable demons who attempt to meet our sinful consciousness and subconscious desire to be gods. But our sin gives life to evil beings which can be brought under control only by people who have been "born from above by water and the Spirit" and empowered by the Holy Spirit to send them to their temporary Hell[420] (abyss: abusso).

Jesus answered, "Truly, truly, I say to you, unless one is born of water and the Spirit, he cannot enter the kingdom of God." (John 3:5)

From their temporary Hell, demons will be cast into the Lake of Fire (gehenna), their permanent Hell, along with the devil, when Jesus

---
[419] Luke 8:31
[420] Luke 8:31

returns.[421] The horrifying truth is that those who believed the "strong delusion," rather than the truth, will be condemned with them.

> *Therefore God sends upon them a strong delusion, to make them believe what is false, so that all may be condemned who did not believe the truth but had pleasure in unrighteousness.*
> (2 Thessalonians 2:11-12)

The kingdom of darkness attempts to counterfeit the genuine works of God the Father, God the Son and God the Holy Spirit with the works of false gods – counterfeit gifts of the Holy Spirit, which include false prophecy and false fruit of the Spirit (the works of the flesh).[422] Demons / evil spirits take on the sinful characteristics of the people who invent (or birth) them, degrading and tormenting them with various symptoms of physical, mental and psychological disorders. Through possession, they commit crimes, murder people and do harm to their victims. Because of their evil invention or birth, they are unredeemable. They are the by-product of their spiritual father, the devil / Satan.

> *You are of your father the devil, and your will is to do your father's desires. He was a murderer from the beginning, and has nothing to do with the truth, because there is no truth in him. When he lies, he speaks according to his own nature, for he is a liar and the father of lies.* (John 8: 44)

The kingdom of Heaven gives freedom and eternal life while the kingdom of darkness brings captivity, slavery, sickness, possession and death. Everything in the kingdom of Heaven has a counterfeit in the kingdom of darkness.

It is almost unimaginable that we have within our sinful hearts the ability to produce such evil beings, but once we have received our new hearts and a new Spirit, the Holy Spirit,[423] the fruit of our lives will be changed and we will do the works that Jesus does.

---

[421] Revelation 20:10,14,15
[422] Galatians 5:19-21
[423] John 3:3-7

> "Truly, truly, I say to you, he who believes in Me will also do the works that I do; and greater works than these will he do, because I go to the Father." (John. 14:12)

With salvation and the baptism of the Holy Spirit, using the gifts of the Holy Spirit, we can be witnesses for Jesus, doing ministry with the "signs"[424] under His guidance. We can minister with the character of Jesus (the fruit of the Spirit) and the guarantee of our inheritance of eternal life in the New Jerusalem.[425]

> *In Him you also, who have heard the Word of truth, the gospel of your salvation, and have believed in Him, were sealed with the promised Holy Spirit, which is the guarantee of our inheritance until we acquire possession of it, to the praise of His glory.*
> (Ephesians 1:13-14)

Amen!

---

[424] Mark 16:17-20
[425] Revelation 21

Bibliography

Concordances and Lexicons:

A Greek-English Lexicon of the New Testament and Other Christian Literature. Third Edition revised and edited by Frederick William Donker, based on Walter Bauer's Sixth Edition. The University of Chicago Press, 2000.

A Greek-English Lexicon of the New Testament and Other Christian Literature, by William F. Arndt and F. Wilbur Gingrich. The University of Chicago Press, Chicago, Illinois, 1957.

A Greek-English Lexicon of the New Testament and Other Christian Literature, Second Edition revised and augmented by F. Wilbur Gingrich and Fredrick W. Danker from Walter Bauer's Fifth Edition, 1958. The University of Chicago Press, Chicago, Illinois, 1979.

A Hebrew and English Lexicon of the Old Testament by Francis Brown, S. R. Driver and Charles A. Briggs. Oxford at Clarendon Press, 1962.

The Englishman's Greek Concordance of the New Testament, George V. Wigram. Baker Book House, Grand Rapids, Michigan, 1979.

Vine's Expository Dictionary of New Testament Words, by W. E. Vine. MacDonald Publishing Company, McLean, Virginia.

Dictionary of Old Testament Words for English Readers, by Aaron Pick. Kregel Publications, Grand Rapids, Michigan, 1979.

Nelson's Complete Concordance of the Revised Standard Version Bible. John W. Ellison. Thomas Nelson Sons, New York & Toronto, 1957.

Strong's Exhaustive Concordance of the Bible, James Strong, Abingdon Press, 1890, 26th Edition, 1965.

Concordance of the Greek Testament, edited by Rev. W. F. Moulton and Rev. A. S. Geden. Fourth Edition revised by Rev. H. K. Moulton, T. & T. Clark, 38 George Street, Edinburgh, 1963.

Bibles:

The Interlinear Bible. Hebrew-Greek-English, J. P. Green, Sr. General Editor and Translator. Sovereign Grace Publishers, Lafayette, Indiana 47903 USA, 1985.

Interlinear for The Rest of Us, William D. Mounce, Zondervan, Grand Rapids, Michigan, USA, 2006.

The Englishman's Greek New Testament, Zondervan Publishing House of the Zondervan Corporation, Grand Rapids, Michigan, 1974.

Greek-English New Testament, Kurt Aland & Erwin Nestle, Deutsche Bibelgesellschaft, Stuttgart, 1992.

The Holy Bible, The Authorized King James Version, The World Publishing Company, Cleveland and New York, 1945.

The Harper Study Bible, Revised Standard Version, Editor Harold Lindsell. Zondervan Bible Publisher, Grand Rapids, Michigan, 1971.

Other Books and Articles:

Old Testament Parsing Guide, Todd S. Beall, William A Banks, Colin Smith. Broadman & Holman Publishers, Nashville, Tennessee, 2000.

A Parsing Guide To The Greek New Testament, Nathan E. Han. Herald Press, Scottdale, Pennsylvania, 1971.

A Grammatical Analysis of the Greek New Testament, Fifth Edition by Max Zerwick, S.J., Mary Grosvenor. Editrice Pontificio Instituto, Roma, 1996.

Mysteries of the Unexplained, Project Editor: Carroll C. Calkins, The Reader's Digest Association, Inc., Printed in Pleasantville, New York, United States of America, Ninth Printing, February 1990.

Like A Rushing Mighty Wind, Rev. Gordon Williams with Diane Roblin-Lee, by Gordon & Gordon Associates, Inc., Canada, Second Printing, 2002.

Charisma, Philip Rieff, Pantheon Books, New York, N.Y., Random House Inc., 2007.

The Screwtape Letters, C.S. Lewis, The Macmillan Company, New York, N.Y., 1982.

An Idiom Book of New Testament Greek, C. F. D. Moule, Second Edition, Cambridge at the University Press, 1960.

New Testament Greek For Beginners, J. Gresham Machen, The MacMillan Company, New York, 1958.

New Testament Greek, G. Jay. Published by S.P.C.K. and printed by William Clowes and Sons, Limited, London and Beccles, 1958, Reprinted 1961.

Greek Grammar, Herbert Weir Smyth, Revised by Gordon M. Messing, Harvard University Press, Harvard, Massachusetts, USA, 1984.

Wilson's Old Testament Word Studies, William Wilson, MacDonald Publishing Company, McLean, VA, 1992.

Webster's New World Dictionary, College Edition, The World Publishing Company, Nelson, Foster & Scott Ltd., Toronto, Canada, 1960.

A Critical and Exegetical Commentary on The Epistle to the Romans, The International Critical Commentary, by the Rev. William Sandy and Rev. Arthur C. Headlam, Fifth Edition, The T. & T. Clark, 38 George Street, Edinburgh, 1971.

To book
Evangelistic Meetings
or Crusades,
*or for information on our
Home Churches*

Please phone or fax

*The Gordon Williams
Evangelistic Association Office*
(G.W.E.A.)

Phone 519-940-1940
Fax 519-940-8365

11 Bayberry Road, Mono
Ontario, Canada L9V 6G5

E-mail: *gordwea@rogers.com*
Website: *gordwilliams.com*

Books, Booklets, CDs, DVDs, Cassettes & Videos
by Rev. Gordon Williams

Like a Rushing Mighty Wind
by Rev. Gordon Williams with Diane Roblin-Lee
Book: $20.00 donation   Quantity _____ Total _____

Spirit-led Days Daily Devotional
by Rev. Gordon Williams with Diane Roblin-Lee
Book: $10.00 donation   Quantity _____ Total _____

The Forgotten Key to Christian Marriage
by Rev. Gordon Williams with Diane Roblin-Lee
Book: $20.00 donation   Quantity _____ Total _____

Victory Over the Kingdom of Darkness
by Rev. Gordon Williams
Edited by Diane Roblin-Lee & Rev. Dennis Baker
Book: $20.00 donation   Quantity _____ Total _____

Generational Curses-Gone Forever (booklet)   Quantity _____ Total _____
Exciting Praise! (booklet)   Quantity _____ Total _____
Clock-Watchers Incorporated: End-Time Ministries (booklet)   Quantity _____ Total _____

* Booklets: ea. $8.00 donation

The Testimony of Gordon Williams
Making Yourself Available to Jesus Christ
DVD: $10.00 donation   Quantity _____ Total _____

The Baptism & Gifts of the Holy Spirit
Using the Spiritual Gifts Skillfully
DVD: $10.00 donation (3 for $25.)   Quantity _____ Total _____

From Caterpillar to Butterfly
The Key to Christian Maturity
DVD: $10.00 donation (3 for $25.)   Quantity _____ Total _____

Prices include taxes, shipping and handling.   **TOTAL** _____

```
Name _____
Address _____
City _____  Province/State _____
Country _____  Postal/Zip _____
E-mail _____
```

Please send order form and payment to:
Gordon Williams Evangelistic Association or **G.W.E.A.**
11 Bayberry Road, Mono ON L9V 6G5